Early Childhood Experiences in Language Arts

Third Edition

Jeanne M. Machado

Delmar Publishers inc.

To my ever-encouraging husband Frank, and Danielle, Katrina and Claire. Each is a uniquely special gift in my life. And to my father, Emil Hamm, who always saw the best in me.

Cover photo: Joseph Schuyler Photography

Delmar Staff
  Administrative Editor: Adele M. O'Connell
  Production Editor: Carol A. Micheli

10 9 8 7 6 5 4 3 2

Printed in the United States of America
Published simultaneously in Canada
by Nelson Canada,
A division of International Thomson Limited

Library of Congress Cataloging in Publication Data

Machado, Jeanne M.
  Early childhood experiences in language arts.

  Bibliography: p. 413
  Includes index.
  1. Language arts (Preschool) I. Title.
LB1140.5.L3M33 1985   372.6   84-23001
ISBN: 0-8273-2253-4
ISBN: 0-8273-2254-2 (instructor's guide)

Early Childhood Experiences in Language Arts

Third Edition

Contents

SECTION 1 LANGUAGE DEVELOPMENT
IN THE YOUNG CHILD

SECTION 2 LISTENING — A LANGUAGE ART

SECTION 3 SPEAKING — A LANGUAGE ART

SECTION 4 WRITING — A LANGUAGE ART

SECTION 5 READING — A LANGUAGE ART

SECTION 6 LANGUAGE ARTS —
IN CLASS AND AT HOME

To The Student

Since you are a unique, caring individual who has chosen an important career, early childhood teaching, this text hopes to help you discover and share your innate and developing language arts abilities and talents! Create your own activities, author when possible your own "quality" literary, oral, and prewriting opportunities for young children. Share your specialness, and those language arts-related experiences which excite and delight you both now and when *you* were a child.

In this text I urge you to become a skilled interactor and conversationalist, "a subtle opportunist," getting the most possible out of each child-adult situation, while also enjoying these daily exchanges yourself.

Collect, select, construct, and practice those appropriate activities so that you can present them with enthusiasm. Your joy in language arts then becomes the child's joy. A file box and/or binder collection of ideas, completed sets, patterns, games, etc. carefully made and stored for present or future use is suggested. Filling young children's days with developmental, worthwhile experiences will prove a challenge, and your collection of ideas and teaching visual aids will grow and be adapted over the years.

Suggested activities and review sections at the end of units give immediate feedback on your grasp of unit main ideas and techniques. You'll find the answers to the review questions in the back of the text.

In this text, I attempt to help you become "ever better" at what you may already do well, and help you grow in professional competence. Since I'm growing too, I invite your suggestions and comments so in future revisions I can refine and improve this text's value to new students.

Preface

Early Childhood Experiences in Language Arts is an up-to-date, state-of-the-art teacher training text designed to help early childhood education students and practicing preschool and child care personnel provide an opportunity-rich program full of interesting, appropriate, and developmental language arts activities. Beginning units present a detailed account of language acquisition, young children's emerging communicative capacities, growth milestones, and age-level characteristics, along with suggested professional techniques for promoting each child's self-esteem and potential. It is both a practical "how-to" text and a resource collection which includes a large number of classic, tried and true activities, complete with step-by-step directions.

Because a comprehensive, dynamically planned early childhood language arts curriculum consists of four broad, interrelated areas — speaking (oral), listening, prewriting, and prereading — each is fully explored and described in its own section within the text. It is hoped that the confidence and skill gained by the readers of this text will give young children enthusiastic, knowledgeable teacher-companions who enjoy and encourage them in their discovery of the language arts.

Changes in this Third Edition include more in-depth material on infant and toddler language abilities, developmental theory, cross-cultural and individual differences in language acquisition and use, and an increased emphasis on "quality" literature for children. Such issues as bilingualism, language disturbances, giftedness, and the impact of computers on language arts in the early childhood curriculum are explored. A helpful discussion concerning the recent emphasis on academics and early reading instruction for young children is presented, and advocates dedication to traditional play, discovery, and basic skill-building and readiness activities. Many new and innovative activities suitable for use in a variety of child care settings have been added, and group instructional methods have been further clarified and expanded. Resource lists have been added to many of the units in this new edition, providing further enrichment of the learning experience, and a new glossary has been added to the back of the text. An extensive appendix with numerous classroom ideas and activities and lists of additional resources also appears at the end of the text. Traditional learning aids, such as learning objectives, review questions, and learning activities, have been retained from the previous edition.

ABOUT THE AUTHOR

The author is employed as a full-time instructor with the San Jose Community College District. Currently, as department chairperson, she supervises students (both early childhood education majors and parents) at two on-campus laboratory child development centers at San Jose City College and Evergreen Valley College, in addition to child care centers within the community. Her teaching responsibilities encompass early childhood education, child development, and parenting courses. The author received her Masters degree from San Jose State University and her vocational community college life credential with course work from The University of California at Berkeley. Her experience includes working as a teacher and director in public early childhood programs, parent cooperative programs, and a self-owned and operated private preschool. Ms. Machado is an active participant in several professional organizations which relate to the education and well-being of young children and their families. Her writing efforts include, in addition to this text, the publication of *Early Childhood Practicum Guide*, which was co-authored with Dr. Helen Meyer of the University of California at Hayward and published in 1984, by Delmar Publishers Inc.

Section 1
Language Development in the Young Child

Unit 1
Beginnings of Communication

OBJECTIVES

After studying this unit, you should be able to

- describe one theory of human language acquisition.
- identify factors which influence language development.
- discuss the reciprocal behaviors of infants and parents.

Each child is a special combination of inherited traits and the influence of his environment. The qualities a child receives from both parents and the events that occur help shape language development.

In a short four to five years after birth, the child's speech becomes purposeful and adultlike. This growing language skill is a useful tool for satisfying needs and exchanging thoughts, hopes, and dreams with others. As ability grows, the child understands and uses more of the resources of oral and recorded human knowledge, and the natural capacity for categorizing, inventing, and remembering information aids a child's language acquisition.

Although unique among the species because of the ability to *speak*, human beings are not the only ones who can *communicate*. Birds and other animals can imitate sounds and signals and are known to communicate. For instance, chimpanzees exposed to experimental language techniques (American Sign Language, specially equipped machines, and plastic tokens) have surprised researchers with their abilities. Some have learned to use symbols and follow linguistic rules with a sophistication that rivals some two-year-olds, and researchers con-

tinue to probe the limits of their capabilities (de Villiers, 1979).

Speech itself, however, is a human trait; much more complex than simple parroting or a primitive level of functioning. The power of language enables humans to dominate other life forms. The ability to use language creatively secured our survival by giving us a vehicle to both understand and transmit knowledge and to work cooperatively in concert with others (Hoy and Somer, 1974). Language facilitates peaceful solutions between people.

DEFINITIONS

Language, as used in this text, refers to a system of intentional communication through sounds, signs (gestures), or symbols which are understandable to others. The language development process includes both sending and receiving. Input (receiving) comes before output (sending); input is organized mentally by an individual long before decipherable sending takes place.

Communication is a broader term, defined as giving and receiving information, signals, or messages. A person can communicate with or receive communications from animals, infants, or foreign speakers. Even a whistling teakettle sends a message that someone can understand.

INFLUENCES ON DEVELOPMENT

A child's ability to communicate involves an integration of body parts and systems allowing hearing, understanding, organizing, and using language. Most children accomplish the task quickly and easily, but many factors *influence the learning of language*.

Sensory-motor development, which involves the use of sense organs and the coordination of motor systems (body muscles and parts) are all vital to language acquisition. Sense organs gather information through sight, hearing, smelling, tasting, and touching, figure 1-1. These sense-organ impressions of people, objects, and life encounters are then sent to the brain. Each *perception* (impression received through the senses) is recorded and stored, serving as a base

for future oral and written language. Sensory-motor tasks are covered in greater depth in Unit 5.

The child's social and emotional environments play a leading role in both the quality and quantity of beginning language. Much learning occurs through contact and interaction with others in family and then in social settings, figure 1-2. Basic attitudes towards life, self, and other people form early as life's pleasures and pains are experienced. The young child depends on parents and other caregivers to provide what is needed for growth and *equilibrium* (a balance achieved when consistent care is given and needs are satisfied). This side of a child's development has been called the *affective sphere,* referring to the affectionate feelings (or lack of them) shaped through experience with others, figure 1-3.

Another important factor which is related to all others is the child's mental maturity, or ability to think. The ages, stages, and sequences of increased mental capacity are very

FIGURE 1-1 Look at his exploring concentration!

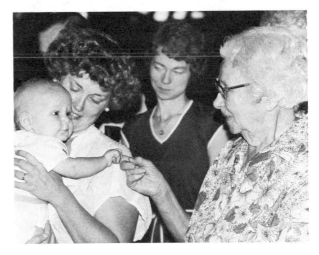

FIGURE 1-2 Positive experiences and interactions are important for language acquisition. *(From Machado and Meyer,* Early Childhood Practicum Guide, *Copyright 1984 by Delmar Publishers Inc.)*

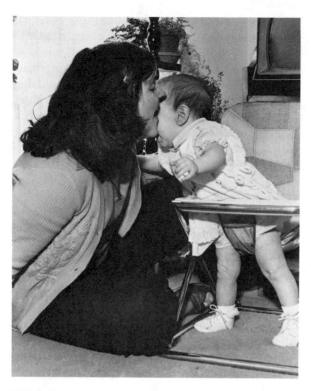

FIGURE 1-3 Loving care and attention in the early years can influence language development.

closely related to language development. Yet, at times, language skill and intellect seem to be growing independently, with one or the other developing at a faster rate. The relationship of intelligence and language has been a subject of debate for a long time. Most scholars, however, agree that these two topics are closely associated.

Cultural and social forces touch young lives with group attitudes, values, and beliefs. These have a great impact on a child's language development. Some cultures, for instance, expect children to look down when adults speak, showing respect by this action. Other cultures make extensive use of gestures and signaling. Still others seem to have limited vocabularies. Cultural values and factors can indeed affect language acquisition.

CURRENT THEORIES OF LANGUAGE ACQUISITION

Many scholars, philosophers, linguists, and researchers have tried to pinpoint exactly how language is learned. The view most early childhood educators hold focuses on *hearing* and *imitating,* and the child's realization that speech is useful in getting what he wants and needs. People in major fields of study: human development, linguistics, sociology, psychology, anthropology, speech-language pathology, and animal study (zoology) have contributed to current theory. The following are major theoretical positions.

Behavorist (or Stimulus-response) Theory

Theorists taking this position emphasize that language is only partially learned through imitation. As parents reward, correct, ignore, or punish the young child's communication, they exert considerable influence over both the quantity and quality of language usage and the child's *attitudes* toward communicating. The most important factor to consider in trying to promote language using this theory focuses upon the reactions of the people in a child's environment. In other words, positive, neutral, and/or negative reinforcement plays a key role in the emergence of communicating behaviors.

The child's sounds and sound combinations are thought to be uttered partly as imitation and partly at random, on impulse, without pattern or meaning. The child's utterances grow, seem to stand still, or are stifled depending on feedback from others. This theory is attributed to the work of B. F. Skinner, a pioneer researcher in the field of learning theory.

Predetermined Theory

In this theoretical position language acquisition is seen as being *innate* (a predetermined human capacity). Each new being is believed to possess a mental ability "wired-in" which equips that being to master *any* language. Chomsky (1968), a linguistic researcher, theorizes that each person has an individual Language Acquisition Device (LAD). Chomsky also theorizes that this device (capacity) has several sets of language-system rules (grammar) which are common to all known languages. As the child lives within a favorable family climate, his perceptions spark the device and the child learns the "mother tongue." Imitation or reinforcement are not ruled out as additional influences.

Chomsky notes that two and three year olds can utter understandable, complicated sentences that they have never heard. The child has to either possess remarkable thinking skills to do so, or very special skills as a language learner. Chomsky favors the latter explanation. Theorists who support this position note the infant's ability to babble sounds and noises used in languages the child has never heard.

Cognitive-transactional Theory

In a third theory, language acquisition is said to *develop* from basic social and emotional drives. The child, within this theory, is naturally active, seeking, adapting, and is shaped by transactions with the people in his environment. Drives stem from a need for love and care and the *need* prompts language acquisition. The child is described as a reactor to the human social contact that is so crucial to survival and well being. The child's view of the world consists of the mental impressions built as life events are fit into existing ones or categories are created for new ones. Language is an integral part of living, consequently the child seeks to fit its occurrence into some pattern which allows understanding. With enough exposure and with a functioning sensory receiving system the "code" is cracked slowly and the child eventually becomes a fluent speaker. The work of Jean Piaget, Jerome Bruner, and J. McVicker Hunt has prompted wide acceptance of this theory by early childhood professionals.

Maturational (Normative) Theory

The writings of Arnold Gesell and his colleagues represent the position that children are primarily a product of *genetic inheritance* with environmental influence being secondary. Children are seen as moving from one predictable stage to another with *readiness* the precursor of actual learning. This position was widely accepted in the 1960s when linguists studied children in less than desirable circumstances and discovered consistent patterns of language development. Using this theory as a basis for planning instruction for young children includes (1) identifying predictable stages of growth in language abilities, and (2) offering appropriate readiness activities to aid the child's graduation to the next higher level.

Other Theories

There is no all-inclusive theory of language acquisition which has been substantiated by research, rather there is some truth in each possibility; many relationships and mysteries are still under study. Current teaching practices involve many different styles and approaches to language arts activities although some teachers may prefer using techniques in accord with one particular theory. One common goal among educators is the desire to provide instruction for the child that encourages social and emotional development while also offering activities and opportunities in a warm, language-rich, supportive classroom, center, or home. Eveloff (1977) identified three major prerequisites of development and language acquisition. They are:

- thinking ability.
- a central nervous system allowing sophisticated perception.
- loving care.

These are all present if children are in good health and in quality day care and preschool facilities.

This text presents many challenging activities which go beyond simple rote memorization or passive participation. There's an attempt to offer an enriched program of literary experience which provokes thinking and enhances the child's ability to relate and share what's on his or her mind.

Dr. Maria Montessori, well known for her work with young children, described a sequence of development in language gathered from her observations, figure 1-4. It's offered here to stimulate your observation of the young child, and to urge you to be consciously alert to the child's emerging abilities.

COMMUNICATIVE BEGINNINGS IN INFANCY

Development of the ability to communicate begins even before the child is born since the prenatal environment plays such an important role. Factors can affect the development and health of the unborn such as emotional and physical stress of the mother and her health and nutrition. These, in turn, may lead to complications later in the child's language-learning capabilities.

The newborn quickly makes its needs known. The baby cries; mother or father responds. The parent feeds, holds, and keeps the child warm and dry. The sound of the parents' footsteps or voices, and their caring touch, often stops the baby's crying. The baby learns to anticipate. The sense perceptions received begin to be connected to stored impressions of the past.

As the child grows, he or she makes vocal noises; cooing after feeding, for instance, seems to be related to the child's feeling of comfort. During cooing, sounds are relaxed, low-pitched, gurgly, and are made in an open-mouthed, vowel-like way — for example, e (as in see), e (get), a (at), ah, and o, oo, ooo, figure 1-5. The infant appears to be in control of this sound making. Discomfort, by comparison, produces

1. Individual sounds.
2. Syllables.
3. Simple words, often doubled syllables like "dada." This is when the child first is said to speak, because the sound he produces communicates an idea.
4. Understanding and saying words that are the names of objects (nouns).
5. Understanding and saying words that refer to qualities of objects named (adjectives).
6. Understanding and saying words that refer to the relationship of objects named.
7. Explosion into language (verbs and the exact form of nouns and adjectives, including prefixes and suffixes).
8. The forms for present, past, and future tenses of verbs, use of the pronoun as a word that "stands in place of" a name.
9. Construction of sentences with mutually dependent parts.

FIGURE 1-4 Montessori sequence of language acquisition *(From Maria Montessori's* The Discovery of the Child, *translated by M. Joseph Costelloe, Notre Dame, IN: Fides Publishers, 1967.)*

consonantlike sounds, made in a tense manner with lips partly closed.

Infants differ in numerous ways from the moment of birth. Freedman's research (1979) concludes that significant ethnic differences and similarities exist in a newborn's reactions to various stimuli. However, in most cases, milestones in language development are reached at about the same age and in a recognizable sequence.

Eye Contact

Babies learn quickly that communicating is worthwhile since it results in actions on the part of another. Have you ever watched a baby gaze intently into his parent's eyes? Somehow, the child knows that this is a form of communication — and he is avidly looking for clues to fur-

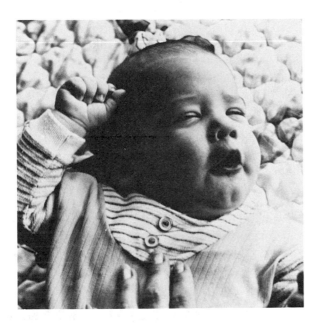

FIGURE 1-5 Cooing is related to a child's comfort level.

ther his meager knowledge. If the parent speaks, the baby's entire body seems to respond to the rhythm of the human voice. The *reciprocal* nature of the interactions aids development. Clarke-Stewart (1981) reported a high degree of relationship between a mother's responsiveness and the child's language competence. In a longitudinal study of infants from nine to eighteen months of age, more responsive mothers had children with greater language facility and growth.

Infants quickly recognize subtle (fine) differences in sounds. A parent's talk and touch increases sound making. Condon and Sanders have observed infants moving arms and legs in synchrony to the *rhythms* of human speech. Random noises, tapping, and disconnected vowel sounds don't produce the behavior (1982).

Research continues to uncover responding capabilities in both infants and their parents which have previously been overlooked. In one such experiment, newborns learned to suck on an artificial nipple hooked to a switch that turned on a brief portion of recorded speech or vocal music. They did not suck as readily when they heard instrumental music or rhythmic sound as when they heard a human voice (de Villiers, 1982).

The special people in the infant's life adopt observable behaviors when "speaking" to him just as the child seems to react in special ways to their attention. Mothers sometimes raise their voice pitch to a falsetto, shorten sentences, simplify their syntax, use nonsense sounds, and maintain prolonged eye contact during playful interchanges. Infants display a wide-eyed, playful, and bright-faced attitude toward their fathers and mothers (Brazelton, 1982). A mutual readiness to respond to each other appears built-in to warm relationships. The infant learns that eye contact can hold and maintain attention, and that looking away usually terminates both verbal and nonverbal episodes.

Around the fifth to tenth week of life, a significant event happens — the baby's first social smile. This is a giant first step to the many parent-child two-way conversations which will follow. Ainsworth and Bell (1972) concluded that responsive mothers (those who are alert in caring for the infant's needs) have babies who cry less frequently and have a wider range of different modes of communication. These responsive mothers create a balance between showing attention and affording the infant autonomy (offering a choice of action within safe bounds) when the infant became mobile. They also provide body contact and involve themselves playfully at times.

Babbling

Early random sound making is often called *babbling*. Infants the world over make sounds they've not heard, and will not use in their native language. This has been taken to mean that each human infant has the potential to master any world language (Jacobson, 1968). Close inspection shows repetitive sounds and "practice sessions" present. Babbling starts at about the fourth to sixth month and continues in some children through the toddler period, however, a peak in babbling is usually reached between nine and twelve months. Periods before the first words are marked by a type of babbling which repeats syllables over and over, as in "dadada-dadada." This is called *echolalia;* infants seem to echo themselves and others. Babbling behavior overlaps the one and two (or more) word-making stages, ending for some children at about eighteen months of age.

Deaf infants also babble and in play sessions will babble for longer periods without hearing either adult sound or their own sounds as long as they can see the adult responding. However, they stop babbling younger than hearing children do. It is not clearly understood why babbling occurs, either in hearing or non-hearing children, but it is felt that babbling gives the child the opportunity to use and control the mouth, throat, and lung muscles. Possibly, a child's babbling amuses and motivates him, acting as stimulus which adds variety to his existence.

In time, there is an increasing number of articulated (clear, distinct) vowel-like, consonant-like, and syllabic sounds. Although babbling includes a wide range of sounds, as children grow older they narrow the range and begin to focus on the familiar, much-heard language of the family. Other sounds are gradually discarded.

Physical contact continues to be important, figure 1-6. Touching, holding, rocking, and other types of physical contact bring a sense of security and a chance to respond through sound making. The active receiving of perceptions is encouraged by warm, loving parents who share a close relationship. A secure child responds more readily to the world around him. The child who lacks social and physical contact, or lives in an insecure home environment, falls behind in both the number and range of sounds made; differences start showing at about six months of age.

Simple imitation of language sounds begins early. Nonverbal imitated behavior such as tongue protrusion also occurs, figure 1-7. Sound

FIGURE 1-6 Touching brings feelings of security.

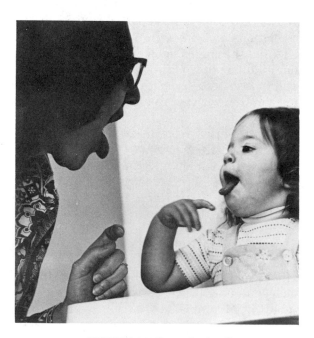

FIGURE 1-7 "I can do that."

imitation becomes syllable imitation, and short words are spoken about the end of the child's first year.

UNDERSTANDING

At about ten months of age, some infants start to respond to spoken word clues. A game such as "pat-a-cake" may start the baby clapping and "bye-bye" or "peek-a-boo" brings other imitations of earlier play activities with the parents. The child's language is called passive at this stage, for he or she primarily receives (or is receptive). Speaking attempts will later become active (or expressive). Vocabulary provides a small portal through which adults can gauge a little of what the child knows.

The infant communicates with the parents through many nonverbal actions; one common way is by holding the arms up, which most often means "I want to be picked up." Others include facial expression, voice tone, voice volume, posture, and gestures, such as an infant's "locking in" by pointing both fingers and toes at attention-getting people and events. For additional examples, see figure 1-8.

Although the infant can now respond to words, speaking does not automatically follow, because at this early age, there is much more for the child to understand. Changes in a parent's facial expression, changes in tone of voice and volume, and actions and gestures are all things which carry feelings and messages important to the child's well-being. Understanding the *tone* of the parents' speech comes before understanding the words, and that comes prior to the child trying to say them.

FIRST WORDS

Before an understandable close approximation of a word is uttered, the child's physical organs need to function in a delicate unison, and the required mental maturity needs to be reached. The child's respiratory system sup-

Gesture	Meaning
Allows food to run out of mouth	Satisfied or not hungry
Pouts	Displeased
Pushes nipple from mouth with tongue	Satisfied or not hungry
Pushes object away	Does not want it
Reaches out for object	Wants to have it handed to him
Reaches out to person	Wants to be picked up
Smacks lips or ejects tongue	Hungry
Smiles and holds out arms	Wants to be picked up
Sneezes excessively	Wet and cold
Squirms and trembles	Cold
Squirms, wiggles, and cries during dressing or bathing	Resents restriction on activities
Turns head from nipple	Satisfied or not hungry

FIGURE 1-8 Some common gestures of babyhood (*From Child Development by Elizabeth B. Hurlock, 1972 — used with permission of McGraw-Hill Company.*)

plies the necessary energy. As the breath is exhaled, sounds and speech are formed with the upward movement of air. The larnyx's vibrating folds produce voice: called *phonation*. The larnyx, mouth, and nose influence the child's voice quality: termed *resonation*. A last modification of the breath stream is *articulation;* a final formation done through molding, shaping, stopping, and releasing voiced and non-voiced sounds which reflect language heard in the child's environment.

Repetition of syllables such as ma, da, and ba in a child's babbling happens toward the end of the first year. If "mama" or "dada" or a close copy is said, parents show attention and joy. Language, especially in the area of speech development, is a two-way process; reaction is an important feedback to action.

Generally, first words are nouns or proper names of foods, animals, and toys, figure 1-9.

FIGURE 1-9 The name of the family pet may be among the first words a child learns.

Words first spoken are usually ones which contain p, b, t, d, m, and n (front of the mouth consonants). They are shortened versions, such as da for daddy and beh for bed. When two-syllable words are attempted, they are often strung together using the same syllable sound: as in dada and beebee. If the second syllable is different, however, the child's attempt at reproduction will come out dodee for doggy or papee for potty.

At this stage, words tend to be segments (parts) of wider happenings in the child's life. A child's word "ba" may represent a favorite often-used toy (such as a ball). As the child grows in experience, *any* round object seen in the grocery store for instance, will also be recognized, and called ba. This phenomenon has been termed *overextension*. The child has embraced "everything round" which is a much larger meaning for ball than the adult definition of the word ball.

Lee (1970) describes the child's development from early situation-tied first words to a broader usage:

> All words in the beginning vocabulary are on the same level of abstraction. They are labels of developing categories of experiences.

A child finds that words can open many doors. They help the child to get things, and cause caretakers to act in many ways. Vocabulary quickly grows from the names of objects to words which refer to action. This slowly decreases the child's dependence on context (a specific location and situation) for communication and gradually increases the child's reliance on words — the tools of abstract thought.

Toddler Speech

Toddlerhood begins and the child eagerly names things and seeks names for others. As if playing an enjoyable game, the child echoes and repeats to the best of his ability. At times, the words are not recognizable as the same words the parents offered. When interacting with young speakers, an adult must listen closely, watch for nonverbal signs, scan the situation, and use a good deal of guessing to understand the child and respond appropriately. The child's single words accompanied by gestures, motions, and intonations are called *holophrases*. They usually represent a whole idea or sentence.

While the child is learning to walk, speech, for a short period, may take a back seat to this developing motor skill.

> Between 15 to 18 months, while energy is concentrated upon walking, progress in talking may be slow. However, at this time the child may listen more intently to what others say (Scott, 1968).

The slow-paced learning of new words, figure 1-10, is followed by a period of rapid growth in vocabulary. The child pauses briefly, listening

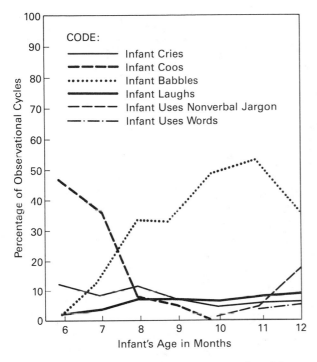

FIGURE 1-10 Infant vocalization to caretaker *(From Ziajka, Alan, Prelinguistic Communication in Infancy, Praeger Publishers, CBS Educational and Professional Publishing, 521 Fifth Ave., New York 10175.)*

and digesting, gathering his forces to embark on the great adventure — becoming a fluent speaker.

IMPLICATIONS FOR INFANT CENTER STAFF MEMBERS

The importance of understanding the responsive, reciprocal nature of optimal caregiving in group infant centers cannot be underestimated. As Honig (1981) points out, "caregivers who boost language are giving the gift of a great power to babies."

Infants can benefit from sensitive, alert, skilled adults — ones who read both nonverbal and vocalized cues, and react appropriately, and who are also attentive and loving. Learning to read each other's signals is basic to the *quality* of the relationship. Liberal amounts of touching, holding, smiling, and looking promote language as well as the child's overall sense that the world around him is both safe and fascinating. (1) Noting individualness, (2) reading nonverbal behaviors, and (3) reacting with purposeful actions are all expected of professional infant specialists. Specific suggestions to promote sound-making and subsequent first spoken words follow.

- Hold infant firmly yet gently, making soft, gentle sounds, and move smoothly while holding close.
- Your tone of voice is important for showing love and tenderness.
- Make a game of smiles, sounds, and movements at times.
- Imitate child's sounds in babbling, cooing, or other sound making between four and six months of age.
- Speak clearly.
- Encourage the child to look at you while you speak.
- Don't interrupt the child's vocal play, jargon, or self-communication.
- Engage in word play, rhyme, chants, and fun-to-say short expressions at times.
- Be an animated speaker frequently.
- Try simple fingerplays.
- Plan concrete participatory activities with textures, sights, and sounds.

Tarrow and Lundsteen (1981) have identified additional caregiver activities in figure 1-11.

CLASSIC LANGUAGE PLAY

The first two of the following language and body action plays has brought delight to generations of infants.

Level	Objective	Activity
Birth to 1 month	1. To develop intimacy and awareness of communication based on personal contact.	1. Whisper into the child's ear.
	2. To introduce the concept or oral communication.	2. Coo at the child.
	3. To introduce verbal communication.	3. Talk to the child.
	4. To stimulate interest in the process of talking.	4. Let the child explore your mouth with his or her hands as you talk.
1 to 3 months	1. To develop oral communication.	1. Imitate the sounds the child makes.
	2. To develop auditory acuity.	2. Talk to the child in different tones.
	3. To develop the concept that different people sound different.	3. Encourage others to talk and coo to the child.
	4. To develop the concept of oral and musical communication of feelings.	4. Sing songs of different moods, rhythms, and tempos.
3 to 6 months	1. To develop the concept of positive use of verbal communication.	1. Reward the child with words.
	2. To stimulate excitement about words.	2. Talk expressively to the child.
	3. To develop the concept that words and music can be linked.	3. Sing or chant to the child.
	4. To develop the ability to name things and events.	4. Describe daily rituals to the child as you carry them out.
6 to 9 months	1. To develop use of words and reinforce intimacy.	1. Talk constantly to the child and explain processes such as feeding, bathing, and changing clothes.
	2. To develop the concept that things have names.	2. Name toys for the child as the child plays, foods and utensils as the child eats, and so on.
	3. To develop the concept that there is joy in the written word.	3. Read aloud to the child, enthusiastically.
	4. To develop the concept that language is used to describe.	4. Describe sounds to the child as they are heard.
9 to 12 months	1. To develop the concept that body parts have names.	1. Name parts of the body and encourage the child to point to them.
	2. To reinforce the concept that things have names.	2. Describe and name things seen on a walk or an automobile trip.
	3. To stimulate rhythm and interest in words.	3. Repeat simple songs, rhymes, and finger plays.
	4. To stimulate experimentation with sounds and words.	4. Respond to sounds the child makes, and encourage the child to imitate sounds.

FIGURE 1-11 Sequential objectives and activities for language development *(Sara Wynn Lundsteen and Norma Bernstein Tarrow,* Activities and Resources for Guiding Young Children's Learning, *1981. Reproduced with permission from Mc-Graw-Hill Book Company.)*

This Little Piggie

(While holding and wiggling each toe gently — starting with the big toe and continuing down toward the smallest toe as each line is said.)

This little pig went to market,
This little pig stayed home,
This little pig had roast beef,
This little pig had none,
This little piggie cried, "Wee, wee, wee,
　　wee!" all the way home.

Pat-a-cake

(While helping him imitate hand-clapping, and pat-a-caking.)

Pat-a-cake, pat-a-cake, baker's man,
Bake me a cake as fast as you can.
Pat it and prick it and mark it with a "B",
And put it in the oven for baby and me.

So Big

Say, "How big are you?" and then help him answer by saying "So-o-o-o-o big!" as you raise his hands above his head. Repeat.

Say "Ah" as you slowly bring him to your face, and then gently say "Boo!". Repeat. "Ah-h-h-h-h . . . Boo!" (Pushaw, 1976)

SUMMARY

Each child grows in language ability in a unique way. The process starts before birth with the development of sensory organs. Parents play an important role in a child's growth and mastery of language.

Perceptions gained through life experiences serve as a base for the later learning of words and speech. Babbling, sound-making, and imitation occur, and first words appear.

A number of related factors influence a child's language acquisition. Most children progress through a series of language ability stages at about the same ages, figure 1-12, and become adultlike speakers during the preschool period. The way children learn language is not clearly understood, and so there are a number of differing theories of language acquisition.

Early in life infants and parents form a reciprocal relationship, reacting in special ways to each other. The quality and quantity of parental attention becomes an important factor in language development.

The child progresses from receiving to sending language, which is accompanied by gestures and nonverbal communication. From infancy, the child is an active participant, edging closer to the two-way process required in language usage and verbal communication.

Staff members in infant care programs can possess interaction skills which offer infants optimum opportunities for speech development.

Age	Developing Language Behaviors and Occurrences
Birth–one month	Cries to express desires (food, attention, etc.) or displeasure (pain or discomfort); small throaty sounds; tense, active movement, or relaxed posture (nonverbal).
2–3 months	Coos, pleasurable noises; babbling; blowing and smacking sounds; open vowel-like babbles; fewer consonant-type babbles; markedly less crying; smiles, squeals; may coo for half a minute; pitch changes apparent.
4–6 months	Sound play; single syllable-like sounds (phonemes); babbles; smiles; responds to human sounds more intently; eye searches speakers; consonant-like sounds; turns head toward speaker; responds by raising arms at times; reacts to friendly or angry voice; looks at speaking family members, and may look at a "named" object or person.
6–8 months	Repeats syllables; imitates motions; uses nonverbal signals; vocalizes all 14 vowels; reduplication of utterances; more distinct intonation.
9–10 months	Gurgling or bubble blowing, may start jargon-like strings of sounds; gestures; grunts.
11–17 months	First words; may master 10 words; gestures used to add meaning; two-word sentences; starts to label familiar objects and people; overgeneralizes words; babbling and jargon decrease during the end of this period.
18 months	Uses up to 50 words; understanding progressing rapidly; recognizes up to 12 objects by name; points to 3 body parts; simple commands understood; babbling includes intricate intonation patterns.

FIGURE 1-12

Learning Activities

- Observe two infants (birth to 12 months). Note situations in which the infants make sounds and how adults (parent or teacher) react to the sound-making.

- Describe nonverbal communication that you notice or receive in any situation with a group of people — such as in a classroom, cafeteria, family group, social group, or anywhere a group of people are assembled.

- Sit with a young infant facing you. Have a note pad handy. Remain speechless and motionless. Try to determine what moment-to-moment needs the child has, and try to fulfill each need you recognize. Try not to add anything new; just respond to what you feel the child needs. Write a description of needs observed and your feelings.

- Using the form in figure 1-13, read and review a magazine article or a research article concerning children's language development. Be prepared to briefly review your findings to fellow students. Make a few statements concerning your reaction to the article's main conclusions.

Topics:

LANGUAGE DEVELOPMENT, LANGUAGE ACQUISITION, PSYCHOLINGUISTICS, STUDIES IN ANIMAL COMMUNICATION.

Use the *Reader's Guide to Periodical Literature* or another resource guide to locate an article.

Title of article _____

Author(s) _____

Source name _____

Date of publication _____

Number of pages _____

General findings of the research article (number of subjects, ages, testing device or procedure, results, or article main points).

SUGGESTED JOURNALS: Child Development, Young Children, Today's Education, Journal of Clinical Psychology, Journal of Personality and Social Psychology, Journal of Marriage and Family, Teacher, Children, Learning, Journal of Psychology, Journal of Social Psychology, Child Welfare, Exceptional Children, Journal of Speech and Hearing Research, School Review, Reading Teacher, Journal of Special Education.
MAGAZINES: Parents, Family Circle, Good Housekeeping, Instructor, Child Care and Early Education.
BOOKS: Readings in Child Development, Readings in Early Childhood Education.

FIGURE 1-13

- Try the following with a 4–12 month old. Touch the child as you say the words. Report the child's reactions at the next class meeting. (Watson, 1978, Reprinted by permission)

    Here comes a mouse
    Mousie, mousie, mouse

    With tiny light feet
    And a soft pink nose
    Tickledy tickle
    Wherever he goes

    He runs up your arm
    And under your chin
    Don't open your mouth
    Or the mouse will run in

    Mousie, mousie, mouse!

Unit Review

A. Write your own theory of how children learn language.

B. Finish the following: Caregivers working in group infant care programs who wish to give infants opportunities to acquire language should carefully monitor their ability to . . . (List specific techniques.)

C. Write definitions for:

   phonation   resonation   echolalia

D. Discuss and finish "Language is a kind of game infants learn. A game played with precise recognizable rules like. . . . 'First, I talk, then you talk.' To learn the game it's best to have adults in your life who . . . ?"

E. Answer the following questions based on the information in the unit.
   1. What are the two basic factors which influence language development?
   2. How can parents help the young child develop language?
   3. What is one purpose of a child's babbling?
   4. Why is language development described as a two-way process?
   5. What are the names of the sense organs which receive and transmit messages?
   6. What is the name for impressions received through the senses?

F. Select the best answer.
   1. Environmental factors which can affect future language development start
      a. at birth.   c. during infancy.
      b. before birth   d. during toddlerhood.

2. The tone of a parent's voice is
   a. understood when a child learns to speak in sentences.
   b. less important than the parent's words.
   c. understood before actual words are understood.
   d. less important than the parent's actions.

3. In acquiring language the child
   a. learns only through imitation.
   b. is one participant in a two-part process.
   c. learns best when parents ignore the child's unclear sounds.
   d. does not learn anything by imitating.

4. Select the true statement about babbling.
   a. Why babbling occurs is not clearly understood.
   b. Babbling is unimportant.
   c. Babbling predicts how early a child will start talking.
   d. Babbling rarely lasts beyond one year of age.

5. How a child acquires language is
   a. clearly understood.
   b. not important.
   c. only partly understood.
   d. rarely a subject for study.

G. Explain the difference between language and communication.

H. Match the words in Column I with the appropriate meaning or example in Column II.

Column I
1. perception
2. babbling
3. tone
4. B. F. Skinner
5. imitation
6. speaking vocabulary at 12 months
7. nonverbal communication
8. deprivation
9. repeated syllables
10. one of five senses
11. first words
12. recognized English language sounds
13. authorities agree

Column II
a. random sound production
b. mama, dada, bye-bye
c. the Behaviorist Theory
d. close reproduction of alphabet letter sounds
e. 0–4 words
f. language and thought are interrelated
g. the way words are spoken rather than the meaning of the words
h. repeating sounds and actions
i. thumb sucking, smiling, tears
j. lack of warm, loving care
k. impressions sent from sensory organs to brain
l. touching
m. usually represent objects or people experienced daily

References

Ainsworth, M. D. S. and S. M. Bell, "Mother-Infant Interaction and the Development of Competence," ERIC Document. ED 065 180, 1972.

Bee, Helen, *The Developing Child,* Harper and Row, 1981.

Brazelton, T. Berry, in Richard M. Restak's "Newborn Knowledge," Article 15, 1982, *Human Development,* Annual Editions 83/84, The Dushkin Publishing Group Inc., 1983.

Chomsky, Noam, *Language and Mind,* New York; Harcourt, Brace, and World, 1968.

Clarke-Stewart, K. A., *Interactions Between Mothers and Their Young Children; Characteristics and Consequences,* Monographs of the Society for Research in Child Development 38, nos. 6–7 (1973).

Condon and Sanders in Restak, R. M., "Newborn Knowledge," *Science 82 Magazine,* copyright 1982. The American Association for the Advancement of Science.

Egolf, D. and S. Chester, *Nonverbal Communication and Disorders of Speech and Language,* ASHA, 1973.

Eveloff, Herbert H., "Some Cognitive and Affective Aspects of Early Language Development" in S. Cohen and T. Comiskey (eds.) *Child Development Contemporary Perspectives,* Itasca, IL: F. E. Peacock Publishers, Inc., p. 149, 1977.

Freedman, Daniel G., "Ethnic Differences in Babies," *Human Nature,* 1979.

Hoy, J. and I. Somer, editors; *The Language Experience,* Dell Publishing Co., Inc., New York, 1974.

Jacobson, R., *Child Language,* The Hague: Monton, 1968.

Lee, Laura L., "The Relevance of General Semantics to Development of Sentence Structure in Children's Language" in Lee Thayer (ed.) *Communication: General Semantics Perspectives,* New York: Spartan Books, 1970.

Pushaw, David R., *Teach Your Child To Talk,* Dantree Press, Inc., 1976.

Scott, Louise Binder, *Learning Time With Language Experiences for Young Children,* McGraw-Hill Book Co., 1968.

Stewig, John W., "Teaching Language Arts in Early Childhood," *CBS College Publishing,* 1982.

Tarrow, Norma Bernstein and Sara Wynn Lundsteen, *Activities and Resources for Guiding Young Children's Learning,* McGraw-Hill Book Company, New York, 1981.

Watson, Clyde, *Catch Me and Kiss Me and Say It Again,* Philomel Books, a Division of Putnam Publishing Group, 1978.

Suggested Readings

de Villiers, Peter A. and Jill G. de Villiers, *Early Language,* Harvard University Press, Cambridge, MA, 1979.

Honig, Alice Sterling, "What Are the Needs of Infants?", *Young Children,* Vol. 37, no. 1, Nov. 1981.

Unit 2
The Tasks of the Toddler

OBJECTIVES

After studying this unit you should be able to

- discuss phonology, grammar, and the toddler's understanding of semantics.

- list three characteristics of toddler language.

- identify adult behaviors which aid the toddler's speech development.

If you were amazed at the infant's and year-old's ability, wait until you meet the toddler! Toddlerhood marks the beginning of a critical language growth period — named for the child's speed in gaining language competency. This period seems to be the prime time for speech development. Never again will words enter the vocabulary at the same rate; abilities emerge in giant spurts almost daily. When a child stops and focuses, whether on specks on the floor or something larger than himself, concentration is total — every sense organ seems to probe for data, figure 2-1.

There are three major tasks in language acquisition which face the toddler. These are (1) the child's growing understanding of *phonology* (the sound system of a language), (2) *grammar* (a system of rules governing word order and combinations which give sense to short utterances and sentences), and (3) *semantics* (word meanings).

PHONOLOGY

Toddlers learn the phonology of their native language: its phonetic units, and its particular and sometimes peculiar sounds. A *pho-* *neme* is the smallest unit of sound which distinguishes one utterance from another — inferring a difference in meaning, figure 2-2. English has 46–50 phonemes depending on what expert is consulted.

Languages are divided into vowel sounds and consonants. In vowels the breath stream flows freely from the vocal cords, in consonants it is blocked and molded in the mouth-throat area by soft tissue, muscle tissue, and bone with

FIGURE 2-1 Focusing on a new object

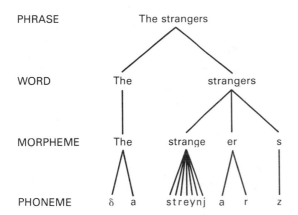

SENTENCE   The strangers said hello.

PHRASE   The strangers

WORD   The   strangers

MORPHEME   The   strange   er   s

PHONEME   δ a   streynj a   r   z

FIGURE 2-2 From phonemes to sentences

tongue and jaw often working together. The child focuses on those sounds heard most often, using repetition and rhythm speech-play. Toddler babbling of this type continues and remains pleasurable during early toddlerhood. Sounds which are combinations of vowels and consonants increase. Some sounds, which take close listening and are difficult to form, will continue to be spoken without being close approximations of adult sounds until the child reaches five or six years of age or even slightly older. Early childhood teachers realize they will have to listen closely and watch for nonverbal clues to understand child speech in many instances.

It is a difficult task for the child to make recognizable sounds with mouth, throat, and breath control working in unison. Lenneberg (1971) comments on the difficulties of perfecting motor control of speech-producing muscles, noting that this sophisticated skill comes ahead of many other physical skills.

Speech, which requires infinitely precise and swift movements of tongue and lips, all well-coordinated with laryngeal and respiratory motor systems, is all but fully developed when most other mechanical skills are far below levels of their future accomplishment.

Much of early speech has been called jargon or gibberish. The toddler seems to realize that conversations come in long strings of sound. Rising to the occasion, he imitates the *rhythm* of the sound, but utters only a few understandable words.

Toddlers hear a word as an adult hears it. Sometimes they also know the proper pronunciation but are unable to reproduce it: the child may say "pway" for play. If the parent says "pway," the child objects, showing confusion and perhaps frustration. Toddler talk, sometimes called baby talk, represents the child's best imitation given his present ability. Adults may be tempted to respond in a playful baby-talking mode because of the perceived cuteness of the toddler's speech. This isn't recommended because it offers immature forms of words rather than correct pronunciations. Play with words with a toddler can easily be undertaken with adults using simple, clear speech.

Views on adult use of baby talk include the idea that the practice may limit modeling of more mature word forms and emphasize dependency. On the other hand, parents may offer simplified, easily-pronounced forms like "bow-wow" for barking poodle. They later quickly switch to adult, harder-to-pronounce forms when the child seems ready. In the beginning, though, most adults automatically modify their speech when speaking with toddlers by using short sentences and stressing *key* words.

Children progress with language at their individual rates and with varying degrees of clarity. Some children speak relatively clearly from their first tries. Other children, who are also progressing normally, take a longer time before their speech is easily understood. All fifty basic sounds (fifty including diphthongs) are perfected by most children by age seven or eight.

Morphology

A *morpheme* is the smallest unit of language standing by itself with recognized meaning. It can be a word or part of a word. Many prefixes (un-, ill-) and suffixes (-s, -ness, -ed, -ing) are morphemes with their own distinct meaning. The study of morphemes is called *morphology*. There are wide individual differences in the rates toddlers utter morphemes, figure 2-3. It is unfortunate if early childhood teachers or parents attempt to compare the emerging speech of toddlers or equate greater speech usage with higher ability or "give the squeeky wheels the grease" thus giving the quiet toddler(s) perhaps less of their time.

GRAMMAR RULE FORMATION

Languages have word orders and rules, and young children speak in the word order and fol-

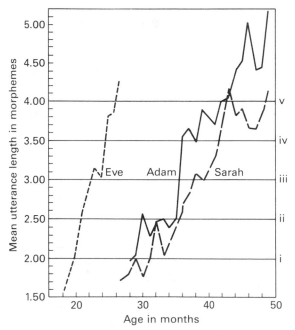

FIGURE 2-3 Individual rates in morpheme usage *(From "The Child's Grammar from I to III," by R. Brown, C. Cazden, and U. Bellugi-Klima, John P. Hill (ed.), Minnesota Symposium on Child Psychology, Vol. 2, 1969. Reprinted by permission of the University of Minnesota Press.)*

low the rules of their native tongue. In one language, the subject of a sentence follows the verb; in other languages, it precedes the verb. Modifiers (describing words) in some languages have gender (male and female forms), while in others they do not. Plurals and possessive forms are unique to each language. Young speakers will make mistakes, but adults marvel at the grammar the child does use correctly, having learned the rules without direct instruction.

Of all the perceptions received, the words spoken to and about him, the child has noted regularities and unconsciously formed rules, which are continually revised. Chukovsky (1965) describes this task:

> It is frightening to think what an enormous number of grammatical forms are poured over the poor head of the young child. And he, as if it were nothing at all, adjusts to all the chaos, constantly sorting out in rubrics the disorderly elements of words he hears, without noticing as he does this, his gigantic effort. If an adult had to master so many grammatical rules within so short a time, his head would surely burst . . . In truth, the young child is the hardest mental toiler on our planet. Fortunately, he does not even suspect this.

Understanding general rules of grammar develops before the exceptions to the rules do. Correct grammar forms may change to incorrect as the child forms new rules. Slobin (1971) has an interesting example of this phenomena:

> In all of the cases which have been studied (and these are children of homes where standard English is spoken, and are usually first-born children) the first past tenses used are the correct forms of irregular verbs — came, broke, went, and so on. Apparently these irregular verbs in the past tense — which are the most frequent past tense forms in adult speech — are learned as

separate vocabulary items at a very early age.

Then, as soon as the child learns only one or two regular past tense forms — like helped and walked — he immediately replaces the correct irregular past tense forms with their incorrect over-generalizations from the regular forms. Thus children say "it came off," "it broke," and "he did it" before they say "it comed off," "it breaked," and "he doed it." Even though the correct forms may have been practiced for several months, they are driven out of the child's speech by the overregularization, and may not return for years.

In later years, during elementary school, the child will formally learn the grammar rules of his native language. What the child has accomplished before that time, however, is monumental. The amount of speech that already conforms to the particular syntactical and grammatical rules of language is amazing. The child has done this through careful listening and mentally reorganizing the common things in language that have been perceived.

The toddler's growing use of intonation and inflection (changes in loudness of voice) adds clarity, as do nonverbal gestures. The child is often insistent that adults listen.

English sentences follow a subject-verb-object sequence. Bruner (1966) notes three fundamental properties of sentences: verb-object, subject-predicate, and modification, and explains their universal use:

> There are no human languages whose sentences do not contain rules for these three basic sentential structures, and there are no nonhuman languages that have them.

Learning the grammar rules helps the toddler express ideas (Bellugi, 1977). Understanding *syntax* (the arrangement of words to show relationship) relates to the child being understood:

It is our knowledge of the rules of combination — the syntax of the language — that governs how we construct and understand an infinite number of sentences from a finite vocabulary. Syntax gives language its power.

If one listens closely to the older toddler, sometimes self-correction of speech errors takes place. Toddlers talk to themselves and their toys often, figure 2-4. It seems to aid storage and remembering.

MEANINGS (SEMANTICS)

Semantics is the study of meanings. It probes how the sounds of language are related to the real world and life experiences (Clarke-Stewart & Koch, 1983). The toddler absorbs meanings from both verbal and nonverbal communication sent and received. The nonverbal refers to expressive associates of words — rhythm,

FIGURE 2-4 "Beebee"

stress, pitch, gesture, body position, facial changes, and so on. Adults perform important functions in the child's labeling and concept formation by giving words meanings in conversations. Adults and teachers seem to unconsciously realize there are different levels of specificity in naming most objects. One offers dog before spaniel and collie, money before quarter, cookie before chocolate chip. As de Villiers (1982) explains:

So a child will typically learn the word flower before he separates roses from daffodils and tulips and before he can call flowers, trees, and grass *plants.*

In toddler classrooms, teachers have many opportunities to name objects and happenings as the day unfolds. Using gesturing along with words (or pointing in simple picture books and magazine pictures) helps the toddler form a connection between what is heard and said. Repeating words with voice stress can be done in a natural way while monitoring if the child is still interested.

A *concept* is the recognition of one or more distinguishing features of a set of events, per-

FIGURE 2-5 "Give me the ball."

sons, or objects, figure 2-5. Some parents supply, help the child discover, and point out the differences; others may not. The following passage deals with the concept of "thimbles."

A person who espies a thimble is recognizing what he sees, and this certainly entails what he has already learned and not forgotten about what thimbles look like. He has learned enough of the recipe for the looks of thimbles to recognize thimbles when he sees them . . . (Ryle, 1946).

A toddler may overuse concepts in new situations. Perhaps a Band-Aid® on the tip of brother's finger will be called a thimble. For a short time, all men are daddies; a cow may be called a big dog; and all people in white are feared. As mental maturity and life experiences increase, concepts change; small details and exceptions are noticed.

Concepts, often paired mentally with words, aid categorizing. Concept words may have full, partial, or little depth of meaning. The toddler's level of thought is reflected in speech. When counting to three, he may or may not know what "three-ness" represents. Words are symbols; Huey (1965) explains their importance:

A concept, to be communicable, must be represented by a symbol that is understood by others to carry the same meaning that the child intends. The symbol is usually a word. Symbols are aids to thinking that enable the individual to reflect upon objects or situations which are not actually present.

A toddler's first-hand sensory experiences are very important. Stored mental perceptions are attached to words. Spitzer (1977) points out that words are only as rich as the experiences and depth of understanding behind them:

Words are the basic elements of language, but they are too often misunderstood. Our society puts tremendous emphasis on the acquisition of a large vocabulary in young children. But few realize that words without experiences are meaningless. They are empty concepts. Language allows humans to communicate meaningfully with others. The more experiences and meaning that backs up words, the more rewarding the communication process will become.

The activities and experiences found in later units help the early childhood teacher enrich the child's concepts by providing deeper meanings in a wide range of language arts. Every activity for young children — a total school program — gives them a language arts background full of exploring opportunities for handling, manipulating, tasting, smelling, and touching, besides seeing and listening.

PRAGMATICS

The subtleties of our language are many faceted. *Pragmatics* is the study of how language is used effectively in a social context, or the practical aspect of oral communication. It's the study of "who can say what, in what way, where and when, by what means and to whom" (Hymes, 1971). Language is a tool in questioning, ordering, soothing, ridiculing, and other social actions. One can request quiet in the form of a question "Can't anyone get a peaceful moment around here?" or talk longingly about the candy in a store for the purpose of obtaining it, as in "Oh they've got my favorite kind of chocolate bar!", without making a direct request.

The language that young children use to express desires, wishes, concerns, and interests becomes a reflection of their social selves (Yawkey, Askov, Cartwright, DuPuis, Fairchild, 1981). When a toddler communicates effectively feedback is received from others. Many times a sense of well-being elicited by positive happenings help the child shape a feeling of competency and self esteem. Not yet socially subtle in speech, the toddler has not learned the pragmatically useful or appropriate behaviors of older children. There seems to be one

intent, to get the message across by gaining adult attention regardless of who is present and in what situation . . . the world — in his opinion — revolves around him and his need to communicate what is on his mind.

FIRST SENTENCES

The shift from one word to a two (or more) word stage at approximately 18 months is a milestone. At that time the toddler has a speaking vocabulary of about 50 words; by thirty-six months upwards of 1,000 words.

If one looks closely at two-word utterances, two classes of words become apparent. Braine (1973) termed the smaller group "pivot words." Examples of the toddler's two-word sentences, with pivot words underlined, are shown in figure 2-6. They are used more often than nonpivots, but seem to enter the vocabulary more slowly, perhaps because pivot words are stable and fixed in meaning.

Understanding grammar rules at this two-word stage is displayed even though many words are missing. Braine also points out the frequency with which toddlers use a simple form, and almost in the same breath, clarify by expansion (by adding another word). The invention of words by toddlers is commonplace. Meers

Two-word Sentences	Meanings
Daddy there.*	Location
See kitty.	Identification
More cookie.	Repetition
Milk allgone.	Nonexistence
Sit chair.	Action — location
No car.	Negation
Todd shoe.	Possession
Big cup.	Attribute description
Jim walk.	Agent — action
Kiss you.	Action — direct object
Where ball?	Question

*underlined words are pivots

FIGURE 2-6 Pivot words in toddler's two-word sentences

(1976) describes an 18-month old who had her own private word for "sleep" consistently calling it "ooma." Parents trying to understand their toddler get good at filling in the blanks. They then can confirm the child's statement, and can add meaning at a time when the child's interest is focused.

TODDLER-ADULT CONVERSATIONS

Toddlers are skillful communicators. They converse and correct adult interpretations, gaining pleasure and satisfaction from language exchanges. The following incident shows more than toddler persistence.

A first-time visitor to the home of a twenty-month-old toddler is approached by the toddler. The visitor eventually rises out of his chair, accompanies the toddler to the kitchen, gets a glass of water, and hands it to the child. The toddler takes a tiny drink, and returns, satisfied, to the living room. Parents were not involved. Thirst, itself, was unimportant. The pleasure gained by the child seemed to motivate his actions.

For the child to accomplish his ends, the following actions occurred:

- Visitor behavior
  1. Focuses attention on child.
  2. Realizes a "talking" situation is occurring.
  3. Listens and maintains a receiver attitude.
  4. Corrects own behavior, guesses at child's meaning, and tries new actions.
  5. Realizes conversation is over.
- Child behavior
  1. Stands in front of visitor, searches face to catch eye, makes loud vocalization dropping volume when eye contact made, observes visitor behavior.
  2. Repeats first sound (parents understand, visitor doesn't), observes visitor reaction.

3. Grabs visitor's hand, vocalizes loudly, looks in visitor's eyes.
4. Tugs at hand, uses insistent voice tone, gestures toward kitchen.
5. Pulls visitor to sink, uses new word (visitor doesn't understand), corrects through gestures when visitor reaches for cooky jar.
6. Corrects visitor's guess (milk), gestures towards water, holds out hand.
7. Drinks and hands back glass, smiles, and walks away.

This type of behavior has been called *instrumental expression* since vocalization and nonverbal behaviors were used to obtain a certain goal.

The toddler seeks out people willing to listen and learns from each encounter.

CHARACTERISTICS OF TODDLER LANGUAGE

The speech of young children speaking in two-word sentences is termed *telegraphic* and *prosodic*. It is telegraphic because many words are omitted because of the child's limited ability to express and remember large segments of information; the most important parts of the sentence are usually present. Prosodic refers to the child's use of voice modulation and word stress with a particular word(s) to give special emphasis and meaning.

NEGATIVES

No discussion of the older toddler's language would be complete without mention of the child's use of "no." There seems to be an exasperating time when the child says no to everything . . . seemingly testing whether there is a choice. Young children's first use of "no" indicates non-existence (Bloom, 1970). Later it is used to indicate rejection and denial. Even when the child can speak in sentences longer than three words, "no" often remains the first in a sequence of words. A typical example is "No want go bed." Soon children insert negatives properly between the subject and the verb into longer utterances as sentence length increases. Of all speech characteristics, toddlers use of negatives, and their avid, energetic demands to be "listened to" stick in the memories of their caretakers.

AIDS TO TODDLER SPEECH DEVELOPMENT

Holmes and Morrison (1979) offer adults advice concerning providing an optimum toddler center environment for language stimulation.

- Expose the child to language with speech neither too simple nor too complex, but just slightly above the child's current level.
- Stay "in tune" with the child's actual abilities.
- Omit unreasonable speech demands, yet encourage attempts.
- Remember positive reinforcement is a more effective tool than negative feedback.
- Accept the child's formulating a language concept on his own.
- Channel progress by providing a correct model.
- Make a point of being responsive.
- Follow the child's interest by naming and simple discussion.

Tarrow and Lundsteen (1981) suggest toddler activities identifying their objectives in figure 2-7. Other toddler activity ideas can be found by Sterling (1983) in *Early Childhood Practicum Guide*, Delmar Publishers, pages 279–80. A toddler movement play follows.

Take your little hands and go clap, clap,
clap
Take your little hands and go clap, clap,
clap

Take your little hands and go clap, clap,
clap
Clap, clap, clap your hands.

Take your little foot and go tap, tap, tap
Take your little foot and go tap, tap, tap
Take your little foot and go tap, tap, tap
Tap, tap, tap your foot.

Take your little eyes and go blink, blink,
blink
Take your little eyes and go blink, blink,
blink
Take your little eyes and go blink, blink,
blink
Blink, blink, blink your eyes.

Take your little mouth and go buzz, buzz,
buzz
Take your little mouth and go buzz, buzz,
buzz
Take your little mouth and go buzz, buzz,
buzz
Buzz like a bumblebee.

Take your little hand and wave bye, bye,
bye
Take your little hand and wave bye, bye,
bye
Take your little hand and wave bye, bye,
bye
Wave your hand bye-bye.

INTRODUCING TODDLERS TO BOOKS

Toddlers show an interest in simple, colorful books and pictures and enjoy adult closeness and attention. Pointing and naming can become an enjoyed game. Sturdy pages which are easily turned help the toddler too. A scrapbook of photographs of favorite objects mounted on cardboard individualize the experience. Clear contact and lamination will add life and protection. Since a toddler may move on quickly to investigating other aspects of the environment, adults offering initial experiences with

12 to 18 months	1. To develop the ability to label things and follow directions. 2. To expand vocabulary and lay the foundation for later production of sentences. 3. To reinforce the concept of names and the ability to recognize names and sounds. 4. To encourage verbal communication. 5. To reinforce the concept of labels and increase vocabulary.	1. Line up various objects and, naming one, ask the child to get it. 2. Act out verbs ("sit," "jump," "run," "smile," etc.). 3. Use animal picture books and posters of animals. 4. Let the child talk on a real telephone. 5. Describe things at home or outside, on a walk or an automobile trip.
18 to 24 months	1. To stimulate imitation and verbalization. 2. To improve the ability to name objects. 3. To encourage repetition, sequencing, and rhythm. 4. To develop auditory acuity, passive vocabulary, and the concept of language constancy. 5. To stimulate verbalization, selectivity and — eventually — descriptive language. 6. To stimulate conversation.	1. Tape-record the child and others familiar to the child, and play the tapes back for the child. 2. On a walk around the home or neighborhood with the child, point out and name familiar objects. 3. Play counting games, sing songs, and tell and retell familiar stories. 4. With the child, listen to the same recording of a story or song over and over. 5. Cut out of magazines and mount on stiff cardboard: pictures of foods, clothing, appliances, etc. Have the child identify them as you show them. Use memorable descriptions: "orange, buttery carrots"; "the shiny blue car." 6. With the child, prepare and eat a make-believe meal.

FIGURE 2-7 Toddler activities and objectives *(Sara Wynn Lundsteen and Norma Bernstein Tarrow,* Activities and Resources for Guiding Young Children's Learning, *1981. Reproduced with permission from McGraw-Hill Book Company.)*

books need to remember that when interest has waned it's time to respect the search for other adventures.

An infant and toddler book bibliography is suggested by Pushaw (1976), figure 2-8.

SUMMARY

Language ability grows at its fastest rate of development during the toddler period. Young children accomplish difficult language tasks. They learn their native language sounds (phonetics) and produce an increasing number successfully. Grammar rules form and reform, coming closer to mature speech. The child listens more carefully, noticing regularities and meanings (semantics) of words and gestures.

Concepts develop, serving as categories which help the child organize life's events. Many concepts are paired with words. Word symbols aid

Six to Twelve Months

Baby's Book of Animals, James & Jonathan, Inc. Ideal for six-month-old child. Colorful pictures; pages not easily torn.
What the Animals Say, James & Jonathan, Inc. Cloth picture book with brief text; good pictures.
Baby Animals Board Book, illustrated by Gyo Fujikawa, McLoughlin Brothers.
Farm Animals Board Book, illustrated by Irma Wilde, McLoughlin Brothers.
Baby's Mother Goose, illustrated by Alice Schlesinger, McLoughlin Brothers. Colorful pictures; simple, suitable content.
Tall Book of Mother Goose, The, illustrated by Feodor Rojankovsky, Harper and Row. The bold colors of the pictures are attractive to youngsters.
Real Mother Goose, The, illustrated by Blanche Fisher Wright, Rand McNally. Appealing pictures.

One to Two Years

Come Walk With Me; I Look Out My Window; This Is My House; My Toys; Let's Go Shopping; A Trip to the Zoo; designed by Aurelius Battaglia, Playskool Play Books, Playskool Manufacturing Company, Inc.
Baby Farm Animals, by Garth Williams, Golden Press. Just a few words of text — and charming pictures. The pages are made of strong cardboard.
Child's Good Night Book, A, by Margaret Wise Brown, illustrated by Jean Charlot, Addison-Wesley. A thoroughly satisfying book, and one that may be a calming preliminary to going to bed.
Goodnight Moon, by Margaret Wise Brown, illustrated by Clement Hurd, Harper and Row. Part of the fun of this book is locating the mouse in each picture.

FIGURE 2-8 Infant and toddler book list

communication and language by allowing the child to speak and be understood. Parents' conversations and the child's first-hand exploring by sense organs give depth to new words.

The toddler is active in conversations, speaking and listening, sometimes correcting, trying to get the message across to whoever in the family will listen. The toddler talks to himself and his toys in one and then two (or more) word sentences. These sentences are barely recognizable at first, but gain more and more clarity as age progresses.

Learning Activities

- Form a group of three fellow students. Using the following three statements, explore changing word stress, rhythm, and pitch. Analyze changed meaning.
  1. What am I doing?
  2. It was his book.
  3. You're a fine person.

- Using only gestures, get the person sitting next to you to give you a Kleenex or handkerchief or tell you that one is not available.

- Observe three toddlers (15–24 months). Write down consonant sounds you hear. Record the number of minutes for each observation.

- Using the following scale, rate each of the following statements.

Strongly Agree	Agree	Can't Decide	Mildly Disagree	Strongly Disagree

1. Toddlers can be best understood when adults analyze their words instead of their meanings.
2. Some parents seem to have a knack of talking to young children which they probably don't realize they possess.
3. The labeling stage is a time when children learn concepts rather than words.
4. Learning language is really simple imitation.
5. The study of semantics could take a lifetime.

Talk about your ratings in a group discussion.

- On a piece of paper, list as many toddler language milestones or accomplishments as you can remember.

Unit Review

A. Match each word in Column I with the phrase it relates to in Column II.

Column I
1. jargon
2. phonology
3. grammar
4. dis? dat?
5. pivot
6. alphabet
7. symbol

Column II
a. "Allgone cookie."
   "Shoe allgone."
b. toddler goes through a naming or labeling stage
c. toddler unconsciously recognizes word order
d. though they are limited in number, many serve a double purpose
e. each world language has its own
f. "Ibbed googa oodle."
g. a word represents something

B. Write a brief description of experiences that could promote a toddler's learning the word "hat." (Example: Parent points to a picture of a hat in a picture book, and says "hat.")

C. List five identifying characteristics of the following concepts:
needle, giraffe

D. Return to Review Question B. How many of your examples involved the child's sensory exploration of a hat? Why would this aid the child's learning?

E. Why is the toddler period called the prime or critical time for learning language?

F. Write definitions for the following words. Check your definition with the ones found in the Glossary at the end of the text. Add your definition if one is absent.

    syntax   phonetic   modifier   phoneme   morpheme

G. Select the best answer.
   1. Most children clearly articulate all English letter sounds by age
      a. 7 or 8.   c. 5.
      b. 6.   d. 24 months.
   2. Most concept words used correctly by toddlers are
      a. labels and imitative echoing.
      b. fully understood.
      c. used because identifying characteristics have been noticed.
      d. rarely overused.
   3. From beginning attempts, children
      a. reverse word order.
      b. use full simple sentences.
      c. use stress, intonation, and inflection in speaking.
      d. are always clearly understood.
   4. One should _____ insist the toddler pronounce "tree" correctly if he is saying "twee."
      a. always   c. never
      b. usually   d. tactfully
   5. A toddler's one word sentence, "Wawa" may mean:
      a. "I want a drink of water."
      b. The child's dog, Waiter, is present.
      c. The child's father's name is Walter.
      d. Any one or none of the above.

H. What parent behaviors are helpful in the toddler's acquisition of language?

References

Anglin, J. M., *Work, Object, and Conceptual Development,* Norton Publishers, New York, 1977.

Bellugi, Ursula, "Learning the Language" in Robert Schell (ed.) *Reading in Psychology Today,* New York: Random House, 1977.

Bloom, L., *Language Development: Form and Function in Emerging Grammars,* MIT Press, Cambridge, MA, 1970.

Braine, M. D. S., "The Ontogeny of English Phrase Structures: The First Phase," in C. A. Ferguson and D. I. Sloben (eds.) *Studies of Child Language Development,* New York: Holt, Rinehart, and Winston, Inc., 1973.

Bruner, Jerome et al., *Studies in Cognitive Growth,* New York: John Wiley and Sons, 1966.

Clarke-Stewart, R. and Joanne Barbara Koch, *Children,* John Wiley and Sons, Inc., 1983.

de Villiers, Peter A. and Jill G. de Villiers, *Early Language,* Harvard University Press, Cambridge, MA, 1982.

Holmes, Deborah L. and Frederick J. Morrison, *The Child,* Brooks-Cole Publishing Co., Monterey, CA, 1979.

Huey, Francis, "Learning Potential of the Young Child," *Educational Leadership,* Nov. 1965, Vol. 23.

Hymes, D., "Competence and Performance in Linguistic Theory" in Huxley, R. and E. Ingram, (eds.) *Language Acquisition: Models and Methods,* New York: Academic Press, Inc., 1971.

Lenneberg, Eric H., "The Natural History of Language," in John Eliot (ed.) *Human Development and Cognitive Processes,* New York: Holt, Rinehart and Winston, Inc., 1971.

Meers, Hilda J., *Helping Our Children Talk,* Longman Group Limited, New York, 1976.

Pushaw, David K., *Teach Your Child to Talk,* Dantree Press, Inc., 1976.

Ryle, Gilbert, *The Concept of Mind,* London: Hutchinson House, 1949.

Slobin, Dan I., *Psycholinguistics* (Glenview, IL: Scott, Foresman and Co., 1971).

Spitzer, Dean R., *Concept Formation and Learning in Early Childhood,* Charles E. Merrill Publ., Co., 1977.

Tarrow, Norma B. and S. W. Lundsteen, *Activities and Resources for Guiding Young Children's Learning,* McGraw-Hill Book Co., 1981.

Yawkey, Thomas D., et al., *Language Arts and The Young Child,* F. E. Peacock Publishers Inc., 1981.

Suggested Readings

Chukovsky, Kornei Ivanovich, *From Two to Five,* University of California Press, Berkeley, 1965.

Machado, J. and H. Meyer, *Early Childhood Practicum Guide,* Delmar Publishers, Albany, NY, 1984, pp. 279–85.

Meers, Hilda J., *Helping Our Children Talk,* Longman Group Limited, New York, 1976.

Unit 3
Preschool Years

OBJECTIVES

After studying this unit you should be able to

- identify characteristics of typical preschool speech.

- describe differences in the language of younger and older preschool children.

- discuss the child's vocabulary growth.

The preschool child's speech reflects sensory, physical, and social experiences as well as thinking ability. Parents and teachers accept temporary limitations, knowing that almost all children will reach adult language levels.

A main concern of teachers is to interact and provide growing opportunities and activities. An understanding of typical preschool speech characteristics can help the teacher to do this.

Background experiences with children and child study gives a teacher insight into children's language behavior. The beginnings of language, early steps, and factors affecting the infant and toddler's self-expression were covered in Units 1 and 2. This unit pinpoints language use during preschool years. Although speech abilities are emphasized, growth and change in other areas is also covered as it relates to speech.

Next to the influence of the child's home, playing with other children is a major factor influencing language development. Finding friends one's own age is an important part of attending an early childhood center. In a place where there are fascinating things to explore and talk about, language abilities blossom, figure 3-1.

It is almost impossible to find a child who has *all* of the speech characteristics of a given age group, but most children possess *some* of the characteristics that are typical for their age level. There is a wide range within normal age-level behavior, although each child's individualism is always present.

FIGURE 3-1 "Lookit, lookit, lookit, caterpillar!"

For simplicity's sake, the preschool period is divided here into early (2 to 3 years) and later (4 to 5 years) age groups.

THE EARLY PRESCHOOL YEARS

Preschoolers communicate needs, desires, and feelings through speech and action. Close observation of a child's nonverbal communication can help to uncover true meanings. A raised arm, fierce clutching of playthings, or lying "spread eagle" over as many blocks as possible may express more than the child is able to put into words.

Squeals, grunts, and screams are often part of play. Imitating animals, sirens, and environmental noise is common. The child points and pulls to help others understand meanings. Younger preschoolers tend to act as if others can read their thoughts because, in the child's past, adults anticipated what was needed. A few children may have what seems to be a limited vocabulary at school until they feel at home there.

The words used most often are nouns and short possessives: my, mine, Rick's. Speech focuses on present happenings, things observed "newscaster" style, and "no" is used liberally.

Volume may be loud, with high-pitched speech when excited, or barely audible and muffled speech when the child is embarrassed, sad, or shy. Speech of two- and three-year-olds tends to be uneven in rhythm, stopping and starting, rather than flowing like the speech of older children.

VERB FORMS

In English, most verbs (regular ones) use -ed to indicate past tense. Unfortunately, many frequently-used verbs happen to be irregular with past tense forms — came, fell, hit, saw, took, and gave among others. Since the child begins using often-heard words, early speech contains correct verb forms. With additional exposure to the language around him, the idea that past happenings are described with -ed signals on verb endings becomes noticed unconsciously. At that point children tack the -ed on both regular verbs and irregular ones, coming up with broked, dranked, and other charming past tense forms. This beautiful logic often brings inner smiles to adult listeners. Verbs ending with "ing" are used more than before. Even auxiliary verbs are scattered through speech — "Me have," "Daddy did it" (Pflaum, 1974). Words such as wanna, gonna, and hafta seem to be learned as "wholes," and stick in the child's vocabulary, being used over and over.

TELEGRAM SENTENCES

The early preschooler, as the toddler, omits many words in sentences. The remaining words remind one of a telegram in which only the essentials are present. These words are key words and convey the essence of the message. Without relating them to real occurrences, meaning might be lost to the listener. Sentences now are about four words long. Some pronouns and adjectives — such as pretty or big — are used. Very few, if any, prepositions (by, on, with), or articles (a, an, the), or conjunctions (and, but, so) are spoken with high frequency. Some words are run together, and are spoken as single units, such as "whadat?" or "eatem," as are the verb forms mentioned in the previous paragraph. The order of words (syntax) may seem jumbled at times, as in "outside going ball," but basic grammar rules are observed in most cases.

Pronouns are often used incorrectly and confused — "Me all finish milk," and "him Mark's." Concepts of male and female, living things, and objects may be only partly understood, as shown in the following example:

And when a three-year-old says of the ring she cannot find, "Maybe it's hiding!" the listener wonders if she hasn't yet learned that hiding can be done only by an animate object (Cazden, 1972).

1 Child: Ages	Yes-No Questions	Wh-Questions
Period A (28 mths)	Expressed by intonation only: Sit chair? Ball go?	Limited number of routines: What('s) that? Where NP go? What NP doing?
Period B (38 mths) More complex sentences being questioned, but no development of question forms themselves, except the appearances, probably as routines, of two negative auxiliaries *don't* and *can't* Development of auxiliary verbs in the child's entire grammatical system. Inversion of aux. and subject NP in Yes-No, but not in Wh-questions	Dat black too? Mom pinch finger? You can't fix it? Are you going to make it with me? Will you help me? Does the kitty stand up? Can I have a piece of paper?	What soldier marching? Where my mitten? Why you waking me up? What I did yesterday? Which way they should go? Why the Christmas Tree? How he can be a doctor?
Period C–F (42–54 mths)	Development of tag questions from *Huh?* to mature form: I have two turn, huh? We're playing, huh? That's funny isn't it? He was scared wasn't he? Mommy, when we saw those girls they were running weren't they?	Inversion of aux. and subject NP, first in affirmative questions only: Why are you thirsty? Why can't we find the right one? Later, starting in Period F, negative question also: Why can't they put on their diving suits and swim? Development of complex questions, including indirect Wh-questions: You don't know where you're going. He doesn't know what to do. We don't know who that is.

FIGURE 3-2 Development of question forms (*From Child Language and Education by Courtney B. Cazden. Copyright © 1972 by Holt, Rinehart and Winston, CBS College Publishing*)

QUESTIONS

"Wh" questions (where, what, why, who) begin in speech. During the toddler period rising voice inflection and simple declarative utterances such as "Dolly drink?" are typical. Now questions focus on location, objects, and people, with causation (why), process (how), and time (when) appearing. This reflects more mature thinking which probes purposes and intentions in others. Figure 3-2 shows one child's questioning development. Questions are frequent, and the child sometimes asks for an object's function, or reasons behind happenings. It is as if the child sees that things exist for a purpose which in some way relates to him or her. The answers that adults provide stimulate further "wanting to know."

Vocabularies now range from between 250 to over 1,000 words, figure 3-3. An average of fifty new words enter the child's vocabulary each month.

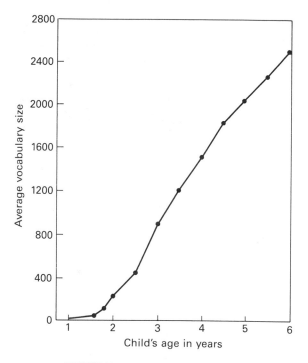

FIGURE 3-3 Growth of vocabulary

Word	Object or Event for Which the Word Was Originally Used	Other Objects or Events to Which the Word Was Later Applied
mooi	moon	cakes, round marks on windows, writing on windows and in books, round shapes in books, tooling on leather book covers, round post-marks, letter *O*
buti	ball	toy, radish, stone spheres at park entrance.
sch	sound of train	all moving machines
em	worm	flies, ants, all small insects, heads of timothy grass.
fafer	sound of trains	steaming coffee pot, anything that hissed or made a noise
va	white plush dog	muffler, cat, father's fur coat

FIGURE 3-4 Some examples of overextensions in the language of 1- and 2-year-old children. *(From Eve V. Clark, "Knowledge, context, and strategy in the acquisition of meaning." In Gurt 1975: Daniel P. Dato, ed.,* Developmental Psycholinguistics: Theory and Applications. *Copyright 1975 by Georgetown University, Washington, DC.)*

OVERLAPPING CONCEPTS AND UNDEREXTENSION

Younger preschoolers commonly call all four-footed furry animals "dog," and all large animals "horse." The child has *overextended* and made a logical conclusion because these animals have many of the same features, can be about the same size, and therefore fit the existing word. This phenomena: termed overlap or overgeneralization, is seen in the examples given in figure 3-4.

Underextension is somewhat the opposite. It refers to the child's tendency to call all male adults "daddy" or all dogs by the family dog's name, even though the child can clearly recognize the difference between his dad and all other males, and his dog from other dogs.

Concept development, defined in Unit 2 as the recognition of one or more distinguishing features or characteristics, proceeds by leaps and bounds during preschool years, and is essential to meaningful communication. Details, exceptions, and discrepancies are often present in child conversations. The excitement of discovery and exploring — particularly something new and novel — is readily apparent in preschool classrooms. Crowding around to see, touch, experience, and talk about happenings is typical. Teachers notice the "all consuming focusing," the long periods of watching or touching usually followed by verbalizing and questioning an event or experience.

Running Commentaries

As children play, their actions are sometimes accompanied by running self-commentaries of what they are doing or what is happening, figure 3-5. Brophy (1977) offers a reason for this type of speech:

Children talk to themselves to give themselves directions for the same reason that they use their fingers in counting. They need sensorimotor activity as a reinforcement or "crutch," because their cognitive schemes are not yet developed well enough to allow them to think silently without such props.

Talking to self and talking to another can occur alternately. Toys, animals, and treasured items still receive a few words. Statements directed to others do not usually need answers: they tend to alert others to what the child is doing. This is called *egocentric* speech — speech which does not consider another's point of view. A conversation between young preschoolers may sound like two children talking together about different subjects. Neither child is really listening or reacting to what the other says. When a young child does wish to talk directly to another child, it is sometimes done through an adult. A child may say, "I want truck," to an adult, even if the other child is standing close by, playing with the truck.

Repetition

Repetition in speech occurs often. Sometimes it happens randomly at play, and at other times

FIGURE 3-5 "Coming out now."

it is done with a special purpose. A young child may repeat almost everything said to him, word for word. Most young preschoolers repeat words or parts of sentences regularly. They quickly imitate a word that they like; sometimes excitement is the cause. Chukovsky (1963) points out that rhyming words or syllables may promote enjoyable mimicking: "The younger the child, the greater his attraction to word repetition that rhymes." Some reasons for repetition are (1) it is a way to promote remembering [just as adults mentally repeat a new telephone number], (2) it is a way to reduce stress, and (3) there is enjoyment in repetitive sound making.

Free associations (voiced juggling of sounds and words) occurs at play and at rest, and may sound like babbling. It is as if having learned a word, the child must savor it or practice it, over and over. Occasionally, a child even makes up words to fit play situations.

LACK OF CLARITY

About one in every four words of the young preschooler is not readily understandable. This lack of clarity is partially caused by an inability to control mouth, tongue, and breathing, and to hear subtle differences and distinctions in speech. Typically, articulation of all English speech sounds is not accomplished until age seven or eight; the preschooler is only 40–80% correct in articulation. This lack of intelligibility in children can also be partly attributed to the complexity of the task of mastering the sounds. So though right on target in development, he's still hard to understand at times.

He may have a difficulty with speech or a combination — rate of speech, phrasing, inflection, intensity, syntax, and voice stress. Misarticulation and defective sound making can also contribute to the problem. The child who attempts to form the longest utterances is usually the one who is hardest to understand. The child who omits sounds is less clear than the one who distorts them. As a rule, expect omissions, substitutions, and distortions in the speech of two- and three-year-olds for they will be plentiful.

Young children typically omit sounds at the end of words — "ba" for ball. Middle consonants in longer words are also passed over lightly — "ikeem" for ice cream, or "telfone" for telephone. Even beginning sounds may be omitted, as the common "ellow" for yellow.

Substitutions of letter sounds are also common; for example, "aminal" and "pasghetti." Until the new sound is mastered one consonant may even take the place of another; "wabbit" for "rabbit" is a common example.

Parents sometimes worry about a child who stops, stammers, or stutters when speaking. Calling attention to this and making demands on the child can cause tension, making the situation worse instead of better. All children hesitate, repeat, stop, and start — it is typical behavior. Searching for the right word takes the child time; thoughts may come faster than words. Adults need to relax and wait. Speech is a complex sending and receiving process. Maintaining patience and optimism is the best course of action for the adult.

THE OLDER PRESCHOOLER

Between 4 and 5 years of age, most preschoolers approach adultlike speech, their sentences are longer and almost all words are present instead of only key ones.

Their play is active and vocal and they copy each other's words. A word such as "monster," or more colorful ones, may swiftly gain in interest and spread rapidly from child to child. Remember the joy which both younger and older children exhibited with the phrases: "Zip-a-dee-doo-dah!", "Bibbidi-bobbidi-boo!", "Scoobi-scoobi-do!", "Super-cali-fragi-listic-expi-ali-docious!", "Ooey-gooey!", "Fuzzy-wuzzy!"?

Social speech and conversations are now heard and interpreted to a greater degree by others of the child's own age. Joint planning of play activities and active make-believe and role playing take place, figure 3-6. When playing "mama," the child acts like one; adults often see themselves in the role play of the child.

More and more relational words appear as the child begins to compare, contrast, and revise stored concepts with new happenings. The following teacher-recorded anecdote during a storytelling activity shows how the child attempts to relate previously learned ideas to a new situation.

During storytelling, Michael repeated with increasing vigor, "He not berry nice!" at story parts when the wolf said "I'm going to blow your house down." Michael seemed to be checking with me the correctness of his thinking based on his internalized rules of proper moral conduct. (Busy Bee Preschool, Santa Clara, CA)

Impact Words

Not all speech used by the older preschooler is appreciated by adults. Namecalling and offensive words and phrases may be used by the active preschooler to get attention and reaction from both adults and children. The child discovers that some phrases, sentences, and words cause unusual behavior in others. He actively explores these and usually learns what is appropriate and when it can be used. The child learns that most of this type of talk has "impact value." If it makes people laugh or gives the child some kind of positive reward, it is used over and over.

Some children discover that by increasing volume or changing tone they can affect others' behavior. They also may discover that speech can show anger and be used aggressively to hurt another.

Young children may mimic the speech of television characters. Acts of aggression can

Situation:	Two girls are playing with water.	
	Commentary	**Characteristic**
Debbie:	"Two of those make one of these." (playing with measuring cups.)	Talking to self.
Debbie:	"Two cups or three cups . . . whoops it went over."	Talks about what happened.
Tifine:	"Stop it or else I'll beat you up." (said to Debbie)	Doesn't respond to another's speech.
Debbie:	"This is heavy." (Holding the 2-cup measuring container full of water.)	Describes perception.
Christine:	"Is it hot?" (Chris just dropped in.)	
Debbie:	"Feel it and see."	Hears another; answers appropriately.
	"It's not hot." (Feeling the water.)	Child talking to self.
Debbie:	"I'm finished now. Oh this is awfully heavy — I'm going to pour it into the bottle."	Talking about what she is doing.

FIGURE 3-6 Conversation during play activity

become part of this type of play, clothed in the character's imitated speech and actions.

Purposeful echoing or baby talk may be used to irritate or tease. Excessive talking is sometimes used to get one's way, and "talking back" may occur.

Silence can get as much attention from adults as loud speech, but bragging, boasting, and continuous "look at me" statements are common. These are often used to gain recognition and acceptance, which builds self-confidence. Tattling on another may simply be checking for correctness, or it can be purposeful.

Through trial and error, and feedback, the child finds that words can gain friends or favor, hurt, or satisfy a wide range of needs. Being an emotion-packed human being, a preschooler's statements can range from "you're my buddy" type expressions to "you're my enemy" ones, figure 3-7.

FIGURE 3-7 "You're my friend, huh?"

What appears to adults to be violent statements may be just role playing or cooperative competition play. To some adults, the preschooler might appear loud and wild in speech. Speech seems overly nasal and full of moisture which sprays out in some words. A young child may have frequent nasal colds and congestion during this period. He tends to stand close, and volume goes up when he is intense about his subject.

Bathroom words are explored and used as "put downs" and attention getters. Giggles and uproarious laughter ensue when they are used. Adding to the child's enjoyment, new teachers may not know how to handle these situations. Knowing the school's position can be a subject for staff discussion. Commonly, newly-spoken bathroom talk is ignored unless it's hurtful, or the child is matter-of-factly told that the place to use the word is in the bathroom. Since it's no fun without an audience this frequently remedies the behavior. Otherwise a firm "That's a word that hurts. His name is Michael," might suffice.

Common Speech Patterns

Rhyming happens frequently in the play speech of four-year-olds, and teachers sometimes join the fun.

Often self-chatter is present. At this age, it seems to be an attempt to relate what is happening with what the child already thinks and feels; a kind of thinking out loud.

The older preschooler still makes errors in grammar and in the past tense of verbs — "He didn't *caught* me"; adjectives — "It's *biggerer* than yours"; time words — "The *next tomorrow*"; and negatives — "I *didn't did* it." But skill is increasing, and forms of the irregular verb 'to be' improve: "I *am* so," or "They're hot and yours *are* cold." Sentence structure becomes more adultlike including relative clause use and using both complex and compound forms. Articulation of letter sounds is still developing; about 75% of English letter sounds are made correctly. Omissions of letter sounds: *'merca* for America, or substitutions: *udder* for other, are still present.

The older preschooler has a vocabulary of over 2,000 words. The child is very concerned about the correct names of things, and can find the errors in the speech of others. Being an active explorer, the child's questions still probe the "purposefulness" of objects or actions, such as "Why is the moon in the sky?" The 4-year-old becomes an active "problem solver" and tends to explain, when possible, through visual attributes, "A cow is called that 'cause of its horns'." Elkind (1971) describes the preschooler's inability at times to talk about his solutions:

Although the preschooler can respond to and solve problems posed verbally, he is not able to verbalize his solutions.

The child can transform questions; for example, if asked to carry a message asking mom if *she's* ready, he will correctly ask her, "Are *you* ready?"

At this time of early childhood, most children can enjoy books, stories, and activities with words. More and more of a child's time is spent on these pursuits, figure 3-8.

The child may still stutter, clutter, and stop speech when there is stress or excitement. The less-mature speech of a best friend might be copied, and nonverbal expression is always a part of communication.

Most 4- and 5-year-olds are avid speakers. They are interested in exploring the real world as well as make-believe ones.

Chukovsky (1963) prizes the child's ability to fantasize, and encourages teachers and parents to accept and value it:

Fantasy is the most valuable attribute of the human mind, and it should be diligently nurtured from earliest childhood, as one nurtures musical sensitivity.

A wide range of individual speech behavior is both normal and possible. Knowing some

FIGURE 3-8 Enjoying a favorite book

typical behaviors can help the teacher understand young children. Some younger preschoolers may have the speech characteristics of older preschoolers; while some older preschoolers have the characteristics of younger ones, figure 3-9. Each child is unique in his own progress and rate of acquiring language skill.

SUMMARY

Knowing typical and common language development characteristics helps the teacher to understand that children are individuals. The

Consonant Sounds	Average Age of Control
f, h, m, n, ng, p, w, y	3
b, ch, d, g, k, s, sh, r	4
l, t, th, v	5–6
z, zh, j, sl, sk, br, tr	7
all letter sounds	8

FIGURE 3-9 Average ages of clear reproduction of English consonants

speech of the young preschooler (aged 2 to 3) is partly understandable. Teachers can use their knowledge in many ways, such as alerting the staff about a child's need for special help, and helping parents who are concerned with their child's speech patterns.

The older preschool child (aged 4 to 5) has almost adultlike speech. Some newly learned speech may be irritating to school staffs and parents, but it indicates physical, mental, and social growth. It shows positive development in language arts. Exploring both real and make-believe worlds with words becomes the child's active pursuit during the early childhood years.

There is no "average" child when it comes to language development; individual differences exist and are treated with acceptance and optimism.

Learning Activities

- Observe a 2-, 3-, 4-, and 5-year-old for fifteen minute periods. Try to write down what is said and a brief description of the setting and actions. Underline typical characteristics described in this unit. Make comparisons between older and younger preschool children.

- Interview two teachers. Ask if any preschool child within their care seems to have special speech or language problems. Write down the teachers' comments and compare them to typical characteristics mentioned in the unit.

- What rules or restrictions concerning the use of inappropriate speech (name-calling, swearing, and screaming) would you expect to find in a preschool center?

- Write definitions for:
    egocentric speech
    running commentary
    fantasy
    overextension

Unit Review

A. Associate the following characteristics with the correct age group. Some may seem to fit both categories; choose the *most* appropriate one. Write the characteristics under the headings: Younger Preschooler (2 and 3 years) and Older Preschooler (4 and 5 years).

   75% perfect articulation   nonverbal communication
   "Look, I'm jumping."   2,000–2,500 word vocabulary

telegram sentences

rhyming and nonsense words

name-calling

repetitions

omission of letter sounds

adultlike speech

bathroom words

talking about what one is doing

stuttering

talking through an adult

substitutions

role playing

planning play with others

B. Select the correct answer. Many questions have more than one correct response.

1. The younger preschool child (2–3 years)
   a. may still grunt and scream in communicating.
   b. always replies to what is said to him by another child.
   c. articulates many sounds unclearly.
   d. speaks in complete sentences at two years of age.

2. A truly typical or average child
   a. would have all the characteristics for his age.
   b. is almost impossible to find.
   c. is one who speaks better than his peers.
   d. sometimes makes up words to fit new situations.

3. Repetition in the speech of the young child
   a. needs careful watching.
   b. is common for children aged 2 to 5.
   c. can be word play.
   d. happens for a variety of reasons.

4. Name-calling and swearing
   a. may take place during preschool years.
   b. can gain attention.
   c. shows that children are testing reactions with words.
   d. only happens with poorly behaved children.

5. A word like "blood" or "ghost"
   a. may spread quickly to many children.
   b. has impact value.
   c. can make people listen.
   d. is rarely used in a preschool group.

6. Most younger preschoolers
   a. cannot correctly pronounce all consonants.
   b. omit some letter sounds.
   c. have adultlike speech.
   d. will, when older, reach adult-level speech.

7. Stuttering during preschool years
   a. happens often.
   b. should not be drawn to the child's attention.
   c. may happen when a child is excited.
   d. means the child will need professional help to overcome it.

8. "Me wented" is an example of
   a. pronoun difficulty.
   b. a telegram sentence.
   c. verb incorrectness.
   d. the speech of some 2- or 3-year-olds.

9. Planning word play with two or more children is found more often in
   a. the 2- to 3-year-old.
   b. the 4- to 5-year old.
   c. slowly developing children.
   d. male children.

10. Knowing typical speech characteristics is important because teachers
    a. must answer parents' questions.
    b. can help individual children.
    c. interact daily with young children.
    d. should be able to recognize normal behavior.

References

Brophy, Jere E., *Child Development and Socialization,* Chicago, IL: Science Research Associates, Inc., 1977.

Cazden, Courtney B., *Child Language and Education,* New York: Holt, Rinehart and Winston, Inc., 1972.

Chukovsky, Kornei, *From Two to Five,* Berkeley, CA: University of California Press, 1963.

Elkind, David, "Cognition in Infancy and Early Childhood" in John Eliot (ed.) *Human Development and Cognitive Process,* New York: Holt, Rinehart and Winston, Inc., 1971.

Pflaum, S. W., *The Development of Language and Reading,* Columbus, OH: Charles Merrill Publishers, 1974.

Suggested Readings

Charlesworth, Rosalind, *Understanding Child Development,* Delmar Publishers, 1983, Units 17 and 18.

Feeney, Stephanie et al., *Who Am I in the Lives of Young Children?,* Second edition, Chas. E. Merrill Publishing Co., 1983, pp 205–213.

Hendrick, Joanne, *The Whole Child,* Third edition, C. V. Mosby, 1984, Chapter 16.

Honig, Alice S., "Language Environments for Young Children," *Young Children,* 38:1, 1982, pp 56–67.

Unit 4
Growth Systems Affecting Early Language Ability

OBJECTIVES

After studying this unit you should be able to

- describe sequential stages of intellectual development.
- list three perceptual-motor skills which preschool activities might include.
- discuss the importance of a center's ability to meet young children's social and emotional needs.

The child is a total being and so language growth cannot be isolated from physical, mental, and social-emotional well-being. All body systems need a minimum level of movement (exercise) to keep the body in good working order and to stimulate brain growth. A proper intake of nutritious foods and living conditions which provide emotional security and balance can affect the child's acquisition of language and his general health and resistance to disease. A preschool, child care center, or day care setting intent on developing language skills focuses on satisfying both physical and emotional needs while also providing intellectual opportunity and challenge by offering a variety of age-appropriate activities.

PHYSICAL GROWTH

Physical development limits or aids capabilities, thereby affecting the child's view of himself as well as the way he is treated by others. Early childhood teachers are aware of these fundamental physical changes which take place in the young child. For instance, a slightly taller, physically active, strong, and well-coordinated child who can ride a two wheeler, figure 4-1, and drop kick a football may be admired by his peers. A wide range of physical skills in individual children exists within preschool groups as in all developmental areas.

Preschoolers grow at the rate of 2–3 inches in height, and 4–6 pounds in weight a year. At about 18–24 months, the child's thumb is used in opposition to just one finger. The ability to use tools and drawing markers begins. The nutritional quality of the child's diet exerts an influence on both body and neural development. Monitoring nutrient intake, height, weight gain, and emotional well being can alert parents to possible deficiencies.

Illness during accelerated growth may produce conditions affecting language development if it damages necessary body systems. Hearing loss and vision difficulties impair the child's ability to receive communications and

FIGURE 4-1 A two-wheel bike takes balance and coordination.

FIGURE 4-2 Interesting equipment encourages exploration.

learn the native language. A brain impairment may hinder the child's ability to sort perceptions; efficiently slowing progress.

Preschools and day care programs plan a wide range of motor activities; lots of time is devoted to children playing with interesting equipment in both indoor and outdoor areas, figure 4-2. The well known adage "healthy body/healthy mind" should be translated into "well-exercised and coordinated small and large muscles" for people who plan young children's daily programs.

PERCEPTION

As the child matures perceptual acuity increases; finer detail is seen. Most children achieve 20/20 vision (adult optimum) at age 14. At ages 2 to 5 vision is in the 20/45 to 20/30 range (Weymouth, 1963). Hearing acuity increases from birth through age 4 and 5 (Weiss & Lillywhite, 1981). At this point the hearing mechanisms are essentially mature and will not change greatly except through disease or injury.

Young children are noted for their desire to get their hands on what interests them. If a new child with particularly noticeable hair joins a group, hands and fingers are sure to try to explore its texture. If a teacher wears a soft, fuzzy jacket there will be stroking and snuggling. Perceptions are gathered with all sense organs.

Researchers exploring infant visual preferences have pinpointed a series of changes in attention-drawing features from infancy to age 5:

Two months — change from having attention captured by movement and edges of people and objects to active search and explore.

Age 2–5 — change from unsystematic exploring to systematically examining each feature carefully. (Gibson, 1969)

Children get better and better at focusing on one aspect of a complex situation: selective attentioning, and ignoring the irrelevant and distracting. In complex situations the child does best when perceptual distractions are minimized allowing deep concentration (Gibson, 1969).

Individual differences have been described in the way children explore their environment and react to problems. Kagan (1971) has described *conceptual tempo,* where the child who answers quickly and may make mistakes (impulsive) is contrasted with the child who spends considerable time examining alternatives (reflective). A second difference in perception identifies field-independent and field-dependent styles of perceiving. Field-independent children are those good at ignoring irrelevant context while field dependents tend to focus upon the total context. See how long it takes you to find the hidden objects in Ahlberg's *Each Peach Pear Plum* illustration in figure 4-3. How would you describe your perceptual style?

Perceptual-motor Skills

Piaget, the noted Swiss psychologist and researcher, has greatly affected early childhood educators' interest in perceptual-motor activities. Piaget and others observed that reflective (automatic) movements such as crying, sucking, and grasping in infants became controlled, purposeful body movements as the child grew. He speculated that physical movement

FIGURE 4-3 *(From Janet and Allan Ahlberg,* Each Peach Pear Plum, *Reprinted by permission of Penguin Books Ltd., London.)*

served as a base for later mental abilities necessary for thinking and speaking. His theory (1952) includes stages in the development of human intelligence, which are condensed in the following:

1. *Sensorimotor period* (birth to 18–24 months) Reflex actions become coordinated and perfected by physical movement and exploration of real objects and events.
2. *Preoperational period* (18–24 months to 7–8 years) Mental symbols represent what is experienced; imitation occurs. As the child matures meanings attached to symbols grow and become detailed and precise, and physical actions combine with mental actions.
3. *Concrete operations period* (7–8 years to 11–12 years) Child's thinking now is less dependent on physical involvement or immediate perceptual cues which aid classifying, ordering, grouping, numbering, and "inner" and "cross" subgrouping of concepts.

Manipulation and body activity during preschool years (2 to 5 years old) is equally as important as developing language abilities. The close ties between motor activities and thought processes indicates that the child needs motor activity involving the five sense organs plus larger body muscle use, figure 4-4. Exactly how much of a child's mental activity is dependent upon or promoted by physical activity is unknown. Most educators of young children feel that a definite, strong connection exists.

Motor skill develops in an orderly, predictable, head-to-toe fashion. Head, neck, and upper body muscles are controlled first, large before small muscles, and center of body muscles are coordinated before extremities (fingers and toes). Handedness (left or right) is usually stable by age 5 or 6.

Montessori's approach (1967) to educating young children is noted for direct manipulation

FIGURE 4-4 Exercising large muscles is an important preschool activity.

of real objects presented in sequenced form. This led to her design and construction of many tactile (touching) exploring materials for the young child. She explains her motives in the following:

The training and sharpening of the senses has the obvious advantage of enlarging the field of perception and of offering an ever more solid foundation for intellectual growth. The intellect builds up its store of practical ideas through contact with, and exploration of, its environment. Without such concepts the intellect would lack precision in its abstract operations.

Preschools are full of appealing equipment and programs which offer a planned approach to sensory-motor skills. They are seen as integral parts of the curricula. Spitzer (1977) believes that sensory exploration and motor skill development takes place jointly:

> Perceptual and motor abilities are almost completely interdependent, particularly in terms of early childhood learning. Actually, when we think of sensory exploration, we must consider motor skills. When we look at an object, we must move our bodies to explore it or manipulate it in some way.

School success in later elementary years may also be influenced by the development of perceptual-motor skill.

There seems to be no clearly accepted or defined separate place within the preschool curriculum for sensory skill development. Some centers identify a series of sequential activities and label them perceptual or sensory-motor; their main goal is skill development. In other centers, every activity is seen as developing perceptual-motor skill. Commonly, music activities and physical games deal with physical coordination and endurance. Other programs plan for perceptual-motor activities within their language arts curriculum. What remains important is that this type of emphasis be part of every center's program.

This list of objectives designed to refine perceptual-motor skills is drawn from a number of schools' and centers' goal statements. It includes developing:

- awareness of self in space.
- awareness of self in relation to objects.
- flexibility and ability.
- body coordination, figure 4-5.
- awareness of spatial relationships.
- posture and balance.

FIGURE 4-5 Both coordination and flexibility are needed to master rope climbing.

- rhythmic body movements.
- the ability to identify objects and surfaces with the eyes closed.
- awareness of temperatures by touch.
- ability to trace form outlines with fingers.
- ability to discriminate color, shapes, similar features, different features, sizes, textures, and sounds.
- ability to match a wide variety of patterns and symbols.
- ability to identify parts of figures or objects when a small part of a whole is presented.
- eye-hand coordination, figure 4-6.
- familiarity with the following terms:
  same, different
  long, longer, longest

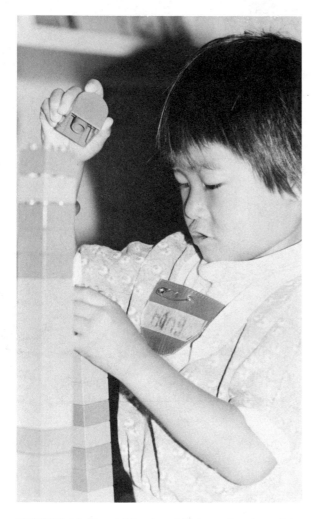

FIGURE 4-6 The child gains skill in eye-hand coordination by fitting the pieces in the puzzle. *(From Machado and Meyer,* Early Childhood Practicum Guide, *Copyright 1984 by Delmar Publishers Inc.)*

small, smaller, smallest
big, little
tall, short
wide, narrow
high, low
above, below
on, in
hard, soft
sweet, salty, sour

- ability to identify food by tasting.
- ability to identify smells of a variety of items.
- ability to identify common sounds.

ACTIVITIES FOR PERCEPTUAL-MOTOR DEVELOPMENT

It is difficult to think of one piece of preschool equipment or one activity which does not contain some aspect or component of perceptual-motor development. Figure 4-7 lists activities and equipment and has been gathered from a broad range of early childhood books and sources. It can serve as a beginning.

INTELLECTUAL GROWTH

Two major views concerning the link between language and thought are opposites. One is that language is the foundation of thought; language is seen as being vital to a person's awareness of the world. The second view suggests language is dependent on thinking; as intelligence grows, language grows, reflecting thoughts. It is difficult to determine which of the two ideas is closer to the truth.

Teachers need to realize that there are differences between adult concepts and child concepts. The child's view of the world is usually based on immediate, present happenings and beginning thought processes which use symbols, figure 4-8. A child's speech is full of many unique misconceptions, conclusions, and errors (as judged by adult standards). These errors arise because of each child's unique way of sorting out experiences — a continuous process of trying to make sense and order out of daily events. Errors based on just a few happenings may be quite logical conclusions. Many "funny" or "incorrect" children's statements, when carefully examined by adults, are shown to be correct and logical according to the child's maturity and experience. The child who offers "milk comes from the store" is a good example.

Experiences Dealing With:	Possible Materials and Equipment

Visual Discrimination

long, longer, longest	felt or paper strips; sticks; ribbons
small, smaller, smallest	nested boxes; blocks; buttons; measuring cups
big, little	blocks; jars; buttons; balloons; toys
tall, short	felt figures; stuffed toys
wide, narrow	pieces of cloth and paper; scraps of wood; boxes
high, low	jump rope; small ball; see-saw made from small board with tiny block in middle
above, below	table-shaped piece of felt with box-shaped felt pieces to place above and below box
on, in	with colored stones

Auditory Discrimination

quiet, noisy	two boxes: one containing something that rattles (such as stones or beads) and one containing cloth or paper
bell sounds	bells of varying shapes and sizes for a variety of tones
falling sounds	feather; leaf; stone; block of wood; cotton
shaking sounds	maracas; baby rattle; pebbles inside coffee can
musical sounds	variety of rhythm instruments

Tactile Discrimination

textures	sandpaper; tissue; stone; waxed paper; tree bark; velvet; wool; fur; cotton
outline of shapes	thin wooden circle, square, triangle, rectangle; letters cut from sandpaper
recognition of objects	four different-shaped objects, each tied in end of sock — children guess what each is by feeling it (change objects often)
hard, soft	handkerchief; rock; cotton batting; nail; sponge

Taste Discrimination

identifying food: sweet, salty, sour	small jars: filled with salt, sugar, unsweetened lemonade
trying new foods	variety of vegetables children may not know; samples of fruit juices; honey, molasses, maple syrup

FIGURE 4-7 Perceptual activities

Experiences Dealing With:	Possible Materials and Equipment
Smell Discrimination	
identifying object by smell	cake of soap; vial of perfume; pine sprig; onion; vials of kitchen spices; orange
Kinesthetic Discrimination	
lifting, racing downhill, swinging, throwing, running, jumping, climbing, bending, stretching, twisting, turning, spinning, balancing.	yard and motor play materials

FIGURE 4-7 Cont.

The Teacher's Role

Working with children on a daily basis, teachers strive to understand the logic and correctness behind children's statements. The balance a teacher maintains between gently correcting false impressions and having the child discover the misconceptions for himself is not easy to maintain. Piaget (1952) encourages teachers to concentrate on discovery techniques:

FIGURE 4-8 There are lots of opportunities for intimate conversations. *(From Machado and Meyer,* Early Childhood Practicum Guide, *Copyright 1984 by Delmar Publishers Inc.)*

Each time one prematurely teaches a child something he could have discovered for himself, that child is kept from inventing it and consequently from understanding it completely.

Skillful questioning by and sensitive responses from the teacher preserve a child's secure feeling about expressing worthwhile ideas and makes him more willing to speak and share. These examples illustrate:

- "I can see you want to have a turn talking too, Becky, and we want to hear you."
- "Would you tell us, Mark, about the boat you put together this morning?"
- "You thought of a different way to make a hole in your paper. I think your friends would like to hear about it."
- "Did anyone see what happened to Tim's shoe?"
- "I wonder if there's a way for three people to share two pairs of scissors?"

The following is an example of a kindergartner's answer to the question, "What is a grandmother?" Note the concepts based on lack of experience and examples of overgeneralization.

What A Grandmother Is

A grandmother is a lady who has no children of her own, so she likes other people's little girls. A grandfather is a man grandmother. He goes for walks with the boys, and they talk about fishing and tractors and things like that. Grandfathers wear glasses and funny underwear. They can take their teeth off. Grandmas are the only grownups who have time.

Huey (1965) lists suggestions for teaching young children which help them to use both mental and language abilities.

1. Set the stage for abundant sensory experiences varied so as to promote discrimination learnings and abundant associations.
2. Provide abundant opportunities for self-selected learning activities especially of the manipulative and experimental types.
3. Provide many opportunities for children to observe work activities of adults so that they will have experiences to think about.
4. Encourage children with toys, other play accessories, conversation, and art materials to symbolize their experiences through play, art, and language.
5. Direct children's attention to learning opportunities they may miss, to opportunities to use their previous associations, and to opportunities for abstracting common elements (e.g., "all blue things").
6. Provide an environment of simple language that helps clothe each child's experience with language while he is absorbing the experience.
7. Encourage each child to use the language that he has to clothe his own experiences in his own language.
8. Plan opportunities for experiences that will help children discover new concepts and redefine a concept already met, including differentiation of concepts.
9. Provide opportunities for vicarious experiences through stories, pictures and conversation that relate to recent direct experiences.
10. Pace learning opportunities, not too many at one time, for the group and for the individual child, so that clear images are possible, new learnings are reinforced to the point of usefulness, and the hazard of overstimulation is avoided.

Figure 4-9 presents additional suggestions for teachers which match activities to children's intellectual characteristics and needs.

While keeping these suggestions in mind, look at figure 4-10 which illustrates how the preschooler's ability to process information is improving and expanding during this period.

SOCIAL AND EMOTIONAL GROWTH

Interaction with other people is always a major factor of the child's language learning. Children who have positive feelings about themselves — feelings of self value and security — speak frequently. New contacts with adults outside the home run smoothly as the child branches out from the home.

Feelings and emotions are part of each human conversation. A child's feelings toward adults are generalized to teachers in early school years. The parent-child bond and its influence on language learning has been described by Douglass (1959):

The feeling relationships between parents and child appear to be a tremendous factor in the child's learning of language. The child who avoids talking because he fears lack of acceptance, the child whose feelings are not understood, the standards of eating, toilet training, and behaviors which are imposed too soon, and emotional tensions existing

Characteristics	Needs	Suggestions for the Classroom Teacher
Intellectual Are curious: learn best through active involvement through their senses, and through direct experiences with things in the environment.	Opportunities to have sensory experiences — to see, touch, taste, smell and hear things around them. Opportunities to handle materials and make their own discoveries.	Provide firsthand experiences. For example, bring a guinea pig to the classroom and provide enough time and space for a small group of children to sit around and watch and handle the animal. Questions will most likely come from the children. For instance: "What is this?" "Where do guinea pigs come from?" The teacher is there to provide clear and simple explanations as well as to ask questions when necessary.
Are concerned primarily with things that affect them personally.	Opportunities to investigate things that they see around them or experience in their everyday lives. Opportunities to see their names, their photographs, and their work as part of the classroom materials and displays.	Provide activities that enable the children to explore familiar materials like water, soap, and plastic containers. Classroom meetings may include discussions about the children's families and the work their parents do. Snacks can include many foods that the children also eat at home. The children can also make their own snacks — like French toast or pancakes — and can be encouraged to observe and discuss each step in the process. Books can be made about the children's experiences, including names of people they know.
Are concerned primarily with the present.	Opportunities to distinguish between reality and "make-believe."	Stories should be concerned with feelings and experiences that are familiar to the children.
Are increasing their attention span.	Opportunities to have a variety of experiences that are interesting to children.	For younger children, provide many different materials for similar learning experiences. Schedule group activities for relatively short periods of time. Provide games and toys which are open-ended (have more than one way of being played or played with) or which require a relatively short amount of time.

FIGURE 4-9 Chart of teaching ideas, matching child's needs and intellectual abilities to appropriate activities *(From* Open for Children, *by Danoff et al., 1976. Used with permission of McGraw-Hill Book Company.)*

		Gradually introduce activities that require a longer attention span.
Are developing a sense of time.	Opportunities to recall experiences. Opportunities to plan and organize play.	At snack time the children can be asked what they did earlier in the morning. Classroom discussions on Monday morning should include what the children did over the weekend. The children should be asked to choose where they want to work each day — for example, a child might choose the block area. Block structures can be left intact and added to each day for as long as the children are interested.
Are developing the ability to "symbolize" experiences.	Opportunities to express ideas in a variety of ways. Opportunities to symbolize their experiences through art, language, dramatic play, music, and movement. Opportunities to use materials imaginatively and creatively.	If the children take a trip, they can be encouraged to discuss the experience, and the teacher can write down some of what they say. They can also reproduce some of the sounds they heard with rhythm instruments, or they can make a mural of their visual impressions, or recreate the experience with blocks.
Are developing the ability to deal with complex, abstract ideas.	Opportunities to note similarities and differences between things around them. Opportunities to sort, group, categorize, and classify the things around them.	At a group time, the children can be asked, "Who is wearing pants today?" "Who is not wearing pants?" The children can be asked to compare any two pieces of clothing from the housekeeping area in terms of color, size, or function. A box full of clothes can be sorted in many different ways. For instance, the children can put together all the things that are worn on the head or all the clothes that have stripes.

FIGURE 4-9 Cont.

in the home, can create surface symptoms produced by a child who attempts to cope with an unsatisfying and hostile world.

During preschool years, children form ideas of self-identity. It becomes difficult for a child to believe in himself — or his language ability — if self-esteem is constantly undermined. Figure 4-11 suggests teacher communications and behaviors which promote social growth.

Erikson's writings (1950) have identified a series of social-emotional developments in the young child.

• (Infancy) *Trust vs. Mistrust.* Trust develops from consistent care which fulfills ba-

1. Seeking information. (Focusing)

2. Seeking word labels. (Concept building)

3. Naming, classifying, categorizing, and grouping experiences mentally — objects, ideas, etc. (General to specific; revising concepts)

4. Responding and remembering. (Memorizing and recalling)

5. Comparing and contrasting information. (Abstracting)

6. Making inferences and predicting in general ways. (Predicting)

7. Generalizing. (Inductive thinking)

8. Applying known information to new situations. (Transferring)

9. Making hypotheses (educated guesses) and predicting in specific ways. (Deductive thinking)

FIGURE 4-10 The child's emerging intellectual skills

sic needs (food, warmth, holding, etc.) leading to stable and secure feelings rather than anxiousness. A positive view of life forms.

- (Toddlers and Twos) *Autonomy vs. Shame and Doubt*. The child gets to know himself as a separate person. What he controls, decisions he can make, and freedom he may have while still being very dependent, becomes apparent. Awareness of inabilities and helplessness is sensed. Behavior may be testing and full of the word "no."

- (Preschooler) *Initiative vs. Guilt Feelings*. Experimenting and active exploring of new skills and directions happens. There are strong emotions at times in resistance to authority figures and rules, yet he is still dependent on adult approval.

Preschoolers begin to learn labels for feelings such as happy, sad, jealous, fear, and so on. They begin to think of others' feelings. The conscience is forming and interest in "right" and "wrong" is expressed. Teachers who speak of their own feelings as adults set an example and provide a climate in which children's feelings

In communication, the teacher:

- cares and is ready to give of self.

- listens intent on understanding.

- puts in simple words what the child can't.

- doesn't correct speech when this might break down willingness to speak further.

- is available for help in clarifying ideas or suggesting new play and exploring possibilities.

- senses child interests and guides to new real experiences.

- is available when problems and conflicts happen.

- enjoys time spent in child activities.

- establishes friendships with each child.

- talks positively about each child's individual uniqueness.

- is an enthusiastic and expressive communicator.

- offers friendly support while redirecting undesirable social behavior or stating rules.

- notices and respects each child's work.

FIGURE 4-11 Teacher behaviors helpful to child's social growth

are also accepted and understood (Greenberg, 1969).

Most children explore social actions and reactions. Strong emotions accompany much of the child's behavior; his total being speaks. When a child feels "left out," life becomes an overwhelming tragedy, and a party invitation may be a time to jump for joy.

The following activities develop a sense of self. They are just a few suggestions; many more are possible.

- Mirror activities
- Child photograph activities (home movies)
- Tracing the child's outline
- Touch and name body parts
- Nametags, names on belongings, drawings, lockers, and projects
- Family pictures and discussions about families

- Statements he hears others make which describe him
- Activities which identify and discuss feelings

Teachers strive to supply a center atmosphere where a sense of trust and security thrives. Danoff, Breitbart, and Barr (1977) feel this is crucial to each child's opportunity to learn.

Basic to the learning process is children's ability to trust themselves and the adults who teach them. This is totally interactional. Children must trust people in their world, or else they reject all that these people want to teach them. They learn to have faith in those who respect them and accept their feelings. In turn, they learn to trust themselves. In a climate that engenders trust, they want to learn and are able to learn.

SUMMARY

Physical, intellectual, and social-emotional growth is connected to and influences child speech and language. Understanding these growth systems promotes more appropriate teacher techniques and behavior.

Perceptual-motor activities are an integral part of many centers' language arts programs. Many educators feel that there is a strong correlation between physical activity during this period and mental growth.

Adults need to react to and sense the correctness of what seem to be errors in children's thinking. Guiding the child's discovery of concepts is an integral part of early childhood teaching.

A child who trusts can learn. Teachers' must accept a child's feelings, and concentrate on establishing a bond between themselves and the child. This encourages growth of abilities. The feeling tone which lies beneath each human contact and conversation creates a setting for learning.

Learning Activities

- Observe young children (2 to 4 years) in a public place (restaurant, laundromat, grocery store, park, bus, department store). What do the children seem to notice, and how do they investigate what they notice? Write down those environmental objects, people, etc., and what features capture the child's interest. (Example — sound, color, texture)

- With a group of fellow students, pinpoint possible concepts which underlie the following quotes of children which were taken from Chukovsky's, *From Two to Five* (Berkeley, CA: University of California Press, 1963).
  a. "Mommie, Mommie, the ship is taking a bath." (e.g. — All objects found in water are bathing.)
  b. "Can't you see? I'm barefoot all over!"
  c. "Daddy, when you were little, were you a boy or a girl?"
  d. "The stars in the sky are real ones not like the ones we see on holidays."
  e. "Mother, shut off your radio."
  f. "Mommie, please give birth to a baby or a puppy. You know how much I'll love them."
  g. "An ostrich is a giraffe-bird."

- Using the blackboard or a large piece of newsprint (or shelfpaper) list, with a small group of others, the teacher behaviors which might develop a sense of trust in children on the first day of school.

- Plan and conduct two activities with preschool children which concentrate on a perceptual-motor skill. Report your successes and failures to the group.

- Describe your reaction to the following statements from children:
  a. "Milk comes from a truck."
  b. "You're ugly!"
  c. "You like her best!"
  d. "He always gets to be first!"
  e. "I don't like Petey." (another child)
  f. "Don't touch me!"
  g. "My dad kills all our bugs."

- With your eyes closed, identify three objects given you by another person.

Unit Review

A. Give a definition of:

    abstract   motor development   reflex   conceptual tempo

B. Write a brief description of Piaget's stages of intellect development or Erikson's stages of social-emotional development.

C. Choose the category which fits best, and code the following words with the headings (a) Perceptual-motor development, (b) Social-emotional development, or (c) Mental development.

1. trust	6. categorizing	11. security
2. concepts	7. predicting	12. generalizing
3. tasting	8. avoiding people	13. balance
4. self-awareness	9. eye-hand skill	14. conscience
5. self-image	10. body image	15. abstracting

D. Write the numbers of those teacher behavior examples that follow which you feel would help a child develop healthy social-emotional skills.
  1. Recognizing each child by name as he enters.
  2. Pointing out (to others) a child's inability to sit still.
  3. Telling a child it's all right to hate you.
  4. Keeping a child's special toy safe for him.
  5. Encouraging a child's saying, "I don't like that," or "I'm not finished" when another child grabs his toy.
  6. Saying, "Jerome thinks we should ask the janitor, Mr. Smith, to eat lunch with us."
  7. Saying, "It makes me angry when you hit me. It hurts."
  8. Planning activities which are either "girls only" or "boys only."

9. Rewarding children who show kindness to others.
10. Allowing a child to make fun of another child without speaking to the first child about it.
11. Changing the rules and rewards often.
12. Ignoring an irritating behavior which seems to be happening more frequently.

E. Discuss children's vision and hearing acuity during preschool years.

F. Why is it important to know that children may have differences in perceiving?

G. Choose the best answer.
1. Most centers agree that perceptual skills belong
   a. somewhere in the program.
   b. in the language arts area.
   c. in the music and physical education area.
   d. to a separate category of activities.
2. The younger the child the more he needs
   a. demonstration activities.
   b. to be told about the properties of objects.
   c. sensory experience.
   d. enriching child conversations.
3. Trust usually _____ being able to risk and explore, when considering early childhood school attendance.
   a. follows
   b. combines
   c. is dependent upon
   d. comes before
4. Young children's thinking is focused upon
   a. first-hand current happening.
   b. abstract symbols.
   c. pleasing adults for rewards.
   d. the consequences of their behavior.
5. There is a _____ relationship between language and thought.
   a. well understood
   b. well researched
   c. clear
   d. cloudy

References

Danoff, Judith, Breitbart, Vicki, and Elinor Barr, *Open for Children*, McGraw-Hill Book Co., New York, 1977.
Douglass, Robert, "Basic Feeling and Speech Defects," *Exceptional Children*, March, 1959.

Erikson, Erik, *Childhood and Society,* W. W. Norton, New York, 1950.

Gibson, E. J., *Principles of Perceptual Learning and Development,* Appleton-Century-Crofts, New York, 1969.

Greenberg, Dr. Herbert M., *Teaching With Feeling,* The Pegasus Press, 1969.

Huey, J. Francis, "Learning Potential of the Young Child," *Educational Leadership,* Nov. 1965, Vol. 23.

Kagan, J., *Change and Continuity,* Wiley, New York, 1971.

Montessori, Maria, *The Discovery of the Child,* Ballantine Books, 1967.

Osborn, Janie Dyson and D. Keith Osborn, *Cognition In Early Childhood,* Education Associates, Athens, GA, 1983.

Piaget, Jean, *The Language and Thought of the Child,* Rutledge and Kegan Paul, London, 1952.

Spitzer, Dean R., *Concept Formation and Learning in Early Childhood,* Charles E. Merrill Publishing Co., 1977.

Weiss, Curtis E., and Herold S. Lillywhite, *Communicative Disorders,* 2nd ed., The C. V. Mosby Co., 1981.

Weymouth, F. W., "Visual Acuity of Children," in M. J. Hirsch and R. E. Wick (eds.), *Vision of Children, A Symposium,* Philadelphia, 1963.

Suggested Reading

Lewis, M. M., *Language, Thought, and Personality,* New York: Basic Books, 1963.

Unit 5
Identifying Goals and Planning the Language Arts Curriculum

OBJECTIVES

After studying this unit you should be able to

- describe the development of early childhood language arts programs and curricula.

- discuss the possible uses of assessment instruments and data obtained.

- write an activity plan for one language arts activity.

This text divides language arts into four interrelated subdivisions — listening, speaking, writing (or prewriting), and reading (or prereading). Increasing the child's *understanding* of how language arts combine and overlap in everyday preschool activities helps to increase language use. To that end, a unified approach is recommended, one in which the teacher purposefully shows and stresses connections between areas, figure 5-1.

LANGUAGE USE IN ALL CURRICULUM AREAS

Every planned and unplanned preschool activity uses language in some way. Past experience is basic to all language arts because a child's success often depends on understanding what is happening. Language helps children learn, retain, recall, and transmit information (Lerner, 1976). Messages are received through words and nonverbal means. The teacher's speech, behavior, and use of words in planned activities are discussed in Units 6, 13, and 14.

Daily routines, play with peers, and unplanned happenings stimulate language as well as the center's planned program. Teachers use every opportunity to add meanings in a natural conversational way during the preschool day. This generally begins with the teacher's "hello" to the child as he or she enters the child care center. The "hello" is a part of the ritual in preschools that aims to recognize each child's presence each morning.

Daily routines are regular features of a school's program which occur about the same time every day — snacks, toileting, and get together times — in which language is an associate function, figure 5-2.

Group times range from short roll-taking and announcement times to planned child language arts (or other content area) experiences. Instruction may take place with one child, a few, or with a group.

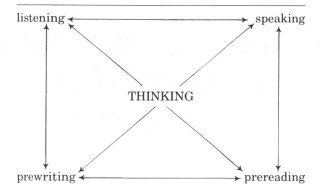

Listening (receptive language)
One hears speech.
One can listen to another reading orally.
One can listen and write what one hears.

Speaking (oral expressive language)
One can speak to a listener.
One can put speech into written form.
One can read orally.

Writing (prewriting)
One can write what's spoken and heard.
One's writing can be read.
One's writing can be read and spoken.

Reading (reading readiness)
One can read written words.
One can listen to another reading.
One can read speech when it's written.

FIGURE 5-1 Interrelation of early childhood language arts

LANGUAGE ARTS PROGRAMMING

Preplanned language arts programs develop from identified goals: the knowledge, skills, and attitudes that the school intends to teach. Early childhood teachers also base their goals and teaching techniques upon what they feel is best, right, appropriate, and prudent. This, in turn, is connected to views they hold about how, what, when, and where children learn to communicate and use language. The following views

FIGURE 5-2 Snack time is a get-together time

about language learning are commonly expressed or implied by staff members involved in planning language arts programs.

- Language permeates all planned and unplanned activities.
- A dynamic, rich-in-opportunity classroom stimulates communicating and exchanging ideas.
- Real experiences are preferred to second-hand ones when practical and possible.
- The reciprocal nature of exploring and discovering together should be promoted by teachers.
- Play provides many opportunities to learn language.
- Teacher's instructional techniques should be skilled and be alert to child readiness.
- Stressing relationships between objects, events, and experiences is a useful teaching technique.
- Individual planning as well as group planning is desirable.
- Program activities should center upon child interests.
- The entire teaching staff should be committed and enthusiastic about their planned program, and clearly understood stated objectives.

Determining Program Effectiveness

Goals pinpointed through staff meetings and solicited parent input can be finalized in written form to serve as a basis for planning. For one child or many, goals are achieved when the teacher or staff plans interesting and appropriate activities for daily, weekly, monthly, or even longer periods. In addition to the actual program, materials, classroom equipment and arrangement, teacher techniques and interactions, and other resources aid in goal realization, figure 5-3.

Teacher observation and assessment instruments — teacher-designed and commercial — add extra data that helps in planning programs. Tests, rating scales, and checklists gather information which alerts teachers to levels of development, child interest and abilities, and aids them in finding what Hunt (1961) terms "the match," that is, activities neither too easy nor too difficult. If the activities are "just right," the child experiences inner satisfaction and does not require praise or outside influence to be involved.

Early childhood centers often try to determine the center's effectiveness by rating children at both the beginning and ending of a school year. When this is done with a young child at the beginning of his first group experience — and possibly his first time away from his home setting — results may not be favorable or accurate. Spodek (1972) points out:

Administration of tests early in a child's career has certain inherent pitfalls. Many young children are unfamiliar with testing procedures and do not know appropriate response behavior, thus making test results invalid. It may be well to postpone administering tests to young children until they have been in school long enough to have been acculturated to the ways of the school.

FIGURE 5-3 Outdoor equipment can help children with goal realization.

A teacher or assistant teacher may have the responsibility of administering a test to a group of young children. This is usually accomplished by taking each child aside and asking him to answer questions or perform tasks. The teacher or assistant must have a clear understanding of the test's instruction manual beforehand, figure 5-4.

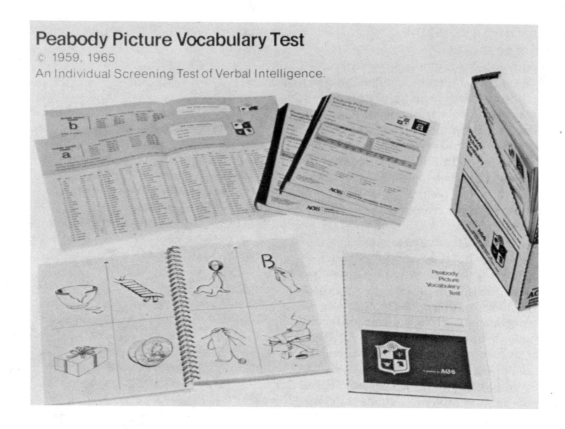

FIGURE 5-4 A picture vocabulary test for young children

There are many different types of assessments. Figure 5-5 is a screening instrument for 2½- to 5-year-old children. Some assessments attempt to determine ability and accomplishment in a number of language and communication areas; others may be limited to one skill. A list of commercial language instruments is included in the Appendix.

To ensure a language program's quality, plans are changed, updated, and revised based on both the children's progress and staff members' ideas and observations.

Each center's goals are concerned with (1) attending children's needs (2) parents and community input and (3) the personalities, training, and experience of staff.

GOAL STATEMENTS

A particular center may have many or few goal statements, which can be both general and specific.

In infant and toddler centers the following specific objectives might be included in goal statements.

- Making comfort and discomfort sounds
- Following an object with eyes and reaching for it
- Smiling and laughing
- Turning head in a sound's direction
- Anticipating consequences of a heard sound
- Recognizing familiar people
- Picking up small objects

	Present	Date Observed
Two Year Olds		
Receptive:		
Understands most commonly used nouns and verbs		
Responds to 2-part command		
Enjoys simple story books		
Points to common objects when they are named		
Understands functions of objects, e.g. cup-drink		
Expressive:		
Verbalizes own actions		
Uses 2–3 word phrases		
Asks what and where questions		
Makes negative statements		
Labels action in pictures		
Approx. 50-word vocabulary (2 yrs.)		
Answers questions		
Speech sounds:		
Substitutes some consonant sounds, e.g., w for r, d for th		
Articulates all vowels with few deviations		
Three Years Olds		
Receptive:		
Understands size and time concepts		
Enjoys being read to		
Understands IF, THEN, and BECAUSE concepts		
Carries out 2–4 related directions		
Responds to or questions		
Expressive:		
Gives full name		
Knows sex and can state girl or boy		

FIGURE 5-5 A center-designed screening instrument (*Adapted from E.S.P. Inc.* Developmental Checklist, *1983.*)

	Present	Date Observed
Three Year Olds (*Continued*) Expressive: Uses 3–4 word phrases		
Uses /s/ on nouns to indicate plurals		
Uses /ed/ on verbs to indicate past tense		
Repeats simple songs, fingerplays, etc.		
Speech is 70%–80% intelligible		
Vocabulary of over 500 words		
Four Year Olds Receptive: Follows 3 unrelated commands		
Understands sequencing		
Understands comparatives: big, bigger, biggest		
Expressive: Has mastery of inflection (can change volume and rate)		
Uses 5 + word sentences		
Uses adjectives, adverbs, conjunctions in complex sentences		
Speech about 90%–95% intelligible		
Speech sounds: S, SH, R, CH		
Five Year Olds Receptive: Demonstrates preacademic skills such as following directions and listening		
Expressive: Few differences between child's use of language and adults'		
Can take turns in conversation		
May have some difficulty with noun-verb agreement and irregular past tenses		
Communicates well with family, friends, and strangers		
Speech sounds: Can correctly articulate most simple consonants and many digraphs		

FIGURE 5-5 Cont.

- Babbling with vowels and consonants
- Making physical responses to words
- Gesturing in response — as in waving bye-bye
- Engaging in vocal play
- Imitating sounds made by others
- Mimicking nonverbal actions
- Using jargon suggestive of meaning
- Using one word sentences
- Pointing to body parts when requested
- Pointing to objects to elicit object's name
- Using telegram speech
- Using an 8–10 word spoken vocabulary
- Knowing name

Goal statements for preschoolers, 2½–5 years, are usually categorized into the four language arts areas and can include goals dealing with imaginative and creative use of language. *Auditory skill* (listening — receptive language) includes awareness, discrimination, memory, comprehension, and direction following. Possible goal statements follow.

- Listens to stories
- Is able to retell short parts of stories — plot particulars, main ideas and character traits
- Hears rhyme
- Becomes increasing understandable, less dependent on context in speech
- Gives attention to verbal instructions
- Replies in a relevant fashion to others' remarks
- Identifies familiar sounds from the environment
- Describes past experience from a listening happening
- Discriminates sounds
- Possesses a sense of the rhythm, sequence, and patterns of something heard

Expressive speaking skills for 2 ½–5 year olds may include the following:

At 2½:
- Uses correct word order most of the time
- Averages at least 75 words per hour during play

- Uses 2–3 or more word sentences
- Uses pronouns such as I, me, mine, it, who, and that
- Uses adjectives and adverbs at times
- Names common object and pictures
- Repeats two or more items from memory
- Announces intentions before acting
- Asks questions of adults

At 3:
- Has a 900 word vocabulary
- Gives name
- Tells simple stories
- Uses plurals and some prepositions
- Can describe at least one element of a picture
- Talks about past and future happenings
- Uses commands, is critical at times, makes requests
- Uses "wh" questions and offers answers

At 3½:
- Has a 1,200 word vocabulary
- Uses 4, 5 or more word sentences
- Averages over 200 words per hour in play
- Tells an experience in sequential order at times
- Recites simple rhymes or fingerplays or sings simple songs

At 4:
- Has a 1,500 or more word vocabulary
- Speaks in adultlike sentences
- Repeats 9 word sentences from memory
- Enjoys and uses nonsense words at times
- Exaggerates and uses imaginative speech at times
- Often requests the reason for things
- Uses why
- Can tell a simple story with picture clues
- Evaluates his own activities in words periodically

At 4½:
- Has an 1,800 or more word vocabulary
- Uses compound or complex sentences
- Problem solves in language with peers
- Creates simple stories
- Dramatizes simple stories with others

- Is 85–95% fluent in speech
- Speaks mainly in complete sentences

Prewriting Goals

Centers concentrate on exposing children to printed words rather than starting actual writing practice in alphabet letter formation. The following are center goals statements in *prewriting:*

- Tracing
- Cutting out shapes
- Using marking tools
- Displaying a curiosity about alphabet letters and numerals
- Trying to printscript name or asking name to be printed on work
- Giving dictation
- Contributing to group dictation on charts, experience stories, etc.
- Creating his own short book with dictated print and his illustrations
- Attempting simple dot-to-dot drawing activities

Prereading Goals

Prereading skills are multiple and complex, often involving the coordination of skills and abilities.

- Reads pictures
- Shows an interest and enjoyment in stories and books
- Is able to arrange pictures in sequence that tells a story
- Finds "hidden" objects in pictures
- Guesses at meaning based on context cues
- Reads own and others' names
- Predicts events
- Recognizes letters of own name in other words
- Senses left-right direction
- Guesses a word to complete sentences
- Chooses a favorite book character
- Treats books with care
- Authors own books through dictation

- Sees finely detailed differences
- Recognizes and names alphabet letters at times
- Shows interest in libraries
- Shows interest in the sounds of letters
- Watches or uses puppets to enact simple stories

Some schools are under considerable pressure to leap into prereading skills, rather than to plan a program of activities which fully develops all areas. Language arts, carefully planned, provide children with basic experiences that can help make future reading both successful and pleasurable. Reading is certainly a *key* skill in elementary schooling, but no more so than the child's view of his own competence and a positive attitude toward reading and books. That is why preschoolers need a wealth of important exploring and discovering activities based on their own choice and agenda.

Nedler (1977) reviewing The Bilingual Early Childhood Program, mentions the following categories of goals which were included in the project:

- Visual training
- Auditory training
- Ideas and concepts
- Syntax of English
- Building vocabulary
- Prewriting
- Exploring and discovering

COMMITMENT TO GOALS AND OBJECTIVES

A number of factors determine whether goals are met:

- Enthusiasm and commitment of staff
- Staff ingenuity, resourcefulness
- Methods and techniques used
- Resources available
- Child abilities, interest, and motivation

- General center feeling tone
- Examination of sequence (easiest to complex)

Effort translates goals into daily activities.

DAILY ACTIVITY PLANS

Recognizing child interests stimulates activity planning ideas based on what captures the child's attention and holds it. Part of the challenge and excitement of teaching is using teacher creativity in daily activity planning.

Lesson plans (activity plans) differ widely. Although two staff members work toward the same goal, they may approach the task in a different way.

Lesson plans enable teachers to foresee needs — settings, materials, and staffing. The time that children spend waiting can be minimized. Some teachers pinpoint exactly what words and concepts will be emphasized or what questions asked.

Activities in language arts may require teacher practice beforehand. Others may require visual aids or materials that must be gathered in advance. Planning time is time well spent. Teacher tension is reduced, knowing that everything is ready. Much preparation lies below the surface of many smoothly-run child activities.

Three examples of different approaches and types of activity planning are on pages 69 to 74.

Written lesson plans done in a detailed fashion also help the beginning teacher feel prepared and relaxed, figure 5-6. After a period of time teachers internalize lesson-planning components and discontinue detailed written plans although they usually continue to use lists and outlines.

A notebook in the pocket is a valuable aid to remembering the interests of a young group. Good guideposts for unearthing what's interesting and useful in program-planning attempts offer what's already captured their attention: What's talked about often?, What's crowded around?, What's questioned frequently?, What's got the longest waiting list?, What are children exploring with their hands?, Who wants to share something discovered or created? To illustrate — if butterflies interest a group, additional butterfly experiences can add depth.

Activities based on teacher enthusiasm for living and growing, skills, talents, hobbies, and pursuits can fit beautifully into language arts goals. Parent and community resources, including borrowed items and field trips increase the vitality of programs.

Example 1 — Individual Activity

Understanding Locational Words

Purpose: The child will, on the first try, correctly place objects "under," "over," "behind," and "in front of" when given verbal directions.

Materials: Large box (large enough for a child to climb into), cup and plastic man, cloth and bar of soap.

Procedure:
1. Place large box in front of child. Put all objects inside.
2. Ask child to find what is in the box. Say to child, "Tell me about what you find in the box."
3. Pause and let the child talk about objects.
4. Ask, "Can you hide *under* this box?" Encourage the child to do so. "Show me how the plastic man could hide *under* the cup. What can you hide *under* the cloth?"
5. "Put your hand *over* the box. Can you step *over* the cup?" etc.

LANGUAGE ACTIVITY PLAN GUIDE

1. Language Activity Title _____

   _____

2. Materials needed _____

   _____

   _____

3. Location of activity (To be used when plan is developed for a particular classroom or area) _____

   _____

4. Number of children _____

5. Language goal or objective _____

   _____

6. Preparation (Necessary teacher preparation including getting materials or objects, visual aids, etc. ready)

   _____

   _____

   _____

7. Getting started (Introductory and/or motivational statement.) _____

   _____

   _____

8. Show and explore (Include possible teacher questions or statements which promote language ability)

   _____

   _____

   _____

   _____

   _____

9. Discussion key points (What vocabulary and/or concepts might be included?) _____

   _____

   _____

   _____

   _____

   _____

   _____

FIGURE 5-6 Sample activity plan form

_____

_____

_____

10. Apply (Include child practice or application of newly learned knowledge or skill when appropriate)

_____

_____

_____

11. Evaluation: (1) Activity, (2) Teacher, (3) Child participation, (4) Other aspects such as setting, materials, outcomes, etc. _____

_____

_____

_____

_____

_____

_____

_____

_____

FIGURE 5-6 Cont.

6. "Let's put everything *in front of* the big box. Now let's hide everything *behind* the box." etc.

7. "You tell me what I should put *under* the cloth. Did I do it? Is it *under?*" Continue in the same manner with over, behind, and in front of.

8. Ask the child to put the objects any way he wishes. "Are any *in front of? Behind? Under? Over?* Tell me where you chose to put them."

9. "Is there anything *under* your shoes? What's *over* your chest? Tell me something you see that's *in front of* your eyes. Guess what's *behind* you right now."

(Move your hand behind the child.)

Example 2 — Group Activity

Visual Reception

Purpose: To match identical mittens from an assortment.

Materials: Picture of three little kittens and twelve pairs of construction paper mittens. All mittens are to be made from the same color paper. Each pair of mittens should be decorated differently. Do not use color or size as the differentiating element. (Trace around a child's hand for size of mittens.)

Procedure:

1. Show children a picture of the three little kittens. Ask, "Do you remember what the three little kittens lost?" (Children answer) "That's right, they lost their mittens. I have some mittens here."

2. Show the children a pair of mittens. "Look at these mittens. How are they the same? What do the mittens have on them? Yes, they each have a flower." Have a child point to both flowers.

3. Show another pair of mittens. "Look! I have another pair of mittens. Are they the same? How are they the same? Yes, these mittens are the same. Children say, 'The mittens are the same.' "

4. "Now we're going to play a game. You're just like the three little kittens. Let's start with *(Child's name)*." (Give the child one mitten, and place its mate and one other mitten in the center of the table.) "*(Child's name)*, find the mitten that's the same as yours." If the child has difficulty, let him put his mitten next to one of the mittens and compare the patterns.

5. Continue the procedure until all children have had several turns. Stress often that the mittens are the same.

6. Separate five pairs of mittens into two sets. Place the right-hand mittens in one set and the left-hand mittens in the other. Ask a child to choose a mitten he likes from one of the sets and find the matching mitten in the other set. Then say, "Good! *(Child's name)* has two mittens that look the same."

7. Continue the procedure until each child has had a turn. Repeat the activity two or three times, putting out more pairs of mittens each time.

NOTE: At Easter time, the teacher may use eggs for matching patterns. In fall, leaf patterns may be used.

Criterion Activity:

During a play period, ask each child to come with you and play the Mitten Game. Arrange the mittens on the table. "Find a mitten, and then find another one that looks the same. Good." Have the child continue the procedure until he has matched all the mittens. The child must match three pairs to reach criterion.

Reinforcement:

For extension lessons on the concept of "same" and "not

the same," Picture Cards, Set 2, Picture Dominoes can be used.

NOTE: A review of the lesson can help the reader think of similar activities that may be used in future lessons. For example, the gloves and mittens worn to school by the children can also be used as a basis for a lesson. In climates where mittens are not worn, shoes can be used. One of the strengths of the curriculum is its flexibility and adaptability. For example, in one classroom made up of Indian children, the teacher used pairs of feathers, colored beads, and cutouts of tepees (Karnes, 1972).

Example 3 — Multiple-goal Approach

NOTE: This is a portion of a longer description. The words in italics show how the teacher works toward a variety of goals.

This episode is an account of a sequence of planned activities culminating in a cooking experience for four 4-year-old children. Part 1 of the episode details the preparation in the classroom for the purchase of the food and the group's trip to a local store. Part 2 describes the cooking.

The fresh pears at lunch evoked the excited comment "Apples!" from Spanish-speaking Fernando.

"Well, this is a fruit," said Miss Gordon, encouragingly, "but it has another name. Do you remember the apples we had last week?"

"They were hard to bite," said Joey.

"And we made applesauce," said Rosina.

"This fruit is called a pear, Fernando; let's taste this pear now. We'll have apples again."

The teacher responds to what is correct in the child's response, valuing his category association. First, she wants to support communication and willingness to experiment with language; later she gives the correct name. The children strengthen the experience by relating it to previous experience in which they were active.

"Mine's soft," said Joey.

"Can we make applesauce again?" begged Rosina.

The teacher replied, "Perhaps we could do what Janice wanted to do. Remember? To take some home to her family?"

"To my mommy, and my grandma, and Danny."

"Not to my baby," said Rosina. "He's too little. Him only drink milk."

"Tomorrow we'll buy lots of apples," said Miss Gordon.

The teacher is building a sense of continuity by recalling earlier intentions that had been expressed by the children.

She rarely corrects use of pronouns for four-year-olds. She knows the child will learn through greater social maturity and hearing language.

After rest, Miss Gordon asked the children how they could take home their applesauce. "What can we put it in?"

Rosina ran to the house corner and returned with two baby food jars. "I bringed lots," she said. Miss Gordon remembered that Rosina had come to school lugging a bag full of baby food jars, many of which she had put away. "A good idea! And your mommy said she would keep more for us. Let's write a note to tell her we need them tomorrow."

Rosina dictated a note: "I got to bring bunches of jars to school. We are going to make applesauce. I love you, Mommy." And painted her name with a red marker.

The teacher helps children to think ahead to steps in a process.

The use of a tense form, though incorrect, represents learning for the child. The teacher does not correct at this moment, when she is responding to the child's pleasure in solving the practical problem that had been posed. She is strengthening the connection between home and school.

The teacher helps the children learn that writing is a recording of meaning and a way of communicating.

The next day was jar washing and arranging time. Each of the four children put his jars on a tray on which there was a large card with his name.

Janice put on one jar for her mother, one for her grandmother, one for her brother, and after a pause, one for herself.

Rosina changed her mind. "My baby can have a little tiny bit," she said. So she needed a jar for her father, her mother, her baby and herself.

Joey and the teacher figured out that he needed six, and that Fernando needed nine!

The children are actively involved in the steps preparatory to the planned activity — an experience in organization which has personal meaning.

The teacher's plan calls for recognition of one's own name and one-to-one counting of family members.

The teacher turned their attention to a chart near the cooking corner. She had made a recipe chart, pasting colored (magazine) pictures next to the names of the items they would need to make the applesauce and had taped a stick of cinnamon to the chart.

Miss Gordon said, "Let's look at the recipe chart. I have a list so we can remember to buy everything."

The children said, "Apples."

Miss Gordon checked her list.

Then, "Sugar."

The children were silent as they looked at the stick of cinnamon taped to the chart.

Miss Gordon suggested, "Smell it. Have we had it before?"

Joey remembered: "Toast! What we put on toast!"

"Yes," said Miss Gordon, and then gave the word, "cinnamon."

The children are having a dual experience — pictorial representation and formal symbol usage.

The teacher supplies the word after the children have revived their direct experience with the phenomenon (Biber, Shapiro, Wickens, 1977).

EVALUATION

Thinking back over planned activities helps teachers analyze the benefits, and possibly leads to additional planning along the same line or with the same theme. Oversights in planning may occur or activities may develop in unexpected ways. Hindsight is a useful and valuable tool in evaluating activities.

SUMMARY

Language is part of every preschool activity. This text recommends an integrated approach to early childhood language arts — that is, a program that involves listening, speaking, prewriting, and prereading.

Centers identify language arts goals through a group process. Activities are then planned based on these goals. Daily plans increase awareness of what is intended. Assessment instruments and staff observation provide data on children's abilities, interests, and levels, giving additional insight useful in activity planning. Every center has a unique set of goals and teachers' approaches, so designing child experiences is done in a variety of ways.

Evaluating a planned activity after it is presented can pinpoint strengths and weaknesses. This also serves as the basis for further activity planning.

Learning Activities

- Form a discussion group with a few fellow students. Take out one item from your pocket or purse. Describe an activity you could use with children to promote the following skills:
  a. Memory (naming or recalling)
  b. Discrimination
  c. Problem solving
  d. Perceptual-motor

  Be aware that each activity planned should
    — be interesting and enjoyable.
    — help children feel competent and successful.
    — stimulate an excitement in "finding out."
    — promote sensory exploration.
    — include learning by doing.
    — promote language.

  Go on to discuss what activities could be planned which would promote the same four skills using a box of Kleenex or a doll.

- Design an activity plan form which includes:
  a. Title (What?)
  b. Materials and tools needed (With what?)
  c. An objective (language arts) (Why?)
  d. A preparation section
  e. Setting or location description
  f. Number of children who are to participate at one time
  g. Identification of child skills and abilities necessary for success
  h. A statement which introduces the activity to children
  i. A description of how the activity will proceed (How?)

- Study the publisher's instructions and administer a language-development assessment instrument to three different children (ages 2–5 years). Share your results with the class. In what ways could the results serve as a basis for activity planning? List your answers.

- Invite teachers to describe their center's language arts curriculum.

- Using any activity plan form, make a written plan for a language development activity. Share your plan with others at the next class meeting. Rate the quality of your participation in the discussion using the following scale.

No Input	Very Little	Contributed About As Much As Classmates	A Fair Amount	Offered Lots of Ideas

- Ask an early childhood teacher to speak about the use of assessment instruments in a language program.

- Ask a school psychologist to describe testing and test construction.

Unit Review

A. Name the four interrelated language arts areas, arranging them in what you feel is their order of appearance in young children.

B. Compare lesson plan Examples 2 and 3 in this unit. How do they differ? In which ways are they similar?

C. Write three language arts goal statements (what you would want children to have the opportunity to experience and learn). These should be ones that would be included in a program where you were (or will be) employed.

D. Select the correct answer(s). Each item may have more than one correct answer.
   1. Assessment instruments can be
      a. a checklist.
      b. a child interest inventory.
      c. counted upon to be valid.
      d. teacher made.
   2. Compiling and identifying a center's goal statements ideally involves
      a. children's input.
      b. staff.
      c. parents.
      d. interested community members.
   3. Early childhood language arts should be offered to children using
      a. an approach which helps children see relationships between areas.
      b. techniques which promote the child's realization that spoken words can be written.
      c. separate times of day to explore prereading and prewriting without combining these skills.
      d. identified goal statements as a basis for activity planning.
   4. When goals are identified, a school (or center) could
      a. lose its flexibility in activity planning.
      b. use its ability to fulfill children's individual needs if once developed activity plans are used from year to year.
      c. keep its program "personal" by continually evaluating and updating.
      d. periodically take a close look at goals to see if staff commitment is strong or weak.

5. "There is only one correct way to plan and present activities to children." This statement is
   a. true.
   b. false.
   c. partly true because each individual strives to find the one plan which helps planned activities run smoothly and successfully.
   d. incorrect because the plan itself doesn't insure success or goal realization.
6. Evaluating an activity is
   a. rarely necessary if it's well planned.
   b. admitting that teachers can learn a lot through hindsight.
   c. busy work with little value.
   d. necessary if teachers wish to improve their abilities.
7. Test results are
   a. always valid if a test is standardized.
   b. used primarily to judge children's inherited ability.
   c. used to help teachers plan growing experiences.
   d. always reliable if the teacher has studied the publisher's instructions.
8. Before administering a test to a young child, the teacher
   a. needs to know how to score the test.
   b. must have read the testing instructions carefully.
   c. needs to know if the test was standardized.
   d. should know that most tests are really used to judge a teacher's effectiveness.

References

Biber, Barbara, Edna Shapiro, and David Wickens, *Promoting Cognitive Growth: A Developmental-Interaction Point of View,* National Association for the Education of Young Children, Washington, DC, 1977.

EPIE Report — Education Product Report, No. 68, EPIE Exchange Institute, 1975, p. 77.

Hunt, J. McVicker, *Intelligence and Experience,* The Ronald Press, 1961.

Karnes, Merle B., *Goal Language Development Program,* Milton Bradley Co., 1972.

Lerner, J., *Children With Learning Disabilities,* 2nd ed., Houghton Mifflin Co., Boston, 1976.

Nedler, Sharie, "A Bilingual Early Childhood Program," in *The Preschool in Action,* Mary Carol Day and Ronald K. Parker (eds.), Allyn and Bacon, Inc., 1977.

Spodek, Bernard, *Teaching in the Early Years,* Prentice-Hall Inc., 1972.

Suggested Readings

Danoff, Judith, Vicki Breitbart, and Elinor Barr, *Open for Children,* New York: McGraw-Hill Book Co., 1977.

Draper, Mary Wanda and Henry E. Draper, *Caring for Children,* Charles A. Bennett Co., Inc., 1975, appendix pp. 535–538 (Suggests possible themes for planned activities.)

Rainey, Ernestine W., *Language Development for the Young Child,* Humanics Press, 1978.

Tarrow, Norma B. and S. W. Lundsteen, *Activities and Resources for Guiding Young Children's Learning,* McGraw-Hill Book Co., 1981.

Van Allen, Roach and Claryce Allen, *Language Experience Activities,* Houghton Mifflin Co., 1982.

Unit 6
Promoting Language

OBJECTIVES

After studying this unit you should be able to

- list three roles of a teacher in early childhood language education.
- discuss the balances needed in teacher behavior.
- describe ways a teacher can promote language growth.

A teacher (or assistant teacher) tries to encourage as much language arts growth as possible in the young child. The teacher has three main functions in teaching language.

1. The teacher serves as a daily *model* of language. *What* is communicated and *how* it is communicated is important.
2. The teacher is a *provider* of experiences. Many of these events are planned; others simply happen in the normal course of activities.
3. The teacher is an *interactor,* sharing experiences with the children and encouraging conversation, figure 6-1.

These three functions are kept in balance and in relation to each child's level and individual needs. The teaching role requires constant decision making; knowing when to supply or withhold information to help self-discovery, and knowing when to talk or listen are only two important decisions. At the center, sensitivity and predictable behavior can make the teacher the child's best ally in the growth of language skills.

TEACHER AS A MODEL

During the preschool years "a teacher model" speaking in complete sentences in standard English is appropriate. Teachers not only model speech, but also attitudes and behaviors in listening, writing, and reading. Children watch

FIGURE 6-1 As the teacher interacts in everyday experiences, a smile is a way of showing interest. (*From Machado and Meyer,* Early Childhood Practicum Guide, *Copyright 1984 by Delmar Publishers Inc.*)

and listen to the adult's use of grammar, intonation, and sentence patterns. They imitate and use the adult as an example.

Adults should use clear, descriptive speech at a speed and pitch easily understood. Articulation should be as precise as possible. Weiss and Lillywhite (1981) describe appropriate models during infancy and toddlerhood. These characteristics are also desirable in teachers of preschoolers.

> But being a good model involves more than merely speaking clearly, slowly, and appropriately. A good model uses a variety of facial expression and other forms of nonverbal communication; associates talking with love, understanding, affection; provides happy, pleasant experiences associated with talking; demonstrates the importance of clearly spoken words. A good model takes advantage of various timely situations . . .

and speaking further about infancy:

> A good model imitates what the child says or echos the sounds the child makes and provides many opportunities for the child to experiment with the vocal mechanism and rewards these early efforts.

Preschool teachers also need to be sure reward is present in their teaching behavior as they deal with young children's attitudes, skills, and behaviors in language arts activities.

Teachers should use language patterns with which they feel comfortable and natural and analyze their speech — working toward providing the best English model possible. Familiar language patterns tend to reflect each teacher's personality as well as ethnic culture (Weir and Eggleston, 1975), so knowing what kind of model one presents is important. Knowing that there is always room for improvement can help a teacher become more professional. Finally, employment prospects and parent attitudes toward less than the best need to be considered along with influences on young children who are learning vocabulary at amazing speeds.

Modeling the correct word or sentence is done by simply supplying it in a relaxed, natural way rather than in a corrective tone. The teacher's example is a strong influence; when a teacher adds courtesy words (please and thank you, for instance), they appear in the child's speech.

After hearing corrections the child will probably not shift to correct grammar or usage immediately. It may take many repetitions by teachers and adults over a period of time. What's important is the teacher's acceptance and recognition of the child's idea within the verbalization, and the addition of pertinent comments along the same line.

If the adult focuses on the way something was said (grammar) rather than the meaning, they miss opportunities to increase awareness and extend child interest. Overt correction often ends teacher-child conversation. Affirming is appropriate; emphasize the child's intended message.

Adults can sometimes develop the habit of self talk and self listening: it's hypnotic and can be a deterrent to *really* hearing the child. If one's mind wanders or one listens to refute, agree, or jumps to judge validity, it interferes with receiving. Weiss and Lillywhite (1981) urge teachers to not be afraid of silences, and to pause slightly when necessary before answering. They make the following listening suggestions:

- Develop the attitude that you'll work as hard to listen as to talk.
- Try to hear the message behind the words.
- Consciously practice good listening.

One teacher behavior is simple modeling of grammar or filling in missing words and completing simple sentences. It is even more valuable for the teacher to promote wider depth of meaning or spark interest by contributing or suggesting an idea for further exploring. Additional conversation usually happens.

Example A.

Child: "It's chicken soup."

Teacher: "Yes. I see chicken pieces and something else."

Child: "It's noodles."

Teacher: "Yes, it's different from yesterday's red tomato soup."

Child: "Tastes good. It's 'ellow."

Teacher: "Do you like it better than red tomato soup?"

Compare Examples B and C.

Example B.

Child: "Cup breaked."

Adult: "Yes, the cup is broken."
(Teacher affirms but also corrects.)

Example C.

Child: "Cup breaked."

Adult: "Yes, there are many sharp pieces on the floor."

Child: "Lots of pieces."

Adult: "The pieces are sharp and might cut your fingers if you try to pick them up. I'll hold the dustpan. You can sweep with our hand broom." (Demonstrating)

Child: "Sweep pieces." (While sweeping.)

Adult: "Your pieces are all in the dustpan. Here's our garbage can. Now, we'll dump them." (Holds dustpan gently over child's hand. Turns over with child. Teacher extends interest and knowledge.)

The teacher is a model for listening as well as speaking, figure 6-2. Words, expressions, pronunciations, and gestures are copied as is listening behavior. A quiet teacher may have a quiet classroom; an enthusiastic, talkative teacher (who also listens) may have a classroom where children both talk, listen, and share experiences.

FIGURE 6-2 A teacher is a good listener, too.

The way children feel about themselves is reflected in their behavior. When teachers listen closely children come to feel that what they say is worthwhile.

Modeling good printscript form (classroom or center manuscript print) will hopefully result after studying Units 18–20 of this text. Since children seem to absorb everything in their environment, correctly formed alphabet letters and numerals on children's work, charts, bulletin boards, and recipe cards are in order.

Teacher's use and care of books is modeled, as well as her attitude toward story and nonfictional book experiences. Beginning ideas of ways to handle and store books are observed by children.

TEACHER AS PROVIDER

Fortunately, the number of interesting language arts activities to offer to children is almost limitless. Teachers rely on both their own creativity and the many resources available to plan experiences based on identified goals. Early childhood resource books, other teachers, teacher magazines, workshops, and conferences all contribute ideas. A listing of language arts activity ideas and resource books is included in the Appendix.

Gathering activity ideas and beginning your own resource file is suggested. Since it is almost impossible to remember all the activity ideas one comes upon, a file serves this purpose. An activity file can be described as "new" or "tried and true" activity ideas. Developing a usable file starts with identifying initial categories (file headings) and adding more heads as the file grows. Some teachers use large file cards, others use binders or file folders. Whatever the size, teachers find that files are very worthwhile when it comes to daily, weekly, and monthly planning. Often, files are helpful when ideas on a certain subject or theme are needed, or when a child exhibits a special interest.

A large number of activity ideas are presented in coming units. Your creativity can produce other ideas. Separate file headings (categories) suggested in this text are listed.

- Audiovisual Activities
- Bulletin Board Ideas
- Chalkboard Ideas
- Chants
- Charts
- Child Drama Ideas
- Children's Books
- Circle Time Ideas
- Dramatic Play Stimulators
- Experience Stories
- Field Trip Ideas
- Flannel Board Ideas
- Finger Plays
- Language Game Ideas
- Listening Activities
- Listening Center Ideas
- Magazine (child's) Activities
- Patterns
- Poetry
- Perceptual-motor Activities
- Printscript Ideas
- Puppets
- Reading Readiness Ideas
- Rebus Stories
- Seasonal Ideas
- Speaking Activity Ideas
- Stories for Storytelling
- Visitor Resources

As a provider of materials, a teacher must realize that every classroom object can possibly become a useful program tool to stimulate language. From the clock on the wall to the door knob, every safe item can be discussed, compared, and explored in some way. Since most school budgets are limited, the early childhood teacher finds a way to use available equipment and materials to their fullest.

PROVIDING FOR ABUNDANT PLAY

Emphasis needs to be placed on the importance of abundant play opportunities as a valuable aid in contributing to child language acquisition. Child's play is complex and the subject of considerable research. It's rich with child talk, verbal rituals, topic development and maintenance, turn taking, intimate speech in friendships, follower-leader conversations, besides a variety of additional language situations. Story comprehension may enhance the children's ability to recreate stories among themselves (Pellegrini and Galdi, 1982). Children who were "fantasy-trained," and verbally constructed stories with peers were also more adept in understanding, retelling stories, and answering questions about the storytelling experience. Peer play is a vehicle leading to a wide range of communicative skills (Garvey, 1977). Encouraging children to pretend in play — letting children decide how pretend play is to flow — without adult interference is recommended. Children will want to talk to teachers about their play, and teacher's role is to show interest and to be playful themselves at times.

TEACHER AS INTERACTOR

An interactor can be defined as a person who is always interested in what a child is saying or doing, figure 6-3. This person encourages conversation on any subject the child selects. An interactor is never too busy to talk and share interests and concerns. Time is purposely planned for conversations (daily, if possible) with each child. These private, personal, one-to-one encounters build "I value you" feelings, and open communications. A "full of talk" day can begin with a morning greeting such as:

"Alphonse, I've been waiting to talk to you. Tell me about your visit to Chicago."

or

"How is your puppy feeling today, Andrea?"

or

"Those new blue tennis shoes will be good for running in the yard, and for tiptoeing, too."

When a teacher answers a child by showing interest, this rewards the child's speaking. This interest is one type of *positive* reinforcement; defined here as something good that happens to a person after having performed an activity or shown certain behavior. *Negative* reinforcement is the opposite; either something bad happens, or nothing happens. Rewarded actions tend to be repeated. The child's speech and listening should be rewarded so that the child will continue to speak and to listen. The rewards given most often by a teacher are attention by listening to, looking at, smiling at, patting, answering, or acting favorably to what a child has said or done.

Tough (1973) offers teachers interactional techniques to extend conversations:

- Invite children to speak by developing a relationship that encourages talking through being a good listener — smiling, nodding, and saying "mm," "yes," and "really" tell the child to go ahead and you're listening.
- Reflecting back on what the child has said showing your understanding.
- Using questions that are indirect and give the child the choice of answering or not.
- Letting the child know it's ok not to answer your question such as: "Do you want to tell me about . . . ?" or "If you'd like, I like to know how . . ."
- When the child's eager to talk, use more direct open-ended questions — "What do you see?"

Additionally, she suggests that conversations need to be adultlike; one needs to make comments, tell about happenings, how one feels, and exchange information.

The teacher who interacts in daily experiences can help to improve the child's ability to see relationships. Although there is current disagreement as to the teacher's ability to promote *cognitive* growth (the act or process of knowing), attention can be focused and help provided by answering and asking questions. Often, a teacher can help children see clear links between material already learned and new

FIGURE 6-3 As an interactor, the teacher enjoys participating in an activity that interests the child. *(From Machado and Meyer,* Early Childhood Practicum Guide, *Copyright 1984 by Delmar Publishers Inc.)*

material. Words are related to the child's mental images which have come through the senses. Language aids memory because words attached to mental images help the child to retrieve stored information.

Intellectually valuable experiences can involve the teacher or parent as active participants in the task with the child. They can assist in labeling, describing, comparing, classifying, and questioning, and so support intellectual development (Stevens, 1981). Good examples of this type of interaction follow:

Sara looks at a worm crawling on the ground. Teacher: "It's a worm. It's long and brown, sort of like a stick. See, it's smaller than your finger."

Sonja (24 months old) says something about a circus. Mother: "No, you didn't go to the circus — you went to the parade." Sonja: "I went to the parade." Mother: "What did you see?" . . . Sonja: "Big girls." Mother smiles. "Big girls and what else?" . . . Sonja: "Trumpets." Mother: "Yes, and fire engines. Do you remember the fire engines?" Sonja: "You hold my ears a little bit." Mother smiles. "Yes, I did, just like this," and puts her hands on Sonja's ears. Sonja laughs. (Carew, 1980)

As the teacher interacts by supplying words to fit situations, it should be remembered that often a new word needs to be repeated in a subtle way. It has been said that at least three repetitions of a new word are needed for adults to master it; young children need more. Teachers often hear the child repeating a new word, trying to become familiar with it.

A teacher can help the child focus on something of interest. The child's "desire to know" can be motivated. Repetition of words and many firsthand activities on the same theme will help the child to form an idea or concept. The child may even touch and try something new with the teacher's encouragement.

The teacher's reaction supplies the child with feedback to his actions. The teacher is responsible for reinforcing the use of a new word and ensuring that the child has a good attitude about himself as a speaker.

Every day, the teacher can take advantage of unplanned things that happen to promote language and speech. Landreth (1972) provides an illustration:

While children were sitting in a story group, John noticed that a mobile, hung from the ceiling above, was spinning. "Look," said John pointing, "it's moving!" "How come?" said another child. "Someone must have touched it," said Mary. "Stand up, Mary, and see if you can touch it," added the teacher, standing up and reaching, herself. "I can't reach it either." "Maybe it spins itself," contributed Bill. "No, it can't spin itself," said another child. "Let's see," said the teacher. She got a piece of yarn with a bead tied to the end and held it out in front of the children. It was still. Then she held it near the mobile, which was in a draft of a window. The string swayed gently. "The window, the window is open," suggested the children. "Yes, the wind is coming through the window," said John. "And making it move," said all the children, pleased with their discovery. The teacher held the string so the children could blow at it. "Look, I'm, the wind," said one of them. That afternoon, outside, the children were given crepe paper streamers to explore wind direction. They were also read *Gilberto and the Wind*, which tells what happens when wind blows the sail of a boat, the arm of a windmill, the smoke from a chimney, and a child's hat and hair.

Being able to make the most of an unexpected event is a valuable skill. The key is to be alert to the child's interests. Moving into a situation with skill and helping the child discover something and tell about it is part of promoting word growth.

Teachers need a clear understanding of how children learn words and concepts. The chart in figure 6-4 includes guidelines for the teacher's actions to accompany the child's progress toward new learning.

Incorporating the child's ideas and suggestions into teacher conversation, and giving credit, makes children aware of the importance of their expressed ideas.

"Kimberly's idea was to . . ."
"Angelo thinks we should . . ."
"Christal suggests we . . ."
"Here's the way Trevor would . . ."

An early childhood center is a *child's* center, where children are actively involved with exciting and interesting things to discuss. It is *not* a place where teachers do all the talking.

One approach to teacher interaction during structured, planned, or incidental activities, described by Maria Montessori, is called *three stage interaction*. It shows movement from the child's sensory exploration to showing understanding, and then to verbalizing the understanding. An example follows:

Step 1: Associating sense perception with words. A cut lemon is introduced and the child is encouraged to taste it. As the child tests, the adult says, "The lemon tastes sour," pairing the

Child Activity	Teacher Actions
• Focuses on an object or activity.	• Name the object, or offer a statement describing the actions or situation. (Supplies words)
• Manipulates and explores the object or situation using touch, taste, smell, sight, sound organs.	• Try to help child connect this object or action to child's past experience through simple conversation. (Builds bridge between old and new)
• Fits this into what he already knows. Develops some understanding.	• Help the child see details through simple statements or questions. (Focus on identifying characteristics)
	• Ask "Show me . . ." or "Give me . . ." questions which ask for a nonverbal response. (Prompting)
	• Put child's action into words. (Example: "John touched the red ball.") (Modeling)
	• Ask the child for a verbal response. "What is this called?" "What happened when . . . ?" (Prompting)
• Uses a new word or sentence which names, describes, classifies or generalizes a feature or whole part of the object or action.	• Give a response in words indicating the truth factor of the response. "Yes, that's a red ball." or "It has four legs like a horse, but it's called a cow." (Corrective or reinforcing response)
	• Extend one-word answers to full simple sentence if needed. (Modeling)
	• Suggest an exploration of another feature of the object or situation. (Extend interest)
	• Ask a memory or review question. "Tell me about . . ." (Reinforcing and assessing)

FIGURE 6-4 Language learning and teacher interaction

word *sour* with the sensory experience. Repetition of the verbal pairing strengthens the impression.

Step 2: Probing understanding. A number of yellow cut fruit are presented. "Find the one that tastes sour," teacher suggests. The child shows by his actions his understanding, or lack of it.

Step 3: Expressing understanding. A child is presented a cut lemon and a grapefruit, and asked, "Tell me how they taste." If the child is able to describe the fruit as sour, he has incorporated the word into his vocabulary and has some understanding of the concept.

When using the three-step approach, Montessori (1967) suggests that if a child is uninterested, the adult should stop at that point. If a mistake is made, the adult remains silent. The mistake only indicates the child is not ready to learn — not that he is unable to learn.

This verbal approach may seem mechanical and ritualistic to some, yet it points out clearly the sequence a child travels from *not knowing* to *knowing*.

Interacting does require teachers to "wonder out loud." They express their own curiosity while at the same time noticing each child's quest to find out what makes others tick and what the world is all about.

THE TEACHER AS A BALANCER

In all roles, the teacher needs to maintain a balance. This means:

- giving, but withholding when self-discovery is practical and possible.
- interacting, but not interfering or dominating the child's train of thought or actions.
- giving support, but not hovering.
- talking, but not overtalking.
- listening, but not remaining totally silent.
- providing many opportunities for the child to speak.

To maintain such a balance, the teacher is a model, a provider, and an interactor, suiting the ability of each child. As a model, the teacher's example offers the child a step above — but not too far above — what the child is already able to do. In doing this, the teacher watches and listens while working with individual children, learning as much from the child's misunderstandings or mistakes as from correct or appropriate responses and behavior. This does not mean that the motive is always to *teach,* for the teacher also enjoys just talking with the children, figure 6-6. It does mean that the teacher

FIGURE 6-5 "Look at me, teacher!"

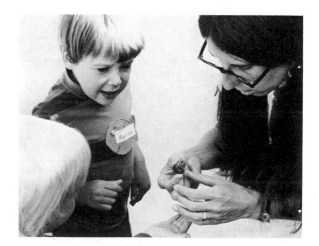

FIGURE 6-6 Sharing the child's discoveries helps him verbalize.

is ready to make the most of every situation as teacher and child enjoy learning together.

A teacher's attitude toward child growth in language should be one of optimism; provide the best learning environment and realize the child will grow and learn new language skills when he is ready. Early childhood centers plan for as much growth as possible in language abilities with teachers who model, provide, and interact during activities, figure 6-7.

SUMMARY

Teachers function as models, providers of opportunities for language growth, and interactors. Children copy behaviors and attitudes of both adults and peers.

Words are symbols for objects, ideas, actions, and situations. The teacher can increase the learning of new words and ideas by helping

FIGURE 6-7 The child depends on the teacher as a model, provider, and interactor.

children to recognize links between past and present.

A delicate balance exists in early childhood education. Decisions are made which will affect each child's maximum growth opportunities.

Rewarding a child's actions tends to make those actions happen again. Learning and accomplishing may have its own reward value for the child.

Learning Activities

- Observe a teacher interacting with a preschool child. Note the teacher's speech and actions which make the child feel that what he says is important.

- Describe three typical preschool situations that would make it necessary for a child to speak.

- Listen intently to three adults. (Take notes.) How would you evaluate them as speech models? (good, average, poor) State the reasons for your decision.

- Describe what is meant by the following terms:
  standard English   image   example
  symbol   motivation   cognitive
  positive reinforcement   interactor

- Record a conversation with another classmate. Have the recording analyzed for standard English speech usage.

- Tape record or videotape your interaction with a group of young children for a period of 15 minutes. Analyze your listening, questioning, sentence structure, extending ability, and pronunciation.

- Discuss "How do teachers model reading and writing in preschool classrooms?"

- Fill out the following checklist and compare your ratings with those of your classmates.

	Agree	Can't Decide	Disagree
1. Every center happening should encourage speech.			
2. It takes considerable time and effort to have personal conversations with each child daily.			
3. Each child is entitled to a personal greeting and goodbye.			

	Agree	Can't Decide	Disagree
4. "How are you?" is a good opening remark.			
5. A child who bursts out with something to say which has nothing to do with what's presently happening must have something important on his mind.			
6. Pausing silently for a few moments after speaking to a shy child is a good idea.			
7. Most new vocabulary words are learned at group times.			
8. Saying "John stepped over the green block" is unnecessary, for the child knows what he has done.			
9. All children have home interests that teachers can discuss with them.			
10. At mealtimes, it's best to remain quiet while children enjoy their food.			
11. If the child talks about a bathroom function, ignore it.			
12. When Phil says, "Girls can't drive trucks" tell him he's wrong.			
13. Teachers really need to talk more than they listen.			
14. Saying "Tell him you don't like it when he grabs your toy" is poor technique.			
15. I don't think it's possible to use a lot of language building techniques and still speak naturally and comfortably with a child.			
16. Teacher should model a playful attitude at times.			

Unit Review

A. Name the three basic functions of the early childhood teacher.

B. List five examples of each of the functions you listed for question A.

C. Following is an observation of a teacher and children. After reading it, indicate what you feel was appropriate behavior and inappropriate behavior on the part of the teacher in regard to language development.

Situation: *Teacher is conducting a sharing time with Joey, Mabel, Maria, and Chris.*

Teacher: "It's time for sharing. Please sit down, children."

Joey: "I want to share first!"

Teacher: "You'll have your turn. You must learn to wait."

Mabel: "I can't see."

Teacher: "Yes, you can."

"Maria, you're sitting quietly and not talking. You may go first."

Maria: "This is a book about Mickey. Mickey clips."

Joey: "What's clips, teacher?"

Teacher: "You're next, Joey."

Joey: "Mickey on T.V. teacher. Tomorrow I went to the fire station. The fireman let me wear his badge, like this."

Chris: "Fireman's truck red. Goes whee — whee."

Teacher: "It's Joey's turn, Chris. Would you wait to talk?"

Mabel: "I want to go, now!"

Teacher: "Mabel, you must have your turn to share before you can go."

Mabel: "I see a butterfly on the window."

Teacher: "Later, Mabel. You can go outside later."

D. What two factors should be considered by the teacher in trying to keep the main functions of teaching in balance?

E. Select the correct answers. All have more than one correct reply.
1. The teacher is a model for
   a. speech.
   b. attitudes.
   c. speech more often than parents may be.
   d. speech only during planned activities.
2. It is more important for the young child to
   a. like to speak than to speak correctly.
   b. participate than sit quietly.
   c. speak than to listen.
   d. have the teacher tell him about something than to explore it himself.

3. Teachers reinforce learning by
   a. using speech to solve problems.
   b. praising the child's use of a new word.
   c. motivating the child's "wanting to know."
   d. linking the old with the new ideas.
4. When speaking, the teacher should
   a. attempt to use natural language patterns.
   b. speak in full sentences.
   c. make sure each child responds by speaking.
   d. refrain from "overtalking."
5. Preschool children
   a. are also speech models.
   b. rarely teach others new words.
   c. play and use words in play.
   d. have growing vocabularies only when teachers act appropriately.
6. Words are
   a. symbols for real happenings.
   b. related to stored images.
   c. learned through the senses.
   d. not labels for concepts.

F. Write a short ending to the following. "A teacher who is not speaking standard English should . . . ."

G. Robert D. Hess and V. C. Shipman have shown that different adults have different styles of communicating with young children. The following is a comparison of two mothers trying to teach the same task to their child.

First Mother: All right, Susan, this board is the place where we put the little toys; first of all you're supposed to learn how to place them according to color. Can you do that? The things that are all the same color you put in one section; in the other section you put another group of colors, and in the third section you put the last group of colors. Can you do that? Or would you like to see me do it first?
Child: I want to do it.

Second Mother: (Introducing the same task): Now I'll take them all off the board; now you put them all back on the board. What are these?
Child: A truck.
Second Mother: All right, just put them right here; put the other one right here; all right, put the other one there."

From R. D. Hess & V. C. Shipman, "Early Experience and the Socialization of Cognitive Modes in Children." *Child Development,* 1966.

Write a brief comparison of the two mothers, but pretend they are two teachers.

H. Finish the following statement. "Simple expanding of child comments to make full sentences is not as valuable as extending conversations because . . . . ."

REFERENCES

Carew, J. V., "Experience and the Development of Intelligence in Young Children at Home and in Day Care," *Monographs of the Society for Research in Child Development 45,* Serial No. 187, 1980.

Garvey, Catherine, *Play,* Harvard University Press, Cambridge, MA, 1977.

Landreth, Catherine, *Preschool Learning and Teaching,* Harper and Row, 1972.

McCandless, Boyd R., *Children,* Holt, Rinehart, and Winston, New York, 1967.

Montessori, Maria, *The Absorbent Mind,* Holt, Rinehart, and Winston, NY, 1967.

Pellegrini, Anthony and Lee Galda, "Effects of Thematic-Fantasy Play Training on the Development of Children's Story Comprehension," *American Educational Research Journal,* Vol. 19, No. 3, 1982.

Stevens, Joseph H. Jr., "Everyday Experience and Intellectual Development," Research in Review, *Young Children,* Vol. 37, No. 1, Nov. 1981.

Tough, J., *Focus on Meaning: Talking to Some Purpose with Young Children,* George Allen and Unwin, Ltd., 1973.

Weir, Mary E., and Pat Eggleston, "Teachers First Words," *Day Care and Early Education,* Nov./Dec., 1975.

Weiss, Curtis E., and Herold S. Lillywhite, *Communicative Disorders,* 2nd ed., C. V. Mosby Co., 1981.

SUGGESTED READINGS

Hendrick, Joanne, *The Whole Child,* 3rd ed., 1984, Chapter 1, C. V. Mosby Co.

Hess, R. D., & V. C. Shipman, "Early Experience and the Socialization of Cognitive Modes in Children," *Child Development,* 1966.

Pellegrini, Anthony and Lee Galda, "The Effects of Thematic-Fantasy Play Training on the Development of Children's Story Comprehension," *American Educational Research Journal,* Vol. 19, no. 3, 1982.

Section 2
Listening — A
Language Art

Unit 7
Developing Listening Skills

OBJECTIVES

After studying this unit you should be able to

- list five levels of listening
- discuss teaching techniques which promote good listening habits.
- demonstrate how to plan an activity which promotes auditory perception.

Auditory perception refers to the process of being aware of sounds and their meanings. The world, with its many sounds, bombards the infant. Although no one formally teaches an infant to listen, certain sounds become familiar and take on meanings from this mass of confusion. The infant has begun to listen.

Many children develop the ability to listen *carefully* to the speech of others during early childhood; others do not. Since language growth has been described as a receiving process followed by a sending process, a child's listening ability is very important. This ability to listen develops before the child speaks.

Hearing and listening are quite different. Hearing is a process involving nerves and muscles which reach adult efficiency by age 4–5. Listening is a learned behavior; a mental process: concerned with hearing, attending, discriminating, understanding, and remembering. It can be improved with practice. Listening affects social interactions, one's level of functioning, and perhaps one's overall success in life (Weiss and Lillywhite, 1981). Nichols (1948) estimates that we listen to 50% of what we hear and comprehend only 25% of that.

There are usually many opportunities to listen in early childhood centers. Teacher-planned or child-created play is a source of many sounds, figure 7-1. A quality program sharpens a child's listening and offers a variety of experiences. Listening is not left to chance; planned programs develop skills.

LISTENING LEVELS

Listening occurs in a variety of ways. A person does not always listen for knowledge, but may listen to a sound because it is pleasing to hear. The first time a child discovers the sound made by pots and pans, he is fascinated. Preschoolers often make their own pleasurable or rhythmic sounds with whatever is available.

The human voice can be interesting, threatening, or monotonous to a child, depending on past experience. Silence also has meaning. Sometimes teachers suspect that a child has a hearing problem, only to find that the child was inattentive for other reasons.

A child may listen but not understand. He may miss sound differences, or listen without evaluating what he hears. Listening involves a

FIGURE 7-1 Teacher-planned or child-created play is a source of many sounds. *(From Machado and Meyer,* Early Childhood Practicum Guide, *Copyright 1984 by Delmar Publishers Inc.)*

variety of skills and levels. In order to provide growing opportunities, teachers should be aware of various listening levels, as shown in figure 7-2.

The goal of a good program in early childhood language arts is to guide the young child toward development of these levels. Semel (1976) has analyzed the listening process, and describes three stages which the child moves through in efficient listening, figure 7-3.

When a sound occurs, it is remembered by thinking about its features: direction, pitch, intensity, newsness, and so on.

TODDLER LISTENING EXPERIENCES

Parents of the toddler and center staff members can engage in a number of activities to stimulate listening. Body action play of the old "coo-chee-coo" variety, "this little piggy," and simple rhymes and repetitions are recommended. Connecting noises and sounds with toys and objects, and encouraging the child to playfully imitate helps joy and sound-making go hand in hand. Rhythmic clapping, tapping, and pan beating in sequence or patterns can be enjoyable. Musical toys and records add variety and ear pleasure. Encouraging face watching as different human sounds are produced, and locating environmental sounds together are additional hints in listening development attempts.

Adults should exercise care in sound volume and quality; at all age levels extra loud, shrill, vibrating, or emergency alert sounds can be frightening — the service station "flush" can terrorize. (Note: The service station bathroom is often a strange and foreign place for young children. For some reason many toilets there flush violently and very loudly, causing a child to cling and cry.)

Appreciative listening. The child finds pleasure and entertainment in hearing music, poems and stories. It is best to begin with this type of listening because it is passive, but personal for each child.

Purposeful listening. The child follows directions, and gives back responses.

Discriminative listening. The child becomes aware of changes in pitch and loudness. He differentiates sounds in the environment. Eventually, he is able to discriminate the speech sounds.

Creative listening. The child's imagination and emotions are stimulated by his listening experiences. He expresses his thoughts spontaneously and freely through words, or actions, or both.

Critical listening. The child understands, evaluates, makes decisions, and formulates opinions. To encourage this critical listening, the teacher may pose such questions as: "What happens when we all talk at once?" "What if everyone wanted to play in the playhouse at the same time?" The child must think through the responses, decide the most logical solution to the problem, and present a point of view.

FIGURE 7-2 Some of the ways a child listens *(From Louise B. Scott,* Learning Time With Language Experiences, *New York: McGraw-Hill Book Co., 1968.)*

Responding to Stimuli	Organizing the Stimuli	Understanding the Meaning
Awareness Focus Figure-Ground Discrimination	Sequencing and Synthesizing Scanning	(Classification; Integration; Monitoring)

←———————— Memory ————————→

Stage 1 — Responding to stimuli: Was there sound? Where was it? Which sound was it? Was there more than one sound? Were the sounds the same?
Stage 2 — Organizing the stimuli: What was the sequence of the sounds? What was the length of time between sounds? Have I heard that sound before? Where have I heard it?
Stage 3 — Understanding the meaning: What do the sounds and words mean?

FIGURE 7-3 Stages of the listening process

TEACHER SKILLS

Good listening habits are especially important in school situations. Instructions from teachers should be clear and simple, with a sequence of what comes first, next, and last. Usually instructions need not be repeated when given clearly and simply. Often, when the attention of the group is required, a signal is used. Ringing a small bell, playing a piano chord, or a flick of the lights can be a signal that it's time to listen. The silent pause before beginning an activity can be used effectively to focus attention on listening.

Teachers also use a short song, finger play, or body movement activity to stimulate interest and draw the group together, figure 7-4. This helps children focus on what is to follow.

Praise and smiles at any time of the day can reward individual listening. Positive, specific statements such as "Michael, I liked the way you listened to what Janet had to say before you started talking," or, "Thank you, Berti, for waiting so quietly. Now we can all hear the beginning of the story," give children feedback on expected listening behavior.

These are sample teacher statements that can promote a group's ability to listen:

At the Beginning

- "When I see everyone's eyes, I'll know you're ready to hear about . . ."

FIGURE 7-4 A clapping game is used to draw a group together and "ready them" for listening.

- "Let's zip the lips (draw hand across the mouth) and open our ears (pretend to turn an imaginary knob at ears) . . ."
- "We'll begin when we can all hear the clock ticking."
- "Pedro's listening. He's ready. Lulane's listening . . ." (until all are quieted)
- "I'm waiting until everyone can hear before I start. Raise your hand if you can't hear me. Listen." (After starting, if hand goes up — "Michael can't hear. We need to be quiet so Michael can hear about . . .")
- "We're all listening; it's time to begin."
- "We take turns speaking. Bill's first, then . . ."

During Activity

- "Jack wants to tell us, himself, about his idea." (or what happened, etc.)
- "It's Maria's turn to tell us . . ."
- "We can hear best when just one person is talking. Louis, you go first, then Cristalee."
- "Bill, it's hard to wait when you want to tell your friends something. Gloria's talk-ing now; you can be next." Later, add, "Bill, thank you for waiting for Gloria to finish. Now we want to hear what you wanted to tell us."
- "Everyone wants to tell us about their own pets. Raise your hand — I'll make a waiting list so we can hear everyone." (Make list quickly and hold it up.) "Isaac, your name's first," (or next, etc.)

At Activity's End

- "We listened so quietly. We all heard every word of that story."
- "Thank you for being such good listeners."
- "I like the way everyone listened to what their friends said."
- "We listened and found out a lot about . . ."

Rewarded behavior is usually repeated and becomes a habit. Teachers should consistently notice correct listening behavior, and comment favorably about it to the children.

AUDITORY PERCEPTION

Ears respond to sound waves. These sounds go to the brain and become organized in relation to past experience. The same process is used in early childhood and later when the child learns to read. Language development depends upon the auditory process.

Educational activities which give practice and help perfect auditory skills usually deal with the following objectives:

- Sustaining attention span
- Following directions or commands
- Imitating sounds
- Identifying and associating sounds
- Using auditory memory
- Discriminating between sounds (intensity, pitch, tempo)

The *intensity* of a sound is its degree of force, strength, or energy. *Pitch* is the highness or lowness of sound. *Tempo* is the rate of speed of a sound, in other words, the rhythm of the sound which engages the attention.

AUDITORY ACTIVITIES

A wide range of auditory activities can be planned. The following goals often serve as the basis for planning. Simple skills come before more difficult ones:

- Recognizing own name when spoken
- Repeating two nonsense words, short sayings, chants, poems, finger plays, or any series of words
- Reporting sounds heard at home
- Imitating sounds of toys, animals, classroom, rain, sirens, bells
- Telling if a sound is near or far, loud or soft, fast or slow, high or low, same or different
- Identifying people's voices
- Identifying and repeating rhythms heard
- Retelling a story, poem, or part of one
- Trying to perform first one-, then two-part directions
- Recalling sounds in sequence
- Coordinating listening and moving the body in a requested way
- Enjoying music, stories, poems, and the many other language arts, both individually and in groups

SETTINGS FOR LISTENING

When preparing listening activities, the teacher can plan for success by having activities take place in room areas with a minimum of distracting sounds or objects, figure 7-5. Screens, dividers, and bookcases are helpful. Heating and lighting are checked and comfortable seating is provided. Decisions concerning the size of a group are important. In general, the younger the group, the smaller it should be, and the shorter the length of the lesson.

Since listening cannot be forced, the key is to motivate, figure 7-6. Some schools offer chil-

FIGURE 7-5 Proper placement of a piece of furniture or cabinet can reduce distractions.

FIGURE 7-6 A teacher promotes active speech and tries to motivate listening too. (*From Machado and Meyer,* Early Childhood Practicum Guide, *Copyright 1984 by Delmar Publishers Inc.*)

dren the choice of joining a group listening activity or playing quietly nearby. Teachers find that an interesting experience attracts children who are nearby. When activities are enjoyable and successful, the child who was hesitant may look forward to new experiences. A teacher can *turn on* or *turn off:* ending, changing, or modifying activities when necessary. Carefully watching for feedback is part of developing active listening in the child. One of the skills of the successful teacher is to complete the learning activity before the group becomes restless. The active preschooler may struggle to remain seated for any length of time. This fact is important to consider when listening is necessary to the activity.

LISTENING CENTER

Special listening areas, sometimes called listening posts, can become a part of early childhood classrooms. Enjoying a quiet time by oneself or listening to recorded materials fascinates many children. Headsets plugged to a jack or terminal help to block out room noise. Partitions cut distractions. Clever listening places to settle into are favorite spots, such as:

- large packing boxes lined with soft fabrics and pillows.
- old, soft armchairs.
- a bunk or loft.

Phonographs, cassette tape recorders, photographs, picture sets, and books offer added dimensions to listening centers. Recordings of the teacher reading a new or favorite story can be available at all times for children's use.

Children can record their own descriptions of special block constructions together with accompanying drawings or photos. "Why I like this book" talks can be made about a special book. Children can record comments about their own pieces of art. A field trip scrapbook may have a child's commentary with it. Recorded puppet scripts and flannel board stories can be enjoyed while the child moves the characters and listens. The child can explore small plastic animals while listening to a prepared cassette tape story. Possibilities for recorded activities are limited only by preparational time and staff interest.

Children's ages are always a factor in the use of audiovisual equipment. Listening centers need teacher introduction and explanation.

Records

Some companies specialize in children's records that improve listening skills. These records involve the child in listening for a signal, listening to directions, or listening to sounds. Some records include body movement activities along with listening skills.

Not all records contain appropriate subject matter for young children. Before using a record with children, the teacher should listen to it. The following criteria may be used to judge a record's worth:

1. Is the subject matter appropriate for young children?
2. Is it clearly presented?
3. Is it interesting to the young child?
4. Does it meet the teaching objective?

Many records have been made of children's classics. These can also help to improve children's listening skills.

Tape Recorders

Tape recorders can both fascinate and frighten children. They can be valuable tools for listening activities. Under the teacher's supervision, children can explore and enjoy sounds using tape recorders.

Language Master

A language master is a sturdy, portable piece of equipment. It can record and then play back instantly. Cards are inserted in a left-to-right fashion. Although children need supervision in its use, they can learn how to use it in a short time. This machine has many listening-activity possibilities. More information about it is given in Unit 22 of this text.

SUMMARY

The ability to listen improves with experience and exposure, although young children vary in their *ability* to listen. Listening ability can be divided into a series of levels — appreciative, purposeful, discriminative, creative, and critical.

Planned activities, teacher interaction, and equipment can provide opportunities for children to develop their perception skills.

Listening cannot be forced, but can be motivated. Signals and positive reinforcement can help to form habits. Settings which limit stimuli and control the size of groups are desirable. When teachers are watchful and act when children seem restless or lacking in interest during planned activities, listening remains active. One of the responsibilities of the teacher is to plan carefully so that young children consistently want to hear what is being offered.

Learning Activities

- With a small group of classmates, discuss some of the ways a home or school environment can make young children "tune out."

- Watch a listening activity in a preschool center. Then answer the following questions:
  a. How did the teacher prepare the children for listening?
  b. What elements of the activity captured interest?
  c. How was child interest held?
  d. Did the teacher have an opportunity to praise listening?
  e. Did children's behavior during the activity seem important to the teacher?
  f. Was this the kind of activity that should be repeated? If so, why?

- Observe preschoolers in group play. Write down any examples of appreciative, purposeful, discriminative, creative, or critical listening.

- Plan a listening activity. Describe the materials needed, how the activity will start, what is to happen during the activity, and what auditory perception skills were included in your plan.

- In a paragraph, describe the difference between motivating a child to listen and forcing a child to listen.

- Find a source for recorded stories in your community.

- Record a child's picturebook using a cassette tape recorder. Decide on a "turn-the-page" signal for which you will instruct the child to listen.

Unit Review

A. Five levels of listening have been discussed. After each of the following statements, identify the listening level which best fits the situation.
   1. After hearing an indian drum on a record, Brett slaps out a rhythm of his own on his thighs while dancing around the room.

2. During a story of "The Three Little Pigs," Mickey pops out with "He's not berry nice!" in reference to the wolf's behavior in the story.

3. Kimmie is following Chris around. Chris is repeating "Swishy, fishy-co-co-pop," over and over again; both giggle periodically.

4. Debbie tells you about the little voice of small Billy Goat Gruff and the big voice of big Billy Goat Gruff in the story of the "Three Billy Goats Gruff."

5. Peter has asked if he can leave his block tower standing during snacktime instead of putting the blocks away as you requested, because he wishes to return and build it higher. He then listens for your answer.

B. Name five objectives that could be used in planning listening activities for auditory perception.

C. Select the correct answers. All have more than one correct reply.
  1. Most parents unconsciously teach preschoolers
    a. to develop auditory perception.
    b. attitudes toward listening.
    c. to listen to their teachers.
    d. many words.
  2. A teacher can promote listening by
    a. demanding a listening attitude.
    b. using a signal to listen.
    c. praising a child.
    d. telling a child he is not listening.
  3. Critical listening happens when the
    a. child relates what is new to past experience.
    b. child disagrees with another's statement.
    c. child makes a comment about a word being good or bad.
    d. teacher plans thought-provoking questions, and the child has the maturity needed to answer them.
  4. Children come to early childhood centers with
    a. individual variation in ability to listen.
    b. habits of listening.
    c. all the abilities and experiences needed to be successful in planned activities.
    d. a desire to listen.
  5. A child's ability to follow a series of commands depends on
    a. his auditory memory.
    b. how clearly the commands are stated.
    c. how well his ears transmit the sounds to his brain and how well the brain sorts the information.
    d. how well he can imitate the words of the commands.

D. Explain what is meant by *intensity, pitch,* and *tempo.*

E. Assume the children are involved in an activity when they are suddenly distracted by a dog barking outside the window. List four things you could say to the children to draw their attention back to the activity.

References

Barker, Larry L., *Listening Behavior,* Prentice-Hall Inc., NJ, 1971.

Hennings, Dorothy Grant, *Communication in Action,* Rand McNally, 1978.

Lamberts, Frances, et al., "Listening and Language Activities for Preschool Children," *Language, Speech and Hearing Services in Schools,* April 1980, pp. 111–117.

Margolin, Edythe, *Teaching Young Children at School and Home,* Macmillan Publishing Co., NY, 1982, pp. 157–58.

Marten, Milton, "Listening Review," *Classroom-relevant Research in the Language Arts,* Assoc. for Supv. and Curriculum Development, Washington, DC, 1978, pp. 48–60.

Nichols, R., "Factors in Listening Comprehension," *Speech Monographs,* 15:154–163, 1948.

Stewig, John Warren, *Teaching Language Arts in Early Childhood,* Holt, Rinehart and Winston, NY, 1982, Chap. 3.

Van Allen, Roach and Claryce Allen, *Language Experience Activities,* 2nd ed., Houghton Mifflin Co., Boston, 1982, Chap. 10.

Weiss, Curtis E., and Herold S. Lillywhite, *Communicative Disorders,* 2nd ed., C. V. Mosby Co., 1981.

Suggested Readings

Beaty, Janice J., *Skills for Preschool Teachers,* Bell and Howell Co., 1979. Module E, p. 115.

Hymes, James L., *Teaching the Child Under Six,* 2nd Edition, Charles E. Merrill Publishing Co., 1974, pages 102–109.

Children's Books with Listening Themes

Borten, Helen, *Do You Hear What I Hear?,* Abelard-Schuman, NY, 1960. (Describes the pleasures to be found in really listening.)

Brown, Margaret Wise, *The Summer Noisy Book,* Harper and Row Publ., NY, 1951. (Can be easily made into a "guess-what" sound game.)

Guilfoile, Elizabeth, *Nobody Listens to Andrew,* Follett Publishing Company, 1957. (The "no one ever listens to me" idea is humorously handled.)

Johnson, LaVerne, *Night Noises,* Parents Magazine Press, 1967. (Listening to noises in bed at night.)

Showers, Paul, *The Listening Walk,* Thomas Y. Crowell Co., 1961. (Good book to share before adventuring on a group sound walk.)

Spier, Peter, *Gobble, Growl, Grunt,* Doubleday and Co., 1971. (Lots of variety in animal sounds, with brilliant illustrations.)

Zolotow, Charlotte, *If You Listen,* Harper and Row, Publishers, 1980. (A touching tale of a child who, missing her father, turns to listening.)

Unit 8
Listening Activities

OBJECTIVES

After studying this unit you should be able to

- describe three listening activities, stating the auditory perception skill that is discussed in each.

- plan and present a listening activity.

- tell a story which involves purposeful child listening.

Listening activities are used to increase enjoyment, vocabulary, and attention span. In this unit, the activities focus on the development of auditory skills through listening and responding interactions. Activities which further develop these skills through the use of books and stories are found in later units.

Group activities found in this unit concentrate on developing listening skills: Unit 15 will give you lots of encouragement and help in conducting the activities. If you will be trying out activities in this unit first, it's best to skip ahead to Unit 15.

One of your first tasks will be how to gather an interested group. Every classroom has some signal which alerts children to a change in activities or a new opportunity. This can range from flicking lights to piano chords or more creative "attention getters." Usually a short invitational and motivating statement will be used to peak child curiosity such as:

- "Gail has a new game for you in the rug area today."

- "Time to finish what you are doing if you want to join Madelyn in storytime with a book about Clifford the Big Red Dog."
- "Our clapping song begins in two minutes; today we are going to be Jack-In-The-Boxes."

In some centers children are simply requested to finish up and join their friends in a particular room area. The enjoyment of already-started finger plays, chants, songs, or movement captures their attention and they are drawn in. This is a great time to recognize all the children by name, as in the following: (To the tune of "She'll be coming 'round the mountain.")

"Susie is here with us, yes, yes, yes."
(Clap on yes, yes, yes.)

"Larry is here with us, yes, yes, yes."
(Continue until all children are recognized, ending with)

"We are sitting here together,
We are sitting here together,
We are sitting here together, yes, yes, yes."

"CAN YOU SAY IT LIKE I DO?"

Objective
To imitate sounds.

Materials
None

Introduction and Activity
The teacher says, "Can you change your voice like I can?"

"My name is _____." (softly
teacher's name
whispering) With changes of voice, speed, and pitch, the teacher illustrates: loudly, low voice, high voice, fast, slow, with mouth nearly closed, with mouth wide open, and when holding nose, among others.

The teacher then selects a child who talks easily.

"Now, let's see if we can change our voice like Billy. Try it in a whisper, Billy. Do it any way you want, Billy. We'll try to copy you."

The teacher then gives others who wish to take a turn a chance. This activity may be followed up with a body-action play with voice changes, like Mr. Tall and Mr. Small, page 203.

WHAT'S CRUNCHY?

Objective
Discriminative listening and sound memory.

Materials
Small celery sticks, carrot sticks, cotton balls, miniature marshmallows, uncooked spaghetti.

Introduction and Activity
Put materials in a bag behind your back. Reach in and show a celery stick as your start.

"Celery is long and green, long and green, long and green," (to the tune of "Mary Had a Little Lamb"). Repeat first line. "When you eat it, it goes crunch." Pass out a celery stick to each child who wishes one, and sing through again making a crunch at the end. Follow up with "What else is crunchy?" Sing with child crunchy suggestion substituted for celery. Then introduce the following lyrics while passing out the items to each child from your bag.

Carrot sticks are long and orange. When you eat them, they go crunch. Cotton balls are soft and white. When you touch them, they feel soft. Spaghetti is long and thin. When you break it, it goes snap. Marshmallows are small and white. When you squeeze them they pop back.

Variation
Try children's names next if group is still with you. "Jayne is a girl that's four." Repeat. "When you ask her she says . . ." pause waiting for child to finish sentence, if not, add "Hello," and try other children.

PARAKEET TALK

Objective
To imitate sounds.

Materials
Popsicle sticks and colored construction paper. Cut out parakeets from colored construction paper and paste them on popsicle sticks. All forms can be traced and cut from one pattern.

Introduction and Activity
Discuss birds that imitate what people say. Distribute parakeet forms, figure 8-1. Begin with something like, "We can pretend to be parakeets, too."

Teacher: Hi, parakeets!
Children: Hi, parakeets!

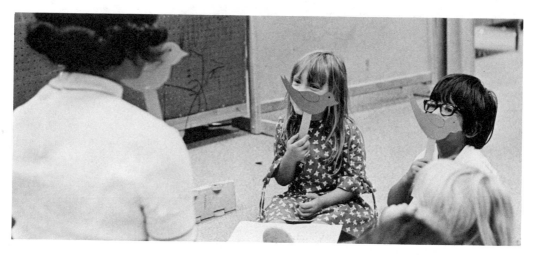

FIGURE 8-1 Parakeet talk

Teacher: Pretty bird.
Children: Pretty bird.

Teacher: Now let's hear from Julie, the yellow parakeet. Can the blue parakeet (Mike) say whatever the green parakeet (Sue) says? Let's see."

This activity leads well into a record with children pretending to be flying. Suggest that the children flap their wings through a door to an outdoor area, or take a walk to listen for bird sounds.

"LISTEN, OOPS A MISTAKE!"

Objective
To associate and discriminate word sounds with objects.

Materials
Four or five common school objects (pencil, crayon, block, toy, cup, doll, etc.); a low table.

Introduction and Activity
Talk about calling things by the wrong name. Then name the objects on the table. Begin with something like, "Have you ever called your friend by the wrong name?"

Teacher: When you call your friend by the wrong name, you've made a mistake. Look at the things on the table. I am going to name each of them. (Teacher names them correctly.) All right, now see if you can hear my mistakes. This time I'm going to point to them, too. If you hear a mistake, raise your hand and say, "Oops, a mistake!" Let's say that together once: "Oops, a mistake!" Good. Are you ready? Listen: crayon, ball, doll, cup.

Change objects and give one of the children a chance to "make a mistake" while the others listen, figure 8-2.

This activity can later be followed with the story of *Moptop* (by Don Freeman, Children's Press) in which a long-haired red-headed boy is mistaken for a mop.

ERRAND GAME

Objective
To follow verbal commands.

Materials
None

FIGURE 8-2 "If you hear a mistake, raise your hand."

Introduction and Activity

Start a discussion about doing things for parents. Include getting objects from other rooms, from neighbors, etc. Tell the children you are going to play a game in which each person looks for something another has asked for.

Teacher: "Get me a book, please."
            "Can you find me a leaf, please."

Items to ask for include a rock, a blade of grass, a piece of paper, a block, a doll, a crayon, a toy car, a sweater, a hat, clothes, a hanger, a blanket, etc. Send children off one at a time. As they return, talk to each about where they found their item. While the group waits for all members to return, the group can name all the returned items, put them in a row, ask children to cover their eyes while one is hidden, and then ask the children to guess which item was removed, or chant, "We're waiting, we're waiting for _____(child's name)."

If interest is still high, the teacher can again give the command that the items be returned, and repeat the game by sending the children for new items.

JACK-IN-THE-BOX

Objective

To discriminate sounds by listening for a signal, and responding to it.

Materials

None. (To increase fun, cardboard boxes may be used. Tops should open easily. Be sure that the child is not afraid to climb inside the box. A back door large enough to climb through works best.)

Introduction and Activity

Recite the following rhyme in a whispered voice until the word "pop" is reached. Using hand motions, hide thumb in fist, and let it pop up on the word "pop" each time it is said.

Jack-in-the-Box, Jack-in-the-Box, where can you be?
Hiding inside where I can't see?
If you jump up, you won't scare me.
Pop! Pop! Pop!

Suggest that children squat and pretend to be jack-in-the-boxes. Ask them to listen and jump up only when they hear the word "pop." Try a second verse if the group seems willing.

Jack-in-the-Box, Jack-in-the-Box, you like to play.
Down in the box you won't stay.
There's only one word I have to say.
Pop! Pop! Pop!

PIN-ON SOUND CARDS (ANIMALS AND BIRDS)

Objective
To associate and imitate sounds, and to use auditory memory.

Materials
Safety pins or masking tape, file cards (3″ x 5″) with pictures of birds and animals (gummed stickers of animals and birds are available in stationery stores and from supply houses). Suggestions: duck, rooster, chick (peep-peep), owl, goose (honk-honk), woodpecker (peck-peck), horse, cow, cat, dog, sheep, lion, mouse, turkey, bee, frog, donkey, seal (clap-clap).

Introduction and Activity
Have a card pinned on your blouse before the children enter the room. This will start questions. Talk about the sound your card makes. Practice it with the children. Ask who would like a card of his own. Have the children come, one at a time, while you pin on the cards, figure 8-3. Talk about the animal and the sound it makes. Imitate each sound with the group. Play a game where one of the children makes an animal noise and the child with the right card stands up and says,

"That's me, I'm a _____."
                              name of animal

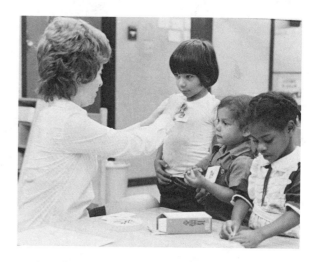

FIGURE 8-3 Pinning on sound cards

Children usually like to wear the cards the rest of the day and take them home if possible.

GUESS WHAT?

Objective
To identify and discriminate common sounds.

Materials
A bell, hand eggbeater, paper bag to crumple, baby rattle, tambourine, drum, stapler, any other noisemaker; a room divider, screen, table turned on its side, or blanket taped across a doorway. (This activity also works with a pre-recorded tape cassette.)

Introduction and Activity
Ask children to guess what you have behind the screen.

Teacher: "Listen; what makes that sound?"

NOTE: With younger children, it is best to introduce each item with its name first. Ask a child to come behind the screen and make the next noise.

Variation

Clap simple rhythms behind the screen and have children imitate them. Rhythms can be made by using full claps of the hands with light claps and pauses at regular intervals; for example, a loud clap followed by two light ones and a pause repeated over and over.

Ask a child to sit in the "guessing chair" with his back to the group. From the group, select a child to say, "Guess my name." If the first child answers correctly, he gets a chance to select the next child who is to sit in the guessing chair.

PLAY TELEPHONES

Objective

To focus on listening and responding.

Materials

Paper, blunt toothpicks, string, two small tin cans with both ends removed (check for rough edges).

Introduction and Activity

Cover one end of each tin can with paper. Make a small hole. Insert a long string in the hole. Tie the string around blunt toothpicks. (Paper cups can be substituted for the tin cans.) Make enough sets for the group. Demonstrate how they work.

SOUND STORY

This story contains three sound words. Every time one of the words is mentioned, the children should make the appropriate sound.

Say: "When you hear the word spinach, say "yum, yum, yum." When you hear the word dog, bark like a dog. When you hear the word cat, meow like a cat."

Once upon a time there was a little boy who would not taste SPINACH. Everyone would say, "Marvin, why won't you taste SPIN-

ACH?" Marvin would say, "I think SPIN-ACH is yuk!!!"

Marvin's DOG Malcolm loved SPINACH. Marvin's cat Malvina loved SPINACH. If Marvin didn't eat his SPINACH, Malcolm the DOG and Malvina the CAT would fight over who would get the SPINACH. The DOG and CAT would make so much noise fighting over the SPINACH that everyone in the neighborhood would say, "If you don't stop that noise, you will have to move away from here."

Marvin loved his house and he didn't want to move away from the neighborhood. Malcolm the DOG loved his house and he didn't want to move away from the neighborhood. Malvina the CAT loved her house and she didn't want to move away from the neighborhood.

WHAT COULD THEY DO ?????????

Let the children tell you the answer. This game is a lot of fun and the children never tire of hearing the story.

You can make up your own sound stories. You can also add rhythm instruments to make the sounds instead of voices. (Weissman, 1979)

LISTENING RIDDLES FOR GUESSING

Animal Riddles

A tail that's skinny and long.
At night he nibbles and gnaws
With teeth sharp and strong
Beady eyes and tiny paws
One called Mickey is very nice
And when there's more than one
We call them _____.

(MICE)

He has a head to pat.
But he's not a cat.
Sometimes he has a shiny coat.
It's not a hog, it's not a goat.
It's bigger than a frog.
I guess that it's a _____.

(DOG)

No arms, no hands, no paws.
But it can fly in the sky.
It sings a song
That you have heard.
So now you know
That it's a _____.

(BIRD)

Sharp claws and soft paws.
Big night eyes, and whiskers, too.
Likes to curl up in your lap,
Or catch a mouse or a rat.
Raise your hand if you know.
Now all together, let's whisper it's name
    very slow. _____.

(ccaatt — CAT)

Riddle Game. (Children take turns calling on others with raised hands.)

I'll ask you some riddles.
Answer if you can.
If you think you know,
Please raise your hand.
Don't say it out loud
'Til _____calls your name.
That's how we'll play
This riddling game.

A beautiful flower we smell with our nose.
Its special name is not pansy but

_____.

(ROSE)

I shine when you're playing and having
    fun.
I'm up in the sky and I'm called the

_____.

(SUN)

If you listen closely you can tell,
I ring and chime because I'm a

_____.

(BELL)

You've got ten of me, I suppose,
I'm on your feet and I'm your

_____.

(TOES)

I'm down on your feet, both one and two.
Brown, black, blue, or red, I'm a

_____.

(SHOE)

I sit on the stove and cook what I can.
They pour stuff in me, I'm a frying

_____.

(PAN)

It is helpful to have magazine pictures of a rose, the sun, toes, shoes, and a pan, plus a real bell to ring behind you as you speak. These are appropriate for young children who have little experience with rhyming.

Body Parts Riddle

If a bird you want to hear,
You have to listen with your

_____.

(EAR)

If you want to dig in sand,
Hold the shovel in your _____.

(HAND)

To see an airplane as it flies,
You must open up your _____.

(EYES)

To smell a pansy or a rose,
You sniff its smell with your

_____.

(NOSE)

When you walk across the street
You use two things called your

_____.

(FEET)

If a beautiful song you've sung,
You used your mouth and your

_____.

(TONGUE)

All these parts you can feel and see
Are parts always with you on your

_____.

(BODY)

Tracing hands, or drawing in any body part they choose (on a picture with missing hands, feet, etc.) is a fun follow-up activity.

LISTEN AND FOLLOW DIRECTIONS — STORIES AND GAMES

Sit-down — Stand-up Story

Teacher: Let's see if you can stand _up_ and sit _down_ when I say the words. Listen: Stand _up!_ Good, you all are standing. Sit _down!_ Good listening; we're ready to start.

When I woke _up_ this morning, I reached _down_ to the floor for my slippers. Then I stood _up_ and slipped them on. Next, I went _down_stairs to the kitchen. I opened the refrigerator, picked _up_ the milk and sat _down_ to drink. When I finished drinking, I tried to stand _up_ but I was stuck in the chair. I pulled and pulled, but I was still sitting _down_.

"Don't sit on the chairs," my _____ (dad, mother, brother) called from _up_stairs. "I painted them."

"It's too late! I'm sitting _down_." I answered. "Hurry _down_ here and help me."

_____(Dad, Mother, Brother) pulled and pulled, but I didn't come _up_.

"I'll go get our neighbor, Mr. Green. Maybe he can pull you _up_," _____ said. "I'll ask him to come _down_ here."

_____ and Mr. Green pulled and pulled. "What'll I do?" I said. "The children will be waiting at school for me." Then I got an idea.

"Go get the shovel," I said. Well, that worked; they pushed the shovel handle _down_ and I came _up_.

"You know, I think I'm stuck in this chair, too. Look, I am. _____(child's name)

and _____(child's name), please help me. Everyone else sit _down_."

"After my story, let's see if just _____ (child's   name)   and   _____ (child's name) can show us with their hands which way is _up_, and which way is _down_."

A good follow-up is to talk about what we see in the room that is "_up_ above our heads" and "_down_ below our heads," or say this poem together:

When you're up — you're up,
And when you're down — you're down.
But when you're halfway in between,
You're neither up nor down.

Funny Old Hat Game

Gather a bag of old hats (such as discarded paper party hats). Pass the hats out to the children, or let the children choose one.

Say, "We're ready when our hat is _on_ our _head_. We're going to put our hats in some funny places and do some funny things. Listen.

Put your hat between your knees.
Put your hat under your arm.
Put your hat over your shoes.
Put your hat under your chin.
Touch the top of your hat.
Sit on your hat.
Stand on your hat.

Encourage the children to choose a place to put the hat.

"Where's the hat? Where's the hat? _____ (child's name), tell me where the hat is at." (This can be chanted.) "Under the chair, under the chair — that is where the hat is at."

See If You Can Game

Collect objects from around the classroom (examples: scissors, ruler, eraser, cup, chalk). Put them on the floor on large paper.

"I'm not going to say its name. See if you can tell me what object I am talking about. Raise your hand if you know." (Keep giving hints until the children guess.)

"What has two circles for two fingers?" (Scissors)

"It's long and thin with numbers printed on one side." (Ruler)

"What makes pencil marks disappear?" (Eraser)

"You can fill it with milk." (Cup)

"What's white and small, and writes on the blackboard?" (Chalk)

Make up some of your own.

Listen for Your Name Story

"I'm going to ask each one of you for help. Listen for your name and do what I ask you to do. We'll all do it after you."

Once upon a time, a boy named Mark went to his friend's house. He knocked at the door. _____, [child's name], knock on the floor. His friend Cindy said, "Come in." She shook hands with Mark. _____[child's name] and _____[child's name] stand up and shake hands.

"Let's play school," said Mark. "I'll be the teacher. Cindy, put your finger on your nose."

"I want to be the teacher," said Cindy.

"We'll take turns," said Mark. "Cindy, scratch your ear."

"Time for a snack," Mark said as he pretended to be the teacher.

"I don't want a snack today," said Cindy.

"It's popcorn and kooky juice," Mark answered. Raise your hand, _____ [child's name].

"Oh boy, kooky juice!" said Cindy. _____[child's name], tell us, is kooky juice green or blue? Cindy pretended to drink all her kooky juice. _____ [child's name], hold your stomach.

"My turn to be teacher," said Cindy.

"We're going to fingerpaint," said Cindy.

Mark pretended to fingerpaint. _____ [child's name], show us how you fingerpaint with just one finger.

"School's over," said Cindy.

The teacher can end the story here, or use the following as a transition to another activity:

"Everyone, tiptoe to the door and back."

Learning Activities

- Choose one of the activities found in the suggested resource list or one from this unit. Present the activity to a group of preschoolers. Then answer the following questions.
  a. Was the activity interesting to the children?
  b. Were they able to perform the auditory perception tasks?
  c. Would you change the activity in any way if you presented it again?

- Find or create five additional listening activities. After the *source* state the title of the book where you found the activity idea. If the idea is original, indicate this by using the word "self." Use a tape recorder in one activity.

  Source   Materials Needed   Objective
  Name of Activity   Description of Activity

- Select a popular children's television program to watch. Study the following questions before watching. Answer them after viewing the program.
  a. What is the name of the program, and the time and date of viewing?
  b. Were there attempts to build listening skills? If so, what were they?

    c. Do you have any criticism of the program?

    d. Could teachers of early childhood education use any techniques from the show in their auditory perception activities?

- Practice one of the listening stories in this unit. At the next class meeting, tell it to a classmate. Share constructive criticism.

Unit Review

A. List three listening activities, stating the objective of each activity and a description of the activity.

B. What is a good follow-up to some listening activities?

Reference

Weissman, Jackie, "Sound Story," *Hello Sound,* Gryphon House, Inc., 1979.

Resources for Additional Listening Activities

Beaty, Janice J., *Skills For Preschool Teachers,* 2nd ed., Charles E. Merrill Publishing Co., 1984, p. 120.

Chandler, Bessie E., *Early Learning Experiences*, The Instructor Publications, Inc., Dansville, NY 14437.

Cochran, E. V., *Teach and Reach That Child,* Palo Alto, CA: Peek Publications.

Croft, Doreen J. and Robert Hess, *An Activities Handbook for Teachers of Young Children,* Boston: Houghton Mifflin Co.

Engel, Rose C., *Language Motivating Experiences for Young Children,* Educative Toys and Supplies, 6416 Van Nuys Blvd., Van Nuys, CA 91401.

Lundsteen, Sara W., *Children Learn to Communicate,* Prentice-Hall Inc., NJ, 1976, pp. 99–103.

Mayesky, M., Neuman, D., and Wlodkowski, R., *Creative Activities for Young Children,* Albany: Delmar Publishers.

Rainey, Ernestine W., *Language Development for the Young Young Child,* Humanics Press, Atlanta, GA, 1978.

Scott, Louise B., *Learning Time with Language Experiences for Young Children,* St. Louis: Webster Division, McGraw-Hill.

Van Allen, Roach, *Language Experiences in Early Childhood,* Encyclopedia Britannica Educational Corp.

Van Allen, Roach and Claryce Allen, *Language Experience Activities,* 2nd ed., Houghton Mifflin Co., Boston, 1982.

Yawkey, Thomas D. et al., *Language Arts and the Young Child,* F. E. Peacock Publishers, Inc., 1981, pp. 75–8.

Unit 9
Reading to Children

OBJECTIVES

After studying this unit you should be able to

- state three goals for reading books to young children.
- describe the criteria for book selection.
- demonstrate suggested techniques for reading a book to a group of children.

Books provide an excellent source of listening activities for the young child. Seeing, touching, and interacting with books is part of a quality program in early childhood education. Books play an important part in language development.

Many parents have read to their children at home; others have not. That means that a teacher may have the joy of offering some children their first contact with stories and books, figure 9-1. The discovery of a very pleasant experience is shared.

Early childhood teachers agree that book-sharing sessions are among their favorite times with children. Each new group of children is introduced to teachers' and children's favorite books which seem never to lose the magic they contain.

There will be those times when young children are all ears in rapt enjoyment in picture book reading sessions; it's then you'll feel the power of literature, and realize your role as an orchestrator of a vast treasure. The responsibility of offering quality books in a skilled way after thoughtful selection becomes readily apparent.

What exactly do picture books offer young children? An opportunity:

- to explore, re-create, and obtain meaning in human experience.
- to come in contact with the diversity and complexity of life.

FIGURE 9-1 Children may have their first experiences with picture books at an early childhood center.

- to feel the texture of others' experiences.
- to look at vulnerability, honesty, and drama in a unique literary form (Hoggart, 1970).
- to experience, in well-conveyed literature, an art that leaves a lasting radiance (Sebesta and Iverson, 1975).
- to gain a sense of well being.
- to experience the concise charm of heightened language and form (Lewis 1976).
- to experience that sense of deepened self — children might call good feelings — that comes from involvement with important human emotions (Lewis, 1976).
- to unearth human truths.
- to nurture and expand imagination (Norton, 1983).
- to understand, value, and appreciate cultural heritage (Norton, 1983).
- to develop language, stimulate thinking, and develop socially (Norton, 1983).
- to gain facts, information, and data (nonfiction).
- to experience visual and aesthetic variety.
- to hear the rhythm and sound qualities of words.
- to gain positive attitudes about books and reading.
- to gain prereading skills.
- to sharpen listening.

Each child gets his own meaning from picture book experiences. Although this art form can't substitute for the child's real life experiences, interactions, and discoveries it can help make life's happenings understandable.

WHERE TO START

This unit contains a beginner's picture book listing, page 128; a starting point. You'll discover other books of quality but, since quality's a value judgement, your favorites may not appear on my list! Develop your own personal collection listing: use your local librarian in your search; book store salespeople will offer additional help. Research lists of Caldecott and Newbery Award books. The Caldecott medal and honor awards have been presented annually, since 1938, by the Children's Service Division of the American Library Association to illustrators of distinguished picture books. Since 1922, the same group has presented medal and honor awards for the year's most distinguished contribution to children's literature published in the United States. Award lists cover literature for all ages of children so examining each for suitability for young children is necessary.

QUALITY

Judging quality means reading and viewing a picture book to find out if it contains something memorable, heartwarming, or worthwhile. For every quality book you discover, you may wade through a stack wondering if the authors have even a nodding acquaintance with young children. Those you feel possess a degree of excellence (and there are many!) will probably appeal to the heart. What's quality material for a four year old, you'll discover, may not suit a younger child.

Each book you select may have one or more of the desirable and valuable features included in the following listing:

- Color
- An example of human courage, cleverness, or grit
- Aesthetic appeal
- A gamelike challenge
- Word play
- Ear pleasure
- Nonsense
- Onomatopoeia (The naming of a thing or action by a vocal imitation of the sound associated with it [as *buzz, hiss*])
- Suspense
- Humor or wit
- Fantasy
- Surprise
- Repetition

- Hope
- Charm
- Sensitivity
- Models admirable traits
- Appealing illustrations
- Reality in dialog
- Cultural insight
- Action

This is a partial listing of possible features. Probably you'll get an "oh yes" or "smile inside" feeling sometimes. You'll say "Life is like that," or "I've been there myself," with other books.

The it's okay to be different theme in Bill Peet's, *Huge Harold,* the gentleness of Uri Shulevitz's *Rain, Rain, Rivers,* or the tenderness of Charlotte Zolotow's *My Grandpa Lew* may fit your criteria of quality. The runaway fantasy of Frank Asch's *Popcorn* and de Paola's *Strega Nona* may tickle your fancy.

The panoramic scenes of *Anno's Counting Book,* the patterns and contrasts in Ezra Jack Keat's *Snowy Day,* the detailed intricacies in *Drummer Hoff* by Ed Emberley, or the fun of discovery in Ahlberg's *Each Peach Pear Plum* may help a book become one of your favorites because of visual appeal.

For humor and wit you may choose Steven Kellogg's *Can I Keep Him?,* Kraus's *Leo the Late Bloomer,* Marshall's *George and Martha,* Mayer's *What Do You Do With a Kangaroo?,* or a selection of others that make you laugh. You may never forget the way you trip over your tongue while reading about Jack, Kack, Lack, Mack, Nack, Ouack, Pack, and Quack in Robert McCloskey's *Make Way for Ducklings* or in *Tikki-Tikki Tembo* by Arlene Mosel. If it's surprise and an ending twist Brinton Turkles' *Deep in the Forest* or Jimmy Kennedy's *The Teddy Bears' Picnic* will delight you. The sound pleasure in Wanda Gag's *Millions of Cats,* or the onomatopoeia in Mabel Brass's *The Little Engine That Could* will stick in your memory.

The reality of city living will be relived if it's in your past in *Tell Me a Mitzi* by Lore Segal.

Perhaps discovering the facts through the colorful, precise artwork in Ruth Hellers' *Chicken's Aren't the Only Ones* will lead you into the world of nonfiction. Unforgettable characters like *Frederick* by Leo Lionni, *Cordoroy* and *Beady Bear* by Don Freeman, and *Harry the Dirty Dog* by Gene Zion, will be counted among your friends as you search for quality. Jewels will stand out and you'll be anxious to share them with children.

ILLUSTRATIONS

In many quality picture books the story stands well by itself, illustrations simply visualize what's written. In others, illustrations play a dominant role and are an integral part of the entire action (Freeman, 1967). Fortunately many picture book illustrations are created by highly-talented individuals. A wide range of artistic styles exists in picture book illustration including line drawings, woodcuts, water colors, and collage, among others. Poltarnees (1972) describes the true artist as one who "is able to enter the realm that the book evokes and move as freely there as if it were the kingdom of his birth. As a consequence he can show us things that we would not have seen as mere visitors."

GOALS

Children can gain much from books; the first goal should be to provide enjoyment. If each child understands that books are interesting, can hold new experiences, and can be enjoyed alone or with others then books will be viewed favorably.

The children's attitudes toward books, and how competent they feel when they are in a book-reading situation, are of prime concern. If learning to read is an unpleasant experience for a child, he may avoid reading. In contrast, children who have enjoyed the experience of learning to read may seek out books.

FIGURE 9-2 Teachers encourage book exploration. *(From Machado and Meyer,* Early Childhood Practicum Guide, *Copyright 1984 by Delmar Publishers Inc.)*

FIGURE 9-3 A book can be a personal experience.

It is the teacher's responsibility to encourage the child's interest, figure 9-2, because not every child in preschool is interested in books or sees them as something to enjoy. Although a child can't be *forced* to like books, he can *acquire* a positive feeling for them. Part of the positive feeling depends on whether the child feels successful and competent during reading time. This, in turn, depends on how skillfully the teacher acts and reacts, and how well the book sessions are planned.

When reading books to children, an important goal is the presentation of knowledge. Books can acquaint the child with new words, ideas, facts, and experiences. These are given in a different form than spoken conversation. In books, sentences are complete; in conversation, they may not be. Stories and illustrations follow a logical sequence in books.

Teachers can show that books may also be used as resources. When one wants to find out about things, picture dictionaries; adult dictionaries; books on special subjects such as animals, birds, fish; child encyclopedias; and similar books are used to find out facts. Teachers, when asked questions, can use books as the source for answers. When the teacher says, "I don't know, but I know where we can find out," this demonstrates that books are used for finding answers. The teacher tells where to look and follows through by showing the child how the information is found. The joy of discovery is shared, and this opens the door to seeking more answers.

The third goal deals with the development of skills. During listening times, children's attention can become focused. Different levels of listening: discriminative, appreciative, purposeful, creative, and critical can all be present in one book.

Teachers should encourage children to learn how to care for books, and where and how they can be used. Attitudes about books as valuable personal possessions need to begin in early childhood, figure 9-3.

Learning to read is a complex skill. It is dependent on smaller skills, some of which children encounter in early reading sessions.

SELECTION

The teacher is responsible for selecting children's books which meet the stated goals. Often, other staff members are asked to choose new books to buy. Some books may fill the needs completely; others only partially meet the goals. The local library offers the opportunity to borrow books which helps to keep storytelling time fresh and interesting.

A book that is liked by one child may not be liked by another. Some stories appeal more to one group than another. Old favorites are usu-ally enjoyed. Children who know the story often look forward to a familiar part or character.

BOOK TYPES

Many types of books and other reading materials are written for young children. The categories in figure 9-4 may overlap, since some books fit equally well in more than one category. The categories outline some of the major types of children's books used in preschool classrooms.

CRITERIA FOR SELECTION

These are a series of questions a teacher could use when selecting a child's book.

Types	Features Teachers Like	Features Children Like
Story books (picture books) • Family and home • Folk tales and fable • Fanciful stories • Fairy tales • Animal stories • Others	Shared moments Children enthusiastic and attentive Making characters' voices Introducing human truths and imaginative adventures Sharing favorites Easy for child to identify with small creatures	Imagination and fantasy Identification with characters' humanness Wish and need fulfillment Adventure Excitement Action Self-realization Visual variety Word pleasure
Nonfiction books (informational)	Expanding individual and group interests Developing "reading-to-know" attitudes Finding out together	Facts, discovery of information and ideas Understanding of reality and how "things" work and function Answers to "why" and "how" New words and new meanings
Wordless books	Promote child speech, creativity and imagination	Supplying their own words to tell story Discovery of meanings Color, action and visual variety
Interaction books (books which have active child participation built-in)	Keeping children involved and attentive Builds listening for directions skills	Movement and group feeling Individual creativity and expression Appeal to senses Manipulative features

FIGURE 9-4 Categories of children's books

Types	Features Teachers Like	Features Children Like
Alphabet and word books (word books have name of object printed near or on top of object: picture dictionaries, child encyclopedias, other favorite word books)	Supplies letters and word models Paired words and objects Useful for child with avid interest in alphabet letters and words	Discovery of meanings and names of alphabet letters and words
Novelty books (pop-ups, fold outs, stamp and pasting books, activity books, puzzle books, scatch and sniff books, hidden objects in illustrations, talking books	Adds sense exploring variety Stimulates creativity Comes in many different sizes and shapes Motor involvement for child	Exploring, touching, moving, feeling, smelling, licking, painting, drawing, coloring, cutting, gluing, acting upon, listening to a mechanical voice and getting instant feedback
Paperback books and magazines (Golden Books Humpty Dumpty Magazine)	Inexpensive Wide variety Many classics available	Children can save own money and choose for themselves
Teacher- and child-made books	Reinforces class learnings Builds understanding of authorship Allows creative expression Records individual, group projects, field trips, parties Promotes child expression of concerns and ideas Builds child's self-esteem	Child sees own name in print Shares ideas with others Self-rewarding
Therapeutic books (books helping children cope with and understand things such as divorce, death, jealousy)	Presents life realistically Offers positive solutions and insights Presents diverse family groups Deals with life's hard-to-deal-with subjects	Helps children discuss real feelings
Seasonal and holiday books	Accompanies child interest May help child understand underlying reasons for celebration	Builds pleasant expectations Adds details
Books and audiovisual combinations	Adds variety Offers group and individual experiencing opportunities Stimulates interest in books	Projects large illustrations Can be enjoyed individually
Toddler pages (durable pages)	Resists wear and tear	Ease in page-turning
Multicultural and cross-cultural books	Increases positive attitudes concerning diversity and similarity Emphasizes the realities in our society	Meeting a variety of people

FIGURE 9-4 Cont.

1. Could I read this book *enthusiastically,* really enjoying the story?
2. Are the contents of the book *appropriate* for the children with whom I work?
   a. Can the children relate some parts to their lives and past experience?
   b. Can the children identify with one or more of the characters?

      Look at some children's classics such as Mother Goose. Almost all of the stories have a well-defined character with whom children have something in common. Teachers find different children identify with different characters — the wolf instead of one of the pigs in "The Three Little Pigs," for example.
   c. Does the book have directly quoted conversation?

      If it does, this can add interest; for example, "Are you my mother?" he said to the cow.
   d. Will the child benefit from attitudes and models found in the book?

Violence and frightening events are part of some fairy and folk tales making them unsuitable for the young child. In analyzing a book for unfavorable racial inference or stereotypes, and sexism consider the following questions.

- Who are the "doers" and "inactive observers"?
- Are character's achievements based on their own initiative, insights, or intelligence?
- Who performs the brave and important deeds?
- Is value and worth connected to skin color and economic resources?
- Does language or setting ridicule or demean a specific group of individuals?
- Are individuals treated as such rather than as one of a group?
- Are ethnic groups or individuals treated as though everyone in that group has the same human talent, ability, food preference, hair style, taste in clothing, or human weakness or characteristic?
- Do illustrations capture natural looking ethnic variations?
- Does this book broaden the crosscultural element in the multicultural selection of books offered at my school?
- Is it accurate and authentic in its portrayal of individuals and groups?

3. Was the book written with an understanding of preschool age-level characteristics? See Kathryn Galbraith's *Katie Did!,* Atheneum, 1983.
   a. Is the text too long to sit through? Are there too many words?
   b. Are there enough colorful or action-packed pictures or illustrations to hold attention? See Robert Mc Closkey's *Blueberries for Sal,* Viking, 1948.
   c. Is the size of the book suitable for easy handling in groups or for individual viewing? See *Anno's Counting Book* by Mitsumasa Anno, Thomas Y. Crowell Co., 1975.
   d. Can the child participate in the story by speaking or making actions? See Esphyr Slobodkina's *Caps for Sale,* William R. Scott, 1947.

4. Is the fairy or folk tale too complex, symbolic, and confusing to have meaning? See *East of the Sun and West of the Moon* (Norway) or *Beauty and the Beast* (France). (Traditional folktales with inappropriate length, vocabulary, and complexity for the young child.)

5. Is the author's style enjoyable?
   a. Is the book written clearly with a vocabulary and sequence the children can understand? See Mercer Mayer's *There's a Nightmare in My Closet,* Dial, 1969. Are memorable words or phrases found in the book?

See Wanda Gag's *Millions of Cats,* Coward-McCann, 1928.

b. Are repetitions of words, actions, rhymes, or story parts used? (Anticipated repetition is part of the young child's enjoyment of stories. Molly Bang's *Ten, Nine, Eight,* Greenwillow, 1983, contains this feature.)

c. Does the story develop and end with a satisfying climax of events? See *Petunia,* by Roger Duvoisin, Knopf, 1950.

d. Are there humorous parts and silly names? The young child's humor is often slapstick in nature (pie-in-the-face, all fall down type rather than play on words). The ridiculous and farfetched often tickles them. See Tomie de Paola's *Pancakes for Breakfast,* Harcourt, Brace, Jovanovich, 1978; a wordless book.

6. Does it have educational value? (Almost all fit this criteria.)

a. Could you use it to expand knowledge in any special way? See Maureen Roffey's *Home, Sweet Home,* Coward, 1983, which depicts animal living quarters in a delightful way.

b. Does it offer new vocabulary? Does it increase or broaden understanding? See Masayuki Yabuuchi's *Animals Sleeping,* Philomel, 1983, for an example.

7. Do pictures (illustrations) explain and coordinate well with the text? Examine Leo Lionni's *Swimmy,* Pantheon Books, 1973 and look for this feature, or Jane Miller's *Farm Counting Book,* Prentice, 1983.

FIGURE 9-5 Many early childhood books have large, colorful pictures.

Some books meet most criteria of the established standards; others meet only a few. The age of attending children makes some criteria more important than others. Schools often select books that are sturdy and low in price. Most teachers try to offer the best in children's literature and a wide variety of book types.

BIBLIOTHERAPY

Bibliotherapy is a term used to describe books which, among other goals, seek to help children with life problems, questions, fears, and pain. Books, some professionals believe, can help children cope with emotional concerns. At some time during childhood children may deal with rejection by friends, ambivalence toward a baby brother, divorce, grief, or death along with other strong emotions (Smith and Foat, 1982). A small sampling of this type of individual book follows:

Mayer, Mercer, *There's a Nightmare in My Closet,* The Dial Press, NY, 1968. (fear)

Viorst, Judith, *The Tenth Good Thing About Barney,* Atheneum, NY, 1973. (death of a pet)

Dragunwagon, Crescent, *Wind Rose,* Harper and Row, 1976. (birth)

A much wider selection of titles is in print. The following resource books are helpful to preschool teachers looking for books dealing with feelings:

Gillis, Ruth J., *Children's Books for Times of Stress,* Indiana University Press, 1978. (An annotated bibliography categorized under headings covering anger, overweight, hospital stays, illness, rivalry, guilt, fear, bravery, hate, rejection, along with other feeling and problem areas.)

Dreyer, Sharon, *The Book Finder,* American Guidance Services, Inc., 1980. (Books are listed by their themes; synopsis and author/illustrator information is included.)

Bernstein, Joanne E., *Books to Help Children Cope with Separation and Loss,* R. R. Bowker Co., NY, 1977. (A listing of book titles.)

Bernstein (1977) urges parents and teachers to use books to open conversations in which children express grief:

It is from adults that they learn their behavior patterns for the future; whether grieving is normal and permissible or whether it is forbidden and wrong and a source of discomfort. Perhaps the most important aspect of helping young people cope with loss is the willingness of adult guides to expose their own grief while at the same time encouraging children to express theirs. For the way in which adults handle trauma determines youngsters' abilities to survive, physically and mentally, and they can come forth from crisis strong and ready once again to celebrate life.

READING BOOKS

Teachers read books in both indoor and outdoor settings, to one child or to many. If a child asks for a story and a teacher is available, the book is shared. Planned reading called *storytimes* are also part of a quality early childhood program.

Building positive attitudes takes skill. A step-by-step outline is helpful.

Step 1. Read the book to yourself enough times to develop a feeling for characters and the story line.

Step 2. Arrange a setting with the children's and teacher's comfort in mind. The illustrations should be at children's eye level. Seating arrangements are chosen for 5 to 15 minute seating. Some teachers prefer small chairs for both children and teachers; others prefer rug areas. Avoid traffic paths and noise interruptions.

Step 3. Make a *motivational* introductory statement. The statement should create a desire to listen or encourage listening. "There's a boy in this book who wanted to give his mother a birthday present." "Monkeys can be funny, and they are funny in this book." "Have you ever wondered where animals go at night to sleep?" "On the last page of this book is a picture of a happy monster.

Step 4. Hold the book to either your left or right side. With your hand in place, make both sides of the page visible. Keep the book at children's eye level.

Step 5. Begin reading; try to glance at the sentences and turn to meet the children's eyes as often as possible, so your voice goes to the children. Also watch for body reactions. Speak clearly, using a rate of speed which enables the children to both look at illustrations and hear what you are reading. Enjoy the story with the children by being enthusiastic. Dramatize and emphasize key parts of the story but not to the degree the children are watching you and not the book. Change your voice to suit the characters if you feel comfortable doing so. A good story will hold attention and often stimulates comments or questions.

Step 6. Answer and discuss questions approvingly. If you feel that interruptions are decreasing the enjoyment for other children, ask a child to wait until the end when you will be glad to discuss it. Then do it. If on the other hand, most of the group is interested, take the time to discuss an idea. Sometimes children suck their thumbs or act sleepy during reading times. They seem to connect books with bedtime; many parents read to their children at this time. By watching closely while reading you will be able to tell if you still have the attention of the children. You can sometimes draw a child back to the book with a direct question like "Debbie, can you see the cat's tail?"

Step 7. You may want to ask a few discussion questions at the end of the book. Questions can clear up ideas, encourage use of vocabulary words, and pinpoint parts that were especially enjoyed. You will have to decide whether to read more than one book at one time. It helps to remember how long the group of children can sit before getting restless. Storytimes should end on an enthusiastic note, with the children looking forward to another story.

ADDITIONAL BOOK-READING TIPS

- Check to make sure all of the children have a clear view of the book before beginning.
- Pause a short while to allow children to focus at the start.
- If one child seems to be unable to concentrate, a teacher can quietly suggest an alternative activity to the child. Clear understanding of alternatives or lack of them needs to be established with the entire staff.
- Moving a distracted child closer to the book, or onto a lap, sometimes works.
- When an outside distraction occurs, recapture attention and make a transition connecting statement leading back to the story. "We all heard that loud noise. There's a different noise made by the steam shovel in our story. Listen and you'll hear the steam shovel's noise."
- Personalize books when appropriate "Have you lost something and not been able to find it?"
- Skip ahead in books, when the book can obviously not maintain interest, by quickly reading pictures and concluding the experience.
- Children often want to handle a book just read. Plan for this as often as possible. Make a quick waiting list at times when all wish to go over the book by themselves.

BUILDING PARTICIPATION

Active child participation helps increase the feeling of being part of the "telling" of a story. Teachers, therefore, plan for child participation when choosing stories to read. Examining story lines closely gives ideas for children's active participation. Some books hold children spellbound and focused — these are usually classics, or become classics. Nonfiction books may not provide as much material for child involvement.

This is a list of ways to promote child participation and "active" listening:

1. Invite children to speak familiar character's dialogue or book sounds. This is easily done in repeated sequences.
   "I don't care," said Pierre.
2. Pantomiming actions.
   "Let's knock on the door."
3. Using closure.
   "The cup fell on the _____ (floor)." When using closure, if children end the statement differently, try saying "It could have fallen on the rug, but the cup in the story fell on the *floor*."
4. Predicting outcomes.
   "Do you think Hector will open the box?"
5. Asking opinions.
   "What's your favorite pie?"
6. Recalling previous story parts.
   "What did Mr. Bear say to Petra?"
7. Probing related experiences.
   "Emil, isn't your dog's name Clifford?"
8. Dramatizing enjoyed parts or wholes.

Younger preschoolers, in general, find sitting without active motor and/or verbal involvement more demanding than older ones.

SETTINGS

Most classrooms have areas suitable for picture book reading in groups, as an individual self-selected activity, or in the company of a few others; if not, staff members can create them. An uninterrupted, low on distraction, comfortable, well lighted area is ideal. A shady spot in the play yard may be the site for teacher's reading on a warm day. A floor lamp in the reading area with all other overhead lights dimmed worked well for group times in one center — it certainly cut distractions and focused the group. The number of children in groups is an important consideration; as size grows:

- intimacy,
- child viewing ease,
- teacher's ability to be physically close,
- teacher's response to each child, and
- touching is decreased.

Some preschools do "instant" replays rather than have large group book-reading sessions. A large stuffed horseshoe-shaped floor pillow can increase child comfort; many centers use small carpet sample squares for comfort and to outline individual space.

FROM BOOKS TO FLANNEL BOARDS AND BEYOND

Teachers find that books can be made into flannel board stories relatively easily; Unit 12 is devoted to these activities.

Five books which are particular favorites have been adapted:

Eric Carle: *The Very Hungry Caterpillar*
Ruth Krauss: *The Carrot Seed*
Maggie Duff: *Jony and His Drum*
Aliki: *My Five Senses*
William Martin: *Brown Bear, Brown Bear, What Do You See?*

Books often open the door to additional instruction through activities or games on the same subject or theme. Whole units of instruction on bears, airplanes, and families can transform a classroom and build on what may have captured child interest and curiosity.

LIBRARY SKILLS

A visit to the local library is often planned for four-year-olds. Librarian-presented story-hours often result in the child's awareness of the library as a storehouse and resource. Selecting and checking out one's choice can be an exciting and important milestone. Most pre-schools do their best to encourage this parent-child activity.

The preschool's book collection can also be viewed as a library. Preschools can allow over-night or weekend check out if a borrowing pro-cedure is developed.

Telling the children the names of authors and illustrators when introducing picture books is a very good idea. One goal is to alert children to the idea that books, their authors and illus-trators have names and are individual identi-ties. Occasionally showing or displaying a photo of authors and illustrators is interesting to most young children. The following books give help-ful background data on authors:

- Hopkins, Lee Bennett, *Books Are By Peo-ple,* Scholastic Magazine, Inc., 1969.
- *More Books by More People,* Citation Press, 1974.
- Doyle, Brian, *Who's Who in Children's Lit-erature,* Schocken Publ., 1971.

CHILD- AND TEACHER-MADE BOOKS

Books authored by children or their teachers have many values.

- They promote interest in the classroom book collection.
- They help children see connections be-tween spoken and written words.
- The material is based on child interests.
- They personalize book reading.
- They prompt self-expression.
- They stimulate creativity.
- They build feelings of competence and self-worth.

If "Antonio's Book" is one of the school's books, the book corner becomes a place where the child's accomplishment is exhibited. Teachers can alert the entire group to new book titles as the books arrive, and make a point to describe them before they are put on the shelves.

Child-made books require teacher prepara-tion and help. A variety of shapes and sizes, figure 9-6, add interest and motivation. Covers made of wallpaper or contact paper over card-board are durable. Insides of the books com-bine child-art and child-dictated words, usually on lined printscript paper. Staples, rings, yarn (string), or brads bind pages together, figure 9-7. Child-dictation is taken word for word with no teacher editing.

The following book dictated by a four-year-old illustrates one child's authorship.

The Window

Page 1 Once upon a time the little girl was looking out the window.
Page 2 Child's Art
Page 3 And the flowers were showing.
Page 4 Child's Art

FIGURE 9-6

Bookbinding

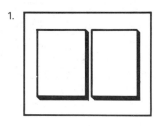

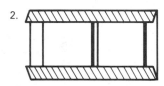

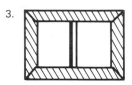

One stitch on outside fold.

Two stitches on inside fold.

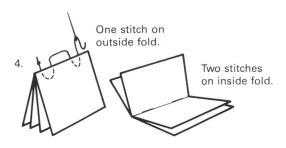

Masking tape with adhesive facing cover boards.

FIGURE 9-7

Page 5 And the water was flushing down and she did not know it.

Page 6 Child's art

Teacher-authored books share teacher's creativity and individuality. Favorite themes and enjoyed experiences can be relived over and over. Books containing the children's, teachers', staff's, parents', or school pets' names are popular. Photographs of familiar school, neighborhood, or family settings are great conversation stimulators.

Group authorship is another idea. Books in which every child has contributed one or more pages are enjoyable projects and discoveries.

BOOK AREAS AND CENTERS

Classrooms with inviting book storage areas beckon curious browsers. Comfort and color attract. Softly textured rugs and pillows, comfortable seating and sprawling spaces prolong time spent there. Books should be at the child's eye level with book front covers in sight, figure 9-8. Quiet, private spaces, shielded from outside distractions and sounds with good lighting, increase the child's ability to stay focused. Climb into's and hideaways where friends can escape together and experience a book that has captured their attention are ideal, figure 9-9. Book jacket wall displays and life-sized book characters (drawings made by using overhead projectors to increase size then tracing on large sheets of paper) have their own appeal.

CARE AND STORAGE OF BOOKS

By setting an example and making clear statements about handling books, the teacher can help children form good book-care habits. However, with time and use, even the sturdiest books will need repairs.

Teachers are quick to show their sadness when a favorite book is torn, crayoned, or used

FIGURE 9-8 A soft rug, some pillows or chairs, and books at child level make this an inviting book corner.

FIGURE 9-9 "Hiding away" with a friend to read

as a building block. Classrooms might have signs reading: Books are friends — Handle with care, or Books are for looking, talking about, and sharing. Teachers are careful to verbally reward children who turn pages gently and return them to shelves or storage areas.

RESOURCES FOR FINDING READING MATERIALS

Public libraries. Many libraries have booklists of suggested early childhood editions. Often, seasonal books are together in special displays.

Ask the librarian about new books, special programs, or resources which can include picture books, films, or slides.

Children's book stores and toy stores. Many stores carry popular new and older titles.

Teachers' supply houses and school supply stores. Often a wide selection is stocked.

Children's book publishers. Catalogs listing new titles, with descriptions of contents, are available for the asking.

Teacher resource books. These books are good sources for finding titles on specific topics or themes. A few teacher and parent resources are listed next.

- *The Horn Book Magazine,* 585 Boyleston Street, Boston, MA 02116
- *Notable Children's Books,* Children's Service Division of the American Library Association, 50 East Huron Street, Chicago, IL 60611

- *Bulletin for the Center for Children's Books,* University of Chicago, 5750 Ellis Ave., Chicago, IL 60637
- *Human Values in Children's Books,* Council on Interracial Books for Children, Inc., 1841 Broadway, New York, NY 10023
- *Multi-ethnic Books for Young Children,* N.A.E.Y.C. Publication Department, 1834 Connecticut Ave., N.W., Washington, DC 20009
- *A Guide to Non-sexist Children's Books,* Academy Press Ltd., 176 W. Adams St., Chicago, IL 60603
- Nancy Larrick, *A Parent's Guide to Children's Reading,* Doubleday and Co., Inc., 1975.
- Book Clubs

  Hard Covers
  1. Grow-With-Me Book Club, Garden City, NY 11530
  2. I Can Read Book Club, 1250 Fairwood Ave., Columbus, OH 43216
  3. Parents' Magazine Read Aloud and Easy Reading Program, Box 161, Bergenfield, NJ 07621
  4. Weekly Reader Children's Book Club, 1250 Fairwood Ave., Columbus, OH 43216

  Paperbacks (Many books under $1.00.)
  1. Lucky Book Club and See-Saw Book Club, Scholastic Book Clubs, 904 Sylvan Ave., Englewood Cliffs, NJ 07632
  2. King Cole Book Club, Simon and Schuster, 1 West 39th Street, New York, NY 10018
  3. Buddy Books, Xerox Paperback Book Clubs, Box 1195, Education Center, Columbus, OH 43216

- Children's Periodicals
  1. *Highlights for Children,* 2300 West Fifth Ave., P.O. Box 269, Columbus, OH 43216
  2. *Peanut Butter,* Scholastic Home Periodicals, P.O. Box 1925, Marion, OH 43302

3. *Sesame Street,* P.O. Box 2895, Boulder, CO 80321
4. *Your Big Backyard* and *Ranger Rick,* National Wildlife Federation, 1412 16th St. N.W., Washington, DC 20036
5. *Children' Playmate,* Saturday Evening Post, A-9, Mountaineer Post, Boone, NC 28607
6. *Humpty Dumpty's Magazine,* Parent's Magazine Press, 80 Newbridge Road, Bergenfield, NJ 07621
7 *Jack and Jill,* P.O. Box 6567B, Indianapolis, IN 46206
8. *Young World* (formerly *Golden Magazine*), P.O. Box 6567B Indianapolis, IN 46206

BOOK SERVICES TO PARENTS

Preschools that have overnight and weekend book borrowing spread book use and promote home enjoyment of books. Manila folders or envelopes preprinted with the center's name protect books in transit. Book pockets and cards are available at stationery or school supply stores. This service can operate with minimal teacher supervision. Parents can help their children pull cards on selected titles, if they thoroughly understand the school's system and rules for book borrowing.

FAVORITE CHILDREN'S BOOKS — BEGINNER'S BOOK LIST

Brown, Margaret Wise, *The Dead Bird,* New York: Young Scott Books, 1938 and 1965. Deals tenderly with the death of a bird.

Carle, Eric, *The Very Hungry Caterpillar,* Collins World, 1969. The hungry caterpillar eats through the pictures and emerges as a butterfly on the last page.

Chorao, Kay, *Lester's Overnight,* New York: E. P. Dutton, 1977. Family humor in a child's overnight plans and his teddy bear.

Ets, Marie Hall, *Play With Me,* New York: Viking Press, 1955. A lesson to learn on the nature of animals.

Flack, Marjorie, *Ask Mr. Bear,* New York: Macmillian, 1932. The search for just the right birthday present for a loved one.

Freeman, Don, *Beady Bear,* New York: Viking Press, 1954. Meet Beady and his courage, independence, and frailty.

Freeman, Don, *Corduroy,* New York: Viking Press, 1968. The department store teddy who longs for love.

Gag, Wanda, *Millions of Cats,* New York: Coward-McCann, 1928. Word pleasure and magic — a favorite with both teachers and children.

Guilfoile, Elizabeth, *Nobody Listens to Andrew,* New York: Scholastic Book Services, 1957. An "adults often ignore what children say" theme.

Hazen, Barbara Shook, *The Gorilla Did It,* New York: Atheneum Press, 1974. A mother's patience with a fantasizing child. Humorous.

Hoban, Russell, *A Baby Sister for Frances,* New York: Harper and Row, 1964. Frances, "so human," deals with the new arrival.

Hutchins, Pat, *Good-Night Owl!* New York: Macmillan, 1976. Riddled with repetitive dialogue; a delightful tale of bedtime.

Hutchins, P. *Changes, Changes,* New York: Macmillan, 1971. Illustrations of block constructions tell a wordless story of the infinite changes in forms.

Keats, Ezra Jack, *Peter's Chair,* New York: Harper and Row, 1967. A delightful tale of family life.

Kraus, Robert, *Leo the Late Bloomer,* New York: E. P. Dutton and Co., 1973. Wonderful color illustrations and a theme which emphasizes individual development.

Kraus, Ruth, *The Carrot Seed,* New York: Harper and Row, 1945. The stick-to-it-tiveness of a child's faith makes this story charming.

Leoni, L., *Little Blue and Little Yellow,* New York: Astor-Honor, 1949. A classic. Collages of torn paper introduce children to surprising color transformations, blended with a story of friendship.

McCloskey, Robert, *Blueberries for Sal,* New York: Viking Press, 1948. The young of the two species meet.

Mosel, Arlene, *Tiki Tiki Tembo,* New York: Holt, Rinehart, and Winston, 1968. A folk tale that tickles the tongue in its telling. Repetitive.

Raskin, Ellen, *Nothing Ever Happens on My Block,* New York: Atheneum Press, 1975. The child discovers a multitude of happenings in illustrations.

Scott, Ann Herbert, *On Mother's Lap,* New York: McGraw-Hill, 1972. There's no place like mother's lap!

Schulevitz, Uri, *Rain Rain Rivers,* New York: Farrar, Straus and Giroux, 1969. Illustrative fine art.

Segal, Lore, *Tell Me A Mitzi,* Farrar, 1970. New York city life.

Slobodkina, Esphyr, *Caps for Sale,* New York: William R. Scott, 1947. A tale of a peddler, some monkeys and their monkey business. Word play and gentle humor.

Turkle, Brinton, *Deep In The Forest,* New York: Dutton, 1976. Interpretation of "Goldilocks and the Three Bears" in an early American setting.

Viorst, Judith, *The Tenth Good Thing About Barney,* New York: Atheneum, 1971. Loss of family pet and positive remembrances.

Viorst, Judith, *Alexander and the Terrible, Horrible, No Good, Very Bad Day,* New York: Atheneum Press, 1976. Everyone relates to the "everything can go wrong" theme.

Zion, Gene, *Harry The Dirty Dog,* New York: Harper and Row, 1956. Poor lost Harry gets so dirty his family doesn't recognize him.

SUMMARY

The goals when reading books to young children are:

- Acquaint children with quality literature
- Enjoyment and attitude development

- Knowledge
- Development of listening and other skills

A careful selection of books makes it easier to reach these goals, and gives reading activities a greater chance for success. Teachers who are prepared can interact with enthusiasm by showing their own enjoyment of language; this helps promote the children's language growth.

Learning Activities

- Select, prepare, and present three books to children. Evaluate your strong points and needed areas of growth.

- Read a children's book to two classmates or to a video camera; take turns evaluating the presentations.

- Discuss "It's easier for a child to identify with small animals acting like people than with photographs of a real child."

- Create a self-authored picture book. Share with a small group of young children. Share results, outcomes, and your feelings with fellow students.

- Visit the local library. Using the form "Analyzing a Children's Book" shown in figure 9-10, review five books.

- A suggested list of children's books is included in the Appendix. Develop an annotated book list using short descriptions, as follows:
  Zion, Gene, *Harry the Dirty Dog,* Harper and Row Publishers. About a family dog who gets so dirty his family doesn't recognize him.

- Make a list of 5 nonfiction books that could be used with preschoolers.

- Present a short oral report about Caldecott Medal books and Newbery Medal books.

Unit Review

A. Read the following descriptions of comments by a teacher who is reading to children. Select those comments which you feel would help the child accomplish a goal mentioned in this unit.
   1. "Sit down now and stop talking; it's story time."
   2. "Kathy, can you remember how the mouse got out of the trap?"
   3. "What part of this story made you laugh?"
   4. "John, I can't read any more because you've made Lonnie cry by stepping on her hand. Children, storytime is over."
   5. "Children, don't look out the window. Look at the book. Children, the book is more interesting than that storm."
   6. "Donald, big boys don't tear book pages."
   7. "Was the dog striped or spotted? If you can't answer, then you weren't listening."
   8. "Mary, of course you liked the story. Everyone did."

Name _____ Date _____

Name of Book _____

Author _____

Illustrator _____

Storyline

1. What is the book's message? _____

_____

_____

2. Does theme build the child's self-image or self-esteem? How? _____

_____

_____

3. Are male and female or ethnic groups stereotyped? _____

Illustrations

1. Fantasy? True to Life? _____

2. Do they add to the book's enjoyment? _____

_____

General Considerations

Could you read this book enthusiastically? Why?

How could you involve children in book? (Besides looking and listening.)

How could you "categorize" this book? (i.e. fireman, alphabet book, concept development, emotions, etc.)

On a scale of 1–10 (1 — little value to 10 — of great value to young child) rate this book. _____

FIGURE 9-10 Form for analyzing a children's book

9. "Tell me, Mario, what was the boy's name in our story? I'm going to sit here until you tell me."
10. "No, the truck wasn't green, Luci. Children, tell Luci what color the truck was."
11. "Take your thumb out of your mouth, Debbie; it's storytime."
12. "I like the way you all watched the book and told me what was in each picture."
13. "One book's enough. We can't sit here all day, you know."
14. "Children, we have to finish this book before we can go outside. Sit back down."
15. "That book had lots of colorful pictures."
16. "Well, now we found out who can help us if we ever lose mama in a store."

B. Answer the following questions:
1. Why is it important for the teacher to read a child's book before it is read to the children?
2. How can a teacher help children learn how books are used to find answers?
3. Why should a teacher watch for the young child's reactions to the story while reading it?

C. Select the phrase in Column II which applies to the item in Column I.

Column I	Column II
1. fairy tales	a. before teacher starts reading to the group
2. first step in planned reading	b. when children show interest in a subject
3. arrange setting with comfort in mind	c. a book about war and killing
4. stop storytelling to discuss it	d. book may not be appropriate for this age level
5. not appropriate for early childhood level	e. may be too frightening
6. children become restless after twenty-five minutes	f. "Tick-tock," said the clock
7. directly quoted conversation	g. teacher reads the book beforehand
8. "And I'll huff and I'll puff and I'll blow your house down."	h. repetition in "The Three Little Pigs"
9. "So they all had a party with cookies and milk." The End.	i. identification
10. "The rabbit's just like me, I can run real fast."	j. a satisfying climax to a story
11. a book should be read and held	k. in an upright position with the front cover showing
12. books are more inviting when stored this way	l. at children's eye level

References

Beaty, Janice J., *Skills for Preschool Teachers,* 2nd ed., Charles E. Merrill Publishing Co., 1984, pp. 126–132. (Annotated book list, Chapter 6.)

Bernstein, Joanne E., *Books to Help Children Cope with Separation and Loss,* R. R. Bowker Co., New York, 1977. (A listing of book titles.)

Bettelheim, Bruno, *The Uses of Enchantment,* Alfred A. Knopf, New York, 1976. (Adds depth to one's understanding of basic human needs and desires and their relationships to stories and literature.)

Bulletin of the Center for Children's Books, The University of Chicago Press, 580 Ellis Ave., Chicago, 1973. (Critiques and reviews picture books.)

Coody, Betty, *Using Literature With Young Children,* 3rd ed., Wm. C. Brown Company Publishers, 1983. (Full of practical activity ideas.)

Children's Books of the Year, Child Study Children's Book Committee, Bank Street College, 610 West 112th St., NY, 1983. (Offers a listing of selected best books in a given year.)

Freeman, Ruth S., *Children's Picture Books,* Century House, NY, 1967. (A comprehensive discussion of picture books and their value.)

Greene, Allen and Madalynne Schoenfeld, *A Multimedia Approach to Children's Literature,* American Library Association, 1972. (Helps one find interesting ways to introduce books to young children.)

Hoggart, Richard, *Speaking to Each Other,* Volume II. About Literature, Chatto and Windus, London, 1970. (Adds insights concerning the use and benefits of books in young children's lives.)

Huck, Charlotte, *Children's Literature in the Elementary School,* 3rd ed., Holt, Rinehart and Winston, NY, 1976.

Lewis, Claudia, *Writing for Children,* Bank St. College, NY, 1976. (A great aid to teachers interested in authoring picture books. Identifies salient features in quality authorship.)

Norton, Donna E., *Through the Eyes of a Child*, Chas. E. Merrill Publ. Co., 1983. (A classic children's literature course textbook with a section devoted to picture book features. Lists and recommends.)

Poltarnees, Welleran, *All Mirrors are Magic Mirrors,* The Green Tiger Press, 1972. (Illustrations and illustrators are the subject matter.)

Sebesta, Sam Leaton, and Wm. J. Iverson, *Literature for Thursday's Child,* Science Research Assoc., Inc., 1975. (Greater depth and understanding of the therapeutic value of literature.)

Smith, Charles and Carolyn Foat, *Once Upon a Mind,* North Central Regional Extension Publication, Kansas State University, 1982. (Using books to help children work out life problems.)

Suggested Readings

Bettelheim, Bruno, *The Uses of Enchantment,* Alfred A. Knopf, New York, 1976.

Coody, Betty, *Using Literature with Young Children,* 3rd ed., William C. Brown, 1983.

Draper, Mary Wanda and Henry E. Draper, *Caring for Children,* Chas. A. Bennett Co., Inc., 1975, pp. 521–532. (Annotated bibliography of books for young children.)

Lewis, Claudia, *Writing for Children,* Bank St. College, NY, 1976.

Townsend, John Rowe, *Written for Children,* The Horn Book, Boston, 1974. (An historical account of the development of picture books.)

Unit 10
Storytelling

OBJECTIVES

After studying this unit you should be able to

- describe how storytelling can help language growth.

- list teacher techniques in storytelling.

- demonstrate the ability to create a story which meets suggested criteria.

Storytelling is an art which an early childhood teacher can develop and use to increase a child's enjoyment of language. When good stories are told the child listens intently; words and ideas are conceived when there is close contact with an enthusiastic adult, figure 10-1. Storytelling also enables teachers to share their life experiences in an individual way.

Early childhood teachers recognize the importance of storytelling in a full language arts curriculum. Good stories that are well told have fascinated young listeners since ancient times. Chambers (1970) feels storytelling is a form of expressive art.

> The art of storytelling remains one of the oldest and most effective art forms. It has survived the printing press, the sound recorder and the camera . . . The oral story, be it aesthetic or pedagogical, has great value. It seems to be a part of the human personality to use it and want it. The art of the storyteller is an important, valuable ingredient in the lives of children. It has been for thousands of years.

The teacher's face, gestures, words, and voice tone tell the story when books or pictures are not used. Eye contact is held throughout the storytelling period. The child pictures the story in his mind as the plot unfolds.

FIGURE 10-1 Children listen intently to a good story.

TELLING STORIES WITHOUT BOOKS

Unit 9 described the merits and use of picture books with young children. Storytelling without books has its own unique set of enjoyed language pleasures. Storytelling is direct, intimate conversation. Arbuthnot (1953) points out the well-told story's power to hold children spellbound.

It is the intimate, personal quality of storytelling as well as the power of the story itself that accomplishes these minor miracles. Yet in order to work this spell, a story must be learned, remembered, and so delightfully told that it catches and holds the attention of the most inveterate wrigglers.

Teachers can observe children's reactions. A quizzical look on a child's face can help the teacher know when to clarify or rephrase for understanding. A teacher's voice can increase the story's drama in parts when children are deeply absorbed.

Many people have noted how quickly and easily ideas and new words are grasped through storytelling. This is rarely the prime goal of early childhood teachers, but rather, an additional benefit. Stories are told to acquaint young children with this enjoyable oral language arts experience. Obvious moralizing or attempts to teach facts by using stories usually turns children away.

Storytelling may occur at almost any time during the course of the day, inside or outside. No books or props are necessary. Teachers are free to relate stories in their own words and manner. Children show by their actions what parts of the story are of high interest. The storyteller can increase children's enjoyment by emphasizing these features, figure 10-2.

USING PICTUREBOOKS FOR STORYTELLING

At times, a picture book is the source for storytelling. The teacher later introduces the book

FIGURE 10-2 An enthusiastic storyteller gets interest and delighted response.

and makes it available in the classroom's book center for individual follow-up. Used this way, storytelling motivates interest in books.

There are many picture books, however, which do not lend themselves to storytelling form because illustrations are such an intregal part of the experience. Books that have been successfully used as the basis for storytelling are handled in a unique way. Schimmel (1978) relates her storytelling experience with *Caps for Sale* by Slobodkina:

I like to make it an audience participation story. I shake my fist at the monkeys; and the audience, with only the slightest encouragement, shakes it's fists at the peddler.

She recommends the following for use with young children:

- *The Fat Cat* by Jack Kent, Parents, 1971.
- *The Journey, Mouse Tales* by Arnold Lobel, Harper, 1972.
- *The Old Woman and Her Pig* by Paul Galdone, McGraw, 1961.
- *The Three Billy Goats Gruff* by P. C. Asbjornsen, Harcourt, 1972.

SOURCES FOR STORIES

A story idea can be found in collections, anthologies, resource books, children's magazines, films, story records, or from another storyteller. A story idea can also be self-created.

A teacher-created story can fill a void. In any group of young children there are special interests and problems. Stories can expand interest and give children more information on a subject. Problems can possibly be solved by the stories and conversations which take place.

New teachers may not yet have confidence in their storytelling abilities, so learning some basic techniques for selecting, creating, and telling stories can help insure success. This, together with the experience gained by presenting the stories to children, should convince the teacher that storytelling is enjoyable for preschoolers and rewarding to the teacher.

SELECTION

The selection of a story is as important as the selection of a book since stories seem to have individual personalities. Searching for a story which appeals to the teller and can be eagerly shared is well worth the time. A few well chosen and prepared stories suiting the individual teacher almost insures a successful experience for all. The following selection criteria is commonly used:

Age level appropriateness. Is the story told in simple, easily-understood words? Is it familiar in light of the child's life experiences? Is it frightening? Can the child profit from traits of the characters?

Plot. Does the setting create a stage for what is to come? Is there action? Something of interest to resolve? A start where something happens? A building to a climax? Maybe some suspense? A timely, satisfying conclusion? Are characters introduced as they appear?

Style. Is there repetition or rhyme? Silly words or a surprise ending? Directly quoted conversations? Child involvement with speaking or movements? A mood which helps the plot develop?

Values. Are values and models presented appropriate for today's children? Does the story hold a human truth?

Storyteller enthusiasm. Is the story well liked by the teller? Does the teller feel "at home" with it?

TYPES OF STORIES

Some stories, particularly folk tales, have been polished to near perfection through generations of use. Classic tales and folk tales may contain dated words and phrases, but they might be important story parts that add to the story's charm. In retelling the story to young children, a brief explanation of these types of terms can be given.

Great stories seem to profit from active child participation or the use of props. Props, such as pictures, costumes and other objects, may spark and hold interest. A cowboy hat worn for a western tale adds to the mood.

Repetitive phrases or word rhythms are used often. Most stories have problems to be solved through the ingenuity of the main character. This sequence can be explored in teachers' self-created stories.

STORY IDEAS

Teachers sometimes begin by telling stories from printed sources.

Classic Tales
Goldilocks and the Three Bears
Little Red Riding Hood
The Three Little Pigs
Billy Goats Gruff

The Little Red Hen
The Gingerbread Boy

From Aesop's Fables

The Lion and the Mouse
The Shepherd Boy and Wolf
The Hare and the Tortoise
The Ant and the Grasshopper

Traditional Stories

Hans Christian Anderson, *Ugly Duckling,*
  The Emperor's New Clothes
Arlene Mosel, *Tiki, Ticki Tembo*
Florence Heide, *Sebastian*

TECHNIQUES

Before presenting a story, the teacher should be familiar with the techniques of good storytelling:

- Know the story well, but not necessarily word for word. Become familiar with the key ideas. Know the key happenings and their order of appearance in the story.
- Practice before a mirror or with another staff member.
- Enjoy and live the story as you tell it in your own words. Use gestures.
- Maintain eye contact; watch for children's interest or restlessness.
- Pace the storytelling by going faster during exciting or fast action parts, and slower in serious parts.
- Use a clear, firm voice. Try changing voice volume to fit the story; in some parts of the story a whisper may be most effective. Change your voice to fit the characters when they speak.
- Make gestures natural complements of the story (large and descriptive for younger children).
- Involve the children often, especially with repetitions, rhymes or actions, silly words,

or appropriate questions if the story lends itself to this.
- Sit close to the group; make sure all are comfortable before beginning.
- Include children's names and familiar places in the community to clarify meanings or add interest to self-created stories.

Even the best of storytellers has an occasional flop. If the storyteller senses that the children are restless, the story may be ended very quickly and tried at a later time, using a revised version or a new story.

CREATING STORIES

After creating a new story, practice it so that it can be retold in a similar way the next time. File cards can be used to jot down the title, beginning, middle, and ending key ideas for future reference. Some teachers find that a popular character in one story can have further adventures in the next story. Don't forget that "bad guys" in stories are enjoyed as much as "good guys." Having a problem that needs to be resolved serves as the basis for many well-known classics. As teachers use their own stories, they tend to cut and add to them based on the reactions of the children. Take care that themes do not always revolve around "mother knows best" episodes and watch for sexism and stereotypes when creating a story.

STORIES FOR STORYTELLING

These stories can be used by the beginning storyteller.

The Little House with No Doors and No Windows and a Star Inside
Author Unknown

(Plan to have an apple, cutting board, and a knife ready for the ending, figure 10-3. A plate full of apple slices is sometimes enjoyed after this story.)

FIGURE 10-3 "This is the little red house with the star inside. Do you see the star?"

Once there was a little boy who had played almost all day. He had played with all his toys and all the games he knew, and he could not think of anything else to do. So he went to his mother and asked, "Mother, what shall I do now?"

His mother said, "I know about a little red house with no doors and no windows and a star inside. You can find it, if you go look for it."

So the little boy went outside and there he met a little girl. He said, "Do you know where there is a little red house with no doors and no windows and a star inside?"

The little girl said, "No, I don't know where there is a little red house with no doors and no windows and a star inside, but you ask my daddy. He is a farmer and he knows lots of things. He's down by the barn and maybe he can help you."

So the little boy went to the farmer down by the barn and said, "Do you know where there is a little red house with no doors and no windows, and a star inside?"

"No," said the farmer, "I don't know, but why don't you ask grandmother. She is in her house up on the hill. She is very wise and knows many things. Maybe she can help you."

So the little boy went up the hill to grandmother's and asked, "Do you know where there is a little red house with no doors and no windows and a star inside?" "No," said Grandmother, "I don't know, but you ask the wind, for the wind goes everywhere, and I am sure he can help you."

So the little boy went outside and asked the wind, "Do you know where I can find a little red house with no doors and no windows and a star inside?" And the wind said, "OHHHH! OOOOOOOOOOOO!" And it sounded to the little boy as if the wind said, "Come with me." So the little boy ran after the wind. He ran through the grass and into the orchard and there on the ground he found the little house — the little red house with no doors and no windows and a star inside! He picked it up and it filled both his hands. He ran home to his mother and said, "Look, Mother! I found the little red house with no doors and no windows, but I cannot see the star!"

So this is what his mother did (Teacher cuts apple.) "Now I see the star!" said the little boy. (to children) DO YOU?

*   *   *   *   *

Laughing Stock and Gastly

Sister Carol Bettencourt
(while an ECE student)

There was a family of elephants that lived in the jungle. There were very large mama and papa elephants, and smaller baby elephants. They were all the color gray — all except one — his name was Laughing Stock. He got his name because all the other elephants had never seen an elephant the color of Laughing Stock. He was the color orange! Have you ever seen an orange elephant? Poor Laughing Stock; everyone made fun of him because he was so different.

In the same jungle lived a family of giraffes. Oh, they were so tall and so nice-looking with their yellow and brown bodies! One day, Laughing Stock was going for a walk when he saw the giraffes eating the leaves right from the top of the trees — those giraffes certainly were tall.

"Hi, giraffes!" said Laughing Stock. "Hi, elephant!" said the giraffes. "Say, elephant," shouted one of the giraffes. "You don't look like an elephant. Your body is the color orange." Then all the giraffes started to laugh. Poor Laughing Stock. One of the giraffes, still laughing loudly, said, "You and Gastly would make a fine pair!" "Who's Gastly?" asked the elephant. "I am," said a quiet little voice. Laughing Stock looked around but didn't see anyone except for the giraffes. Then, he saw something move and Laughing Stock looked closely into the green bushes. "Wha wha wha wha you you . . . ?" (Poor Laughing Stock was having a hard time making the words come out.) "You're green! I've I've I've never seen a green giraffe before!" "Neither have we," laughed the other giraffes. "Oh, but I think you're pretty," said Laughing Stock. "You do?" said Gastly. "Thank you, no one ever said that to me before." "You're welcome," smiled Laughing Stock, and right away they became good friends and each one helped the other. And because they were friends, it didn't hurt so much when others laughed at them, because they had someone who liked them just the way they were.

*　*　*　*　*

This story leads well into discussions about colors. Ask the children if they can find something in the room the same color as Laughing Stock, or the same color as Gastly. This story also leads into a discussion about likenesses and differences:

- Is your hair the same color as one of your friends?
- Can you think of something that makes you different?

PARTICIPATION STORIES

Just Like Metoo!

(Children imitate what "Metoo" does. Metoo does things a little faster each day. Metoo was always late for school. Speedee was always on time.)

Once upon a time Metoo came to live at Speedee's house. He thought "I'd like to do what Speedee does; but I can't learn everything at one time. Each day I'll do one new thing."

On Monday, when the alarm went off, Metoo jumped out of bed and washed his hands and face at 7:30 in the morning. (Jump up, wash hands and face. Sit down.)

On Tuesday, when the alarm went off, Metoo jumped out of bed and washed his hands and face, and brushed his teeth at 7:30 in the morning. (Jump up, wash hands and face, brush teeth. Sit down.)

On Wednesday, when the alarm went off, Metoo jumped out of bed and washed his hands and face, brushed his teeth, and dressed himself at 7:30 in the morning. (Jump up, wash hands and face, brush teeth, dress self, sit down.)

On Thursday, when the alarm went off, Metoo jumped out of bed, washed his hands and face, brushed his teeth, dressed himself, and ate his breakfast at 7:30 in the morning. (Jump up, wash hands and face, brush teeth, dress self, eat breakfast, sit down.)

On Friday, when the alarm went off, Metoo jumped out of bed, washed his hands and face, brushed his teeth, dressed himself, ate his breakfast, and waved goodbye to Speedee's mother who was on her way to work at 7:30 in the morning. (Very rapidly, jump up, wash hands and face, brush teeth, dress self, eat breakfast, wave goodbye, sit down.)

On Saturday, when the alarm went off, Metoo turned over and shut it off. (Move right arm across body slowly, as if shutting off alarm.) He had heard Speedee say, "This is Saturday. *Nobody* wakes up at 7:30 in the morning on Saturday!" And, anyway, Metoo could get to school just as fast as Speedee now, and he could do everything Speedee could do in the morning.

*   *   *   *   *

To Grandmother's House

(Before beginning this story, draw the picture in figure 10-4 on the blackboard or on a large sheet of paper. During the telling let your finger show Clementine's travels.)

One day Clementine's mother said, "I'm making cookies. I need some sugar. Please go to grandma's house and borrow a cup of sugar." "Yes, Mother, I'll go right away," said Clementine.

Clementine climbed up the first mountain. Climb, climb, climb. (Make climbing motions with arms.) Climb, climb, climb.

When she got to the top of the mountain she slid down. (Make sliding motion with hands.)

At the bottom of the mountain was a wide, wide lake. Clementine jumped in and swam across. Swim, swim, swim. (Make swimming arm motions.)

Clementine climbed the next mountain. Climb, climb, climb. (Make climbing hand mo-

tions.) Then she slid down the other side. (Make sliding motions.)

Next, Clementine crossed the bridge. Tromp, tromp, tromp. (Make feet move up and down.) Tromp, tromp, tromp.

Clementine climbed the third mountain. Climb, climb, climb. (motions) Then she slid down the other side. (motions)

Clementine's grandmother was standing next to her house. "Hello, grandmother, may I have a cup of sugar? My mother's making cookies." "Yes, dear," said grandmother, and she came out of the house with a little bag.

"Goodbye, grandmother," Clementine said.

Clementine climbed the mountain. Climb, climb, climb. She slid down the other side and crossed the bridge. Tromp, tromp, tromp. She climbed the middle mountain. Climb, climb, climb. (motions) Then she slid down the other side. (motions) She swam the lake with the bag in her teeth and her head held high. Swim, swim, swim. (motions) Next, she climbed the mountain. Climb, climb, climb. (motions) Then she slid down the mountain (motions) to her house.

When she went into the house she gave her mother the sugar. Her mother said, "This is brown sugar. I wanted white sugar."

"I'll go to grandmother's," said Clementine.

Clementine climbed the first mountain. Climb, climb, climb. (motions) She slid down the other side. (motions) Then she swam the lake. Swim, swim, swim. (motions)

She climbed the second mountain. Climb, climb, climb. (motions) She slid down the other

FIGURE 10-4 Clementine's travels

side (motions) and crossed the bridge. Tromp, tromp, tromp. (motions)

She climbed the third mountain. Climb, climb, climb. (motions) Then she slid down the other side. (motions)

Grandmother was working in her garden.

"Hello, grandmother," said Clementine.

"Two visits in one day. How nice," said grandmother.

"But I can't stay this time either. Mother needs white sugar instead of brown," said Clementine.

Grandmother went into her house and came out with a little bag.

"You look so tired, Clementine!" said grandmother.

"I am," said Clementine.

"Take the shortcut home," said grandmother.

So, Clementine did. She walked straight home on the path at the foot of the mountains.

This story can be lengthened by having the mother request additional ingredients and by Clementine taking cookies to grandmother after they are baked.

*   *   *   *   *

He's a Hat, No He's a Boat, No He's Supershirt

Once there was a hat, a sailor's hat, and the hat could talk! "I don't want to be a hat, I want to be a boat." So the hat folded up like this; (fold to position 2), and did become a boat sailing in the sea. Everything was going just fine until the boat hit a rock, and the front was torn off; (tear off, 3). Then a big whale took a bite out of the other end of the boat; (tear off, 4). A giant wave hit the top of the boat pulling away part of the boat's cabin (5). What was left of the boat drifted to shore. A bird saw it laying there in the sand. "Hey, you don't look like a boat, or a hat! Know what you are? You're a _____." (then unfold and hold up (6)), figure 10-5.

*   *   *   *   *

What Was Behind the Door?

Dog — "Bow Wow"   Bird — "Peep Peep"
Cat — "Meow"   Lion — "Grr (roar)"

(Teacher says the following to children: "I need you to help me tell the story! Do you suppose that you can remember all of the sounds that we have talked about? In this story you can make the animal noises that Granny hears. When the story says, Granny heard a dog say, 'Bow Wow!' etc. Listen carefully."

Granny sat in a big armchair knitting Tommy a sweater. All of a sudden she heard a dog say "_____." (Bow Wow)

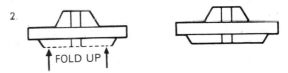

1.
Sailor's hat

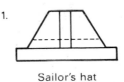

2.
FOLD UP

Folding a hat to look like a boat.

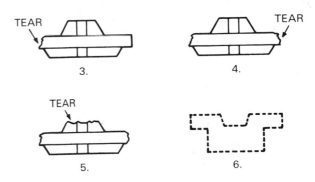

3.   4.
TEAR   TEAR

5.   6.
TEAR

FIGURE 10-5 Tearing parts of the hat to resemble the damaged boat

"Gracious!" said Granny. "I do believe there's a dog behind the door. Should we have a dog in the house?"

"Oh yes," answered the dog behind the door. "I'm a good dog. I don't jump on people."

"Very well," said Granny, and she went on knitting the sweater for Tommy. All of a sudden Granny heard a cat say "_____." (Meow)

"Gracious!" said Granny. "I do believe that there is a cat behind the door. Should we have a cat in the house?"

"Oh yes," answered the cat. "I am a good cat. I do not scratch the furniture."

"Very well," said Granny, and she went on knitting Tommy's sweater. All of a sudden Granny heard a bird say "_____." (Peep Peep)

"Gracious!" said Granny. "I do believe that I heard a bird behind the door. Should we have a bird in the house?"

"Oh yes," answered the bird. "I am a good bird. I sing very nicely."

"Very well," said Granny and she went right on knitting a sweater for Tommy.

All of a sudden Granny heard a lion say "_____!" (Grrrrr!)

"Gracious!" said Granny, "I do believe that there is a lion behind the door. This is too much!" Carefully, Granny opened up the door, because she wasn't sure she liked having a lion in the house.

And what do you think she found hiding behind her door? There was Tommy. He had been making those noises after all!

Suggest: "Can you all make the noises Tommy made?"

Dog = Bow Wow
Cat = Meow
Bird = Peep Peep
Lion = Grrr!

*   *   *   *   *

The Dark House (Halloween Story)

(This story [Tashjian, 1969] is short and needs a discussion about ghosts, but is highly enjoyed for its repetitive quality and surprise ending.)

In a dark, dark wood, there was a dark, dark house.

And on that dark, dark house, there was a dark, dark room.

And in that dark, dark room, there was a dark, dark cupboard.

And in that dark, dark cupboard, there was a dark, dark shelf.

And on that dark, dark shelf, there was a dark, dark box.

And in that dark, dark box, there was a GHOST! (GHOST is done with a dramatic increase in voice volume.)

Additional stories are included in the Appendix.

SUMMARY

The prime goal of storytelling is a feeling of togetherness and enjoyment through the words of a story. Building listening skills, vocabulary development, and expanding interest are other important goals.

Stories for storytelling can be found in printed sources or borrowed from other teachers. A story can also be created by the teacher. By following suggested techniques and criteria, a successful activity for both children and teachers is possible.

Stories are told in the teacher's own words with key happenings well in mind. Watching the children's interest and reactions keeps the teacher aware of how well the experience is accepted. Any skill takes practice; storytelling skills become better with use.

Learning Activities

- Create a story. In outline form, write the beginning, middle and ending. Practice telling it to a fellow student. Use your own title or select one of the following:

    The Giant Ice Cream Cone
    Magic Shoes
    The Dog Who Wouldn't Bark
    Billy Found a Dollar
    The Big Birthday Present
    The Mouse Who Chased Cats
    The Police Officer and Mike
    The Fastest Bike
    I've Got a Bug in My Pocket.

- Tell a story to a group of children.
    a. What parts interested the children the most?
    b. What would you change if you told it again?
    c. What techniques were used to hold interest?

- Try to find an ethnic story that could be told to young children. Cite your source and be ready to share the story with fellow classmates.

- Invite a librarian or experienced teacher who tells stories during story hours to share favorite stories with the class.

- Tell a story and have it recorded on vieeotape. Play it back. Look for strong points and weaknesses.

- Listen to a commercial storytelling record. List the techniques used to hold the child's interest.

- Create a story in which the children's names for a particular class are woven into the story. Share with children, and share children's reactions with your fellow students.

Unit Review

A. Column I lists common preschool characteristics. Select the appropriate storytelling technique or criteria from Column II that matches each item in Column I.

Column I	**Column II**
1. likes to move frequently	a. selects stories without cruel
2. has had experiences at home, school, and in the community	monsters or vivid descriptions of accidents

3. has fear of large animals and bodily harm
4. likes play with words
5. likes to be part of the group
6. likes to talk

b. "Ducky-Ducky and Be-bop-boo went to the park to meet Moo-moo the cow"
c. stories contain familiar objects and animals
d. "What did the big bird say to the baby bird?"
e. "Help Tipper blow out the candle. Pretend my finger is a candle and try to blow it out!"
f. "Stand up and reach for the moon like Johnny did. Good. Now close your eyes; is it dark like night? You couldn't reach the moon, but can you find your nose with your eyes closed?"

B. Briefly answer the following questions.
1. Why should storytelling take place often in early childhood centers?
2. What are some possible problems of a young child that a story might help solve?
3. How can the teacher bring about the learning of words and facts through storytelling?
4. Name three resources for stories.
5. What are stereotypes?
6. What incidents of sexism might be found in young children's stories?

C. Select the correct answers. Each item has more than one correct answer.
1. In storytelling, the storyteller not only uses words but also uses
   a. the hands.
   b. the face.
   c. the eyes.
   d. gestures.
2. Recommended techniques used by storytellers are
   a. changing the voice to fit the character.
   b. changing the personality of a character during the story.
   c. stopping without ending a story so that children will listen quietly the next time.
   d. watching children closely and emphasizing the parts they enjoy.
3. Criteria for story selection includes
   a. believable characters.
   b. a plot with lots of action.
   c. a possible problem to be resolved.
   d. making sure the story is one that can be memorized.

4. Teachers should not
   a. let children be inattentive during their story.
   b. feel defeated if a story occasionally flops.
   c. put bad guys in stories.
   d. tell the story word for word.
5. During storytelling time, the
   a. child can form his own mental pictures.
   b. teacher can share interesting personal life experiences.
   c. teacher models creativity with words.
   d. teacher models correct speech.

References

Arbuthnot, May Hill, *The Arbuthnot Anthology,* Scott, Foresman and Co., 1953. (A collection of children's literature with many classic stories included.)

Bailey, Carolyn and Clara Lewis, *For the Children's Hour,* Platt and Munk, NY, 1943. (Suggested activities and stories for group times.)

Chambers, Dewey W., *Storytelling and Creative Drama,* Wm. C. Brown and Company, 1970. (Helps one develop technique.)

Moore, Vadine, *Preschool Story Hour,* Scarecrow Press, NJ, 1972. (Lots of ideas for storytelling times.)

Tashjian, Virginia A., ed., *Juba This and Juba That: Story Hour Stretches for Large or Small Groups,* Boston: Little, Brown and Company, 1969.

Suggested Readings

Sawyer, Dorothy, *The Way of the Storyteller,* Viking, NY, 1969. (One of the best known and studied references on storytelling technique.)

Schimmel, Nancy, *Just Enough to Make a Story,* Sister's Choice Press, Berkeley, CA, 1978. (A practical guide for beginners. Includes stories.)

Tooze, Ruth, *Storytelling,* Prentice-Hall, NJ, 1959. (A classic reference in storytelling, ever popular and helpful to one who desires to be an outstanding storyteller.)

Unit 11
Poetry

OBJECTIVES

After studying this unit you should be able to

- discuss poetry elements that appeal to young children.
- demonstrate the ability to present a poem.
- create a poem with features that appeal to young children.

Poetry is an enjoyable method of developing listening skills. Activities which involve poetry hold many opportunities to promote language development by associating pleasure with words. By identifying with poetry, children can quickly feel at home with their imaginary pictures.

In addition to fast action and mood building, there is the joy of rhythm and beat of the words. Some rhythms in classic rhymes are so strong that they can motivate the children to move their bodies or clap. The nursery rhymes "Jack and Jill" and "Twinkle, Twinkle, Little Star," are good examples. Not only are poems of this type appealing, they also paint vivid mental images. Other poems appeal to the emotions, figure 11-1.

LEARNINGS

Poetry provides an opportunity for a child to learn new words, ideas, and attitudes, and to experience life through the eyes of the poet. To remember how many days there are in a month, many people still recite a simple poem learned as a child. If you are asked to say the alphabet, the classic ABC song of childhood may come to mind.

FIGURE 11-1 Some poetry brings laughter.

Poetry has form and order. It is dependable. It is also easy to learn. Simple rhymes are picked up quickly, as most parents have seen from their child's ability to remember television commercial jingles. Children in early childhood centers enjoy the accomplishment of memorizing a short verse. They may ask to share the poems they have learned with the teacher, just as they ask to sing songs they know which are often poems set to music.

The teacher should provide encouragement, attention, and a positive comment to the child who responds to poetry. As with reading, storytelling, and other language activities, the goal of the teacher in regard to poetry is to offer children pleasure and enjoyment of the language arts, while expanding the child's knowledge and interest.

Poetry, then, is used for a variety of reasons, including:

- to train the ear to experience the pleasure of hearing sounds.
- to provide enjoyment by silly words, fun, and humor.
- to stimulate the imagination.
- to increase vocabulary and knowledge.
- to build self-worth and give a feeling of self-confidence.

SELECTION

Poetry introduces children to characters with fun-to-say names such as:

Jonathan Bing by Beatrice Curtis Brown
Mrs. Peck Pigeon by Eleanor Farjeon
Godfrey Gordon Gustavos Gore by William Rands

The characters live in familiar and far-fetched settings:

"Under the toadstool" from *The Elf and the Dormouse* by Oliver Herford
"Straight to the animal store" from *The Animal Store* by Rachel Field
"A shining in the sky" from *Aeroplane* by Mary McB. Green

And they have various adventures and difficulties:

"The kids are ten feet tall." from *Grown-Up-Down Town* by Bobbi Katz
"Christopher Robin had wheezles and sneezles." from *Sneezles* by A. A. Milne
"Listen, my children, this must be stopped." from *The Grasshoppers* by Dorothy Aldis

Teachers select poetry they can present eagerly and which they feel children will like. Delight in words is a natural outcome when the poem suits the audience.

TEACHER TECHNIQUES

Read or recited in a conversational manner, rather than in a sing-song fashion, the rhyme is sometimes subtle and under-emphasized — an enjoyable experience for all. Sing-song recitation may become tiresome and difficult to understand by comparison.

Most teachers know that reciting from memory requires practice, so the poems they memorize are a few favorites. At the very least, the teacher should read the poem before reciting it to the children, so it may be offered easily, without stops and hesitation. If it rolls off the tongue with ease, the words savored in the telling, the experience can be delightful for both children and teacher — after all, the most important goal of all in the recitation of poetry.

Posting poems on bulletin boards helps create interest. A poetry tree can be made by placing a tree limb in plaster of paris, and writing poems on the back of paper leaves that can be hung on the tree. Every day a child can be chosen to pick the poem of the day.

Young children sometimes create their own rhymes. The teacher can jot them down for display or to be taken home as a "poem authored by Robby." "Amber, pamber, big fat bamber" created by a child spread like wildfire at one school.

Poetry activities need sensitive handling. Children may recite a favorite poem together.

A teacher can suggest, "Let's say it together," but a child should not be singled out or forced to recite. A number of repetitions of a favorite long verse may be needed before it is totally remembered.

Pictures can be used in poetry presentation to add interest and help children focus on words, figure 11-2. Other props or costumes which relate to the poem (such as a teddy bear or police officer's hat) will gain attention. Some of the best collections of poems have no pictures; others have an illustration for each poem.

A poem can be enjoyed indoors or outdoors, in a train, car, or bus, or between activities as a fill-in when teacher or children are waiting.

Glancing at a 4″ x 6″ card may help a teacher remember a poem, but spontaneity is sometimes sacrificed. Charts are another helpful device, figure 11-3.

Charts can be placed in a position behind a group of children so that if it's not quite mem-

orized by a teacher it can be read without the distraction of looking down at cards or papers. Teacher is then able to maintain partial eye contact.

SOURCES

A fine line divides finger plays, body and movement games, chants, songs, and poems. All involve rhyme and rhythm. Poetry given later in this unit is mainly the "listening to" kind, although some do contain child participation.

Collections, anthologies, and books of children's poetry are available at the public li-

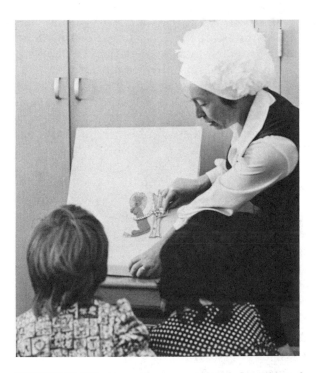

FIGURE 11-2 Poetry can be presented with flannel board cutouts.

FIGURE 11-3 A rhyming chart

brary; children's and teachers' magazines are another source. Teachers can create poetry from their own experiences. The following suggestions for creating poems for young children can help the teacher by pointing out the especially enjoyable features found in popular classics.

- Mental images are found in every line.
- Strong rhythms bring out an urge to chant, move, or sing.
- Frequent rhyming occurs.
- Action verbs are used often.
- Each line has an independent thought.
- A move and change in rhythm are present.
- Words are within the children's level of understanding.
- Themes and subjects are familiar to the young child.

SUGGESTED POEMS

The poems which follow are examples of those which appeal to the young child.

IF I WERE AN APPLE

If I were an apple
And grew on a tree,
I think I'd drop down
On a nice boy like me.

I wouldn't stay there
Giving nobody joy;
I'd fall down at once
And say, "Eat me, my boy!"

Old Rhyme

GOOD-MORNING

One day I saw a downy duck,
With feathers on his back;
I said, "Good-morning, downy duck,"
And he said, "Quack, quack, quack."

One day I saw a timid mouse,
He was so shy and meek;

I said, "Good-morning, timid mouse,"
And he said, "Squeak, squeak, squeak."

One day I saw a curly dog,
I met him with a bow;
I said, "Good-morning, curly dog,"
And he said, "Bow-wow-wow."

One day I saw a scarlet bird,
He woke me from my sleep;
I said, "Good-morning, scarlet bird,"
And he said, "Cheep, cheep, cheep."

Muriel Sipe

ONE STORMY NIGHT

Two little kittens,
* One stormy night*
Began to quarrel,
* And then to fight.*

One had a mouse,
* the other had none;*
And that's the way
* The quarrel begun.*

"I'll have that mouse,"
* Said the bigger cat.*
"You'll have that mouse?
* We'll see about that!"*

"I will have that mouse,"
* Said the eldest son.*
"You shan't have the mouse,"
* Said the little one.*

The old woman seized
* Her sweeping broom,*
And swept both kittens
* Right out of the room.*

The ground was covered
* With frost and snow,*
And the two little kittens
* Had nowhere to go.*

They lay and shivered
    On a mat at the door,
While the old woman
    Was sweeping the floor.

And then they crept in
    As quiet as mice,
All wet with the snow,
    And as cold as ice.

And found it much better
    That stormy night,
To lie by the fire,
    Than to quarrel and fight.

                                    Traditional

WHAT IS RED?

Red is a sunset
Blazy and bright.
Red is feeling brave
With all your might.
Red is a sunburn
Spot on your nose.
Sometimes red
Is a red, red rose.
Red squiggles out
When you cut your hand.

Red is a brick and
A rubber band.
Red is a hotness
You get inside
When you're embarrassed
And want to hide.

From *Hailstones and Halibut Bones* by Mary O'Neill,
Copyright © 1961 By Mary LeDuc O'Neill. Reprinted by
permission of Doubleday and Company, Inc.

GRANDMA RIDES A YAMAHA

Grandma rides a yamaha,
When Grandma comes — hooray!
Grandma takes me everywhere,
I hope she comes today.

"Hold on tight," says my grandma,
The seat feets warm and wide.

My arms hug grandma eagerly,
And snuggled close I ride.

Grandma has her helmet on,
Wind blows against my face.
Houses, poles, go rushing by.
Boom vroom — we roar and race.

Mom says, "Mother act your age!"
Grandma says, "Someday I might."
Grandma laughs and smiles alot.
She loves her motor bike.

Vroom — pop, vroom — ca — boom.
Whoopey — Grandma's here!
I just can't wait until she says
"Ready? Let's go my dear."

                                    Jeanne M. Machado

COUNTING

Today I'll remember forever and ever
Because I can count to ten;
It isn't an accident any more either,
I've done it over and over again.

I used to leave out five and three
And sometimes eight and four.
And once in a while I'd mix up nine
Or seven and two, but not any more.

I count my fingers on one hand first,
And this little pig is one,
And when old thumb goes off to market
That's five, and one of my hands is done.

So then I open my other hand
And start in counting again
From pick up sticks to big fat hen,
Five six seven eight eleven nine ten!

From *Windy Morning*, copyright 1953 by Harry Behn; re-
newed 1981 by Alice Behn Goebel, Pamela Behn Adam,
Prescott Behn, and Peter Behn. Reprinted by permission
of Harcourt Brace Jovanovich, Inc.

THE ANIMAL STORE

If I had a hundred dollars to spend,
    Or maybe a little more,

I'd hurry as fast as my legs would go
   Straight to the animal store.

I wouldn't say, "How much for this or that?"
   "What kind of dog is he?"
I'd buy as many as rolled an eye,
   Or wagged a tail at me!

I'd take the hound with the drooping ears
   That sits by himself alone,
Cockers and Cairns and wobbly pups
   For to be my very own.

I might buy a parrot all red and green,
   And the monkey I saw before,
If I had a hundred dollars to spend,
   Or maybe a little more.

                  Rachel Field

From *Taxis and Toadstools* by Rachel Field. Copyright 1926 by Doubleday and Company. Reprinted by permission of the publisher.

I HAVEN'T LEARNED TO WHISTLE

I haven't learned to whistle
I've tried —
But if there's anything like a whistle in me,
It stops
Inside

Dad whistles,
My brother whistles
And almost everyone I know.

I've tried to put my lips together with
   wrinkles,
To push my tongue against my teeth
And make a whistle
Come
Out
Slow —

But what happens is nothing but a feeble
   gasping
Sound
Like a sort of sickly bird.

(Everybody says they never heard
A whistle like that

And to tell the truth
Neither did I.)

But Dad says, tonight, when he comes
   home,
He'll show me again how
To put my lips together with wrinkles,
To push my tongue against my teeth,
To blow my breath out and really make a
   whistle.

And I'll try!

            Myra Cohn Livingston

Myra Cohn Livingston, "I Haven't Learned to Whistle" from *O Sliver of Liver*. Text copyright © 1979 by Myra Cohn Livingston. Reprinted with the permission of Atheneum Publishers.

FEET

There are things
Feet know
That hands never will:
The exciting
Pounding feel
Of running down a hill;

The soft cool
Prickliness
When feet are bare
Walking in
The summer grass
To most anywhere.

Or dabbling in
Water all
Slip-sliddering through toes —
(Nicer than
Through fingers, though why
No one really knows.)

"Toes, tell my
Fingers," I
Said to them one day,
"Why it's such
Fun just to
Wiggle and play."

But toes just
Looked at me
Solemn and still.
Oh, there are things
Feet know
That hands NEVER WILL.

— Dorothy Aldis

THE GRASSHOPPERS

High
Up
Over the top
Of feathery grasses the
Grasshoppers hop.
They won't eat their suppers;
They will not obey
Their grasshopper mothers
And fathers, who say:
"Listen, my children,
This must be stopped —
Now is the time your last
Hop should be hopped;
So come eat your suppers
And go to your beds —"
But the little green grasshoppers
Shake their green heads.
"No,
No —"
The naughty ones say,
"All we have time to do
Now is to play
If we want supper we'll
Nip at a fly
Or nibble a blueberry
As we go by;
If we feel sleepy we'll
Close our eyes tight
And snoozle away in a
Harebell all night
But not
Now

Now we must hop
And nobody
NOBODY,
Can make us stop."

Dorothy Aldis

THE CHICKENS

Said the first little chicken,
With a queer little squirm,
"I wish I could find
A fat little worm!"

Said the next little chicken,
With an odd little shrug:
"I wish I could find
A fat little bug!"

Said the third little chicken,
With a small sign of grief:
"I wish I could find
A green little leaf!"

Said the fourth little chicken,
With a faint little moan:
"I wish I could find
A wee gravel stone!"

"Now see here!" said the mother,
From the green garden patch,
"If you want any breakfast,
Just come here and scratch!"

Anonymous

MICE

I think mice
Are rather nice
Their tails are long,
Their faces small,
They haven't any
Chins at all.
Their ears are pink,
Their teeth are white.

They run about
The house at night.
They nibble things
They shouldn't touch
And no one seems
To like them much.
But I think mice
Are nice.

Rose Fyleman

From *Fifty-One New Nursery Rhymes*, Doubleday & Co.

The following are poems written by students who created them to use with young children. These beginning attempts show that most teachers are capable of writing enjoyable and interesting poetry to use for language development.

A SLEEPY PLACE TO BE

Oh, it was a yawning day
That nobody wanted to work or play
And everybody felt the very same way.

There was a duckling who quacked and
quacked
He had soft down upon his back.
He was tired of swimming and everything,
So he put his head down under his wing.
And there under the shadowy shade tree
He slept until it was half-past three.

A little old pig gave a big loud squeal
As he ate every scrap of his noonday meal.
And under the shadowy shade tree
He slept as quietly as could be.

A butterfly blue, green and red
Sat with her wings above her head
Up on a branch of the shadowy tree.
Oh, what a sleepy place to be.

Debbie Lauer-Hunter

LITTLE KITTY

Pretty little Kitty
With fur so soft and sweet,

You tiptoe oh so softly
On your tiny little feet.

Fluffy little Kitty
With eyes so big and round,
I never hear you coming,
You hardly make a sound.

Silly little Kitty
Playing with a ball.
Listen! Someone's coming!
You scamper down the hall.

Lazy little Kitty,
Tiny sleepy head,
Curled up, sleeping soundly
In your cozy little bed.

Bari Morgan-Miller

THE PUMPKIN NO ONE WANTED

Out in the pumpkin patch, sad and forlorn,
Sat a funny little pumpkin, shaped like
a horn.
He sat and he waited, through the day and
the night,
For his own special person, someone
just right.

He was thin by his stem,
Flat on the bottom,
Sitting in the corner,
Alone and forgotten.

Along came a Doctor, searching through the
vine.
Looking for some pumpkins, seven,
eight, nine.
She saw the funny pumpkin, sad and
forlorn,
She laughed and said, "You are shaped
like a horn."

He was thin by his stem,
Fat on the bottom,
Sitting in the corner,
Alone and forgotten.

Along came a teacher, walking down the row,
 He came to the pumpkin, laughed and said, "No . . .
For a jack-o-lantern, you won't do at all.
 Here you're thin, there you're fat, you're much too tall."

  He was thin by his stem,
  Fat on the bottom.
  Sitting in the corner,
  Alone and forgotten.

Along came a little girl, all by herself.
 She wanted a jack-o-lantern to sit on a shelf.
She looked for a pumpkin, round, smooth and fat.
 She saw the funny pumpkin and said, "Not one like that."

  He was thin by his stem,
  Fat on the bottom,
  Sitting in the corner,
  Alone and forgotten.

Along came a tall boy, walking all alone,
 Looking for a pumpkin to take to his home.

He saw the funny pumpkin, shaped like a horn,
 Over in the corner, sad and forlorn.

  He was thin by his stem,
  Fat on the bottom,
  No longer in the corner,
  Alone or forgotten.

      Mary Sheridan

SUMMARY

Poetry can be a source of enjoyment and learning for young children. The rhythm, word images, fast action, and rhyme are used to promote listening skill.

Short verses, easily remembered, give children self-confidence with words. Encouragement and attention is offered by the teacher when the child shows interest.

Poems are selected and practiced for enthusiastic, smooth presentations. They can be selected from various sources or created by the teacher. Props help children focus on words. Poems are created or selected keeping in mind the features which attract and interest young children.

Learning Activities

- Select five poems from any source. Be ready to state the reasons you selected them when you bring them to the next class meeting.

- Make a list of ten books that include children's poetry. Cite author, title, publisher, and copyright date.

- Create a poem for young children. Go back and review the features most often found in classic rhymes.

- Present a poem to a group of preschoolers. Evaluate its success in a few sentences.

- Form groups of 3 to 6 students. Using a large sheet of newsprint tacked (or taped) to the wall and a felt pen, list clever ways to introduce poetry to young children. Example: Poem of the Day. Discuss each group's similar and diverse suggestions.

Unit Review

A. List a few reasons why poetry is used with young children.

B. Select from Column II the term which matches each item in Column I.

Column I	Column II
1. poetry	a. an action verb
2. rhyme	b. self-confidence
3. beat	c. a rhythmic measure
4. order and form	d. mental pictures
5. images	e. words with alike sounds
6. remembered	f. consistent and dependable
7. interest	g. teacher attention
8. goal	h. after practice
9. presentation	i. enjoyment
10. reciting	j. promotes listening skill
11. classics	k. never forced
12. song	l. library
13. props	m. Mother Goose rhymes
14. run	n. musical poem
15. source	o. focus attention

C. List the numbers of the statements you feel agree with suggestions mentioned in this unit.
   1. Young children must learn to recite.
   2. Emphasizing the beat of poetry as you read it always increases the enjoyment.
   3. Repeat a poem over and over until a child learns it.
   4. Describe the mental pictures that you see to the children before reading the poem.
   5. It really isn't too important for young children to memorize the poems they hear.
   6. Memorizing a poem can help a child feel competent.
   7. Most poems are not shared because teachers want children to gain the factual information the poem contains.
   8. Poetry's rhythm comes from its form and order.
   9. Memorizing a poem always causes awkward teacher presentation.
   10. Teachers should try to author some of their own poetry.

Resources

Arbuthnot, May H. and Shelton L. Root Jr., *Time for Poetry,* Scott, Foresman and Co., 1968.

Brown, Margaret W., *Nibble, Nibble,* Addison-Wesley, 1959.

Clark, Leonard, *Poetry for the Youngest,* Horn Book, 1969.

Frank, Josette (ed.), *Poems to Read to the Very Young,* Random House, NY, 1961.

Hoban, Russel, *Egg Thoughts and Other Frances Songs,* Harper and Row, 1972.

Katz, Bobbi, *Bedtime Bear's Book of Bedtime Poems,* Random House, 1983.

Manson, Beverlie, *Fairy Poems for the Very Young,* Doubleday, 1983.

Watson, Clyde, *Catch Me and Kiss Me and Say It Again,* Collins, 1983.

Unit 12
Flannel Boards and Activity Sets

OBJECTIVES

After studying this unit you should be able to

- describe flannel boards and types of flannel board activities.
- make and present three flannel board activities.
- list visual aids that can be used to develop listening ability.

Flannel board activities are a rewarding experience for both the child and teacher. Since the attention of young children is easily captured, the teacher finds the use of flannel board activities very popular and effective. Children are highly attentive during this type of activity — straining to see and hear — looking forward to the next piece to be put on the flannel board.

Stories to be used with flannel board activities are selected by the same criteria used for storytelling; see Unit 10. In addition to stories, poetry, and songs, other listening and learning activities can be presented with flannel boards.

FLANNEL BOARD CONSTRUCTION

Boards of different sizes, shapes, and designs are used, depending on the needs of the center. They may be free-standing or propped up in the chalkboard tray, on a chair, or on an easel. Boards can be covered on both sides in different colors. Many are made by covering a sheet of heavy cardboard, display board, styrofoam,

or wood with a piece of solid-colored flannel yardage, figure 12-1. The material is pulled

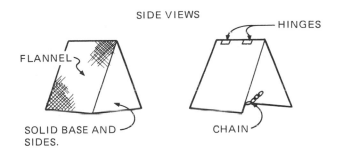

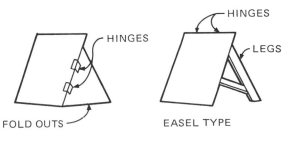

FIGURE 12-1 Free-standing boards

157

smooth and held by tacks, tape, glue, or wood staples, depending on the board material.

Making a board that tilts backward at a slight angle is an important consideration for a free-standing flannel board because pieces applied to a slanted board stick more securely. Stores which sell school supplies have premade boards in various prices.

Flannel and felt are popular coverings for boards but some other materials also work well. Almost all fuzzy-textured material is usable. It is a good idea to press a small piece of felt or pellon to a fabric to see how well it sticks before buying the fabric.

Some boards have pockets in the back so flannel pieces to be used can be lined up and ready beforehand, figure 12-2. There are also childhood centers which have part of the walls or dividers covered with flannel or felt. A simple homemade free-standing board holder is shown in figure 12-3.

Wire mesh inserted beneath the fabric makes it possible to use magnetic pieces on the board. Display fabrics to which three-dimensional ob-

Construction:

   Obtain a piece of cardboard, of the size you desire for the back of your flannel board, and a large sheet of flannel or heavy wrapping paper. The flannel (or paper) should be several inches wider than the cardboard and about twice as long as the finished chart size. One-inch deep with a back three inches high is a good pocket size.

   Measure and mark both sides of flannel (paper) at intervals of three inches and one inch, alternating. Using accordion fold, the first one-inch section is creased and folded forward over the second three-inch section, and so on. Pull tight and secure ends.

   A pocket chart conveniently holds set pieces in sequence for flannel board stories and can be useful in other child activities with flannel set pieces.

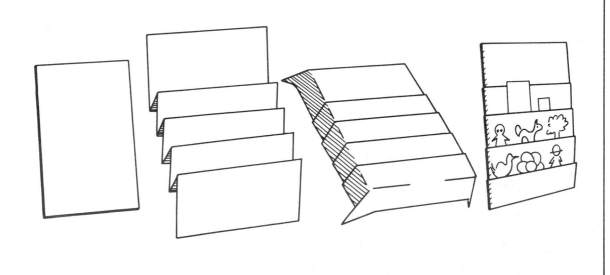

FIGURE 12-2 Pocket chart

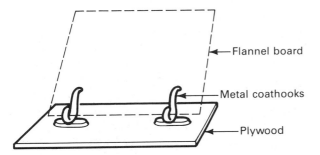

FIGURE 12-3 Two metal coat hooks screwed to a piece of heavy plywood make a good flannel board holder.

jects will adhere are available at commercial audiovisual companies. Special adhesives and tape are needed for this type of flannel board. The following company is one manufacturer of this commercial product.

Charles Mayer Studios, Inc.
140 E. Market St.
Akron, OH 44308

ACTIVITY SETS

Pieces for flannel activity sets can be made in a number of ways and from a number of fabrics and papers. Pellon and felt, because of their low cost and durability, are probably the most popular. Heavy paper figures with flannel backing also stick well. Commercial tapes, sandpaper, fuzzy velour-flocked wallpaper, and used "foam-like" laundry softener sheets are other possibilities. Premade flannel board sets are available at school supply stores and most teacher conferences, figure 12-4.

Shapes and figures can be traced from books, magazines, coloring books, self-drawn and created, or other sources. Tracing paper is helpful for this purpose. Color can be added with felt pen markers, oil pastels, embroidery pens, crayons, paints, and colored pencils. Sets take time to make but are well worth the effort. Favorites will be presented over and over again. Clear contact paper covering pieces or laminating adds durability (fronts only).

Teachers get creative with flannel board sets which can verge on fine art with:

FIGURE 12-4 A commercial flannel board set is in use here.

- Layered felt
- Wiggly eyes commercially available at variety stores
- Hand-stitched character clothing
- Imitation fur fabric
- Liquid glitter and
- Commercial fluorescent crayoning, etc.

Proper storage and care will preserve pieces, thus prolonging their usefulness. A flat stocking box or large mailing envelope or manila folder is practical for storage. If pieces become bent, a warm iron makes most kinds flat again. Sets can be stored in plastic page protectors used in three-ring binders. These are available in stationery stores. Large zip-lock plastic household bags can also offer protection.

PRESENTATION

Like most other listening activities, a semi-secluded, comfortable area is chosen for presentation. The teacher talks about the characters and story, places pieces on the board in proper sequence, and focuses on the children's reactions. Since pieces are usually added one at a time, they should be kept in an open flat box or manila folder in the teacher's lap, or behind the board, stacked in the order they will appear. This is hard to do well if the story or activity is not well in mind.

The teacher should periodically check to see if the set has all its pieces, particularly in large centers where many staff members use the same sets. If pieces are missing or damaged, the teacher can make new pieces. New sets are always appreciated by the entire staff, and can be developed to meet the needs and interests of a particular group of children.

In order to present activities with ease, these steps should be noted for the beginner:

- Read the story and check the pieces to be used.
- Practice until there is a smooth coordination of words and placing pieces on the board.
- Set up the flannel board.
- Check and prepare pieces in order of their appearance.
- Place pieces out of view.
- Gather children.
- Introduce the activity with a motivational statement, if desired.
- Tell the story, watching for reactions from the children.
- Discuss for language development (optional).
- Keep pieces flat. Store.

In addition to storytelling activities, sets may be used for songs, poetry, numbers, language development, and thinking activities, etc.

SUGGESTED STORIES AND ACTIVITIES

There are many resources for story ideas. Stories created by teachers can be enjoyed as much as commercial sets and classic stories. Sets can improve listening skills and enhance vocabulary and concept development, often within one activity. The visual shapes or pieces are linked to words and ideas. Occasionally, a child's picture book can be presented as a flannel board activity before the book becomes part of the school's book collection.

An available — or possibly spare — flannel board placed at children's eye level with an adjacent open box of figures or shapes quickly encourages use and creativity, figure 12-5. Remembered words, lines, and whole stories are relived in children's play. They often go beyond the familiar, devising their own happenings. Even sturdy felt pieces will need to be ironed flat occasionally and replaced due to frequent vigorous use by children.

The following activities and stories are suggested as a start for the beginning teacher. They may also be used to add variety and ideas for new sets. Patterns for the pieces can be found in the Appendix. Additional flannel board stories and patterns may be found in the Appendix also.

THE LION AND THE MOUSE

Author Unknown (A classic story)

(See Appendix for patterns)

Pieces: lion, sleeping   rope
         lion, awake   mouse
         tree   2 hunters

(On the board, place the sleeping lion next to the tree. Place the mouse on the lion's back, moving him slowly while speaking in a soft voice.)

There once was a little mouse who saw a big lion sleeping by a tree. "Oh, it would be fun to climb on top of the lion, and slide down his tail," thought the mouse. So — quietly, he tiptoed close to the lion. When he climbed on the lion's back, the fur felt so soft and warm between his toes that he began running up and down the lion's back.

FIGURE 12-5 The children are placing pellon story pieces on a board covered with flannel.

The lion awoke. He felt a tickle upon his back. He opened one eye and saw the little mouse, which he then caught in his paw.

(Move mouse under lion's paw.)

"Let me go — please!" said the mouse. "I'm sorry I woke you from your nap. Let me go, and I'll never bother you again. Maybe you and I could be friends — friends help each other, you know."

This made the lion laugh. "A little mouse like you, help me? I'm big, I'm strong, and I'm brave!" Then the lion laughed again and he let the mouse go.

(Take the mouse off.)

The mouse ran away, and he didn't see the lion for a long time. But, one day when the mouse was out looking for seeds for dinner, he saw the lion tied to a tree with a rope, and two hunters near him.

(Remove sleeping lion. Add awake lion, placing next to tree with rope on top. Put the two hunters on the other side of the tree.)

One hunter said, "Well, this rope will hold the lion until we can go get our truck and take him to the zoo." So the hunters walked away.

(Remove the hunters.)

The mouse ran up to the lion as soon as the hunters were out of sight. He said, "Hello, lion."

(Add mouse.)

The lion answered, "Well, I guess it's your turn to laugh at me tied to this tree."

"I'm not going to laugh," said the mouse, as he quickly started to chew on the rope.

(Move mouse close to rope. Remove rope.)

The mouse chewed, and chewed, and chewed. The rope fell apart, and the lion was free.

"You are a good friend," said the lion. "Hop on my back and hold on. Let's get away from here before those two hunters come back."

(Place lion in running position with mouse on lion's back.)

"OK," said the mouse. "I'd like that."

So you see, sometimes little friends can help big friends. The size of a friend isn't really too important.

FORTUNATELY-UNFORTUNATELY

(See Appendix for patterns.)

Pieces: boy   haystack   shark
          plane   pitchfork   tiger
          parachute   water   cave
          snake   birthday cake

Once upon a time there was a little boy. Fortunately, he received an invitation to a birthday party. Unfortunately, the party was in Florida, and he was in New York City.

Fortunately, he had a plane. Unfortunately, the plane caught fire. Fortunately, he had a parachute. Unfortunately, the parachute had a hole in it. Fortunately, there was a haystack. Unfortunately, there was a pitchfork in the haystack.

Fortunately, he missed the pitchfork. Unfortunately, he missed the haystack. Fortunately, he landed in the water. Unfortunately, there was a shark in the water.

Fortunately, he could swim, and he swam to shore. Unfortunately, there were tigers on the land. Fortunately, he could run. Unfortunately, so could the tigers.

Fortunately, he found a cave. Unfortunately, there were snakes in the cave. Fortunately, he found a way out of the cave. Unfortunately, it led him to the middle of a formal ballroom.

Fortunately, there was a party going on. Fortunately, it was for him. And, fortunately, it was his birthday!

Remy Charlip, *What Good Luck, What Bad Luck* (New York: Scholastic Book Services, 1969).

THE PUMPKIN THAT GREW
(A Halloween Flannel Board Story/Poem)

(See Appendix for patterns.)

> Once there was a pumpkin
>   And all summer through
> It stayed upon a big green vine
>   And grew, and grew, and grew.
>
> It grew from being small and green
>   To being orange and bright
> And then it said unto itself,
>   "Now I'm a handsome sight."
>
> And then one day it grew a mouth
>   A nose and two big eyes;
> And so that pumpkin grew into
>   A Jack O' Lantern wise!

THE SEED

Margie Cowsert
(While an ECE student)

(See Appendix for patterns.)

Pieces: small roots   leaves
          green shoot   beaver
          deer   bird
          Mr. Man   large trunk
          apples (5 or more)   large leaves
          seed   large roots
          small trunk

Once upon a time there was a seed named Abraham. He didn't know what kind of plant he would be so he asked Mr. Bird. Mr. Bird didn't know, but wanted to eat Abraham. Abraham asked him to wait until after he found out what he would be and the bird agreed to wait.

Abraham grew small roots and green shoots. He asked Mr. Deer if he knew what he would grow up to be. "Do you know what I'll be when I grow up?" Mr. Deer said, "No," but wanted to eat the tender green shoot. Abraham said, "Please wait." So Mr. Deer decided to wait.

Abraham grew a small trunk and leaves. He was glad he was a tree, but still didn't know what kind. He asked Mr. Beaver, "Do you know what I'll be when I grow up?" Mr. Beaver didn't know, but wanted to eat Abraham's tender bark. He decided to wait also.

Abraham grew big roots, a big trunk and more leaves, but still didn't know what kind of tree he was. He asked Mr. Man, "Do you know what I'll be when I grow up?" Mr. Man didn't know but he wanted to chop down Abraham to make a house. He decided to wait.

Abraham grew apples. Hurray! He knew that he was an apple tree. He told Mr. Bird he could eat him now. Mr. Bird said Abraham was too big, but that he would like one of the apples. Mr. Deer thought the tree was too big, too, but he did want an apple.

Abraham Apple Tree was so happy to know what he was and that no one was going to eat him or chop him down, that he grew lots of apples.

JUST LIKE DADDY

(See Appendix for patterns.)

Pieces: little brown bear
little brown bear's
blue vest
flower
brown father bear
red boots for
father bear
yellow coat for
father bear
purple vest for
mother bear
green fish (large)
green fish (small)
brown mother
bear
red boots for little
bear
blue vest for
father bear
yellow coat for
little bear

When I got up this morning, I yawned a
big yawn . . .
Just like daddy.
I washed my face, got dressed, and had a
big breakfast . . .
Just like daddy.

And then I put on my coat and my boots
. . .
Just like daddy.
And we went fishing.

On the way I picked a flower, and gave it
to my mother . . .
Just like daddy.
When we got to the lake, I put a worm on
my hook . . .
Just like daddy.
All day we fished — and I caught a big
fish . . .
Just like mommy!!!

THE TREE IN THE WOODS

(See Appendix for patterns.)

Pieces: grass
tree
tree trunk
tree limb
tree branch
bird's nest
bird's egg
bird
wing
feather

The flannelboard can be used to build the song by placing first the grass (1), the tree (2), the trunk (3), the limb (4), the branch (5), the nest (6), the egg (7), the bird (8), the wing (9), and the feather (10) as each verse calls for it, and placing pieces in appropriate places on the board.

Now in the woods there was a tree,
The finest tree that you ever did see,
And the green grass grew all around,
around, around,
And the green grass grew all around.

And on that tree there was a trunk,
The finest trunk that you ever did see,
And the trunk was on the tree,
And the tree was in the woods,
And the green grass grew all around,
around, around,
And the green grass grew all around.

And on that trunk there was a limb,
The finest limb that you ever did see,
And the limb was on the trunk,
And the trunk was on the tree,
And the tree was in the woods,
And the green grass grew all around,
    around, around,
And the green grass grew all around.

And on that limb there was a branch,
The finest branch that you ever did see,
And the branch was on the limb,
And the limb was on the trunk,
And the trunk was on the tree,
And the tree was in the woods,
And the green grass grew all around,
    around, around,
And the green grass grew all around.

And on that branch there was a nest,
The finest nest that you ever did see,
And the nest was on the branch,
And the branch was on the limb,
And the limb was on the trunk,
And the trunk was on the tree,
And the tree was in the woods,
And the green grass grew all around,
    around, around,
And the green grass grew all around.

And in that nest there was an egg
The finest egg that you ever did see
And the egg was in the nest,
And the nest was on the branch,
And the branch was on the limb,
And the limb was on the trunk,
And the trunk was on the tree,
And the green grass grew all around,
    around, around
And the green grass grew all around.

And on that egg there was a bird
The finest bird that you ever did see
And the bird was on the egg,
And the egg was in the nest,

And the nest was on the branch,
And the branch was on the limb,
And the limb was on the trunk,
And the trunk was on the tree,
And the green grass grew all around,
    around, around
And the green grass grew all around.

And on that bird there was a wing
The finest wing that you ever did see
And the wing was on the bird,
And the bird was on the egg,
And the egg was in the nest,
And the nest was on the branch,
And the branch was on the limb,
And the limb was on the trunk,
And the trunk was on the tree,
And the green grass grew all around,
    around, around
And the green grass grew all around.

And on that wing there was a feather
The finest feather that you ever did see
And the feather was on the wing,
And the wing was on the bird,
And the bird was on the egg,
And the egg was in the nest,
And the nest was on the branch,
And the branch was on the limb,
And the limb was on the trunk,
And the trunk was on the tree,
And the green grass grew all around,
    around, around
And the green grass grew all around.

Riddle

Pieces: Triangles of felt in red, blue, yellow, green, purple, orange, brown, black, and white.

Riddle, riddle, ree,
What color do I see?
_____(child's name) has it on
    his/her _____(shirt, pants.
    etc.).
What color can this be?

Teacher puts triangle of same color on flannel-board. Child whose name was mentioned says name of color. Activity ends with line of triangles which group names as each triangle is removed.

SUMMARY

A flannel board presentation is one of the most popular and successful listening activities for the young child. Stories are told while figures and shapes are moved on the board. The children can learn new ideas and words by seeing the visual model while listening to the story.

Beginning teachers practice presentations with words and pieces until the activity flows smoothly, while the children's behaviors are being noted. Flannel board activities in many other learning areas besides language development take place in early childhood centers.

A wide variety of fabrics are available for both boards and pieces; felt and flannel are the most commonly used materials for boards.

Learning Activities

- Visit a center to watch a flannel board presentation or invite a teacher to present an activity to the class.

- Give a presentation to a small group of classmates. The classmates should make helpful suggestions in written form while watching the presentation, trying to look at the presentations through the "eyes of a child."

- Write an original story for the flannel board on a ditto master. These ditto masters can be purchased from a stationery or office supply store. Include patterns for your pieces on a ditto master also.

- If videotape equipment is available in your classroom, give a flannel board presentation and evaluate yourself.

- Make three flannel board sets using any materials desired.

- Visit a school supply store and price commercial flannel boards. Compare costs for constructing a teacher-made flannel board and report at the next class meeting.

Unit Review

A. List the types of materials used in board construction.

B. Name the kinds of fabrics from which flannel board pieces can be made.

C. In your opinion, what is the best way to color pieces for flannel boards?

D. Why is the use of visual aids valuable?

E. Place in correct order.
   1. Give a flannel board presentation.
   2. Set up area with board.
   3. Check pieces.

    4. Practice.
    5. Place pieces in order of appearance.
    6. Gather children.
    7. Place pieces out of sight.
    8. Discuss what happened during the activity with children.
    9. Store set by keeping pieces flat.
    10. Introduce the set with a motivational statement if you wish.

F. What color flannel would you use to cover your own board? Why?

G. Finish the following statements.
    1. A board is set up slanting back slightly because _____.
    2. A folding flannel board with handles for carrying is a good idea because _____.
    3. If children touch the pieces during a teacher presentation, the teacher should say _____.
    4. The main reason teachers like to store set pieces in a flat position is _____.
    5. One advantage of a flannel board made from a large styrofoam sheet is _____.
    6. One disadvantage of a flannel board made from a large styrofoam sheet is _____.

References and Resources

Anderson, Paul, *Storytelling with the Flannel Board,* Book One and Book Two, T. S. Denison and Co., 9601 Newton Ave. S., Minneapolis, MN. (Useful as a source of additional stories and patterns.)

Jackson, Marilyn, *Finger Play and Flannelboard Fun,* Box 124, Basking Ridge, NJ, 1978. (More activity ideas.)

Pederson, Marcy, *Magic Moments,* (self published), P.O. Box 53635, San Jose, CA, 95135-0635, 1984. (A creative young teacher shares her full-of-child-participation group time ideas and patterns.)

Peralta, Chris, *Flannel Board Activities for the Bilingual Classroom,* La Arana Publ., 11209 Malat Way, Culver City, CA 90232. (A collection of Latin-American traditional stories for the flannel board, patterns included.)

Sweeney, Mary and Jeff Fegan, *Flanneltales,* 310 Sequoia Ave, San Jose, CA 95126. (Classic stories from many cultures.)

Vonk, Idelee, *Storytelling with the Flannel Board,* Book Three, T. S. Denison and Co., 9601 Newton Ave S., Minneapolis, MN. (More patterns and activities.)

Section 3
Speaking —
A Language Art

Unit 13
Realizing Speaking Goals

OBJECTIVES

After studying this unit you should be able to

- state five goals of planned speech activities.
- describe appropriate teacher behavior in daily conversation with children.
- give three examples of questioning techniques.

In a well-planned classroom, a child has many opportunities to speak. While some activities are planned, others just happen. The action happens along with words, when there is both a desire and a need to speak, figure 13-1.

Activities can be classed in groups: structured and unstructured. *Structured activities* are those which the teacher plans and prepares. The teacher is usually at the center of all action — motivating, presenting ideas, giving demonstrations, eliciting child ideas and comments. *Unstructured activities,* on the other hand, may still be prepared by the teacher, but the children lead the action through self-directed play.

PROGRAM GOALS

Each center contains a unique group of children and adults. A center has its own geography and its children come from different segments of society, so the goals and priorities of one program may differ from others. There are, however, some common factors among centers. The following goals are acceptable to most programs. They give the teacher a basis for planning speech activities. Each child should be helped to attain these goals.

- Confidence in the ability to use speech with others.
- Enjoyment of speaking experiences in play, conversations, and groups.

FIGURE 13-1 There should be both a desire and a need to speak.

- Acceptance of the idea that another's speech may be different.
- Interest in the meaning of new words.
- Using speech for ideas, feelings, and needs.
- Using speech to solve problems.
- Using speech both to create and for make-believe.
- Using speech and body actions at the same time.
- Waiting one's turn to speak.

The overall goal in the development of speech communication in language arts is to increase each child's ability to use the speech he already possesses, and to help him move when ready toward the use of standard English. Program goals can be realized mainly through (1) the planning of daily activities, (2) daily staff-child interaction, and (3) the use of equipment and materials.

A wide variety of different experiences can provide many learning opportunities. An activity can follow, review, and add depth to a previous one.

The special interests or needs of a child are considered when planning daily programs. Programs then become more valuable and meaningful, figure 13-2.

DAILY CONVERSATIONS

Some of the best activities happen when the teacher notices what the child or group is focusing on and uses the opportunity to expand interest, knowledge, and enjoyment. A rainbow, a delivery truck, or any chance happening can become the central topic of active speaking by the children, figure 13-3.

Whether limited or advanced, a child's speech is immediately accepted and welcome. Teachers carefully guard and protect each child's self-confidence. Waiting patiently and matter-of-factly, reading nonverbal clues, and using guesswork when necessary, makes teachers understanding listeners.

FIGURE 13-2 A valuable learning experience results from the child's interest in a flower.

Every effort is made to give a logical response, showing the child that the teacher finds value in the communication. Touching, offering a reassuring arm or hand, and giving one's whole attention to the child often seems to relax him or her and increase speech production.

Children are more willing to speak when the following classroom atmosphere is maintained.

- The tone of the room is warm and relaxed, and children have many choices.
- Speaking is voluntary, not mandatory.
- The speaking group is small.
- The group listens attentively.
- Any speaking attempt is welcome.
- Effort and accomplishments are recognized.

A teacher's willingness to engage in light-hearted dialogue may make the child more open

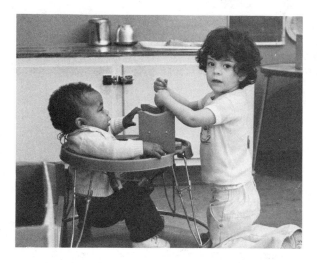

FIGURE 13-3 Children speak and listen while they play. *(From Machado and Meyer,* Early Childhood Practicum Guide, *Copyright 1984 by Delmar Publishers Inc.)*

to talking for the fun of it. When the mood is one of wanting to know, the teacher becomes active in the quest for answers, carefully guiding discovery and expression of discovery, figure 13-4.

Adults who emphasize the reason for happenings and who take a questioning, thoughtful, and systematic approach to problems model this type of behavior. Thinking out loud while sharing activities is a useful device. "I wonder what would happen if you put the block there?" a teacher might ask. In their speech, young children often deal with the reality of what is happening around them; teachers' speech should also be based upon this concept.

SUGGESTED INTERACTION GUIDES

A teacher is a speech model for children. The following guides for teachers in daily verbal conversations is based on understanding the level of each child, since preschoolers range in levels. These guidelines help develop speaking ability when dealing with young nonverbal, or slightly verbal, children.

FIGURE 13-4 Some activities tend to quiet speech while the child is absorbed in what he is doing.

- Let the child see your face and mouth clearly figure 13-5.
- Bend your knees and talk straight to the child, holding eye contact.
- Use simple gestures. Show meanings with your hands as well as with your eyes as you talk.

FIGURE 13-5 Let the child see your face and mouth.

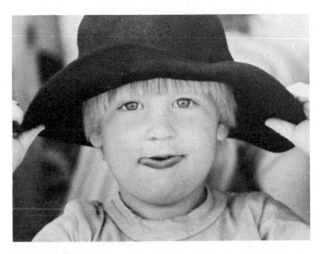

FIGURE 13-6 A face can say a lot to a teacher. *(From Machado and Meyer,* Early Childhood Practicum Guide, *Copyright 1984 by Delmar Publishers Inc.)*

- If possible, let the child touch, feel, smell, taste, and see whatever is interesting as you listen. Talk in simple sentences.
- Watch for nonverbal reactions; the child's face or body actions may show interest, fear, or other things, figure 13-6. Supply words to fit the situation: "Here's the ball." "The dog will not hurt you." "Do you want a cracker?"
- Talk to the nonverbal child slowly, stressing key words such as nouns and verbs. Repeat them if the child does not seem to understand.
- If you cannot understand a word, repeat it back to the child in a relaxed way. Say, "Show me, Mary," if the child tries again and you still cannot understand her.
- Accept a child's attempt to say a word. If a child says "lellow," say, "Yes, the paint is yellow." Articulation will improve with age and observation of good speech models.
- Answer expressive *jargon* (groups of sounds without recognizable words) or jabbering with suitable statements such as "You're telling me," or "You don't say." Go along with the child's desire to put words together in a sentence.

- Play games in which the child copies sounds or words; make games fun. Stop before the child loses interest.
- Watch for the child's lead. If he is interested in some activity or object, talk about it in simple sentences, figure 13-7, "The kitty feels soft." "Pet the kitty." "Bobby's going down the slide."
- Make commands simple. "It's time to go inside, now." Use gestures with the words. "Put the toys in the box." (Indicate actions as you say the words.)
- Reward the child's imitations (whether verbal or nonverbal) with a smile or touch or words. Show that the effort is appreciated.

The next guidelines help develop speaking ability when dealing with the child who speaks in one-word phrases or simple sentences.

- Enlarge a child's one-word sentences into meaningful simple sentences. ("Ball" to "The ball bounces.")
- Use naming words to describe objects and actions. "The *red* ball is *round.*" "The dog wants to *lick* your *hand.*"

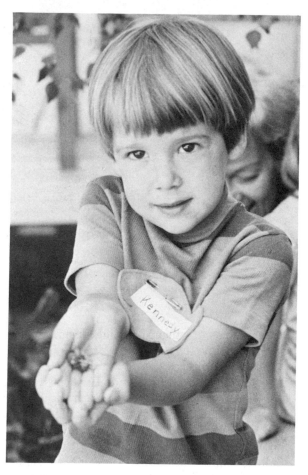

FIGURE 13-7 If the child is interested in some activity or object, talk about it with him.

- In your speech, use conjunctions (and, but, so, also, or) as well as possessives (mine, theirs, ours, Billy's, yours, his, hers), and negatives (is not, will not, do not, isn't, don't, won't, am not).
- Help the child talk about his feelings. "You're angry because he took your toy."
- Use previously learned words with new words. "The black *candy* is called *licorice*." "Your *dog* is a *poodle;* this dog is a *beagle*." "It's a kind of *hat* called a *baseball cap*."
- Ask simple questions which help the child to find out and discover while his interest

is high. "Where did you find that round rock?"
- Play labeling games with pictures and objects.
- Correct speech errors such as "wented" or "goed" by matter-of-factly saying the correct word in a sentence. "Yesterday you *went* to the store." (Omit any corrective tone of voice.) The child may answer by saying it the same as before, but you have modeled correct usage and in time it will be copied.
- Accept hesitant speech and stuttering in a patient, interested way. When a child is excited or under stress ideas may not develop into words properly.
- Wait patiently while a child tries to speak; silently hold eye contact. The thought may get lost, but if you're a good listener, and if you respond with interest to what is said, the child will try again.

When the child speaks in sentences and comes close to mature speech, the teacher should:

- Include appropriate classifications or categories in sentences to help children form concepts. "Dogs and cats are *animals*."
- Ask questions which help the child pinpoint identifying characteristics. "Does it have a tail?"
- Ask questions that help the child see what is alike and what is different.
- After modeling a sentence pattern in conversation, ask a simple question so the child can imitate the proper form while it is still fresh in his mind. "I think this lemon tastes sour." "How does the lemon taste to you?"
- Help the child keep ideas in order. What happened first? What happened next? What came last?
- State instructions clearly, building from one to two or three-part directions. "First wash your hands; then you can choose a cracker."
- Use prepositions in your speech. Say them with gestures. "Put the toy *on* the shelf." "Thank you. The blocks go *inside* the box."

(Use your hand to show position as you speak.)

- Use adjectives (big, little, bright, red, soft, etc.) and comparatives (more, less, lighter, heavier, shorter, tallest). "Tell me about the rubber doll." "Yes, this pink doll is bigger."
- Ask the child to take simple verbal messages to another staff member. "Tell Mrs. Brown it's time to fix the snack." Alert other staff members to the fact that you are trying to promote verbal memory and self-confidence.
- Help the child discover causes and effects. "Teacher, I'm afraid of bugs." "Why do bugs make you afraid, Billy?"
- Remember that what you say in response to the child helps him in many ways. Really listen. Answer every child if possible. When children talk at the same time, say "I want to hear each one." "Mary, please say it again." "John, you can tell us next."
- Give ownership to the ideas children contribute. "Yesterday Nancy told us . . ." "Kate's idea is. . . ."

SETTINGS FOR PREPLANNED SPEAKING ACTIVITIES

Speaking activities occur inside, outside, and when on the move. Preplanned activities are more successful when both children and teachers are comfortable, and when there are no distractions. Peers will be a valuable source of words and meanings.

Close attention should be given to the seating space between children. Lighting and heating in the room must also be considered. Soft textures and rugs add warmth and comfort. A half-circle seating arrangement, with the teacher in the center, provides a good view of both the teacher and what is to be seen.

Ease of viewing depends on eye level and seating arrangement. Whenever possible, the objects children are to look at should be at the child's eye level. Teachers often sit in child-sized chairs while conducting language arts experiences.

Screens, dividers, and bookcases can help to lessen distractions. Also, seating the children so they do not distract each other will give the activity a greater chance for success.

QUESTIONING SKILLS

A teacher's questions often prompt children to think. Questions can also help them see details they would otherwise have missed, figure 13-8. Sometimes questions help a child form relationships between objects and ideas; they may prompt the child to speak about both feelings and thoughts; they can lead the child to a new interest.

Skill in questioning is an important teaching ability. Questions asked by a teacher can often lead children to discovery.

FIGURE 13-8 "Are there any other shapes on the card that are round like a ball?"

The following example illustrates the teacher's role in stimulating the thought process that emerges from play. The teacher, who has created the climate for learning by supplying and arranging the equipment, sees a child playing with cars on ramps that he has constructed with blocks. She knows that if a car is placed on a slope made with blocks, the speed with which it descends and the distance it goes are affected by the slope and length of the ramp. She asks, "Johnny, why did this car go faster than that one?" She also introduces new words to his vocabulary — *slant, ramp, slow, faster, above, below, under, tall, smaller than* — and uses and elicits this vocabulary in conversation. (Danoff et al., 1977)

Teachers need to be sensitive to anxiety which may be present in some children. In past experiences, if a child's answers have been overcorrected, or if adults' questions are associated with punishment, teacher's questions can cause children to be silent and tense.

Also important in asking questions is the teacher's acceptance of the child's answers. Since each child answers a question based on his own experience, each child may give very different answers. The following conversation (observed at the San Jose City College Child Development Center) shows how a teacher handled an unexpected answer.

Teacher: (Conversation has centered around television sets.)
"Where could we go to buy a television set?"
Frank: "Macy's."
Chloe: "At a pear store."
Wanda: "The T.V. store."
Teacher: "Frank says Macy's sells television sets. Chloe thinks we could buy one at a "pear" store. Wanda thought at a T.V. store. "Maybe we could go to three places to buy one. Chloe, have you seen television sets at the 'pear' store?"
Chloe: "The pear store has lots of 'em."
Teacher: "You've been to a 'pear' store?"
Chloe: "Our T.V. broke, and we took it to the 'pair store."
Teacher: "The *repair* shop fixed my broken television set, too. Sets are for sale there sometimes."

The teacher's task is to keep the speech and answers coming, encouraging each child's expression of ideas.

Sometimes a question can be answered with a question. When a child says, "What does a rabbit eat?" the teacher might say, "How could we find out?" The teacher knows that a real experience is better than a quick answer.

When using questions, the level of difficulty should be recognized. Early childhood teachers can use carefully asked questions to find the child's level of understanding. Teachers try to help each child succeed in activities while offering a challenge at the same time. Even snack times can be a time to learn new language skills.

Some teachers are so intent on imparting information to children that they forget to assess the ways it may be assimilated. Thus answers to open-ended questions — "Can you tell me about . . . ?" "What do you think about . . . ?" — are often more revealing than answers to questions with a more specific focus. They can be followed by "Tell me more," "How do you explain that?" "Some people think that . . ." "What do you think?" Learning to ask questions that do not provide children with clues for the expected answer takes both verbal and facial control (Almy, 1975).

Teachers' questions can be classified into seven main types:

- Recall — asks child to remember information, names, words, and so forth.
- Convergent — asks child to compare or contrast similarities or differences, and seek relationships.
- Divergent — asks child to predict or theorize.
- Evaluation — asks child for a personal opinion or judgment, or asks child to explore feelings.
- Observation — asks child to watch or describe what he senses.
- Explanation — asks child to state cause and effect, reasons, and /or descriptions.
- Action — asks child to move body or perform physical task.

The way questions are phrased may produce short or longer answers. Questions using *what* or *where* usually receive one-word or word-phrase answers.

Do you? Did you? Can you? Will you? Have you? Would you? questions can be answered by *yes* or *no*. This type of question fits the level of the very young.

Questions which help a child compare or connect ideas may begin with:

> What would happen if . . . ?
> Which one is longer?
> How are these two alike?
> Why did you say these were different?
> What happened next?
> If it fell off the table, what would happen to it?

> Can you guess which one will be first?
> Could this ball fit inside this can?

The following are examples of questions which encourage problem solving or stimulative creative thought:

> If you had a handful of pennies, what would you buy?
> Tell me what you are going to do when you're big like your dad.
> Can you think of a way to open this coconut?
> How could we find out where this ant lives?

These questions can be answered by the more mature speakers. Through close listening and observing, the teacher can form questions which the child will want to answer.

SUMMARY

Each early childhood educational program is based on goals. Goals state the attitudes and abilities that a center wishes to develop in children. Planned activities and daily teacher-child conversations help the school reach its goals. Teachers plan for both group and individual needs.

Questions are asked by both children and teachers. By observing, listening, and interacting, teachers are better able to promote children's speaking abilities.

Learning Activities

- List five speaking area goals in your own order of priority.

- Interview a preschool teacher (or teachers). Ask the question, "If you could only do one thing to help young children's speaking ability, what would that be?"

- Observe a preschool group. What differences do you notice in the children's ability to solve problems with words? Cite specific examples.

• Observe a preschool classroom. Write down the teacher's questions (word for word). Using the seven question types from this unit, tell which question fits which category. Report your findings to the class.

Unit Review

A. Explain each of the following terms.
   1. structured activities
   2. possessives
   3. negatives
   4. prepositions
   5. comparatives

B. Answer the following questions related to speaking goals.
   1. How can the goals of a program be met?
   2. When children are interested in an object or happening, what should the teacher do in order for the children to learn while motivation is present?
   3. How can the environment around teacher-directed activities be made comfortable?
   4. Where should visual materials be placed?

C. Select the correct answer(s). Each item may have more than one correct answer.
   1. When a child says "wented,"
      a. correct him.
      b. ignore him.
      c. repeat his message correctly.
      d. have him practice "went."
   2. In daily conversations, the teacher should
      a. answer or respond to nonverbal messages.
      b. pair new word meanings with words the child already knows.
      c. ignore the child who yells at you in anger.
      d. accept stuttering and hesitant speech in a relaxed manner.
   3. If a child says "richlotti-gongo" to you,
      a. repeat it back if you can, hoping the child will show you what he wants to say.
      b. ignore it and wait until you understand the message.
      c. go along with the statement saying something like, "Really, you don't say."
      d. ask him to speak more clearly.
   4. In using questions with young children,
      a. suit the question to the child.
      b. always give him the answer.
      c. insist that he answers correctly.

       d. answer some of the children's questions with your own questions, when appropriate.

    5. Planned activities are based on

       a. goals only.

       b. children's current interests only.

       c. goals and children's interests.

       d. knowledge instead of attitudes.

D. Name three ways a teacher can give children confidence in their speaking abilities.

E. Select the appropriate teacher response to the children's comments.

Child	Teacher
1. "Dolly"	a. "Did the door hit you? And then what happened?"
2. "Where do this go?"	b. "Yes, they are."
3. "I fell down. The door hit me." (Child is unhurt.)	c. "They taste good; here's a carrot stick to try."
4. "Horses are big like cows."	d. "Where does the block go? The block goes on the top shelf."
5. "Dem er goodums."	e. "You can play with this dolly."
6. "That's a mouse, teacher."	f. "It has fur like a mouse; it's small like a mouse; but it's called a hamster."

F. Choose the question type from the four listed that matches each question, 1 through 8.

    Recall   Divergent   Convergent   Evaluative

    1. What would happen if we left this glass full of ice on the table?

    2. Will all the people who have socks and shoes which are the same color stand up?

    3. Who can tell me this puppet's name?

    4. If you had a dollar, how would you like to spend it?

    5. What do we need to make a birthday cake?

    6. Why did the basket fall over?

    7. Did the door open by itself?

    8. Who has the smallest cup?

References

Almy, Millie, *The Early Childhood Educator at Work*, New York: McGraw-Hill Book Co., 1975.

Danoff, Judith, Vicki Breitbart and Elinor Barr, *Open for Children*, New York: McGraw-Hill Book Co., 1977.

de Villiers, Peter A. and Jill G. de Villiers, *Early Language,* 3rd ed., Harvard University Press, 1982.

Hendrick, Joanne, *The Whole Child,* 3rd ed., Times Mirror/Mosby, 1984, Chap. 15.

Lundsteen, Sara W., *Children Learn to Communicate,* Prentice-Hall, Inc., 1976, Chap. 4.

Mayesky, Mary, et al., *Creative Activities for Young Children,* 2nd ed., Delmar Publishers, Albany, NY, pp. 2–10.

Stewig, John Warren, *Teaching Language Arts in Early Childhood,* Holt, Rinehart and Winston, 1982.

Van Allen, Roach and Claryce Allen, *Language Experience Activities,* 2nd ed., Houghton Mifflin Co., 1982.

Yawkey, Thomas, et al., *Language Arts and the Young Child,* F. E. Peacock Publishers, Inc., 1981.

Unit 14
Speech in Play and Routines

OBJECTIVES

After studying this unit you should be able to

- describe factors which encourage the development of speaking abilities.

- explain the role of the teacher in dramatic play.

- name activities or describe techniques which promote speaking.

A center should be a place full of interesting and active things for a child to do with other children and teachers, figure 14-1. Speech flows best when a child is relaxed rather than pressured or tense.

PLAY

Play itself produces much child-to-child conversation. Some types of play promote talking more than others. Quiet activities such as painting or working puzzles may tend to limit speech while the child is deeply absorbed.

Teachers plan opportunities for children to play by themselves and with others in small and large groups. Play with another child or a small group almost always requires children to speak. Very young children may play together without speaking in a nonverbal, imitative manner, but as they grow older they use more words. The interaction with other children offers increasing opportunities to grow in speaking ability.

Early in life, children act out and repeat the words and actions of others. During preschool years, this is often called *dramatic play,* and the staffs in early childhood centers plan and

prepare for it. This type of play holds many learning opportunities. It helps the child to:

- develop conversational skills and the ability to express his ideas in words.
- understand the feelings, roles, or work of others.
- connect actions with words. Actions and words go hand-in-hand in dramatic play.
- develop vocabulary.
- develop creativity. The child imagines and acts, making things up as play goes on.
- engage in social interaction with other children, figure 14-2.
- cope with life, sometimes through acting out troubling situations, thus giving an outlet for emotion. Almost every doll in an early childhood center gets a spanking periodically when children play house.
- assume leadership and group-participant roles.

Let's pretend is an enjoyable play activity that helps speech growth. When playing house, the child can start out as the grandfather and end up as the baby or the family dog. Much time and effort is devoted to this type of play in

FIGURE 14-1 When they finish their cut-paper flowers, some of the children will want to talk about their creations.

childhood. The child engages in this type of activity often, and has the ability to slide easily from the real world into make-believe.

Rich home and school experiences (going places and doing things) serve as building blocks for dramatic play. One would have a difficult time playing "restaurant" or "wedding" if there had been no previous experience with either.

Early childhood centers can provide activities that promote dramatic play.

- Field trips
- Visitors and guest speakers
- Books
- Pictures and discussions
- Films, filmstrips, and slides
- Preparation of kits, equipment, and settings for dramatic play

DRAMATIC PLAY SETTINGS

A playhouse area with a child-sized stove, refrigerator, table, and chairs encourages dramatic play. An old boat, a service station pump, and a telephone booth are examples of other pieces of equipment that children enjoy using in their play.

Furniture found at early childhood centers can be moved into room arrangements that suggest a bus, a house, a tunnel, or a store. Large cardboard boxes may become a variety of different props with, or without, word labels. Large paper bags, ropes, blankets, and discarded work clothes or dress-up clothing, figure 14-3, also stimulate the child to pretend. Items for dramatic play can be obtained from shops, secondhand stores, flea market sales, garage sales, and other sources.

DRAMATIC PLAY KITS

Items that go together and suggest the same type of play can be boxed together, ready for use. A shoeshine kit complete with cans of natural shoe polish, a soft cloth, a shoe brush, play money, a newspaper, or a magazine is very

FIGURE 14-2 Dramatic play promotes social interaction.

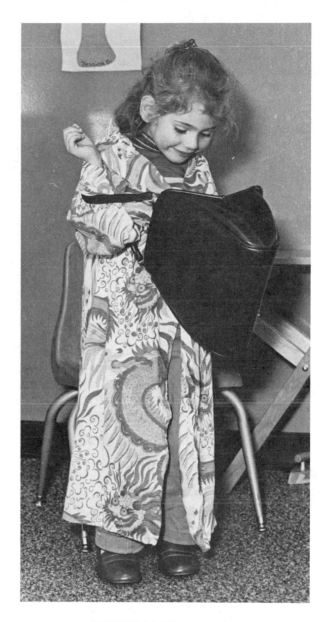

FIGURE 14-3 Dress-up time

popular. Other ideas for kits to be used in dramatic play are listed.

Post office. Large index cards, stamp pads, stampers, crayons or pencils, stamps (Christmas or wildlife seals), shoe box with slot cut in front and name clearly printed on. Old shoulder bag purses for mailbags, and men's shirts.

Cleaning set. Several brooms, mops, sponge mops, dust cloths, sponges, and toweling for windows.

Tea party. Set of cups and saucers, plastic pitchers, napkins, vase, tablecloth, plastic spoons, small grocery containers like cereal boxes, and so on.

Doctor. Stethoscope, medicine bottles, adhesive tape, cotton balls, armband with a red cross on it, bag to carry, paper hospital gowns, white shirt.

Teacher. Notebooks, pencils, plastic glasses, chalk, book about the first day in kindergarten.

Santa Claus. Red jacket and hat, beard that ties behind ears, large sack or pillowcase, assorted toys, reindeer horn hats, flashlight.

Washing tiny babies. Large pieces of toweling to cover the table, several tiny dolls, some sets of toy bathroom furniture, individual plastic pitchers or bowls with soapy water (can be made from plastic bleach bottles), small pieces of toweling, cotton balls, individual talcum cans, doll clothes, clothesline, clothespins.

Supermarket. Cash register, play money, paper pads and pencils or crayons, punchers, paper sacks, empty food cartons, wax fruit.

Beauty parlor. Plastic brushes, combs, cotton balls, powder, scarves, colored water in nail polish bottles, old hair dryer (no plug), curlers, water spray bottle, hairpins, mirror.

Service station. Tire pump, pliers, cans, sponges, and bucket; short length of hose and cylinder (for gas pump); hat, squirt bottle, paper towels, paper and pencil, sign "gas for sale."

Fishing. Hats, bamboo lengths (about 3 feet) with string and magnet at the end, a basin, small metal objects such as paper clips for the fish. Fish shapes can also be cut out and a paper clip attached to each (for the magnet).

More kits can be made for the following:

T.V. repair person	Mail carrier
Baker	Fire fighter
Painter	Car wash
Picnic	Pilot
Restaurant	Circus
Wedding	Birthday
Police officer	Astronaut

TEACHER'S ROLE IN DRAMATIC PLAY

Dramatic play is child-directed instead of teacher-directed. It comes from the child's imagination, with actions to accompany the child's thoughts.

Teachers can motivate a type of dramatic play before they withdraw to remain in the background. They are watchful and sometimes suggest a new direction, but then allow the flow of play to be decided by the children. Their close presence and words can stop or change behavior when the situation becomes unsafe or gets out of hand. If things go smoothly, the ideas, words, and dramatic play actions are those of the children.

Periodic suggestions by the teacher and introduction of materials may extend and enrich play. Care is taken not to dominate but rather to be available as a friendly resource.

COSTUMES

Costumes and clothing props let a child step into a character quickly. Strong, sturdy, child-manageable ties and snaps increase self-help. Elastic waistbands slip on and off with ease. Clothing that is cut down to size (so it doesn't drag) can be worn for a longer time. Items that children enjoy are listed.

- Hats of all types, figure 14-4
- Shoes, boots, slippers
- Uniforms
- Accessories, such as ties, scarves, purses, old jewelry, aprons, badges, key rings
- Outgrown fur jackets, soft fabrics and fancy fabric clothing
- Wigs
- Work clothes

DAILY ROUTINES

Periods for talking are usually included in the program of an early childhood center. Roll call at the start of the day is used to encourage speaking. Snack and lunch periods are set up to promote pleasant conversation while eating, figure 14-5.

Activities are planned and structured to provide for as much child talk as possible. One of the most common pastimes is Show and Tell.

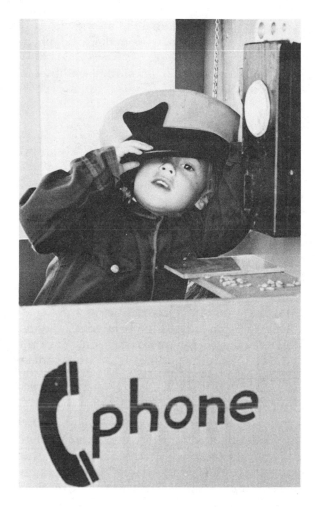

FIGURE 14-4 The center should provide the necessary equipment for dramatic play.

FIGURE 14-5 Pleasant, relaxed conversation can take place at meal times.

This game encourages children to talk about their special interests in front of others. The child brings something from home or shares something made or accomplished at school. Here are some helpful hints for conducting Show and Tell.

- Encourage, don't force the child to speak. If he doesn't want to talk, he can just show what he brought.
- Let the child stand or sit near the teacher. A friendly arm around the shoulders may help.

- Stimulate the other children to ask the child questions. "Mark, your eyes tell me you want to know more about Gustavos' marbles."
- Limit the time for overtalkative children by using an egg timer.
- Be careful the activity does not last too long or the children will become bored.
- Thank each child for his participation.
- Try something new such as:
  a. Display all articles and have the group guess who brought what.
  b. Have children swap what they have brought so they can talk about each other's items.
  c. Bring in a surprise item to share with the children.
  d. Make a caption for each item and display it on a table (for example, Betty's Green Rock).
  e. Have the child hide the object behind his back while describing it to the others. Then the other children guess what the object is.

Show and Tell items are usually kept out of reach to prevent the loss of a valued or favorite toy. Some children think they have to bring an item every day. If desired, the teacher can name "brown eyes" days or "blue eyes" days or "turn" days. The purpose of Show and Tell is to help children develop vocabulary, responsibility, and the ability to speak in front of others. It is helpful to make this purpose known to parents.

Suggestions which can promote more child speech in daily programs are listed.

- Have children give verbal messages or directions to other children often. "Petey, please show Flynn our dustpan and hand-broom. Tell him how we empty it." (Then follow through by thanking him.)
- Let children describe daily projects. "Danielle, tell us about your rocketship. I know you worked hard making it. What did you do first?"
- Relate present ideas and happenings to the children's past when possible. "Shane had a new puppy at his house, too. Did your puppy cry at night? What did you do to help it stop? Kathy has a new puppy who cries at night."
- Promote child explanations. "Who can tell us what happens after we finish our lunch?"
- Promote teacher-child conversations where the teacher records children's words on artwork, constructions, or any happenings or project.
- Periodically make "pin on" badges like the ones shown in figure 14-6.
- Play "explaining games" by setting up a group of related items on a table. The game is to explain how one can use the items.
  Example:
  Group 1.   Mirror, comb, brush, washcloth, soap, basin of water.
  Group 2.   Shoes, white shoe polish, new shoelaces.
  Group 3.   Nuts, nutcracker, bowl.
  Encourage child volunteers to explain and demonstrate by facing the group from the other side of the table. Other possibilities: peeling an orange, making a sandwich with two spreads, or how to make a telephone call.
- Play games which encourage children to speak.

GAMES

The following games promote children's expression of ideas.

Suitcase Game

Teacher: I'm going on a vacation trip. I'm putting suntan oil in my suitcase. What will you put in your suitcase?
Child: A swimming suit.
Child: Candy.

Grocery Store Game

Have a bag handy with lots of grocery items. Pull one out yourself and describe it. Have the children take turns pulling out an item and describing it.

Letter Game

Provide a large bag of letters. Pull one letter out. Talk about a letter you are going to send to a child in the group. "I'm going to give this pretend letter to Frankie and tell him about my new car," or "I want to send this thank you card to Janelle because she always helps me when I ask for clean-up helpers. Who would like to pull out a letter from this bag and tell us who they would like to send it to?"

Guess What's in the Box Game

Collect small boxes with lids. Put small items inside, such as paper clips, erasers, bottle top, plastic toys, a leaf, a flower, etc. Have a child choose a box, guess its contents, open it, and talk about what is in the box.

Talk About a Friend Game

Choose a child out of the group to stand beside you. Describe three of the child's charac-

FIGURE 14-6 Pin-on badges

teristics. Example: red shoes, big smile, one hand in pocket. Ask who would like to choose a friend and tell three things about the friend.

Guessing Picture Messages

Duplicate the drawings shown in figure 14-7 on large newprint. Help the children translate the messages into words.

The Mystery Bag

An activity children enjoy in small groups is called the mystery bag. The teacher collects a series of common objects. Turning away from the group, the teacher puts one of the objects in another bag. The game starts when a child reaches in the second bag and describes the object, but does not look at it. It is then pulled out of the bag and discussed. "What can we do with it? What is it called? It's the same color as what

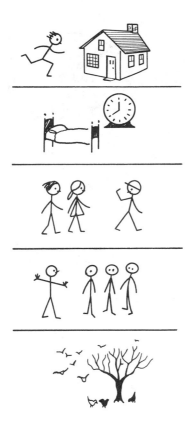

FIGURE 14-7 Guessing picture messages *(Reprinted with permission of the publishers. Allen Raymond, Inc., Darien, CT 06820. EARLY YEARS Magazine, January, 1973.)*

else in the room?" The group should be small since it is hard for a young child to wait for a turn. Examples of objects which could be used — rock, comb, orange, pancake turner, feather, plastic cup, sponge, hole punch, flower, toy animal, whistle.

The Christmas Game
Courtesy of Marian San Fillipo

For this activity, the teacher first constructs a Christmas tree using pellon and color felt pens. Then, individual pellon ornaments are outlined in various shapes (snowman, bell, star, candy canes, balls) and are colored using felt pens. The teacher then prints "directions" on the orna-

ments using a permanent ink pen, after which the ornaments are cut out and placed in a grab bag or box. The directions might read:

- Dance back to your seat.
- Sing "Jingle Bells."
- Say, "Merry Christmas, everyone."
- Gallup back to your seat.
- Wave good-bye as you walk back to your seat.
- Sing, "We Wish You a Merry Christmas."
- Fly like a bird back to your seat.
- Pop like popcorn back to your seat.
- Bounce like a ball back to your seat.
- Sing, "Rudolph The Red-nosed Reindeer."
- Walk backwards to your seat.
- Sing your favorite Christmas carol.
- Pat your head and rub your tummy.
- Do the "Wiggle Webble."
- Turn yourself into a candy cane.
- Sing "Frosty the Snowman."
- Hop back to your seat.

One at a time, each child comes up and chooses an ornament out of the bag (or box). The teacher then reads the directions to the child secretly. The child then places his or her ornament on the tree and does what the ornament said to do. If the child chooses a song that he or she doesn't know, then a friend may be invited to help lead the song, or the teacher may lead the song.

Parts-of-the-Body Guessing Game
I can see you with my _____(eyes).
I can smell you with my _____(nose).
I can chew with my _____(teeth).
I can hear with my _____(ears).
I can clap with my _____(hands).
I walk on my _____(feet).
I put food in my _____(mouth).
This is not my nose, it's my _____. (point to ears)
This is not my eye, it's my _____. (point to nose)

This is not my mouth, it's my _____. (point to eye)

Teacher's Role

Instead of taking the center stage speaking role in planned activities, a teacher analyzes each group activity for places where children may want to speak.

LEADING ACTIVITIES

A child can be chosen to lead others in activities if he is familiar with the routines and activities. The child can alert the others by saying the right words or calling out the names of the children who need a cup or a cookie. One or more children can be in front leading songs or finger plays. (Finger plays will be discussed in the next unit.) Often, individual children can be chosen as the speaker, or speakers, to direct routines with words. A teacher can instruct one child to tell another child something:

"Tell Billy when you want him to pass the wastebasket," or "If you're through, ask Georgette if she wants a turn."

A watchful teacher encourages the children to speak in many ways. The child tends to speak more if his speech is given attention, and if the child is rewarded with a smile and an answer. It is helpful during group times to point out that the teacher and the other children want to hear what everyone says and, because of this, children should take turns in speaking.

SUMMARY

When there is a relaxed atmosphere with interested teachers and many activities, more talking takes place. Playing with others helps vocabulary development and language acquisition in settings where children interact in real and make-believe situations.

The teacher's role in dramatic play is to set the stage but remain in the background so the children can do it on their own. Dramatic play settings and kits are made available, and some are boxed and collected by the teacher.

Part of a teacher's work is to encourage children to talk, to give children opportunities to lead speaking activities, and to ensure that children are talked with and not talked at.

Learning Activities

- Visit a center and record all instances of dramatic play. Note all equipment that seems to promote speaking.

- With a classmate, select one of the dramatic play kit ideas which did not suggest items to be found in the kit. List items you feel would be safe and would promote dramatic play.

- Role play "playing house" with some classmates: assign grandmother, mother, father, brother, sister, baby, family dog, or other family roles.
  Pretend you are having breakfast or dinner; traveling in the car going on vacation; or are in other family situations, such as father or mother telling the family about a raise in pay or a new job. Try a bedtime situation. Did classmates show how the family members cope with life? If not, have the group discuss how young children might do this in the same role-playing situation.

- Conduct a Show and Tell time with a group of young children.

• Observe a full morning program in a center. List the activities or routines in which there was active speaking by most of the children.

Unit Review

A. Define dramatic play.

B. Choose the factors which can help young children develop speaking abilities.
   1. Equipment
   2. Staff members
   3. Parents
   4. Making a child ask correctly for what he wants
   5. A relaxed atmosphere
   6. Interesting happenings to talk about
   7. Lack of play with other children
   8. Asking a child if he wants to tell something
   9. A child's need or desire
   10. A teacher's ignoring the child's nonverbal communication
   11. Daily speaking routines
   12. Teacher attention to speech
   13. Teacher rewarding children's speech
   14. Planned speaking activities

C. Answer the following questions.
   1. What is a dramatic play kit?
   2. Name some of the things a teacher does *not* want to happen during Show and Tell time. (Example: One child talking too long).

D. Select the terms that best define the teacher's role in dramatic play.
   1. Interactor
   2. Background observer
   3. Provider of settings
   4. Provider of props
   5. Redirector of unsafe play
   6. Active participant
   7. Suggestor of ideas during play
   8. Provider of many words
   9. Gatherer of dramatic play items

E. Write a short paragraph which finishes the following.
   The reason some teachers do not actively plan programs with children leading activities up front is . . .

F. In the following description of calling the roll, identify those parts that might make a child feel pressured and tense rather than relaxed. Discuss the attitude of the teacher as well.

"Good morning, children. Everyone say, 'Good Morning, Mrs. Brown.' That's good. Bonnie, you didn't say it. You were playing with your hair ribbon. Say it now, Bonnie.

I'm going to say everyone's name. When I say your name I want you all to say, 'I'm here, Mrs. Brown.' Susie Smith. 'I'm here, Mrs. Brown.' Speak louder, Susie, we can't hear you. Brett Porter. Not 'I'm present,' Brett, say 'I'm here, Mrs. Brown.' David Martinez. David Martinez. Answer please, David. David Martinez. David, you must answer when I call your name! Andy Smith. No, Andy, say 'I'm here, Mrs. Brown,' not 'I'm here' and that's all.

I don't know what's the matter with all of you; you did it right yesterday. We're going to stay here until we all do it the right way. Dana Collins. I can't understand what you said, Dana; say it again. Mark Jefferson. Mark, that's very good, you said it the right way. Chris Peters. No, it's not time to talk to Ronnie now; it's time to speak up. What are you supposed to say, children? I give up, you'll never learn. Let's all go outside now and work out all of our wiggles."

References

Beaty, Janice J., *Skills for Preschool Teachers*, 2nd ed., Charles E. Merrill Publishing Co., 1984, Chap. 6.

Croft, Doreen and Robert Hess, *An Activities Handbook for Teachers of Young Children*, Houghton Mifflin, 1975.

Lorton, Mary, *Workjobs: Activity-Centered Learning for Early Childhood Education*, Addison-Wesley, 1972.

Tiedt, Sidney and Iris Tiedt, *Language Arts Activities for the Classroom*, Penguin, 1971.

Suggested Readings

Hendrick, Joanne, *Total Learning*, C. V. Mosby Co., 1980, pp. 100, 152–53, 198–99.

Maxim, George W., *The Very Young Child*, Wadsworth Publishing Co., 1980, pp. 46–47, 424–426.

Unit 15
Group Times

OBJECTIVES

After studying this unit you should be able to

- describe circle and group time speaking activities.

- perform a finger play with children.

- discuss ways to promote child involvement in simple plays, chants, and circle times.

The activities in this unit give children many speaking opportunities, and as you interact with children you know they will talk about most of their experiences and ideas — if these things are interesting to them. You should also realize that it is difficult to sort activities into just listening or just speaking as they often overlap. Children involved in the activities have the opportunity to imitate speech, to use creative speech, and to express their own ideas and feelings.

GROUPS

Circle and group times are chances for children to develop understanding about themselves as group members. They enjoy language together by using familiar songs, favorite finger plays, chants, and a wide variety of activities. Children gain self-confidence, feelings of personal worth, and group spirit, figure 15-1.

Language activities add sparkle and liveliness to circle times. This is a list of descriptive words that help make a successful group experience.

Descriptives

active
   child participation with motor and speech involvement

enthusiastic
   presented with teacher's obvious commitment showing on face and in manner

FIGURE 15-1 Group time — together time *(From Machado and Meyer,* Early Childhood Practicum Guide, *Copyright 1984 by Delmar Publishers Inc.)*

prepared

all necessary materials at teacher's finger-tips, with smooth verbal presentations

accepting

teacher is open to children's ideas and feelings; appreciative of children's contributions

appropriate

suits particular group

clearly stated concepts

purposeful clarification of concepts which arise

familiar

previously learned and enjoyed material is presented

novel

new ideas and material is presented

relaxed

nonpressuring and nonthreatening

sharing

taking turns

A circle (or groups in semicircles) is begun by capturing group attention. A signal or daily routine can be used. To make sure all children are focused, a short silence (pause) adds a feeling of anticipation and expectation.

Occasionally varying gathering signals keeps one signal from becoming old hat. Flicking lights, a xylophone ripple, a tap on a musical triangle, an attention-getting record, a puppet announcing a group activity, or placing reminder stickers on children's hands related to the activities theme are but a few alternatives.

Opening activities which recognize each individual child help to build group spirit. It is as if the recognition says to each child "You're an important person; we're happy to have you with us." They start the group out on the right note.

The following activities are circle time starters, attention getters, socializers, and wiggle removers.

CIRCLE TIME

I've just come in from outside.
I'm tired as can be.
I'll cross my legs

And fold my hands,
And close my eyes so they can't see.
I WILL NOT MOVE.
My head won't move.
My toes are still.
I'll put my hands on my chin,
And when it's quiet, we'll begin!

WIGGLES

I'll wiggle my fingers,
And wiggle my toes.
I'll wiggle my arms
And wiggle my nose.

And now that all the wiggle's out,
We'll listen to what circle's about.

HANDSHAKE
(Chant or Sing)

Good morning, good morning, good morning to
*   you.*
Good morning, good morning, and how do you
*   do?*
Shake hands, shake hands with someone near
*   you.*
Shake hands, shake hands the other side too.

CLAPPING START

Turn around and face the wall. Clap, Clap, Clap.
Down upon your knees now fall. Clap, Clap,
*   Clap.*
Up again and turn around. Clap, Clap, Clap.
Turn around and then sit down. Clap, Clap,
*   Clap.*
Not a sound.

WHERE ARE YOUR _____?

Where are your eyes? Show me eyes that see.
Where are your eyes? Shut them quietly.
Where is your nose? Show me your nose that
*   blows.*
Where is your nose? Show me your nose and
*   wiggle it so.*
Where is your mouth? Open it wide.

Where is your mouth? With teeth inside.
Smile — Smile — Smile.

I LIKE YOU
(Chant or Sing)

I like you.
There's no doubt about it.
I like you.
There's no doubt abut it.
I am your good friend.

You like me.
There's no doubt about it.
You like me.
There's no doubt about it.
You are my good friend.
There's my friend child's name , and my friend
*   child's name*
*   (Continue around circle).*

THE MORE WE GET TOGETHER
(Chant or Sing)

The more we get together, together, together,
The more we get together, the happier we'll be.
Because (child's name) friend, is (child's name
*   sitting beside) friend, and repeat child's name*
*   is next child's name friend. (Around the cir-*
*   cle).*
Yes, the more we get together, the happier we'll
*   be.*

OH HERE WE ARE TOGETHER
(Chant or Sing)

Oh here we are together, together, together,
Oh here we are together
At (insert school name) Preschool
There's child's name and child's name, and
*   (names of all children)*
Oh here we are together to have a good day.

WE'RE WAITING
(Circle Starter)

We're waiting, we're waiting, we're waiting for
*   (child's name)*

(Repeat until group's formed.)
We're here, because we're here, because we're here,
*   because we're here.*
And my name is _____, and my name
*   is _____. (Around the circle).*

HELLO

Hello child's name. Hello, Hello, Hello.
Shake my hand and around we'll go.
Hello _____. Hello, Hello, Hello.
Shake my hand and around we'll go.
(Teacher starts; children continue around the
*   circle chanting until all are recognized.)*

SECRET

I've got something in my pocket
That belongs across my face.
I keep it very close at hand
In a most convenient place.
I know you couldn't guess it
If you guessed a long, long while.
So I'll take it out and put it on
It's a great big friendly SMILE!

WILL YOU BE A FRIEND OF MINE?

Will you be a friend of mine?
Friend of mine, friend of mine?
Will you be a friend of mine?
Will you? Will you? Will you?

Will you shake my hand every time?
Every time? Every time?
Shake and be a friend of mine
Will you? Will you? Will you?

Shake to the left,
Shake to the right,
Now shake hands with yourself.
What a funny sight!

YOU'RE MY FRIEND

You're my friend.
There's no doubt about it.
You're my friend.

There's no doubt about it.
You and I are friends.

For child's name friend is child's name friend.
And child's name friend is child's name friend.
(Go around circle, filling in each child's name
  in order.)
We are all good friends.

TO LONDON TOWN

Which is the way to London Town
To see the king in his golden crown?

One foot up and one foot down.
That's the way to London Town.

Which is the way to London Town
To see the queen in her silken gown?

Left! Right! Left! Right! Up and down,
Soon you'll be in London Town!

EVERYBODY DO THIS

Refrain:
Everybody do this, do this, do this.
Everybody do this just like me.

Actions:
  Open and close fists
  Roll fists around
  Touch elbows
  Spider fingers
  Pat head, rub tummy
  Wink
  Wave hand good-by
  (Children create others)

WHO'S LISTENING?
(To the tune of Kumbaya)

_____(child's name)'s listening now,
  Kumbaya, _____'s *listening now,*
  Kumbaya.
(Repeat first line.)
Oh, Oh, Kumbaya.
(Continue around group mentioning all chil-
  dren's names.)

PEASE PORRIDGE GROUP

Pease porridge hot,
(Slap knees, clap hands together, push hands
  in air towards leader)
Pease porridge cold,
(Repeat)
Pease porridge in the pot
(Slap knees, clap hands together, push right
  hand forward in air, clap, then push left hand
  in air, clap)
Nine days old.
(clap, clap, clap)
Some like it hot,
(Repeat as above)
Some like it cold,
Some like it in the pot,
Nine days old.

CIRCLE ACTIVITIES

A circle group keeps its lively enthusiasm and
social enjoyment when well planned. Activities
which follow involve both language and coordinated physical movement.

PASSING GAME
Have children arranged in a circle. Pass a small
object around the circle. Start by passing it
in front of the children, then behind, then
overhead, and then between the legs. Directions can be changed upon command of the
teacher, such as "pass it to your left, pass it
to your right," and so on. Ask children for
suggestions for other ways to pass the object.

TEDDY BEAR CIRCLE PASS
(Have bear in bag behind leader)

Love somebody, yes, I do.
Love somebody, yes, I do.
Love somebody, yes, I do.
Love somebody, but I won't tell who
(Shake head sideways).
Love somebody, yes, I do.
Love somebody, yes, I do.

Love somebody, yes, I do.
Now I'll show (him/her) to you!
Here's a hug — Pass it on.
(Group continues to chant as each child hugs and hands Teddy to next child.) When Teddy returns to leader, last verse is repeated, ending with:
"Now back in the bag our hugs are through!"
(Substituted for last line.)

BALL ROLLING CIRCLE

The ball will roll across our circle.
Touch toes with your neighbors.
Here comes the ball, Susie. "I roll the ball to Susie."
(Teacher says: "Susie roll the ball across the circle and say your friend's name")
"I roll the ball to _____."

NAME GAME

"_____ wore her _____, _____, _____."
(Fill in with clothing particulars like brown shoes, red sweater, etc.)
Repeat first line.
"All day at school".
(When the chant gets going, ask children to fill in blanks with what a particular child is wearing.)

courtesy of MAGIC MOMENTS
P.O. Box 53635
San Jose, CA 95153

ECHO GAME

"Echo me, echo me, echo me do
Echo my sound and my movement too."
(Teacher) *"Meow, meow,* (Teacher pretends to lick her arm.)
What am I? Right a cat".
"Echo me, echo me, echo me do
Echo my sound, and my movement too.

Amy, can you be an animal, and make its sound?"

courtesy of MAGIC MOMENTS
P.O. Box 53635
San Jose, CA 95153

OVER THE MOUNTAN
(to the tune The Bear Went Over the Mountain)

"_____ (child's name) went over the mountain".
Repeat.
Repeat.
"To see what he could see".

"_____, what did you see?"

"_____ saw a _____. (child's answer)"
Repeat.
Repeat.

"Pick a friend, _____ (child's name").
Repeat with new child's name.

courtesy of MAGIC MOMENTS
P.O. Box 53635
San Jose, CA 95153

TURNS AT GROUP TIMES

The following are helpful teacher statements:

- "We take turns talking at group time. It's Monica's turn now."
- "Barry's turn to talk so everyone else will listen."
- "Listen to Bonnie. Bonnie's lips are moving, and ours are resting."
- "Remember our group time rule? Just one person talks at a time."
- "I can see you really want to say something Jason, but you're waiting for your turn. Thank you, Jason."

CLOSING GROUP ACTIVITIES

Exciting circles sometimes need quiet settling closers. The "wind-downers" help excited children prepare for the change to another activity or play.

UP AND DOWN

Up and down
Up and down
Clap your hands and turn around.
Up and down
Up and down
Clap your hands and sit down.

RAG DOLL

I'm just a limp rag doll
My arms are limp
My legs are limp
My head is limp
I'm just a limp rag doll.

UP, DOWN, AND REST

Up and down
Up and down
Round, round, round.
Up and down.
I stretch, I stretch, I yawn.
I rest and then I start again.

Up and down, etc.
(2nd time — I rest and I rest)

TRANSITIONS

Disbanding a circle or group at an activity's ending calls for a planned approach. You will need to excuse a few at a time, if the group is of any size. When carpet squares are to be picked up and stacked, or small chairs returned to tables, a reminder is in order. "When you hear your name, pick up your rug square, carry it to the stack. Then you're ready to walk to . . . . ."

Additional Transitions

A fun way to dismiss the children is by saying " _____(child's name) be nimble, _____ be quick, _____jump over the candlestick". (Children clap for the child who jumps over a plastic candleholder and unlit candle.)

Courtesy of Thelma Alaniz
Santa Clara County Headstart

Make a tickler from a piece of three foot doweling and yarn. Say: "Close your eyes. When you feel a tickle on your head, it's time to stand and walk carefully through your friends to the . . . ."

Coutesy of Diane Ferry
Evergreen Child Development Center

Transitory statements which relate to the just-completed activity work well "Crawl like Crictor the Boa Constrictor to the block center," or "Let the wind blow you to the water table like it blew in the little tree."

Some statements that are helpful in moving a group of children in an orderly fashion are listed here. Many identify language concepts and serve a dual purpose.

- "Everyone with brown shoes stand up. Now it's time to . . ."
- "When I see your face I'll know you want to know what we are going to do next. Carrie and Clyde, I see your faces. Please find . . ."
- "If your favorite sandwich is peanut butter and jelly (ham, cheese, tuna, etc.) raise your hand. If your hand is up, please tiptoe to the . . ."
- "Richie is the engine on a slow, slow train. Richie, chug chug slowly to the . . ." "Darlene is the coal car on a slow, slow train, . . ." etc. (The last child is naturally the caboose.)

CHANTS AND CHORUSES

Throughout history, rhythmic chants and choruses have been used in group rituals and ceremonies. The individuals in the group gained a group identity as a result of their participation.

Natural enjoyment of rhythmic word patterns can be seen in a child's involvement in group language chants. Child and teacher can also playfully take part in call and response during the preschool day. "I made it, I made it," the child says. "I see it, I see it," the teacher answers, picking up the child's rhythm.

This verbal play is common. Sounds in the community and schoolyard can be brought to the children's attention by teachers who notice them and make comments.

Urban sounds are sometimes syncopated and rhythmical, such as the fire siren, people walking on sidewalks, jack hammers or nailing in nails. These are rhythms that children imitate verbally and that adults can point out to children. (Weir, Eggleston, 1975)

Chants and choruses are mimicked or sound and word patterns that have regularity and predictability are imitated. Choruses usually involve a back and forth (one individual alternating with another) conversation and involve the rise and fall of accented sounds or syllables.

Children need the teacher's examples and directions, such as, "When it's your turn, I'll point to you," or "Let's say it together," before they can perform the patterns on their own. Chants printed on charts with simple illustrations can enhance chanting and chorus times and tie the oral words to written ones.

The chants that follow are tried and true favorites.

THE DUKE OF YORK

Oh, the Duke of York
Had forty thousand men,

They marched up the hill,
And they marched down again.

And when you're up, you're up!
And when you're down, you're down
And when you're half-way-in-between
You're neither up nor down.

KNICKERBOCKER KNOCKABOUT

Knickerbocker Knockabout
Sausages and sauerkraut
Run! Run! Run! The hogs are out!
Knickerbocker Knockabout.

IT'S RAINING; IT'S POURING

It's raining, it's pouring.
The old man is snoring.
He went to bed and he bumped his head
And he couldn't get up in the morning.
Rain, rain go away — come again some
*   other day.*

MISS MARY MACK

Miss Mary Mack, Mack, Mack
All dressed in black, black, black
With silver buttons, buttons, buttons
All down her back, back, back.

She asked her mother, mother, mother
For fifteen cents, cents, cents
To see the elephants, elephants, elephants
Jump the fence, fence, fence.

They jumped so high, high, high
They touched the sky, sky, sky
And never came back, back, back
'Til the fourth of July, ly, ly.

July can't walk, walk, walk
July can't talk, talk, talk
July can't eat, eat, eat
With a knife and fork, fork, fork.

She went upstairs, stairs, stairs
To say her prayers, prayers, prayers
She made her bed, bed, bed
She hit her head, head, head
On a piece of corn bread, bread, bread.

Now she's asleep, sleep, sleep
She's snoring deep, deep, deep
No more to play, play, play
Until Friday, day, day
What can I say, say, say
Except hurray, ray, ray!

PANCAKE

Mix a pancake.
Stir a pancake.
Pop it in the pan.
Fry a pancake.
Toss a pancake.
Catch it if you can.

THE BIG CLOCK

Slowly ticks the big clock

Chorus:
Tick-tock, tick-tock
(repeat twice)

But the Cuckoo clock ticks double quick

Chorus:
Tick-a-tock-a, tick-a-tock-a
Tick-a-tock-a, tick!

LITTLE BROWN RABBIT

Little brown rabbit went hoppity-hop,

All:
Hoppity-hop, hoppity-hop!

Into a garden without any stop,

All:
Hoppity-hop, hoppity-hop!

He ate for his supper a fresh carrot top,

All:
Hoppity-hop, hoppity-hop!

Then home went the rabbit without any stop,

All:
Hoppity-hop, hoppity-hop!

WHO STOLE THE COOKIES FROM THE COOKIE JAR?

All: Who stole the cookies from the cookie jar?
All: (child's or teacher's name) stole the cookies from the cookie jar. (Teacher points to different child for each verse.)
Named person: Who me?
All: Yes you.
Named person: Couldn't be.
All: Then who?
Named person: (child or teacher) stole the cookies from the cookie jar.
Newly named person: Who me? (etc.)

THE HOUSE THAT JACK BUILT

Chorus: "the house that Jack built"

This is the malt
That lay in

Chorus: the house that Jack built.

This is the rat,
That ate the malt
That lay in

Chorus: the house that Jack built.

This is the cat,
That killed the rat,
That ate the malt
That lay in

Chorus: the house that Jack built.

This is the dog
That worried the cat,
That killed the rat,
That ate the malt
That lay in

Chorus: the house that Jack built.

This is the cow with the crumpled horn,
That tossed the dog,
That worried the cat,
That killed the rat,
That ate the malt
That lay in

Chorus: the house that Jack built.

This is the maiden all forlorn,
That milked the cow with the crumpled horn,
That tossed the dog,
That worried the cat,
That killed the rat,
That ate the malt,
That lay in

Chorus: the house that Jack built.

Using Accessories
LITTLE THINGS
(to the tune of "Oh My Darling" or chanted)

Little black things, little black things
Crawling up and down my arm
I am not afraid of them
For they will do no harm.

(substitute any color for black)

Materials Needed

The following colors of yarn:

red	green	black	pink
orange	blue	brown	gray
yellow	purple	white	

Instructions

NOTE: You will need to make a set of eleven colored things *for each child*. These can be stored easily in zip-lock sandwich bags.

Step 1: For each colored thing, cut 5 yarn pieces, each measuring 8 inches long.

Step 2: Put one yarn piece aside and, keeping the other four together, fold them in half.

Step 3: Using the 5th piece of yarn, tie it around the other four, 1 inch from the folded ends, knotting it well, to form a "head" and "legs." Fold the knotted ends down to form more legs.

Use

Give each child their own bag of "things." Let them tell you what color to use. While singing, have the colored thing crawl up and down arms.

Courtesy of MAGIC MOMENTS

FINGER PLAY

Finger play is an enjoyed preschool group (or individual) activity that parents have probably already introduced children to with "peek-a-boo" or "this little piggy went to market." Finger plays use words and actions (usually finger motions) together. Early childhood play frequently goes beyond finger movements and often includes whole body actions, figure 15-2.

When learning a finger play, the child usually practices and joins in the finger movements before learning the words. Words can be learned and retained by doing the play over and over again.

Finger plays are often done with rhymes, but need not be. Easy-to-remember rhymes give the child ear pleasure and a chance to feel good about himself because (1) the child quickly becomes one of a group having fun and doing the same thing, and (2) the child experiences a feeling of self-worth when a rhyme has been learned.

Teachers use finger plays at any time of the day for speech development, to get the wiggles out, keep children active and interested while waiting, or between activities. They are also useful for special purposes, such as quieting a group or getting toys back on the shelves.

Finger plays can build vocabulary as well as teach facts. They can also help a child release pent-up energy.

Teachers should practice a finger play and memorize it beforehand, to be sure of a clear and smooth presentation. It should be offered enthusiastically, focusing on enjoyment. As with other activities, the teacher can say, "Try it with me." The child who just watches will join in when ready. Watching comes first, one or two

FIGURE 15-2 Finger plays use words and action together.

hand movements next, and after repetitions, both words and actions together. Each child learns at his own rate of speed.

Finger plays appeal to a young child's imagination and keep him active using both words and motions. They also help the child to feel good about himself since he quickly learns to do what the teacher and others are doing and enjoying.

SUGGESTED FINGER PLAYS

Finger plays can be found in many books for early childhood staff members, or can be created by the teacher. The following are recommended because of their popularity with both children and teachers.

HICKORY, DICKORY, DOCK

Hickory, dickory, dock!
   (Rest elbow in the palm of the other hand and swing upraised arm back and forth.)
The mouse ran up the clock;
   (Creep fingers up the arm to the palm of the other hand.)
The clock struck one,
   (Clap hands.)
The mouse ran down.
   (Creep fingers down to elbow.)
Hickory, dickory, dock!
   (Swing arm as before.)

OPEN, SHUT THEM

Open, shut them. Open, shut them.
Give a little clap.
Open, shut them. Open, shut them.
Lay them in your lap.
Creep them, creep them,
Creep them, creep them,
Right up to your chin.
Open wide your little mouth
But do not let them in.

Open, shut them. Open, shut them,
To your shoulder fly
Let them, like the little birds
Flutter to the sky.
Falling, falling, downward falling
Almost to the ground,
Quickly raising all your fingers
Twirl them 'round and 'round and 'round.

CHOO!! CHOO!!

Choo-o! Choo-o! Choo! Choo!
  (Run finger along arm to shoulder slowly.)
This little train goes up the track.

Choo! Choo! Choo! Choo!
  (At shoulder turn "train" and head down arm.)
But this little train comes quickly back.
Choo-choo-choo-choo! choo-choo-choo-choo!

  (Repeat last line.)
  (Run fingers down arm quickly.)
Whoo-o! Whoo-o! Whoo-o!
  (Imitate train whistle.)

FAMILY OF RABBITS

A family of rabbits lived under a tree
  (Close right hand and hide it under left arm.)
A father, a mother, and babies three
  (Hold up thumb, then fingers in succession.)
Sometimes the bunnies would sleep all day
  (Make fist.)
But when night came, they liked to play.
  (Wiggle fingers.)
Out of the hole they'd go creep, creep, creep,
  (Move fingers in creeping motion.)
While the birds in the trees were all asleep.
  (Rest face on hands, place palms together.)
Then the bunnies would scamper about and run
  (Wiggle fingers.)
Uphill, downhill! Oh, what fun!
  (Wiggle fingers vigorously.)
But when the mother said, "It's time to rest."
  (Hold up index finger.)
Pop! They would hurry
  (Clap hands after "Pop.")
Right back to their nest!
  (Hide hand under arm.)

FIRE FIGHTERS

Ten little fire fighters, sleeping in a row,
Ding, dong goes the bell, down the pole they go.
Jumping on the engine, oh, oh, oh.
Putting out the fire, shhhhhhhhhhhhhhhhhh.
And home again they go
Back to sleep again.
All in a row.

THIS IS THE MOUNTAIN

This is the mountain up so high
  (Form triangle.)
And this is the moon that sails through the sky.
  (Circle with thumbs and index fingers)
These are the stars that twinkle so bright.
  (Small circle, thumb and index, other three
  fingers moving)
These are the clouds that pass through the night.
  (Fists)
This is the window through which I peep,
  (Square with thumb and index)
And here am I, fast asleep.
  (Close eyes.)

CLAP YOUR HANDS

Clap your hands high
Clap your hands low,
Pat your head lightly
And down you go.

I'll touch my hair, my lips, my eyes,
I'll sit up straight, and then I'll rise.
I'll touch my ears, my nose, my chin,
Then quietly, sit down again.

BUTTERFLY

Roly-poly caterpillar
Into a corner crept
Spun around himself a blanket
Then for a long time slept
A long time passed (Whisper)
Roly-poly caterpillar wakened by and by
Found himself with beautiful wings
Changed to a butterfly.

SLEEPY TIME

Open wide your little hands,
Now squeeze them very tight.
Shake them, shake them very loose,
With all your might.
Climb them slowly to the sky.
Drop down like gentle rain.
Go to sleep my little hands,
I'll waken you again.

TWO LITTLE BLACKBIRDS

Two little blackbirds sitting on a hill,
   (Place 2 forefingers on shoulders to represent
   birds.)
One named Jack,
   (Hold one forefinger out.)
One named Jill.
   (Hold other forefinger out.)
Fly away Jack; Fly away Jill;
   (Make one hand and then the other "fly
   away.")
Come back Jack; Come back Jill.
   (Bring hands back to shoulders one at a time.)

A FUNNY ONE

'Round the house
'Round the house
   (Fingers around the face)
Peep in the window
   (Open eyes wide.)
Listen at the door
   (Cup hand behind ear.)
Knock at the door
   (Knock on head.)
Lift up the latch
   (Push up nose.)
And walk in
   (Stick out tongue and walk fingers in mouth.)
— I caught you!
   (Bite gently down on fingers!)

TWO LITTLE APPLES

Two little apples hanging on a tree
   (Hand by eyes)
Two little apples smiling at me
   (Smile.)

I shook that tree as hard as I could
   (Shake tree.)
Down came the apples
   (Make falling motions.)
Mmmm — they were good
   (Rub stomach.)

HALLOWEEN

Five little pumpkins sitting on a gate
   (Hold up 5 fingers.)
This one says, "My it's getting late."
   (Wiggle index finger.)
This one says, "There are black cats every-
   where."
   (Wiggle middle finger.)
This one says, "I don't care."
   (Wiggle ring finger.)
This one says, "It's all for Halloween fun."
   (Wiggle little finger.)
And the other one says, "We better run!"
   (Wiggle thumb.)
Woo, goes the wind
   (Blow.)
Out goes the light!
   (Close eyes.)
And the 5 little pumpkins run quickly out of
   sight.
   (Hand runs away.)

BEEHIVE

Here is a beehive
   (Make fist around other hand.)
Where are the bees?
Hidden away
Where nobody sees.
See them creeping
   (Pull out one finger at a time.)
Out of the hive
1-2-3-4-5! Buzz!
   (Make buzzing sound with hand moving in
   air.)

Here is a beehive
   (Make fist.)
Where are the bees?
They're buzzing around

(Buzz around with other hand.)
The flowers and trees.

Soon they'll come home
Back from their fun
　(Put thumb in first then fingers one at a time.)
5-4-3-2-1! Buzz
　(Make buzzing sound.)

MR. BROWN AND MR. BLACK

This is Mr. Brown (Hold up right thumb, fingers outstretched.)

And he lives in this house (Tuck thumb inside fingers.)

And this is Mr. Black (Hold up left thumb, fingers outstretched.)

And he lives in this house (Tuck thumb inside fingers.)

Now one day Mr. Brown decided to visit Mr. Black.

So he opened the door (Extend fingers of right hand.)

Came out (Hold thumb upright.)

Shut the door (Close fingers into fist, leaving thumb upright.)

He went up the hill and down the hill and up the hill and down the hill (Move thumb in directions indicated.)

Until he came to Mr. Black's house (Hold up left fist.)

Knocked on the door (Make knocking motion with right fist on left fist.)

No one was home. (Shake head.)

So he went up the hill and down the hill and up the hill and down the hill until he came to his own house (Follow directions with fist.)

Opened the door (Extend fingers out flat.)

Went in (Put thumb in palm.)

Shut the door (Place fingers over thumb.)

Now one day Mr. Black decided to visit Mr. Brown (Repeat sequence, substituting Mr. Black for Mr. Brown and using left hand.)

One day Mr. Brown and Mr. Black decided to visit each other. (Repeat sequence, using both hands, until:)

They went up the hill and down the hill and up the hill and down the hill and they met (Follow directions with both hands.)

And Mr. Brown said, "Hello, Mr. Black!" (Wiggle right thumb.)

And Mr. Black said, "Hello, Mr. Brown!" (Wiggle left thumb.)

And they shook hands. (Shake hands.)

Then they went up the hill and down the hill and up the hill and down the hill until they came to their own houses (Follow directions with both hands.)

Opened the door (Extend fingers.)

Went in (Place thumbs in palms.)

Shut the door (Close fingers over thumbs.)

PEANUT BUTTER AND JELLY

First you take the peanuts and you crunch them and you crunch them. (Repeat.)
Peanut butter — jelly! Peanut butter — jelly!

Then you take the grapes and you squish them and you squish them. (Repeat.)
Peanut butter — jelly! Peanut butter — jelly!

Then you take the bread and you spread it and you spread it. (Repeat.)
Peanut butter — jelly! Peanut butter — jelly!

Then you take the sandwich and you eat it and you eat it. (Repeat.) (Then with your mouth closed hum the refrain.)
Peanut butter — jelly! Peanut butter — jelly!

("Peanut butter" is said in the following fashion: "Pea" [medium pitch] "nut" [low pitch] "but" (medium) "ter" [high pitch with hands above head, fingers shaking to side in vaudeville-type motion.])

("Jelly" is said in a low, throaty voice, accompanied by hands to opposite side shaking at knee level.)

MR. SNAKE

Mr. Snake, from his hole
Deep in the ground,

Poked out his head
And looked around.
  (From closed right hand, pull thumb out.)
"It's too nice a day
To say in," he said.
"I think I'll go
For a crawl instead,"
So he twitched his tail
  (Jerk right hand back and forth.)
And gave a hiss
And off through the meadow he
Went like this.
  (Make right hand wiggle away.)

FIVE LITTLE ASTRONAUTS

Five little astronauts
  (Hold up fingers on one hand.)
Ready for outer-space.
The first one said, "Let's have a race."
The second one said, "The weather's too rough."
The third one said, "Oh, don't be gruff."
The fourth one said, "I'm ready enough."
The fifth one said, "Let's Blast Off!"
10, 9, 8, 7, 6, 5, 4, 3, 2, 1,
  (Start with ten fingers and pull one down with
  each number.)
BLAST OFF!!!
  (Clap loudly with Blast Off!!)

MR. TALL AND MR. SMALL

There was once a man
  (Stand on tiptoes.)
Who was tall, tall, tall.
  (Reach up as far as possible.)
He had a friend
Who was small, small, small.
  (Kneel and bend way down.)
The man who was small
Would try to call
To the man who was tall,
  (Cup hands near mouth, look up.)
"Hello, up there!"
  (In high voice)

The man who was tall
  (Stand on tiptoes.)
At once would call
To the man who was small,
  (Bend from waist.)
"Hello, down there!"
  (Use deep voice.)

Then each tipped his hat
  (Stand straight.)
And made this reply:
"Good-bye, my friend."
  (Tip an imaginary hat; look up, speak in high
  voice.)

"Good-bye, good-bye."
  (Bow, and speak in low, deep voice.)

Beatrice Wells Carlson, "Mr. Tall and Mr. Small," *Listen And Help Tell the Story* (Nashville, TN: Abingdon Press 1965).

BODY ACTION PLAYS

Encourage the child to jump in rhythm to this jump rope chant while doing what the rhyme says. Use this for working out the wiggles also, figure 15-3.

TEDDY BEAR, TEDDY BEAR

Teddy bear, teddy bear, turn around.
Teddy bear, teddy bear, touch the ground.
Teddy bear, teddy bear, show your shoe,
Teddy bear, teddy bear, that will do.
Teddy bear, teddy bear, go upstairs
  (Alternate hands upwards.)
Teddy bear, teddy bear, say your prayers.
Teddy bear, teddy bear, turn off the light.
Teddy bear, teddy bear, say goodnight.
  (Lay down and pretend to snore.)

HEAD, SHOULDERS

Head, shoulders, knees and toes
  (Stand; touch both hands to each part in
  order.)
Head, shoulders, knees and toes.

FIGURE 15-3 A "body action" play

Head, shoulders, knees and toes.
That's the way the story goes.
  (Clap this line.)
This is my head, this is not
  (Hands on head, then feet)
These are my shoulders, this is not
  (Hands on shoulders, then knees)
Here are my knees, watch them wiggle,
  (Wiggle knees.)
Touch my armpits and I giggle.
  (Hands under armpits with laugh)
Head shoulders, knees and toes
  (Touch in order.)
That's the way the story goes.
  (Clap.)

MONKEY STAMPS

The monkey stamps, stamps, stamps his feet
The monkey stamps, stamps, stamps his feet
Monkey see, monkey do,
The monkey does the same as you.

The monkey claps, claps, claps his hands.
The monkey claps, claps, claps his hands.
Monkey see, monkey do,
The monkey does the same as you.

When you make a funny face, the monkey
  makes a funny face.
When you make a funny face, the monkey
  makes a funny face.
Monkey see, monkey do,
The monkey does the same as you.

When you turn yourself around, the monkey
  turns himself around.
When you turn yourself around, the monkey
  turns himself around.
Monkey see, monkey do,
The monkey does the same as you.

Edith Fowke, *Sally Go Round the Sun: Three Hundred Children's Songs, Rhymes and Games* (Garden City, New York: Doubleday and Company, Inc., 1969).

BEAT ONE HAMMER

My mother told me to tell you
To beat one hammer
  (Pound one fist.)
Like you see me do.
My mother told me to tell you
To beat two hammers
  (Pound two fists.)
Like you see me do.
My mother told me to tell you
To beat three hammers
  (Pound two fists; stamp one foot.)
Like you see me do.
My mother told me to tell you
To beat four hammers
  (Pound two fists; stamp two feet.)
Like you see me do.
My mother told me to tell you

To beat five hammers
  (Add nodding head.)
Like you see me do.
My mother told me to tell you
To beat no hammers
  (Stop!)
Like you see me do.

MY LITTLE THUMBS

My little thumbs keep moving
My little thumbs keep moving
My little thumbs keep moving
  Tra la tra la tra la
My thumbs and fingers keep moving
My thumbs and fingers keep moving
My thumbs and fingers keep moving
  Tra la tra la tra la
My thumbs and fingers and hands keep moving
My thumbs and fingers and hands keep moving
My thumbs and fingers and hands keep moving
  Tra la tra la tra la
My thumbs and fingers and hands and arms
  keep moving
My thumbs and fingers and hands and arms
  keep moving
My thumbs and fingers and hands and arms
  keep moving
  And then I stand right up
My thumbs and fingers and hands and arms
  and feet keep moving
My thumbs and fingers and hands and arms

and feet keep moving
My thumbs and fingers and hands and arms
  and feet keep moving
  Tra la tra la tra la
My thumbs and fingers and hands and arms
  and feet and head keep moving
My thumbs and fingers and hands and arms
  and feet and head keep moving
My thumbs and fingers and hands and arms
  and feet and head keep moving
  Tra la tra la tra la

SUMMARY

Speaking activities are planned for the young child. Some require simple imitation of words while others call for the child's creative or expressive response.

Fingers plays use words and actions together. They are actively enjoyed by children and build feelings of self-worth. Teachers should memorize finger plays and use them daily.

Circle times instill group spirit and social enjoyment of language. Opening activities capture attention. Chants and choruses add rhythmic word play and often involve physical movement. A smooth transition from concluding circle activities takes place when teachers are well-prepared.

Learning Activities

- With a small group of classmates, practice and present a finger play, chant, chorus, or body action play. Have each student present the activity until it is learned by the others.

- Make a list of at least five books which are resources for finger plays.

- Present a finger play, chant, or chorus to a group of young children.

- Find a finger play that is seasonal (generally used at only one time a year). Bring a copy to class.

- Create a finger play, chant, or chorus for young children.

Unit Review

A. Finish the following:
   1. A transitory statement at the end of group time is necessary because _____.
   2. History shows that chants and choruses were used for _____.
   3. A successful circle time for young children can be described by the following terms: _____.

B. Why are finger plays so popular with young children?

C. Rearrange and place in the best order or sequence.
   1. Child knows words and actions of a finger play.
   2. Teacher knows words and actions of a finger play.
   3. Teacher practices finger play.
   4. Child participates with actions only.
   5. Child watches.
   6. Teacher presents finger play to children.
   7. Teacher evaluates the results of the finger play.
   8. Teacher encourages children to join in actions and words.

D. List five signals or attention-getters a teacher could use at the beginning of a circle time.

E. In what ways should an assistant teacher be helpful when another teacher is leading group language activities?

F. Rate the following teacher statements during planned circles.
   G = Good Technique   P = Poor Technique

   1. "It's my turn to talk."
   2. "Stop wiggling, Jimmy."
   3. "Everyone's listening, it's time to begin."
   4. "When Kate, Claire, and Nancy join us, we'll all be together."
   5. "The first one on his feet can be the first one to leave the circle."
   6. "We're finished. Let's go."
   7. "Speak up Gisela. It's time to answer."
   8. "Bert's doing our new finger play the 'right' way."
   9. "Watch closely, and make your fingers move just like mine."
   10. "I like the way everyone listened to what their friends said, and took turns talking today."

Resources for Group Time Planning

Brashears, D., and Sharron Werlin, *Circle Time Activities for Young Children*, 1 Corte Del Rey, Orinda, CA 94563.

Magic Moments, PO Box 53635, San Jose, CA 95153-0635. (Activities, patterns, flannel board ideas, drama with props, puppet activities; from \$.50–\$5.00.)

Wilmes, Liz and Dick, *Everyday Circle Times,* Gryphon House Inc., PO Box 275, Mt. Rainier, MD 20712.

Resources for Finger Plays

Cochran, E. V., *Teach and Reach That Child,* Peek Publications, Palo Alto, CA, 1975.

Croft, Doreen J. and Robert Hess, *An Activities Handbook for Teachers of Young Children,* Houghton Mifflin Co., 1983.

Ellis, Mary Jackson, *Finger Play Approach to Dramatization,* T. S. Denison, and Co., Inc., Minneapolis, MN.

Engel, Rose C., *Language Motivating Experiences for Young Children,* Educative Toys and Supplies, 6416 Van Nuys Blvd., Van Nuys, CA 91401.

Finger Frolics, Gryphon House, 1976.

Glazer, Tom, *Eye Winker Tom Tinker Chin Chopper: Fifty Musical Fingerplays,* Doubleday and Co., Inc., 1973.

Grayson, M., *Let's Do Fingerplays,* Robert B. Luce, Inc., 1962.

Kable, Gratia, *Favorite Finger Plays,* T. S. Denison and Co., Inc., Minneapolis, MN.

Mayesky, Mary et al., *Creative Activities for Young Children,* Delmar Publishers, Albany, NY, 1980.

Scott, Louise B., *Learning Time with Language Experiences for Young Children,* Webster Division, McGraw-Hill.

References

Beckman, Carol, et al., *Channels to Children,* PO Box 25834, Colorado Springs, CO 80936 (A wonderful collection of activities based on a theme approach to teaching. Many crosscultural activities described in last chapter.)

Bos, Bev, San Jose City College Workshop, Creativity, 1983.

Brashears, D. and Sharron Werlin, *Circle Time Activities for Young Children,* 1 Corte Del Rey, Orinda, CA 94563. (A collection of suggested circle time activities.)

Coglin, Mary Lou, *Chants for Children,* Coglin Publ., Box 301, Manilius, NY 13104. (If you enjoy chanting at circle, this will offer you additional chants to try.)

Van Allen, Roach and Claryce Allen, *Language Experience Activities,* 2nd ed., Houghton Mifflin Co., 1976. (Abundant activity ideas)

Weir, Mary E. and Pat Eggleston, "Teachers First Words," *Day Care and Early Education,* Nov./Dec. 1975.

Suggested Reading

Machado, Jeanne and Helen C. Meyer, *Early Childhood Practicum Guide*, Delmar Publishers Inc., 1984, Unit 5. (Pointers on conducting well-planned and interesting group experiences.)

Unit 16
Puppetry and Simple Drama

OBJECTIVES

After studying this unit you should be able to

- use puppetry in language arts programming.
- describe young children's puppet play.
- list five teaching techniques which offer young children opportunities for simple dramatization.

Puppets provide countless opportunities for children's speech growth. They match and fulfill many of the preschooler's developmental needs, besides being of high interest. Puppets can be:

- moved and controlled by the child, figure 16-1.
- a challenge; skill is involved in coordinating speech and movement.
- talked to as an accepting companion.
- used individually and in group play.
- used to create and fantasize.
- used to explore another's personality.
- a way to release pent-up emotions.
- used to "relive" and imitate.
- seen as an "adultlike" activity.
- used to entertain others.
- constructed by children.

Many of these uses build and develop children's confidence in their own speaking ability.

There are many ways the teacher can use puppetry in language development activities: Puppets can:

- motivate.
- gain attention and keep it focused.
- provide variety in the presentation of ideas and words.
- provide a model to imitate.
- present stories.
- promote child creativity and pretending.
- provide a play opportunity which encourages speech and motor coordination.
- introduce new information.
- promote positive attitudes toward speaking and dramatic activities.
- build audience skills.
- provide construction activities.
- help children express themselves.
- build vocabularies.
- offer entertaining and enjoyed activities.
- provide a wide range of puppet personalities for children to explore.

STIMULATING CHILDREN'S USE OF PUPPETS

Teachers can expand children's experiences with puppets in these ways.

- Present puppet plays and skits.
- Find community resources for puppet presentations: puppeteer groups, children's

FIGURE 16-1 Exploring puppetry

theater groups, high school and elementary classes, and skilled individuals.
- Introduce each puppet periodically and provide new ones when possible.
- Store puppets invitingly.
- Provide props and puppet theaters, figure 16-2.
- Keep puppets in good repair.

A puppet carried in a teacher's pocket can be useful in a variety of teaching situations. Children imitate the teacher's use of puppets, and this leads to creative play.

TEACHER PUPPETRY

Children sit, excited and enthralled, at simple skits and dialogues performed by teachers. Continually amazed by young children's rapt attention and obvious pleasure, most teachers find puppetry a valuable teaching skill, figure 16-3.

Prerecording puppet dialogue (or attaching puppet speeches inside the puppet stage) helps beginning puppeteers. With practice, performance skills increase and puppet coordination can then be the main teacher task. Additional puppetry skill-building resource books are listed in the Appendix.

Planning and performing simple puppet plays requires time and effort. The plays are selected for suitability and then practiced until the scene-by-scene sequence is firmly in mind. Good preparation helps ensure a smooth performance, which adds to children's enjoyment.

Several helpful tips on puppetry are listed.

- A dark net peep-hole enables teachers to watch audience reactions and helps dialogue pacing.
- Puppets with strong, identifiable personality traits who stay in character are well received.

FIGURE 16-3 Puppetry is a valuable teaching device. *(From Machado and Meyer,* Early Childhood Practicum Guide, *Copyright 1984 by Delmar Publishers Inc.)*

Speaks in a high-pitched voice.
Lives alone and likes young visitors.
* Use your favorite puppet in at least one activity weekly.

PUPPET ACTIVITIES

Child participation with puppets can be increased when planned puppet activities are performed. The following are but a few of the many puppet play activities.

* Invite children to use puppets (with arms) in the following ways: sleepy, hungry, dancing, crying, laughing, whispering, saying "hello" to a friend, climbing a ladder, waving good-bye, shaking hands.
* A large mirror helps children build skill.
* Ask two volunteers to use puppets in a mother and child "waking up in the morning" situation. The teacher creates both

FIGURE 16-2 Young children enjoy watching a puppet performance.

* Plan your puppet's personality in advance and stick to it.
  Example: Grandma Mabel
    Characteristics:
    Can't hear well.
    Says "Mercy me!" often.
    Likes to talk about her cat, Christobel.
    Lives on a farm.
    Is an optimist.

speaking parts, then prompts two children to continue on their own. Other situations include:

1. Telephone conversation.
2. Child requesting money from a parent to buy an ice cream cone.
3. Puppet inviting another to a party.

- Urge children to answer the teacher's puppet.
  Example:
  Teacher: "Hi! My name is Mr. Smarty Pants. I can sing any song you ask me to sing. Just ask me!"
  OR
  Teacher: "I'm the cook. What shall we have for dinner?"
  OR
  Teacher: "My name is Razzle-dazzle, who are you? Where am I?"

- Record simple puppet directions (such as the following) on a cassette tape recorder. Provide a mirror.
  1. Make your puppet touch his nose.
  2. Have your puppet clap.
  3. Kiss your hand, puppet.
  4. Rub your eyes, puppet.
  5. Reach for the stars, puppet.
  6. Hold your stomach.
  7. Scratch your ear.
  8. Bow low.
  9. Hop.
  Set up this activity in individual, room-divided space.

- Record simple puppet dramas. After a teacher demonstration, make them available to children on a free choice basis. Provide a mirror, if possible.

STORAGE AND THEATERS

Store puppets in an inviting way: face up, begging for handling; shoe racks, wall pockets, or upright pegs within the child's reach are suggested. An adjacent puppet theater tempts children's use. Old television sets (with insides removed) make durable "climb into" theaters. Other theaters can be constructed by the teacher using large packing crates, painted and decorated by the children. For more puppet theater ideas, see the Appendix.

PUPPET PLAYS

Familiar and favorite stories are ready material for puppet dramas. Many contain simple, repetitive lines which most of the children know from memory. Children will often stray from familiar dialogues in stories however, adding their own lines, actions, or settings. Older preschoolers speak through puppets easily; younger children may be more interested in manipulating alone or simple imitating.

OTHER PUPPETRY TIPS

- Some children are fearful of puppets.
- Aggressive puppet play of the "Punch and Judy" type needs redirection if puppets are in danger of being destroyed.
- Most public libraries offer puppet shows periodically.
- Parents and volunteers can help construct sturdy classroom puppets.

PUPPET TYPES

Puppets can be divided into two basic categories — those worked with the hands and fingers, and those which dangle on strings. Hand puppets are popular in the preschool because they are so versatile and practical. Teacher-made, child-made, as well as commercially-manufactured hand puppets are an essential part of most centers.

Moving arms and pliable faces on puppets increase the possibilities for characterization and action. Rubber, plastic, and papier-mache puppet heads are durable. Cloth faces permit a wider variety of facial expressions.

Papier-mache Puppet Heads

Materials:

> styrofoam egg or ball (a little smaller than you want completed head)
>
> neck tube (made from cardboard — about 1½″ wide and 5″ long, rolled into a circle and taped closed, or plastic hair roller)
>
> bottle (this is to put the head on while it is being created)
>
> instant papier-mache
>
> paints (poster paint variety)
>
> spray-gloss coat
>
> white glue

Construction Procedure:

1. Mix instant papier-mache with water (a little at a time) until it is like clay — moist, but not too wet or dry.
2. Place styrofoam egg on neck tube (or roller) securely. Then place egg (or ball) on bottle so that it is steady.
3. Put papier-mache all over head and half way down neck tube. Coating should be about ½″ thick.
4. Begin making the facial features, starting with the cheeks, eyebrows, and chin. Then add eyes, nose, mouth, and ears.
5. When you are satisfied with the head, allow it to dry at least 24 hours in an airy place.
6. When head is dry, paint the face with poster paint. When that is dry, coat with spray gloss finish to seal paint.
7. Glue is useful for adding yarn hair, if desired.

Sock Puppets

Materials:

> old sock, felt, sewing machine

Construction Procedure (see figure 16-4):

1. Use an old wool or other thick sock. Turn it inside out and spread it out with the heel on top.
2. Cut around the edge of the toe (about 3 inches on each side).
3. Fold the mouth material (pink felt) inside the open part of the sock and draw

FIGURE 16-4 Sock puppet construction

the shape. Cut the mouth piece out and sew into position.

4. Turn the sock right side out and sew on the features.

Paper Bag Puppets

Materials:

paper bags, scissors, crayons, paste, yarn or paper scraps, and paint (if desired)

Construction Procedure:

1. Paper bag puppets are quick and easy. Give each child a small paper sack (No. 6 works well).
2. Show them how the mouth works and let them color or paste features on the sack.
3. You may wish to have them paste a circle on for the face. Paste it on the flap part of the bag and then cut the circle on the flap portion so the mouth can move again.
4. Many children will want to add special features to their paper bag puppets, for example — a tail or ears, figure 16-5.

Stick Puppets

A stick puppet is a picture or object attached to a stick, figure 16-6. It moves when the puppeteer moves the puppet up and down or from side to side, holding the stick.

Materials:

paper, glue, scissors, crayons, popsicle sticks (or tongue depressors, or cardboard strips)

Construction Procedure:

1. Characters and scenery can be preoutlined. Depending on the child's age, they can then be colored, or both colored and cut out.
2. Older children may want to create their own figures.

Movable-mouth String Puppets

Materials:

1 styrofoam ball
2 eyes (store-bought or teacher-made)
1 small ball for a nose
felt

FIGURE 16-5 Paper bag puppet

FIGURE 16-6 Stick puppets

pipe cleaners
1 drinking straw
1 nail
smooth string
1 dowel, 18″ long
1 paper cup with plastic lid that fits
material to "dress" puppet
yarn for hair
1 pin

Construction Procedure (see figure 16-7):

1. Cut styrofoam head in two. Cut a wedge out of the top of the head. Cut a felt mouth lining and glue it. (The felt must go all the way around the top, back, and bottom of the mouth.
2. Push dowel into the bottom of the head all the way to the mouth.
3. Pin string to the top of the head. Run string down the back of the head and thread it through the straw. Tape the straw to the dowel and pull the string. The mouth should open!
4. Cut a hole in the bottom of the cup and slide the cup up over the dowel and straw until it hits the head of the puppet.
5. Place lid on the cup and put a nail at the point of the dowel to prevent the cup from sliding back down the dowel.
6. Put pipe cleaner arms through the front of the cup and bend ends to look like hands.
7. Finish puppet by dressing in material or felt. Glue on eyes, nose, and hair.

Large Cloth Hand Puppet

Materials:

fabric, sewing machine, felt scraps, yarn, glue, cardboard sheet (see Appendix for pattern)

Construction Procedure:

1. Sew head darts.

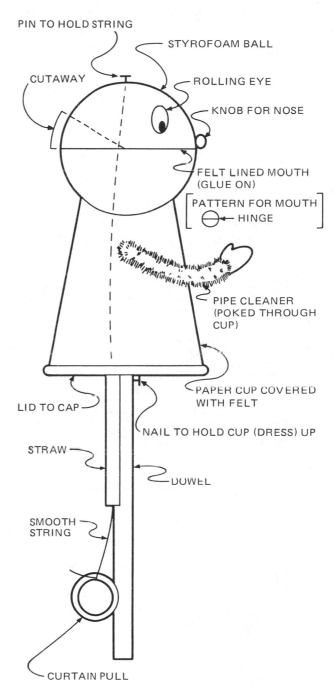

FIGURE 16-7 Movable-mouth string puppet

2. Right sides together, sew back and front ¼".
3. Pin mouth at quarters. Ease mouth piece, and sew.
4. After the mouth is securely in place, glue cardboard to the inside of the mouth. (White glue works fine.)
5. If arms are desired, slash at side, insert arm, and sew.
6. Decorate as desired, figure 16-8.

FIGURE 16-8 Large cloth hand puppets

Box Puppets

Materials:

1 small (individual size) box with both ends intact

1 piece white construction paper, 6″ x 9″

crayons or poster paints and brush

scissors, sharp knife, glue

Construction Procedure (see figure 16-9):

1. Cut box in half as in sketch #1, with one wide side uncut. Fold over as in sketch #2.
2. On construction paper, draw the face of a person or an animal. Color or paint features, and cut out face.
3. Add yarn for hair, broomstraws for whiskers, and so on, if desired.

4. Cut face along line of mouth and glue to box as in sketch #4, so that lips come together as in sketch #5.

Jumping Jacks

Materials:

paper, brads, string, hole punch, dowel, glue, curtain pull (optional)

Construction Procedure (see figure 16-10):

1. Design and cut pattern, making arms and legs long enough to secure behind figure. Cut two body pieces.
2. Glue figure to dowel by inserting between front and back.
3. Brads act like joints. Hole punch and add arms, legs, and string.

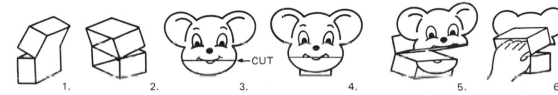

FIGURE 16-9 Box puppets

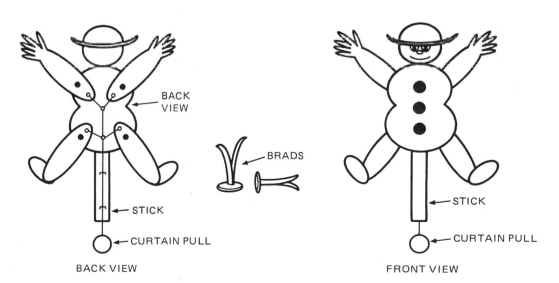

FIGURE 16-10 Jumping jack

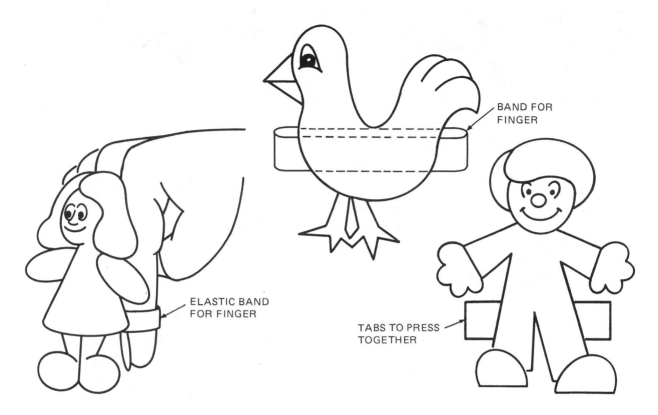

PAPER FINGER PUPPETS (SMALL PATTERN OR TEACHER DRAWING WITH BAND OR TABS FOR FINGER)

FIGURE 16-11 Finger puppets

Frog and Bird Finger Puppets

Materials:
felt fabric, scissors, sewing machine, pattern (see Appendix)

Construction Procedure:
Cut and sew pieces leaving ends open to insert finger.

Additional ideas: (see figure 16-11):
• Dustmop-head puppet.
• Favorite TV character puppet, figure 16-12.
• Garden glove puppets (different faces can be snapped on), figure 16-13.
• Basic puppet body, Appendix.

TEACHER PUPPET PRESENTATIONS

Many simple stories can be shared with children through teacher puppetry. Figures 16-14 and 16-15 show ideas for puppet theaters. See the Appendix for additional puppet patterns.

The following is an example of a tale which lends itself to puppet presentation. Teachers can create their own stories which appeal to the interest of the children with whom they work.

THE PANCAKE

Narrator:
Once upon a time, an old woman made a pan-

FIGURE 16-12 Favorite TV character puppet

cake. When it was nice and golden brown, it hopped out of the frying pan and began rolling down the road, saying:

Pancake:

Whee! I'm free! Nobody will ever eat me! What a nice day! I'll just roll along till — hey! I wonder what that funny looking round thing is that I'm coming to over the river!

Narrator:

He didn't know it, but it was a bridge.

FIGURE 16-13 Garden glove puppets

FIGURE 16-14 Puppet stage

Pancake:

I'll bet I can roll over that thing. Watch this! I'll just get a head start back here — (backs up) one . . . two . . . three! (As the pancake starts over the bridge, frog comes up and grabs it.)

Pancake:

Let me go! Let me go!

Frog:

I want to eat you! I love pancakes! (Pancake pulls away and rolls out of sight.)

Frog:

Oh, dear . . . it got away . . . (Frog down. Bridge down. Pancake rolls in.)

Pancake:

That was a close one! I hope I don't meet any other — (Off stage is heard the sound of barking . . .)

Pancake:

What's that sound? I don't think I like it . . . (Dog in, tries to grab pancake.)

Dog:

I want a bite! I love pancakes! (Pancake cries "No! No!" and rolls off.)

Dog:

It got away. Well, better luck next time . . . (Dog out, pancake rolls in.)

Pancake:

Goodness! Everybody seems to love pancakes, but I don't want to be loved *that* way! (Off stage is heard the sound of "meow!")

Pancake:

Meow? What kind of animal makes *that* sound? (Cat in, tries to grab pancake, pancake escapes as before.)

Cat:

Meow, meow, no breakfast now! (Cat out, pancake rolls in, panting.)

Pancake:

This is dreadful! Everybody I meet wants to eat me! (Bird flies in.)

Bird:

A pancake! Delicious! I'll just peck a few pieces out of it! (Bird starts to peck at pancake, which rolls away crying, "No! No!" Bird follows, then returns alone.)

Bird:

It's too hot to chase it. Besides, it can roll faster than I can fly. (Bird out. Put bridge up again.)

Narrator:

And all day long the pancake rolled 'til it finally found itself back at the same bridge. (Pancake rolls in.)

Pancake:

(wearily) Oh, dear . . . here I am again, back at the same bridge . . . I must have been rolling around in circles. And I'm too tired to roll another inch. I must rest. I'll just lie down here next to this round thing over the river . . . (Pancake lies down flat, or leans against the bridge, if possible. Now puppeteer has two free hands to put on frog and dog. But before they come in, we hear their voices:)

Frog's Voice:

(half-whisper) It's mine!

Dog's Voice:

(half-whisper) No, it's mine. I saw it first!

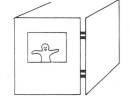

Fiberboard Theatre and Curtain
Use hinges on sides so it can be folded.

Puppet Screen
For shadow puppets. Make by stapling old sheet to picture frame.

Light

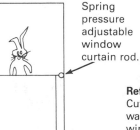

Spring pressure adjustable window curtain rod.

Doorway
Tape sheet across bottom half.

Refrigerator Box
Cut one side all the way down. Cut a window stage about 24″ wide, add curtains and paint.

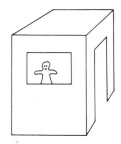

Hat Box
Tie around neck. Place hand through bottom to manipulate puppet.

Table Theatre.
Use a table turned on side. Children work puppets from behind.

Window or Window Shade
On a warm day children go outside, some stay to work puppets from open windows.

Blanket
Hang a blanket from two chairs. Easy and quick.

FIGURE 16-15 Ideas for puppet theaters

Frog's Voice:
(same) You did not! I saw it first!
Dog's Voice:
(same) Who cares — I'm going to eat it! (Dog and Frog enter and grab the pancake between them.)
Pancake:

Let me go! Let me go! (Frog and dog tussle, drop pancake out of sight, look after it.)
Frog:
You idiot! You dropped it in the water!
Dog:
You're the idiot! You're the one who dropped it!

Narrator:

And as the pancake disappeared beneath the water, they heard it say: (faraway voice) "Nobody will ever catch me . . ." And nobody ever did. (Sloane, 1942)

Teachers find that puppet play situations that contain a puppet, animal, or other character which is less knowledgeable and mature than the children themselves promotes a feeling of bigness in children. This situation puts the child in the position of directing and educating an inferior which often produces considerable child speech and self-esteem. A well-known commercial language development kit (program) cleverly contains a puppet who has no eyes . . . children are urged to help this puppet by describing happenings and events.

SIMPLE DRAMA

Children often playact familiar events and home situations. This allows them to both try out and work out elements of past experiences which they remember for one reason or another. Their playacting can be an exact imitation or something created by their active imaginations.

After young children become familiar with stories, they thoroughly enjoy their re-enactment or dramatization. By using both physical motions and verbal comments, children bring remembered story words and actions to life.

Playacting Tips

Remembering that children will act out parts from favorite stories as well as scenes from real life, the teacher sets the stage, keeping some points in mind:

- The child needs to be familiar with the story in order to know what happens first, next, and last.
- Activities in which the child pretends to do an action, to be an animal, or to copy the actions of another, help prepare him for simple drama, figure 16-16.
- A first step is to act without words, or while listening to a good story or record.
- The teacher can be the narrator while the children are the actors.
- Children should be encouraged to volunteer for parts.
- Props and settings can be simple. Ask, "What can be used for a bridge?" or a similar question so children can use their creativity.
- Any of the children's imaginative acts should be accepted, whether or not they are a part of the original story. The teacher remains close without directing or interfering (except when necessary).
- Individual and group actions should be praised and encouraged. Children should take turns playing the parts.

Some classic stories which lend themselves to playacting (drama) include:

FIGURE 16-16 Copying the actions of another helps prepare children for simple drama.

1. Goldilocks and the Three Bears
2. The Three Little Pigs
3. The Little Red Hen
4. Gingerbread Boy
5. Little Red Ridinghood
6. Little Miss Muffet

Patterns for #3 and #6 are in the Appendix.

Fast action and simple story lines are best for the young child. Playacting presents many opportunities for children to develop:

- self expression.
- use of correct speech.
- coordination of actions and words.
- creative thinking.
- self-confidence.
- listening skills.
- social interaction.

DRAMA FROM PICTURE BOOK SOURCES

Bev Bos (1983), a well-known California workshop leader, tells a funny story about children's love of dramatizing. Because picture books are frequently enacted at Bev's center, a child who really identifies with a particular book character often speaks up saying "I want to be the rabbit," long before the picture book reading session is finished.

Many action- and dialog-packed picture books, like the following, lend themselves to child reenactment.

The Funny Thing, by Wanda Gag
Rosie's Walk, by Pat Hutchins
The Gingerbread Boy, by Paul Galdone
Drummer Hoff, by Ed Emberly
One Fine Day, by Nonny Hogragian

PROGRESSIVE SKILL

Dramatizing a familiar story involves a number of language skills — listening, auditory memory of actions and characters' speech lines, and remembered sequence of events — plus audience skills. Simple pantomiming or imitation requires less maturity. Activities which use actions alone are good as a starting place to build children's playacting skills. The child has imitated others' actions since infancy, and as always, the joy of being able to do what he sees another do brings a feeling of self-confidence. A child's individuality is preserved if differences in ways of acting out a familiar story are valued in preschool settings.

CREATIVE DRAMA PROGRAMS

Starting a language program which includes creative drama requires planning and encouragement by the teacher. Props and play materials must be supplied for children to explore. When a child sees simple plays and pantomimes performed by teachers, other children, and adult groups, he is provided with a model and a stimulus. Some drama activity ideas for the older preschool child include:

- Pantomiming action words and phrases: tiptoe, crawl, riding a horse, using a rolling pin.
- Pantomiming words that mean a physical state: cold, hot, itchy.
- Pantomiming feeling words: happy, sad, hurt, holding a favorite teddy bear lovingly, feeling surprise.
- Acting out imaginary life situations: opening a door with a key, climbing in and out of a car, helping to set the table.
- Acting familiar character parts in well known stories. "She covered her mouth so the clown couldn't see her laugh." "The rabbit dug a big hole and buried the carrot." "He tiptoed to the window, raised the shade, and opened it."
- Saying familiar lines from known stories. "And he huffed and he puffed, and he blew the house down."

- Playing a character in a short story which involves both spoken lines and actions, figure 16-17.
- Pantomiming actions of a character in a short, familiar story which the teacher reads (or from a teacher-recorded story tape). A simple story is given as an example.

Little Indian's Adventures

Little Indian (Fingers behind hand for feathers) *went out to look for a buffalo. He took his bow and arrow. Little Indian walked down a path.* (Slap thigh) *Suddenly he thought he heard something.* (Hand behind ear) *He stopped and looked all around.* (Shade eyes) *He saw a squirrel. He walked on.* (Slap thigh) *He saw a hawk fly by.* (Shade eyes) *He walked on.* (Slap thigh) *He*

heard a rustle in the bushes. (Hand behind ear) *Rustle, rustle, rustle.* (Rub palms together) *Little Indian didn't wait a second. He began to run. He didn't stop until he reached his teepee.* (Form triangle with hands)

Imagination and inexpensive, easy-to-make costumes are a great performing incentive. Accessories such as hats can be used in a variety of play and drama situations.

Cutout chartboard or cardboard heads and figures held by the child quickly aid his ability to step into character, figure 16-18. Patterns for figures can be found in children's books and enlarged with the use of an opaque projector. This can produce "face into" props useful in child dramatization.

FIGURE 16-17 Children acting out parts from a favorite story

HAND
HOLES

HAND
HOLES

HAND
HOLES

FIGURE 16-18 Story character boards

SUMMARY

Using puppetry for language development is a widely-accepted practice in preschools. There are many puppet types to choose from. The ability to coordinate puppet actions and words takes practice and maturity. Teachers find that the more children *watch* puppets being used, the more they will use them. Puppets that are stored attractively and upright near puppet theaters encourage children's exploration.

There is a wide range of uses for puppets as instructional devices. Puppets are interest- ing and capture attention as an enjoyable play activity.

Simple child dramatizations of favorite sto- ries begin during preschool years. Language programs provide many playacting opportu- nities. Props, playacting, and pantomime ac- tivities motivate this expressive art. Skills are acquired through increased experiences with dramatic play. Planning by the teacher aids children's acquisition of dramatization abilities.

Learning Activities

- Make a puppet described in this unit.

- Present a simple puppet play with a few classmates.

- Collect ten easy-to-make costume ideas that promote creative drama. Share your ideas with the class.

- Using a lesson (activity) plan form, describe a simple drama activity for a group of preschoolers.

- Record a puppet drama and enact the drama with the help of classmates.

- Construct a puppet theater.

- Invite a local puppeteer group to share ideas with the class.

- Bring one simple puppet play script or drama script to class.

- Create a short puppet play.

- Find commercial resources for multiethnic puppets. Share names of companies and the prices for puppets.

Unit Review

A. Write a short paragraph describing the reasons puppets are a part of preschool language arts programs.

B. Rate the following teachers using this scale.

+	?	−
definitely promotes puppet interest and use	unable to determine or can't decide	will probably "turn off" children

1. Mrs. G. (teacher) pulled a small puppet from her smock pocket. Reaching behind Mark, age 3, she talked through the puppet. "Mark Allen Graham! Rupert sees what you're doing, and he doesn't like children who break crayons." Mark returns the crayon to the container.

2. Miss R. (teacher) is introducing a small group of children to an activity involving a poem on a chart. "Well, there's Petey, Sam, Hubert, Adam, Renee, and Claryce," Miss R. begins. The puppet in her hand moves and claps, and the puppet's voice is low pitched and deep. "I came to talk to you about rabbits. Does anyone know what rabbits look like? I live in a pocket, you know. I've heard about rabbits, but I've never seen one."

3. Mr. O. (teacher) has a large packing carton in the middle of the classroom. Two children notice the carton, and ask, "What's that for?" Mr. O. tells the two children that he noticed the school puppets do not have a puppet theater. "How could we make one from this box?" he asks the children. "You need a window," one child says. "Yes, that's true. I'll draw one. Stand here, please. I'll need the window the right height." The conversation and the project has drawn a larger group of children.

4. Mr. T. (teacher) has noticed a puppet lying on the ground in the playground. He picks it up, examines it, and puts it in his pocket. During circle time, he says, "Orvil (puppet's name) was on the ground

in the yard today. Raise your hand if you know where he should be put after we play with him. Olivia, I see your hand, Would you please put Orvil in the place in the classroom that's just for him. Thank you, Olivia. What could happen to Orvil, our puppet, if we left him on the floor or ground?" "He'd get stepped on," Thad offers. "That could happen, Thad," said Mr. T. "Can anyone else think of what might happen to Orvil on the ground outside?" Mr. T. continues. "The ants would crawl on him," Jessica comments.

5. Ms. Y. announces to a group of children, "It's talking time. Everyone is going to talk to Bonzo (the dog puppet) and tell him their names." She reaches behind her and pulls Bonzo from a bag. "Willy, come up and take Bonzo," Ms. Y. directs. "Now, Cleo, you come up here, too. Willy, have Bonzo say, 'Woof, woof, I'm Bonzo." Willy remains quiet. Ms. Y. repeats. "Woof, woof, I'm Bonzo." Willy fiddles with the puppet and still has not slipped it onto his hand. "We need a barking Bonzo. Who would like to come up, put Bonzo on his hand, and bark?" Ms. Y. asks.

C. Select the best answer for each statement.
1. Because puppets are so appealing, teachers
    a. motivate, model, and plan child activities to enhance the children's experiences.
    b. rarely use puppets in a conventional way for it interrupts children's play.
    c. feel the large expense involved in supplying them is well worth it.
    d. find child language develops best without teacher modeling.
2. Puppets in preschool centers are used
    a. only by children.
    b. most often to present teacher-planned lessons.
    c. by both teachers and children.
    d. only when children ask for them.
3. Creative playacting (dramatization) is probably more appropriate
    a. for younger preschoolers, aged 2 to 3 years.
    b. for older preschoolers.
    c. when children are chosen for familiar characters' parts rather than selected from those children who volunteer for parts.
    d. when teachers help children stick to story particulars rather than promoting new lines or actions.
    e. All of the above.
4. Identifying with a familiar story character through puppet use or playacting may give the child
    a. skills useful in getting along with others.
    b. greater insight into others' viewpoints.
    c. speaking skill.
    d. a chance to use creative imagination.
    e. All of the above.

5. If one is looking for a puppet with an expressive and active movement ability, one should use a
   a. rubber-headed puppet.
   b. papier-mache headed puppet with arms.
   c. cloth-headed puppet with arms.
   d. stick puppet.
   e. All of the above are about equally active and expressive.
6. "Punch and Judy" types of child's play with puppets is
   a. to be expected and needs teacher attention.
   b. a rare occurrence.
   c. best when teacher's performance sticks to the script.
   d. expected and should be ignored.
   e. a good puppetry modeling experience.

References

Bos, Bev, San Jose City College Workshop, Creativity, 1983.
Sloane, G. L., *Fun with Folk Tales,* New York: Dutton, 1942.

Resources

Ackley, E. F., *Marionettes: Easy to Make Fun to Use*, Philadelphia: Lippincott

Batchelder, Marjorie, *The Puppet Theatre Handbook,* New York: Harper & Row

Beaumont, C. W., *Puppets & the Puppet Stage*, Ann Arbor: Finch Press

Bufano, Remo, *Remo Bufano's Book of Puppetry,* New York: Macmillan

Ficklen, B., *Handbook of Fist Puppets,* Philadelphia: Lippincott

Haberl, Sister Marie Anthony, *Marionettes Teach Them,* Denver: Miles and Dryer Printing Co.

Hastings, Sue and Ruthenberg, D., *How to Produce Puppet Plays,* New York: Harper

Hoban, A. M., *Beginners Puppet Book,* New York: Noble and Noble

Inverarity, R. B., *A Manual of Puppetry,* Portland: Binfords & Mort

Joseph, H. H., *A Book of Marionettes,* New York: Viking Press

McPharlin, Paul (ed.) *Puppetry, A Yearbook of Puppets and Marionettes*, Birmingham, Michigan

Millifan, D. F., *First Puppetry,* New York: Barnes

Munger and Elder, *Book of Puppets,* New York: Lothrup

Murphy, Virginia, *Puppetry, An Educational Adventure,* New York: Art Education, Inc.

Rossback, C. E., *Making Marionettes,* New York: Harcourt

Warner, F. S., *The Ragamuffin Marionettes*, New York: Houghton

Unit 17
Understanding Differences

OBJECTIVES

After studying this unit you should be able to

- describe the teacher's role with children who speak a dialect.
- discuss early childhood centers' language programs for bilingual children.
- identifying common speaking difficulties and the techniques which help young children.

Preschool teachers encounter a wide range of language differences in young children. Improvement in speech happens when these children keep talking or trying to communicate. Teachers realize language-different children are just as intelligent and able as those who speak beautifully in standard English. Before we start talking about differences though, let's understand that we are doing so (1) to help the child and (2) to help the child in such a way that we don't actually make matters worse. Let's recognize that something special involving extra teacher sensitivity and knowledge of a cultural group or language-different child may be necessary to plan and aid that particular child's growth. Preserving the child's feelings of adequacy and acceptance is the teacher's prime goal; moving the child toward the eventual learning of standard forms is a secondary one. Meers (1978) states our primary goal with clarity:

. . . to ensure that his idea of himself is positive; of helping the child see himself as a rich source of ideas, as an inventive, resourceful, problem-solving person who can function successfully in personal relationships; at work; in his leisure; as a full member of his community.

STANDARD ENGLISH

Standard English is the language of elementary schools and textbooks. It is the language of the majority of Americans. Within this framework is the child whose speech reflects past experience and the culture (or subculture) to which the child belongs. By practicing the group's way of speaking, its values, attitudes, food preferences, clothing styles, and so on, the child gains acceptance as a group member. Some believe the child's manner of thinking about life's experiences is also influenced.

Dialect, as used here, refers to language patterns which differ from standard English. In the United States today, regional dialects spoken in some areas of the South, Appalachia, and rural New England are good examples of geographic difference. In addition, Dillard (1972) estimates that 80% of Americans with African ancestry use "black" dialect. Teenagers and specific labor groups have their own "dialects" — and teachers, of course, use "educationese."

Dialects evolve naturally over time and possess an element of regularity and systematic usage. Individuals react to dialects by giving prestige, acceptance, or rejection, based on value judgments.

Dialect-speaking teachers, aides, and volunteers (working with children and families of the same dialect) offer children a special degree of familiarity and understanding. A standard English speaking teacher model may sound less familiar but affords the child a model for growth in speaking the dominant language of our society — important to his life opportunities.

Although a dialect may be an advantage in your community, it may be a disadvantage outside of that community. Just as a child who meets another child from a different part of the United States — with a different accent — might say, "You sound funny!" so others may think of dialectic speech as crude or funny.

WORKING WITH BLACK CHILDREN

Much has been researched and debated concerning the best educational techniques to use with young black dialect-speaking children. It's now agreed black English is in no way deficient but is different, with complex syntactic, phonological, and semantic individuality. Children seem to be able to switch from this dialect to standard English, responding in whichever form is acceptable after adequate exposure to both forms. Having this native dialect may affect their ability to read in elementary school, but probably not as much as the teacher's attitude toward socially non-standard dialects, comprehension of such dialects, the relationship of dialect to social class and to self-esteem, and other factors such as nutrition, availability and interest level of reading materials, and community tolerance for reading (Hartwell, 1980). Joiner's table (1981), figure 17-1, presents significant features of black English.

Rapsberry (1979) suggests two important aspects of working with non-standard children which early childhood teachers should note:

The child is not on that account (dialect speaking) less intelligent, less admirable — or less anything else.

and

The teacher must convey the idea standard English is used in the classroom, and other dialects may be appropriate for other circumstances.

One problem which may impede younger disadvantaged black children's learning of standard English is their motivation:

It is especially difficult to motivate younger disadvantaged black children to learn standard English. Teachers can't point out the vocational, social, or academic advantages. As long as they remain in their segregated social environment (and couple this with their natural immaturity), they will not be motivated (Johnson, 1969).

Decreased speed in adopting standard English may also be based on personal preference; young dialect-speaking children who do realize that standard English is advantageous and evaluate it as talking better may not like advantaged individuals or want to be like them (Johnson, 1969).

WORKING WITH DIALECT-SPEAKING FAMILIES

Many centers employ staff members with dialects the children can easily understand — so children feel at home. Teachers who speak the children's dialect may be eagerly sought. Additional insight into the child's culture and the particular meanings of their words is often an advantage for teachers who have the same dialect as the children.

It is important for teachers to know if they are speaking a dialect, and to understand dialectic differences.

(Joiner 1979, p. 343)	Examples
1. The use of the verb <u>be</u> to indicate a reality that is recurring or continuous over time.	1. <u>He be working</u> = He is working every-day.
2. The deletion of some form of the verb <u>to be</u>.	2. <u>Cleo sick today</u> = Cleo is sick today.
3. The use of the third person singular verbs without adding the <u>s</u> or <u>z</u> sound.	3. <u>My mama she talk all the time</u> = My mama talks all the time.
4. The use of the <u>f</u> sound for the <u>th</u> sound at the end of a word.	4. <u>mouf</u> = mouth <u>wif</u> = with
5. The use of an additional word to denote plurals rather than adding an <u>s</u> to the noun.	5. <u>Two boy left for home</u> = Two boys left for home or boys left for home.
6. Non-use of <u>s</u> to indicate possessives.	6. <u>Mr. Green truck got smashed</u> = Mr. Green's truck got smashed.
7. The elimination of <u>l</u> or <u>r</u> sounds in words.	7. <u>hep</u> = help <u>doe</u> = door
8. The use of words with different meanings.	8. <u>bad</u> = great/good
9. The lack of emphasis on the use of tense in verbs.	9. <u>They already walk to the store</u> = They already walked to the store.
10. The deletion of final consonants.	10. <u>toll</u> = told <u>fine</u> = find
11. The use of double subjects.	11. <u>George he here now</u> = George is here now.
12. The use of <u>it</u> instead of <u>there</u>.	12. <u>It ain't none left</u> = There isn't any left.

FIGURE 17-1 Some features of black English *(From C. W. Joiner, "Memorandum Opinion and Order: Martin Luther King Junior Elementary School Children et al. v. Ann Arbor School District Board." 473 F. Supp. 1371 (1979). Reprinted in* Black English and the Education of Black Children and Youth, *ed. G. Smitherman. Detroit, Mich.: Wayne State University Center for Black Studies, 1981.)*

The four most common dialectic differences between standard English and some common dialects occur in verb forms. These differences are in the following areas.

- Subject-verb agreement
- Use of the verb "to be"
- Use of present for past tense
- Use of got for have

In some areas where a language other than English is spoken, part of the rules of the second language may blend and combine to form a type of English, different from standard. Examples of this are (1) English spoken by some Indian children, and (2) English spoken in communities close to the Mexican/American border.

There are differing opinions about the teaching of preferred standard English in early childhood centers. In most centers, however, preserving the child's native dialect while moving slowly toward standard English usage is considered more desirable than immediate, purposeful instruction in standard forms. Joint parent and center discussions can help clarify program goals.

THE TEACHER'S ROLE

Dialectic differences are important to the teacher, so in order to give young children the best model possible, the teacher should speak standard English. It matters very little to children if the teacher speaks a bit differently than they speak. However, the teacher's attitude, warmth, and acceptance of the dialect and the children, themselves, is very important to the child, figure 17-2.

A child may be a very good speaker of his particular dialect, or he may be just a beginner. Staff members working with the young child should respect the child's natural speech and not try to stop the child from using it. The goal is the child's use of natural speech in his native dialect. Since the child's ability to learn new words and new ways is at its peak during early years, standard English can be taught by having many good speaking models available at the center for the child to hear. Interested adults, play activities, other children, and a rich language arts program can provide a setting where children listen and talk freely.

The teacher should know what parts of the center's program are designed to increase the child's use of words. Teachers can show a genuine interest in words in their daily conversations with the children. The teacher also uses the correct forms of standard English in a casual way. Correcting the children in an obvious way could embarrass them and stop openness and enthusiasm. Careful listening, skillful responding, and appropriate questioning during conversations help the child learn to put thoughts into words. The child thinks in terms of his own dialect first and, in time, expresses words in standard English, figure 17-3.

BILINGUALISM

There are two importantly different groups of young preschool children, (1) those who have heard two languages spoken since infancy, and

FIGURE 17-2 Staff attitude can build each child's feelings of self-confidence.

FIGURE 17-3 "Hat."

(2) those who have spoken but one language (other than standard English) before entering school (Bee, 1981). The first are bilingual, the second monolingual. The true bilingual speaks two or more languages well. Children, just learning, may possess different degrees of proficiency in two or more languages.

Bilinguals grasp the idea that one object is represented by a different word in each language rather quickly. Later tests of intelligence and language in elementary school show these children do just as well as other children. One has to also recognize that speaking more than one language has long term career advantages in most cases. Bilingual children, however, can be expected to progress in English usage at slower rates initially than monolingual standard English speaking children.

Creole language speaking children from select areas of the South or Hawaiian Creole speakers are not dialect speakers, but rather speak a distinct language which uses a largely English vocabulary. Often these children will continue to use their native language, maintaining their Creole tradition until their early 20s (Cazden et al., 1981).

A variety of plans and methods to help the bilingual child exist in early childhood centers, figure 17-4.

Being unable to understand or to be understood may be one of the problems facing the bi-

FIGURE 17-4 A program rich in experiences is planned.

lingual child. Learning a second language includes a number of difficult tasks. The child is:

- producing sounds which may not be used in the native language.
- understanding that native speech sounds or words may have different meanings in the new (second) language.
- learning and selecting appropriate responses.
- sorting and revising word orders.
- learning different cultural values and attitudes.
- controlling the flow of air while breathing and speaking.

An important technique — that of admitting and recognizing that a child is a classroom *resource* when it comes to explaining other ways of naming and describing objects, or other ways

FIGURE 17-5 Language learning ability is at its peak during the preschool years.

of satisfying human needs — should be understood by teachers (Clement, 1981). Printscript word cards in both languages can be added to the classroom to reinforce this idea.

The preschooler's language capacity helps the child who learns two languages during the early years. In preschool work it is common to meet children who can switch between fluent conversation in two languages, sorting and switching with speed.

The preschool years are described as the best time to learn a second language, for language learning ability is at its peak, figure 17-5.

The most successful methods for teaching a second language include the same features mentioned in the child's learning of his first language — warm, responsive, articulate adults involved with children's everyday firsthand exploration of the environment. A special project was designed to fit the needs of Spanish-speaking preschoolers in the southwest United States. The curriculum objectives for this well-known bilingual preschool program (called the Bilingual Early Childhood Program) are listed.

1. Development of the child's sensory perceptual skills.

2. Development of the child's language skills in both English and Spanish.
3. Development of the child's thinking and reasoning abilities.
4. Development of the child's positive self-concept. (Nedler, 1977)

Since many centers deal with children who speak a language other than English, or very little English, a center with bilingual children has many decisions to make. The first concern should be the child's adjustment to school. Every effort is made to make the child feel at ease before attempts are made to teach him a second language. Often, the teacher is also bilingual.

Elementary schools teaching reading have relied on a variety of methods. Two common strategies are used with bilingual and dialect speakers.

1. Delay reading instruction until the child has mastered English.
   OR
2. Teach reading in the child's native language (dialect), and switch to English during a later grade in school.

Preschools which encourage children to use two languages are given suggestions by Flores (1980). (Ms. Flores is speaking about the Spanish-speaking child but the comments and suggestions could be applied to other language groups.)

- *Let the children hear both languages.* Speak both languages throughout the day so that children feel comfortable with the second language. Children should have plenty of opportunities to hear the second language without having to speak it.
- *Identify the languages being spoken.* When two languages are being used, identify each language to confirm the child's notion that more than one language is being spoken.
- *Acknowledge and encourage a child's attempt to speak a second language.*

Children eventually will experiment with the sounds and intonations of a second language. Encourage them and comment on what they are doing: "That sounds a lot like Spanish, Mark." When a child addresses you in gibberish, answer in the language they are imitating and then translate. This gives the child the feeling that talking and being understood in the second language is possible.

- *Let a child hear you speak his second language to another child.* For example, read a story in Spanish to a Spanish-speaking child so that an English-speaking child working nearby on a puzzle can overhear.
- *Occasionally give simple commands to the whole group in one language without translating.* "Let's clean up now."
- *Once you get along well with a child in his first language, talk to that child for short periods in the second language.* A child may not understand at first. But by hearing a lot of the second language in a variety of situations, a child will eventually begin to notice, play with, and grasp intonation patterns and sounds.

Teachers faced with a portion of their enrollment speaking another language face unique problems. An interpreter is necessary, and a concerted effort to understand the family's culture is undertaken. Consultants and parents are invaluable. A good place to start on opening days is with a good pronunciation guide of child and parent names. Bilingual teachers or aides are required in a number of centers which serve newly arrived populations. Designing room features and planning curriculum activities which welcome and show acceptance is an important staff task.

Gestures aid communication. Pairing words with actions and naming distinctly helps when working with language-different children.

Both teachers and children can be expected to experience some frustration. Touching and nonverbal behaviors are important cues in communication. The teacher will find that her speech slows, and sentences shorten to one or two words when speaking to the just learning non-English speaking child. Children will rely heavily on showing in actions as they try to communicate and speak. Since preschoolers language ability is amazing — teachers will notice more and more understanding of English — then hesitant naming — followed by beginning phrases. If teacher tries to learn the child's language, the same sequence is apparent.

CULTURAL DIFFERENCES

Cultural differences in communicating are important for teachers to understand. For example, when speaking to adults in some cultures a child lowers his eyes to the floor as a sign of respect. A study of cultural differences can help teachers receive accurate messages.

Cultures are complex and changing, so understanding these cultural similarities and differences can be a life's study in itself. *Culture* is defined here as all the activities and achievements of a society that individuals within that society pass from one generation to the next. Technology, institutions: home, school, religious group; language, values, and customs are typical culture study categories.

Ethnic origin is often a basic ingredient in subcultural groupings: defined as other than a dominant culture. Class structure also exists in societies consisting of upper, middle, and lower income groups. Often, patterns of child-rearing vary between cultures and classes (Broman, 1978). Families may express attitudes and values particular to their class or culture. A poverty attitude, for instance, often includes futility, anger, violence, and loss of trust in anyone or anything.

Teachers try to determine the backgrounds of their attending families — noting the individual nature of children's home communities — housing, income, general numbers and types of cultural groups, in an attempt to better understand children and provide language developing experiences. Their ability to respond and relate to what attending children verbalize is thereby enhanced.

In planning language activities of all types, every effort is made to make children aware of crosscultural similiarities and explore differences. Young children can be exposed to the idea that other people eat, sleep, wear clothing, celebrate, dance, sing, live in groups, and speak to one another in common languages; and that they do these things in ways that may be either the same or different from their family. Planned activities can make comparisions treating diversity with the dignity it deserves. Skin color, hair styles, food preferences, clothing, music, are only starting places. Stories exist in all languages and in most dialects. Librarians can help teachers discover picture books written in dialects or two language translations.

Program goals for children who have had limited opportunities in learning language commonly include

- adding enriching experiences.
- prompting the child's logical thinking abilities.
- reshaping speech *patterns* slowly while increasing speech *usage*.

Each center designs its own activities, giving each child a chance to accomplish new skills. There are many possible program activities. Most program plans emphasize the following ones.

- Activities which develop sensory skills — visual, auditory, and tactile (touch); discriminatory, relational, and sequential abilities.
- Activities which facilitate problem solving and concept development — classifying, organizing, and associating.
- Activities which deal with the language arts, and vocabulary and comprehension devel-

opment — listening, speaking, printscript, and symbolic forms.

Programs are developmental, starting with basics and moving toward higher levels. Supporting, rewarding, and giving language feedback, which expands and clarifies what the children say as they play, is the teacher's role. This includes being an alert listener — really hearing *what* children say, as well as *how* they say it. Good listeners can answer with logical statements and sincere interest. They can ask the child to tell more and to give details. They can suggest ideas or plans for the child to think about related to what was said. A teacher talks with children in a way that helps them grow in understanding and ability. The teacher's time is divided as equally as possible between the quiet children and the talkative ones.

SPEECH-LANGUAGE DISORDERS

Approximately 11–13 million people in the United States have some kind of expressive speech disorder, the most frequent problem involving articulation — an estimated 75% (Weiss and Lillywhite, 1981). The rest, approximately 25%, have language, voice, fluency disorders or a combination of these. Most articulation problems not caused by physical, sensory, or neurological damage respond to treatment. Nonorganic causes of problems can include:

- Lack of stimulation
- Lack of need to talk
- Poor speech models
- Lack of or low reinforcement
- Insecurity, anxiety, crisis

Articulation

If consonant sounds are misarticulated, they may occur in the initial (beginning), medial (middle), or final (ending) positions in words (Weiss and Lillywhite, 1981). It's prudent to point out again that normally-developing children don't master the articulation of all consonants until age 7 or 8.

Teachers sometimes notice differences in children's voice quality which involves pitch, loudness, resonance, and general quality (breathiness, hoarseness, etc.). The intelligibility of a child's speech is determined by how many of the words are understandable. One can expect 80% of the child's speech to be understandable at age 3.

Stuttering and Cluttering

Stuttering and cluttering are categorized as fluency disorders. Stuttering involves the *rhythm* of speech and is a complicated, many-faceted problem. It involves four times as many males as females, and usually responds favorably to treatment. All young children repeat words and phrases, and this increases with anxiety or stress. It's simply typical for the age and isn't true stuttering. Waiting patiently and matter-of-factly is appropriate teacher behavior along with resisting the temptation to say "Slow down."

Cluttering is more of a *rate* of speaking disorder which includes errors in articulation, stress, and pausing. Speech seems too fast with syllables and words run together. Listener reaction and good speech models are critical aspects in lack of fluency. Bloodstein (1975) suggests that adults working with young children should:

- Refrain from criticizing, correcting, helping the child speak, or otherwise reacting negatively or calling the disfluency to the child's attention.
- Improve parent-child relationships if possible.
- Eliminate any factors or conditions that increase disfluency.
- Strengthen the child's expectation of normal fluency and self-faith as a speaker.

COMMUNICATIVE CONCERNS

Most young children (3 to 5 years) hesitate, repeat, and redo as they speak. Imperfections occur for several reasons: (1) A child does not attend as closely as an adult, especially to certain high-frequency consonant sounds. (2) The child may not be able to distinguish some sounds; sounds tend to sound the same. (3) A child's coordination and control of his articulatory mechanisms may not be perfected. For example, he may be able to hear the difference between *Sue* and *shoe* but is not able to pronounce them differently.

Articulation characteristics of young children include:

Substitutions:
   One sound is substituted for another.
   "Wabbit" for *rabbit.*
   "Git" for *get.*

Omissions:
   The speaker leaves out a sound that should be articulated. He says "ca" for *cat,* "icky" for *sticky,* "probly" for *probably.* The left-out sound may be at the beginning, middle, or end of a word.

Distortions:
   Production of a sound in an inarticulate manner.

Additions:
   The speaker adds a sound.
   "Li-it-tle" for *little.*
   "Muv-va-ver" for *mother.*

Transposition:
   Word sounds are switched in position.
   "Hangerber" for *hamburger.*
   "Modren" for *modern.*
   "Aminal" for *animal.*

Lisps:
   A distortion of s, z, sh, th, ch, and j sounds. There are from 2 to 10 types of lisps noted by speech experts.

OTHER PROBLEMS IN COMMUNICATION

Frequent Crying

Occasionally frustrated children will cry or scream to communicate a need. Crying associated with adjustment to a new situation is handled by providing supportive attention and care. Continual crying and screaming to obtain an object or privilege, on the other hand, calls for the following kinds of teacher statements (Osborn, 1983):

"I don't understand what you want when you scream. Use words so I will know what you want."

"Sara does not know what you want when you cry Billy. Saying 'Please get off the puzzle piece,' with your words tells her."

This lets the child know what's expected and gives the teacher the opportunity to reward a child's asking in words.

Avid Talkers and Shouters

Occasionally children may discover that talking incessantly can get them what they want. In order to gain quiet, others give in. This is somewhat different from commonplace give and take in children's daily play conversations, or the child's growing ability to argue and state his case.

Language becomes a social tool. A child may find that loudness in speech can intimidate others and will "outshout" the opposition.

Questioners

At times, children ask many questions, one right after another. This may be a good device to hold or gain adults' attention: "Why isn't it time for lunch?" or "What makes birds sing?" or "Do worms sleep?" The questions may seem endless to adults. Most of the questions are prompted by the child's natural curiosity. Teachers help children find out and, as much as possible, fulfill the needs of the individual child. Along the way there will be many times when questions asked may be difficult or even impossible to answer.

DELAYED LANGUAGE

Adults worry about children who *seem* to understand but speak infrequently in comparison to other children their age. Usually a plan is formulated to only praise and give attention when the child says something. Most staffs are aware of childhood autism, a much more serious condition, whose symptoms include delayed speech and echolalia. Having a speech-language expert observe a delayed language child is often recommended to parents if a child falls more than two years behind his peers.

HEARING

Screening young children's auditory acuity may uncover a hearing loss. The earlier the diagnosis, the more effective the treatment. Since young children can develop ear infections frequently, schools should always alert parents when a child's listening behavior seems newly impaired.

SEEKING HELP

If a child's speech or language lags behind expected development for the child's mental age (mental maturity), school staff members, by observing and listening closely, try to collect additional data. When speech is unusually difficult to understand: rhythmically conspicuous, full of sound distortion, or one must always strain to hear, it is considered serious. Professional help is available to parents through a number of resources. Most cities have speech and hearing centers and public and private practitioners in speech-language pathology and audiology. Other resources include:

- Universities and medical schools
- State Department of Education offices

- The American Speech-Language-Hearing Association Directory (found by checking local medical societies)

A center's director can be alerted to observe a child who the teacher feels may benefit from professional help.

A teacher guards *against:*

- nagging a child about speech usage.
- correcting in a way that makes children doubt their own abilities.
- giving children the idea that they are not trying hard enough to correct or improve their speech.
- discouraging children's speaking.
- allowing teasing about individual speech differences.
- interrupting children who are trying to express an idea.
- hurrying a child who is speaking.
- putting children on stage in an anxiety-producing way.

LANGUAGE GIFTEDNESS

Each child is unique. A few children speak clearly and use long, complex, adultlike speech at two, three, or four years of age. They express ideas originally and excitedly, enjoying individual and group discussions. Some may read simple primers (or other books) along with classroom word labels. Activities that are commonly used with kindergarten or first grade children may interest them. Just as there is no stereotype average child, language-talented children are also unique individuals. They may, however, exhibit many of the following characteristics.

- Attend to tasks in a persistent manner for long periods of time.
- Focus deeply or submerge themselves in what they are doing.
- Block out distractions while concentrating.
- Speak maturely and use a wide vocabulary.
- Show a searching, exploring curiosity.

- Ask questions which go beyond immediate happenings.
- Be avidly interested in words, alphabet letters, numbers, or writing tools.
- Remember small details of past experiences and compare with present happenings.
- Read books (or words) by memorizing pictures or words.
- Offer ideas often and easily.
- If bilingual, rapidly acquire English skills, given exposure (Bernal, 1978).
- Show a mature sense of humor for age (Kitano, 1982).
- Express feeling and emotions, as in storytelling, movement, and visual arts.
- Use rich imagery in informal language (Torrance, 1969).
- Exhibit originality of ideas and persistence in problem solving.
- Retain information.
- Are highly imaginative.

Kitano (1982) recommends planning activities within the regular curriculum which promote attending gifted children's creative thinking. Suggestions include:

Fluency opportunities: defined as promoting many different responses. Example: "What are all the ways you can think of to . . ."
Flexibility opportunities: defined as the facility to change a mind set or seeing things in a different light. Example: "If you were a Christmas tree, how would you feel . . ."
Originality opportunities: "Make something that no one else will think of."
Elaboration opportunities: defined as the embellishment of an idea or adding detail. Example: presenting a doddle or squiggle and asking "Tell what they could be."

RESOURCES

Figure 17-6 lists books with multicultural themes and illustrations.

Bernheim, Marc and Evelyn
  In Africa, A Margaret K. Mc Elderry Book, New York, 1973.
Beskow, Elsa
  Pelle's New Suit, Harper & Row Publishers, New York, 1929.
Binzen, Bill
  First Day in School, Doubleday & Co. Inc., Garden City, NY, 1972.
Calhoun, Mary
  The Hungry Leprechaun, Wm. Morrow & Co., New York, 1962.
Cohen, Miriam
  The New Teacher, The Macmillian Co., New York, 1972.
Ets, Mary Hall
  Gilberto and the Wind, The Viking Press, New York, 1963.
Fraser, Kathleen & Levy, Miriam F.
  Adam's World: San Francisco, Albert Whitman Co., Chicago, 1971.
Freeman, Don
  Corduroy, The Viking Press, New York, 1968.
Greenberg, Polly
  Oh Lord, I Wish I Was A Buzzard, The Macmillian Co., New York, 1968.
Hoff, Syd
  Roberto and the Bull, McGraw-Hill Book Co., New York, 1969.
Keats, Jack Ezra
  Whistle for Willie, Viking Press, New York, 1964.
  Peter's Chair, Harper & Row Publishers, New York, 1967.
  A Letter to Amy, Harper & Row Publishers, New York, 1968.
Otsuka, Yuzo
  Suho and the White Horse (A Legend of Mongolia), Bobbs-Merrill Co. Inc., Indianapolis, 1981.
Politi, Leo
  Pedro, The Angel of Olvera Street, Charles Scribner's Sons, New York, 1946.
  Little Leo, Charles Scribner's Sons, New York, 1964.
  Rosa, Charles Scribner's Sons, New York, 1951.
  Lito the Clown, Charles Scribner's Sons, New York, 1963.
Schick, Eleanor
  City in the Summer, Macmillan Co., Collier-Macmillan Limited, London, 1969.
Scott, Ann Herbert
  On Mother's Lap, McGraw-Hill Book Co., San Francisco, 1972.
Tresselt, Alvin
  It's Time Now, Lothrop, Lee & Shepherd Co., New York, 1969.
Yashima, Mitsu & Taro
  Momo's Kitten, The Viking Press, New York, 1961.

FIGURE 17-6 Books with multi-cultural themes and illustrations

SUMMARY

Teachers work with children who may differ greatly in language development. One of the teacher's roles is to carefully work toward increasing the child's use of words, while providing a model of standard English through activities and daily interaction. Teachers are careful not to give children the impression that their speech is less worthy than that of others.

Program goals should be clearly understood, as should the needs and interests of children who have developed a language which differs from the language of the school. Cultural differences exist, and teachers need to be aware of them in order to understand the young child. Knowing that cultural differences exist, the teacher can provide activities which start at the child's present level, and help the child to grow, know more, and speak in both standard English and their native speech.

Speech differences require observation and study by a center's staff. Parents can be alerted if their child may need further professional language help.

Learning Activities

- List and describe dialects found in your community. Give a few sentence examples of each.

- In small groups, discuss what you feel are essential factors to language growth that may be missing in a disadvantaged child's background.

- Interview the director of a center which cares for bilingual and/or disadvantaged young children. Ask what techniques are used to increase a child's language ability. If there is no early childhood center in your community, give examples of goals or techniques used to increase a child's language ability which you have found from research at a library.

- If possible, have a speech therapist or specialist in speech correction speak with the class.

- Develop a list of community resources or agencies which offer services to children with speech or hearing problems.

- Tape record your voice in a five minute conversation with a friend. Have the recording analyzed for dialect, accent, and standard English usage.

- Observe three preschool children (one at a time) for a period of 10 minutes each. Write down exactly what each child says. Include a description of gestures and nonverbal communications. Analyze your notes. Are there any examples of common speech errors or dialectic differences?

- Compare two languages. What are the differences? What are the similarities?

- Xerox the following cards. Cut into separate cards along the lines. Form discussion groups after each group member rates the cards individually. Compare ratings and discuss.

Rating Scale

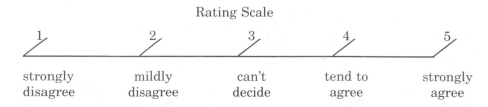

1	2	3	4	5
strongly disagree	mildly disagree	can't decide	tend to agree	strongly agree

Certain cultural groups live only a day-to-day existence. Their children tend to be unable to plan ahead, or work at a task which has no immediate pleasure or reward. These children should be told that learning and education are important.

The culture of the majority of Americans and the speaking of standard English is the natural curriculum of the preschool. Children eventually need to compete for jobs; when they do, they *need* standard English speech skills.

A dialect usually gives others an idea of the person's background and experience. Some dialects and accents are highly prized. A British accent usually indicates properness and "upper class" manners.

If a center has children attending who are bilingual or dialectic speakers, a teacher must be hired who speaks the same language or dialect.

The language of the "street" is as powerful complicated as standard English. We all speak two languages — the one we use at home and the one we use at school.

The child who is bilingual is really advantaged now, for schools and preschools provide extra attention and help. The average child with slight difficulties in language is really the most disadvantaged.

Gifted children have many advantages if they attend early childhood centers.

The reason most young children who use little speech in early childhood centers are silent is because they don't know how to speak well.

School and preschool staffs who spend much time discussing their programs with parents and community groups are foolish. They already know what is best and right for young children.

Teachers who know they are not speaking standard English should take additional courses to improve their speaking ability.

In an interview for a desirable teaching job, the interviewer noted the teacher's use of nonstandard English. The applicant should at that point speak about the advantages of hiring a nonstandard speaker who understands both the speech and culture of attending children.

When working with Spanish-speaking children, teachers should include Spanish names as well as English names for new objects introduced to the children. Celebrations of Spanish holidays should be part of the school's program.

A multicultural program includes activities which give children knowledge of cultural differences. This type of program is necessary only for schools which enroll middle-class children.	Dialectic speaking turns many people off for it usually indicates lack of education. Many view it as inferior, sloppy speech. Actually, it is just as sophisticated as standard English.
Many children could learn a second language easily during preschool years, if preschool teachers planned for it. Some early childhood centers are neglecting this opportunity to teach young children when they have the capacity.	Having the child speak standard English as soon as possible will help him be successful in elementary school reading.
Being bilingual is a real advantage in life.	Most differences in cultures are quite understandable if one traces that cultural group's history.
Disadvantaged children rarely show language giftedness.	The same preschool activities which help the average child grow in language skill rarely help disadvantaged children.
Speech errors such as substitutions, omissions, and transpositions are not common. Teachers should study and refer these children to experts.	The best thing to do for a child who stutters is relax and direct the child to repeat what he's tried to say.

Unit Review

A. Answer the following questions.
  1. How can a teacher learn about the cultural background of a child?
  2. What should be the teacher's attitude toward children whose speech is different from the teacher's?

B. One of the responsibilities of a teacher is to act as a model to the child for correct forms of speech. Another responsibility is to increase the child's ability to express ideas in words. Quality of responses is more important than just talking. In the following exchanges between teachers and small children, why did the child stop speaking?

1. Teacher: "How are you today, Mary?"
   Child: "Fine."
2. Child: "Mrs. Brown, Johnnny hit me!"
   Teacher: "I saw you grab the truck he was playing with. That wasn't nice!"
   Child: (Silence)
3. Child: "Teacher, I want a crayon."
   Teacher: "Do you know how to use a crayon?"
   Child: "Yes."
   Teacher: "Tell me how to use a crayon."
   Child: "To color."
   Teacher: "Say, 'To make colored marks on the paper.' "
   Child: "I want a crayon."
   Teacher: "How are you going to use the crayon?"
   Child: (Silence)
4. Child: "I found a bug."
   Teacher: "That's nice."
5. Child: "Fellow one."
   Teacher: "It's yellow, not fellow."
   Child: "Fellow one."
   Teacher: "You want the yellow one. A fellow is a man, Lindy."
   Child: (Silence)
6. Teacher: "Jason, what's your favorite ice cream flavor?"
   Child: "Huh?"
   Teacher: "What's your favorite ice cream flavor?"
   Child: "Flavorite?"
   Teacher: "Don't you like ice cream?"
   Child: "Yah."
   Teacher: "What's your favorite ice cream flavor?"
   Child: (Silence)

C. Define these speech terms.
   1. dialect
   2. bilingual
   3. stuttering
   4. audiology
   5. cluttering

D. Listed below are comments made by children. Give an example of the response which a teacher could make in order to encourage more thought and stimulate growth on the part of the child.
   1. Child with ball says, "Me play."
   2. Child remarks, "I done went to get a red crayon."
   3. Child says, "I got this thing."
   4. Child says, "I like chitchun choop!"
   5. Child asks, "No run in the street?"
   6. Child exclaims, "I don't wanna play with them childruns."

E. Select the correct answer. Some items have more than one correct answer.
1. Standard English is
   a. the language of textbooks.
   b. often taught slowly to nonstandard speakers.
   c. often different from English spoken in a dialect.
   d. needed for success in any line of work.
2. Early childhood centers try to
   a. teach children standard English during the first days of school.
   b. make sure each child feels secure.
   c. plan activities in which disadvantaged children have interest.
   d. provide for each child's development of word use in his own dialect.
3. Teachers should be careful to guard against
   a. correcting children's speech by drawing attention to errors.
   b. thinking that only standard English is correct and therefore better than English spoken in a dialect.
   c. giving children the idea that they speak differently or "funny."
   d. feeling that children who come from low-income homes are always disadvantaged when compared to children from middle-income homes.
4. Young children with speech errors
   a. rarely outgrow them.
   b. may need special help.
   c. often do not hear as well as adults.
   d. can hear that what they say is different but do not have the ability to say it correctly.
5. Bilingualism in the young child is
   a. always a disadvantage.
   b. sometimes a disadvantage.
   c. a rewarding challenge to the teacher.
   d. a problem when schools make children feel defeated and unaccepted.
6. A disadvantaged child may
   a. also be hyperactice and aggressive.
   b. be more independent and talkative than a middle-class child.
   c. talk a lot but have a smaller vocabulary than the average middle-class child.
   d. need teachers who not only model standard English but also model problem solving with words.

References

Bee, Helen, *The Developing Child,* 3rd Ed., Harper and Row Publishers, 1981, p. 187.

Bernal, E. M., Jr., "The Identification of Gifted Chicano Children," *Educational Planning for the Gifted,* A. Y. Baldwin, G. H. Gear and L. J. Lucito (eds.), Reston, VA, Council for Exceptional Children, 1978.

Bloodstein, O., *A Handbook on Stuttering,* National Easter Seal Society of Crippled Children and Adults, Chicago, 1975.

Broman, Betty, *The Early Years,* Rand McNally College Publishing Co., Chicago, 1978.

Cazden, Courtney B., John C. Baratz, William Labov, and Francis H. Palmer, "Language Development in Day Care Programs," *Language in Early Childhood Education,* revised ed., The National Association for the Education of Young Children, Washington, DC, 1981.

Clement, John, *Prompting Preschool Bilinguialism,* KEYS to Early Childhood Education, Vol. 2, No. 3, March, 1981.

Dee, Rita, *Planning for Ethnic Education: A Handbook for Planned Change,* Revised ed., Illinois State Board of Education, Jan. 1980, ERIC ED191 976.

Dillard, J. L., *Black English,* Random House, 1972.

Flores, Manna I., *Helping Children Learn a Second Language,* KEYS to Early Childhood Education. Vol. 1, No. 6, July, 1980.

Hartwell, P., "Dialect Interference in Writing: A Critical View," *Research in the Teaching of English,* 14 (May, 1980).

Hendrick, Joanne, *The Whole Child,* Times Mirror/Mosby, 1984, Chap. 12.

Johnson, Kenneth, "Pedagogical Problems of Using Second Language Techniques for Teaching Standard English to Speakers of Nonstandard Negro Dialect," *Linguistic Cultural Differences and American Education,* ed. by Aarons, Gordon and Stewart, Florida FL. Reporter, 1969.

Joiner, C. W., "Memorandum Opinion and Order: *Martin Luther King Junior Elementary School Children et al.* v. *Ann Arbor School District Board.*" 473 F. Supp. 1371 (1979). Reprinted in *Black English and the Education of Black Children and Youth,* ed. G. Smitherman. Detroit, MI: Wayne State University Center for Black Studies, 1981.

Kitano, Margie, "Young Gifted Children: Strategies for Preschool Teachers," *Young Children,* Vol. 37, No. 4, May, 1982.

Klopf, Donald W., "Educating Children for Communication in a Multicultural Society," *Paper presented at the Conference on Developing Oral Communication Competence in Children,* Australia, July, 1979, ERIC ED180 026.

Markham, Lynda R., "De Dog and De Cat," Assisting Speakers of Black English as They Begin to Write, *Young Children,* May, 1984.

Meers, Hilda J., *Helping Our Children Talk,* Longman Group Limited, New York, 1976.

Nedler, Shari, "A Bilingual Early Childhood Program," *The Preschool in Action,* Mary Carol Day and Ronald K. Parker (eds.) Boston: Allyn and Bacon, Inc., 1977.

Osborn, Janie Dyson and D. Keith Osborn, *Cognition in Early Childhood,* Education Associates, Athens, GA, 1983.

Rapsberry, W., "Reading, Writing, and Dialect," *Young Children,* Nov. 1979.

Torrance, E., *Creativity,* Dimensions Publ., Belmont, CA, 1969.

Weiss, Curtis E., and Herold S. Lillywhite, *Communicative Disorders,* 2nd Ed., The C. V. Mosby Co., 1981.

Suggested Readings

Dillard, J. L., *Black English,* Random House, 1972.

Hendrick, Joanne, *The Whole Child,* Times Mirror/Mosby, 1984, Chap. 12.

Weiss, Curtis E., and Herold S. Lillywhite, *Communicative Disorders,* 2nd Ed., The C. V. Mosby Co., 1981.

Section 4
Writing —
A Language Art

Unit 18
Printscript

OBJECTIVES

After studying this unit you should be able to

- discuss the child's development of small hand muscle control.
- state three reasons why young children may start making alphabet letters or numerals.
- describe how printscript uppercase and lowercase letters are formed.

At some point, a child learns that written marks have meaning. Just as he sought the names of *things*, he now seeks the names of these marks and what they say. Because each child is an individual, this may or may not happen during the preschool years. One child may try to make letters or numbers. Another child may have little interest in or knowledge of written forms, figure 18-1. Many children are somewhere between these two examples.

Providing experiences which match a child's interests and abilities is the goal of many centers. Most schools plan activities with alphabet letters for those children who ask questions or seem ready, and then proceed if the child is interested. Remember that it is poor practice to ignore obvious interest or to tell the child he will learn to print later, in kindergarten.

If a child asks a direct question, the teacher should help him find the answer; a motivated child learns quickly. This is not to say the teacher should overdo it. The best rule of thumb is to notice the child's lead, and offer what the child can handle successfully without destroying his interest or enthusiasm.

COORDINATION

Muscle control follows a timetable of its own. Control of a particular muscle depends on many factors — diet, exercise, inherited ability, and motivation, to name a few. A baby can control his neck and arms long before his legs. A child's muscle control grows in a head-to-toe fashion. Muscles closer to the center of the body can be controlled long before those of the hands and fingers. Large muscle control comes before small muscle control. Think of a toddler walking; his legs seem to swing from his hips; his large hip muscle is being used. Just as each child starts walking and develops muscle control at different ages, so each one develops the ability to make symbols with a writing tool at different ages.

Early writing instruction is not a new idea. Maria Montessori (a well-known educator and designer of teaching materials) and numerous other teachers have offered instruction in writing (or printing) to preschoolers. Dr. Montessori encouraged the child's tracing of letter forms using the first two fingers of the hand as a pre-

FIGURE 18-1 Some children are interested in alphabet letters; others are not.

writing exercise. She observed that this type of light touching seemed to help youngsters when writing tools were given them. Montessori (1967) designed special *cut out* alphabet letter forms as one of a number of prewriting aids. These forms help exercise and develop small muscles while shapes are learned. Dr. Montessori suggests the following:

When a teacher has a child see and touch the letters of the alphabet, three sensations come into play simultaneously: sight, touch and kinesthetic (muscular) sensation. This is why the image of the graphic symbol is fixed in the mind much more quickly than when it is acquired through sight in ordinary methods.

It should be noted, moreover, that muscular memory is the most tenacious in a small child and is also the readiest. Sometimes even he does not recognize a letter when he sees it, but he does when he touches it.

COGNITIVE DEVELOPMENT

Realization that there are written symbols is a first step in writing. The discovery that written language is simply spoken language is another step. Mental growth, which allows a child to see similarities and differences in symbols, comes before the ability to write. The child recognizes that a written mark is a shape made by the placement of lines.

FIGURE 18-2 A child starts with scribbles and, when older, draws symbols of the world around him.

A young child scribbles if given paper and a marking tool. As the child grows, the scribbles are controlled into lines which he places where desired, figure 18-2. With age, circles appear, then a face, later a full figure, and so on, figure 18-3. Children draw their own symbols of what they see around them. The length of time it takes this process to develop differs with each child. Some children tie shoes, fold paper airplanes, and use forks and knives during preschool years. Others are not able to do these skills until much later. This is also true with the ability to print.

In addition to muscle control, the desire to do what one sees others do, and easy access to writing tools, are important in developing the child's ability to print. Parents can help develop a child's interest in letters by naming alphabet letters with him when he asks.

ART EXPERIENCE

Drawings and paintings not only communicate children's thinking, when they reach the level of drawing which is representative of the environment, but often display early attempts to create symbols. Some of these symbols may be recognized by adults, figure 18-4, but others seem to be unique and represent the world the child's own way. Children often want to talk

FIGURE 18-3 An elaborate detailed human figure — the work of a 4½-year-old

about their work and will create stories to accompany graphics (Kane, 1982). Calkins (1979) believes not only that children can begin writing the first day they enter kindergarten, but that 90% of all children come to school *believing* they can write. She points out that most writer's first drafts concentrate on messages rather than perfection. Her revolutionary idea that "children can learn to write in the same way they learned to talk" hasn't yet gathered many advocates. On the other hand, generations of children are being asked to know the letters of the alphabet, sound-symbol correspondences, and recognize a few vocabulary words by sight before they write. If the same was true of learning to speak, they would be asked to wait until all letter sounds are perfected before attempting speech.

FIGURE 18-4 This is an early attempt to create symbols. Notice the as yet awkward grasp on the brush.

Since alphabet letters are more abstract than representative drawing, some educators suggest that drawing is prewriting skill development. Some feel it's more logical to have children learn to write before learning to read (Kane, 1982) (Chomsky, 1971). Brittain's research (1973) found that children who were making closed forms and recognizable letters in their drawings also made closed forms and recognizable letters if they attempted writing, figure 18-5.

There seems to be a profound connection between experience and ability in drawing and interest in and ability to write alphabet letters (Kane, 1982). Durkin (1969) identifies a characteristic common to almost all children (in her research study) who read early, and continued to hold their lead in reading achievement. Their parents describe them as "pencil-and-paper kids" whose starting point of curiosity about written language was an interest in scribbling and drawing.

Berg (1977) concludes that the acquisition of skills in writing and reading — and develop-

FIGURE 18-5 A closed figure drawing with alphabet letters by a four-year-old

ment of the attitude that books are enjoyable — is not an academic or technical learning, but grow from a warmly physical and emotional base of shared enjoyment and intimacy. Most experts believe considerable support exists for the notion that oral language provides a base for learning to write (Dyson, 1981). Implications for teachers are multiple, not only is access to drawing tools: magic markers, chalk, pencils, and brushes important so children can make "their own marks"; but teacher's ability to form and maintain nurturing, warm interpersonal relationships which promote oral language is equally critical.

A few preschoolers have surprised their teachers by attempting to "write" words and sentences. Chomsky (1971) feels this reflects a "natural order" of writing first, then reading what's written. Some preschoolers develop a sounds of letters and names of letters system of spelling. The excitement early spellers display is reminiscent of the toddler who's just discovered everything has a name. Chomsky states:

> Typically, the speller reaches a point where he begins to ask about words that he sees around him. Either he attempts to pronounce them, reading them off phonetically in order to identify them, or he asks what they say. When this time comes, such a child seems suddenly to notice all the print in the world around him — street signs, food labels, newspaper headlines, printing on cartons, books, billboards, everything. He tries to read everything, already having a good foundation in translating from pronunciation to print. If help is provided when he asks for it, he makes out wonderfully well. It is a tremendously exciting time for him.

The same acceptance and lack of correction on teacher's part which was suggested with beginning speakers is appropriate for beginning writers. Encourage, welcome, and keep it coming by providing attention and a "writing place" is a good course of action. Words which appear may look like a foreign language — DG (dog), JRAGIN (dragon), (Vukelich & Golden 1984, Chomsky 1971).

This discussion is not given here to promote instruction in printscript in preschools but rather to help early childhood teachers in their interactions with children who have interest in printing symbols.

FIRST LEARNINGS

A child may notice marks (letters) in picture books, television, and in the community. The child observes other children or parents reading and writing. Questions and imitation naturally follow.

Letters and numbers are everywhere. "What's that?" the child asks. Many preschoolers add alphabet letters to their drawings. Sometimes they know the name or sound of the letter.

The following early childhood activities help the child use and gain control of small arm and finger muscles in preparation for writing.

- Puzzles
- Pegboards
- Small blocks
- Construction toys
- Cutting with scissors

Most schools plan activities in which the child puts together or arranges small pieces in a puzzle. These are sometimes called tabletop activities, and are available for play throughout the day. A teacher can encourage the use of tabletop activities by suggestion or by having the pieces arranged invitingly on tables or shelves.

Early childhood centers should create rooms that are full of symbols, letters, and numbers in clear view of the child. Many toys have circles, squares, triangles, alphabet letters, and other common shapes. Recommended symbol size for playroom use is at least one to one and one-half inches in height, figure 18-6. Teachers can add printing to playrooms the following ways.

Labeling
Artwork
Nametags
Lockers and storage areas, figure 18-7
Belongings

FIGURE 18-6 Children are busily working on one of the language games the center supplies. Notice the variety of displays on the walls — using both words and pictures.

Common objects in the room such as scissors, paper, crayons, fishbowl, chair, water

School areas such as blocks, library or reading center, playhouse, art center, science center

Placecards for snacks

Display Areas

Magazine pictures with captions

Current interest displays, for example: "Rocks we found on our walk."

Bulletin boards and wall displays with words

Wall alphabet guides (Aa Bb . . .)

Alphabet charts, figure 18-8

Child's work with explanations, such as "Josh's block tower," or "Penny's clay pancakes"

Signmaking for child activities, such as store, hospital, wet paint, and tickets for sale here

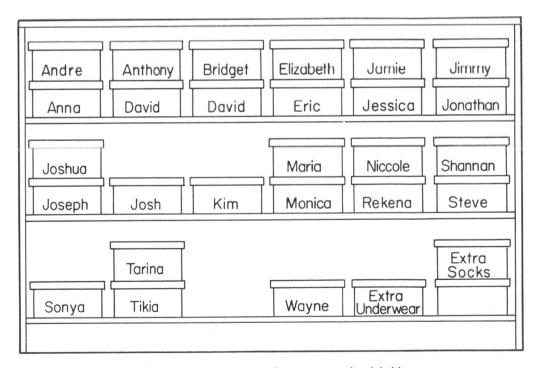

FIGURE 18-7 Large printscript letters are used to label boxes.

INSTRUCTIONS TO MAKE CHARTLINER

Cut a piece of Masonite® 12 inches by 36 inches. Make 7 (seven) sawcuts 1½″ (one and one half inches) apart, beginning and ending 1½″ (one and one half inches) from either end. Then glue or nail ½″ (one half inch) square pieces of wood 12″ (twelve inches) long to each end.

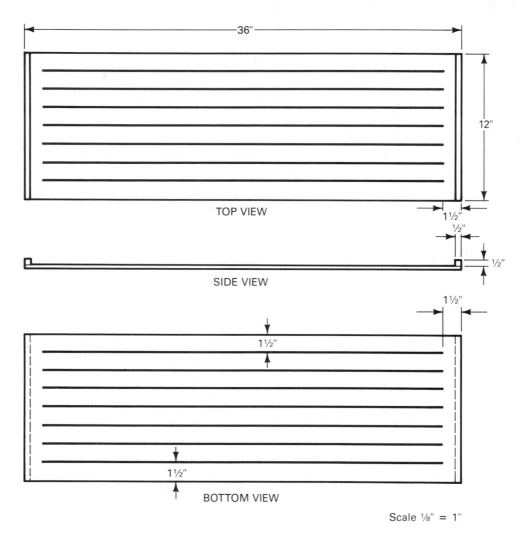

FIGURE 18-8 Making a chartliner

Teacher-made Activities

Brightly colored alphabet letters from felt, cardboard, sandpaper, leather, plastic
Games with letters, numbers, or symbols
Alphabet cards
Games with names and words
Greeting cards
Hats with words

The child's own name is often the first word that is printed. Parents may have taught their child to print with all capitals. Early childhood centers then help introduce the child to the letter forms that are used in the first grades of public school.

FIRST SCHOOL ALPHABETS

In kindergarten or first grade, printing is done in printscript, sometimes called manuscript printing, figure 18-9. Centers can obtain samples from an elementary school in their neighborhood.

Teachers need to be familiar with printscript. It is easier for a child to learn the right way than to be retrained later. All printing seen by young children in a preschool should be printscript, using both uppercase (capitals) and lowercase (small letters). Names, bulletin boards, and labels made by teachers should always show the correct printscript forms. Printscript letters are formed with straight lines, circles, and parts of circles. In figure 18-8, the small arrows and numerals show the direction to follow in making the letters as well as the sequence of the lines. Alphabet letters vary slightly in appearance in different parts of the country, figure 18-10.

Numbers in printed form are called numerals. Children may have used toys with numerals, such as block sets; numbers are everywhere. The young child will probably hold up fingers to indicate his age or tell you he can count. He may start making number symbols before showing an interest in alphabet letters. Numeral forms, figure 18-11, are also available from elementary schools. The numeral forms in one geographic area may also be slightly different from those of another town, city, or state.

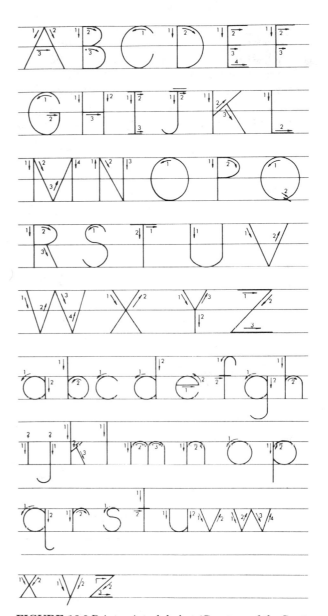

FIGURE 18-9 Printscript alphabet *(Courtesy of the Santa Clara Unified School District, Santa Clara, CA.)*

EARLY ATTEMPTS

The work of young children may include letters that are sideways, backwards, or upside down. The letters may also be upright from the start. These are all normal. Words may appear instead of single letters. The child may, or may not, be able to name the symbol, letter, or word.

Teachers encourage the child's speech and show correct forms, but should not insist that the child copy them. The teacher provides opportunities and observes the child's efforts. Making sure each child feels good about himself, whether he can print symbols or not, is an important part of teaching young children.

In the beginning attempts to write, it is common for children to grasp writing tools tightly and press down hard enough to tear the paper. With time, and mastery of small muscles, children's tense, unschooled muscles relax, and

forms and shapes start to resemble alphabet forms and recognizable shapes. Deep concentration and effort is observed. All attempts are recognized and appreciated by early childhood teachers as a sign of the child's growing interest and ability.

At times, children tutor one another in play with alphabet toys or writing attempts. Brightly colored felt-tip marking pens slide smoothly across the paper, and do not break as easily as crayons, soft large lead pencils, or chalk.

Brand names noticed on common household objects also serve as a stimulus, and are one of many factors that can contribute to a child's interest in writing.

Alphabet letter names or alphabet letter sounds are told to children when they ask, "Teacher, what is this?" Phonetic sounds are preferred in some programming. The Appendix includes a phonetic guide for English alphabet letter pronounciation.

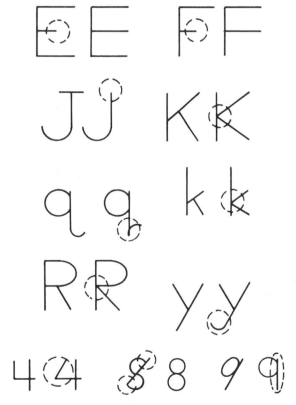

FIGURE 18-10 Some geographical differences in print-script alphabet letters and numeral forms

SUMMARY

The alphabet and printed words are part of preschool life. Centers should not try to teach all children to print. Many children will, however, show interest, and activities are planned around this interest.

Numerals are also interesting to young children. These symbols are part of living; they are seen at school, home, and in the neighborhood. Guides for forming numerals and letters of the alphabet can be obtained from local schools. These guides may vary slightly from city to city.

The ability to print depends upon the child's:

FIGURE 18-11 Printscript numerals *(Courtesy of the Santa Clara Unified School District, Santa Clara, CA).*

- muscle control.
- skill in recognizing symbols.
- ability to note the placement of lines in a symbol.

Printscript is used in preschool, kindergarten, and first grade. Letters are formed with lines and circles in uppercase and lowercase symbols.

Children are ready for printing at different ages. They learn alphabet letters at different rates. Teachers sometimes help children to print. Printscript is used for labeling, display, and other activities at early childhood centers, whenever it is to be seen and understood by children.

Learning Activities

- Without turning back to review the printed alphabet guide given in this unit, print the alphabet in both uppercase and lowercase.

- Obtain a printscript alphabet from the nearest public school. With a red crayon or pen, circle letters which differ (even slightly) from your attempted alphabet. Print all letters you circled on remaining lines using proper form.

- Observe a preschool program. Notice and list all written forms found in the playroom within the view of the children. Report the findings to classmates.

- Find some examples of young children's attempts to make letters and numerals in their drawings. What do you notice about the symbols? Are the lines large, small, slanted, or straight? Are capitals or small letters used? What else do you notice?

- Invite a first grade teacher to speak to the class about methods used to teach printscript in the classroom.

- List all the "marking" tools you find in a classroom you've chosen to visit.

Unit Review

A. Select the correct answer. Most questions have more than one.
1. Child care programs
   a. teach all children to print.
   b. try to teach correct printscript form.
   c. all teach the same printscript.
   d. help children with printing attempts.
2. Small muscle control
   a. comes after large muscle control.
   b. depends on many factors.
   c. is difficult for some preschoolers.
   d. is the only thing involved in learning to print.

3. If drawings have upside-down alphabet letters, teachers should
   a. immediately begin printing lessons.
   b. know that the child may be interested in activities with printed forms.
   c. tell the child the letters are upside down quickly.
   d. worry about the child's ability to do them perfectly.
4. A child's readiness to print may depend upon his
   a. ability to gather information from his senses.
   b. knowledge that letters are formed by placing lines.
   c. home and family.
   d. feelings for the teacher.

B. Place the following in the best order. (What happens, first, next, last for the items in each example.)
   1. a. small muscle control
      b. large muscle control
      c. control of fingers
   2. a. child makes letters
      b. child makes scribbles
      c. child makes circles
   3. a. teacher shows child how to make a Y
      b. child knows the name of the letter Y
      c. child says, "Teacher, make a Y on my paper."
   4. a. child tries to write
      b. child sees parent writing
      c. child prints the letter b
   5. a. child prints letters in artwork
      b. teacher notices and encourages
      c. child know the names of all the letters in the alphabet

C. Answer the following questions.
   1. What are some possible reasons children age 2 to 5 years may start to print?
   2. Give examples of preschool equipment that promotes small muscle and finger control.
   3. What should teachers consider about the printscript form they use?
   4. Why are some preschoolers not interested in letters?
   5. Muscle control is only part of learning to write. Name the other factors that affect readiness for written communication.
   6. When a child says, "Is this M?" how should one reply?
   7. If a child is not interested in printing, what should be done?
   8. If a child says a "b" is an "f", what might a teacher say?

References

Balaban, Nancy, "What Do Young Children Teach Themselves?", *A.C.E.I. International,* 1980.

Berg, Leila, *Reading and Loving,* Henley and Boston: Routledge and Kegan Publ., 1977.

Brittain, W. Lambert, "Analysis of Artistic Behavior in Young Children," *Final Report,* Cornell Univ., 1973.

Calkins, Lucy McCormick, Speech given at Columbia University, 1979.

Chomsky, Carol, "Write Now, Read Later," Reprinted in *Language in Early Childhood Education,* National Association for the Education of Young Children, Washington, DC, 1981.

Durkin, Dolores, *Children Who Read Early,* Teachers College Press, NY, 1969.

Dyson, A. H., "Oral Language: The Rooting System for Learning to Write," *Language Arts,* 58, Oct. 1981, pp. 776–784.

Kane, Frances, "Thinking, Drawing — Writing, Reading," *Childhood Education,* May/June 1982.

Suggested Readings

List, Hindy, "Kids Can Write The Day They Start School," *Early Years,* Jan. 1984.

Markham, Lynda R., "Assisting Speakers of Black English as They Begin to Write," *Young Children,* May, 1984.

Montessori, Maria, *The Absorbant Mind,* New York: Holt, Rinehart, and Winston, 1967.

Paul, R., "Invented Spelling in the Kindergarten," *Young Children,* 31, Mar. 1976.

Vukelich, C. and J. Golden, "Early Writing: Development and Teaching Strategies," *Young Children,* 39, Jan, 1984.

Unit 19
Practicing Printscript

OBJECTIVES

After studying this unit you should be able to

- make the full printscript uppercase and lowercase alphabet.
- list three ways printscript is used daily.
- describe equipment and settings which can be used for printscript development.

Equipment which can motivate interest in writing should be made available to children. Scratch paper (one side already used) or lined paper and crayons placed side-by-side invite use. Most local businesses or offices throw away enough scratch paper to supply a preschool center. This paper can be available every day for play activities.

Felt pens are enjoyed as a change of pace. Colored or white chalk has an appeal of its own and can be used on paper, blackboards, or cement. For variety, use oil pastels which have bright colors, or soft-lead colored pencils.

Most schools install child-high blackboards, figure 19-1; table blackboards are also available. Blackboard paint which can be easily applied to scrap wood pieces, easels, or walls can be obtained at most local hardware stores.

Preprinting activities should take place in a quiet setting where the child can obtain materials from nearby shelves or storage areas. Often, displayed materials have printscript words or letters, figure 19-2.

Letters, words, and pictures are planned for viewing on bulletin boards at children's eye level, figure 19-3. Teachers can apply labels to familiar objects by making printscript signs and attaching the sign to the object with masking tape. Children's names can be printed on labels for lockers, storage areas, or personal belongings.

FIGURE 19-1 Child-high blackboards invite use.

FIGURE 19-2 Children enjoy playing with toys that have alphabet letters, numerals, and symbols.

FIGURE 19-3 Letters and words are planned for children's viewing.

DAILY INTERACTION

Putting the child's name on his work is the most common daily use of printscript, but the teacher should *ask* the child if he wants his name printed on his paper. Many young children think of their creations as their "very own," while others may not want their name on the front of their papers, or on them at all.

All names are printed in the upper left-hand corner of the paper if possible, figure 19-4. This is done to train the child to look at this spot as a preparation for reading; books are read from the left to the right margin. A child's comments about his artwork can be jotted down along the bottom or on the back of his paper. The teacher can be prepared to do this by having a dark crayon or felt-tip pen in a handy place or pocket. Very soon, the child begins to make the

FIGURE 19-4 Children's names are printed in the upper left-hand corner.

FIGURE 19-5 Print the child's name on her work by standing behind her.

Maryellen Donald

FIGURE 19-6 Letters should be large enough for the child to see easily.

connection that a certain combination of shapes *means* something.

The child can learn and practice printing with the teacher standing behind her, working over her shoulder, figure 19-5. In this way, the child sees the letters being formed in the correct position. (If the child and teacher face each other while the teacher writes the letter, the child sees the letter upside down.) Many teachers say the letters aloud as they print the child's name on the art.

Letters or names written for the child should be about one inch to one and a half inches high for uppercase, and half as long for lowercase. This may seem large to an adult, but the letters are much more noticeable and easier to see by the child when they are this size, figure 19-6.

Children may show their printing attempts to the teacher or point out the names of letters they know. A positive statement to the child is appropriate: "Yes, that is an *a*" or "I can see the *a, t,* and *p*" (as the teacher points to each). "Marie, you did print some letters."

FIGURE 19-7 A teacher can ask the "interested" child if he wishes her to print a particular alphabet letter.

With these comments, the teacher encourages and recognizes the child's effort. Often, the child may have the wrong name or form for a letter. The teacher can react by saying, "It is an alphabet letter. Let's go look at our alphabet and see which one."

Asking if the child would like to see the teacher make the letter is another way to supply the child with the correct form, figure 19-7.

The children will make mistakes both in making forms and naming letters and numerals. They have many years ahead to learn; the most important thing now is that they are interested in the forms and can be supplied with correct models and encouragement.

One suggestion is to have children trace over correct letter models or symbols. This can be done with crayons, felt pens, or other writing tools. Since *trace* is a word that needs explanation, the teacher can show the children what to do first.

PRACTICING THE MODEL

Printscript should come automatically to the teacher. Practice is in order if one cannot easily and correctly print the entire alphabet in both uppercase and lowercase.

Before practicing any further, obtain a local printscript guide from a neighboring elementary school, if you do not already have one.

To promote interest in printscript or symbols, a teacher can:

- Make labels for familiar objects.
- Make signs that fit in with child's play.
    John and Jerry's Service Station
    Quiet Please
    Don't Walk on the Grass
    Cookies for Sale
- Create wall displays with words.
- Make alphabet charts.
- Make charts with words.
- Make alphabet and number games.
- Make word games.
- Print stories of children's experiences, as children tell them.
- Point out words in the environment.
- Point out symbols in the environment.
- Print children's names on artwork.
- Supply scrap paper and a variety of writing tools.
- Make table blackboards.
- Cut letters in colorful felt, cloth, sandpaper, and tagboard.

- Help children make their own creative or informative books.
- Make clever nametags.
- Make giant alphabet letters.
- Have children dictate captions for their own photographs.

LINED PAPER

Many companies manufacture lined printing paper for beginners. Some preschoolers acquire the necessary motor control and can use this type of paper. One resource for lined paper is:

Modern Education Corp.
P.O. Box 721
Tulsa, OK 74101

Primary (lined) chart paper is available from:

Union Paper Company
P.O. Box 24164
Oakland, CA 94623

Lines can easily be drawn on a chalkboard by the teacher. This provides a larger working surface and an opportunity for making large-size letters.

CHART IDEAS

Printscript can be added to playrooms by posting charts which have been made by the teacher. Charts can be used just to look at, or can be designed to encourage the child's active involvement. Pockets, parts that move, or pieces that can be added or removed add extra interest. Charts made on heavy chart board or cardboard last longer. Clear contact paper can be used to seal the surface. Some ideas for charts include:

- Color or number chart
- Large clock with movable hands
- Chart showing the four seasons
- Picture story sequence charts
- Calendar
- Room task chart, "Helpers Charts"
- Texture chart (for children to feel)
- Poetry chart, figure 19-8

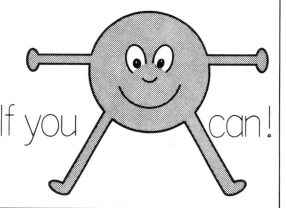

Mix a pancake
Stir a pancake
Pop it in a pan,
Fry the pancake,
Toss the pancake,
Catch it
If you   can!

FIGURE 19-8 Poetry chart

- Recipe chart using step-by-step illustrations
- Classification or matching-concepts chart
- Birthday charts
- Height and weight chart
- Alphabet chart

In making a chart, first draw sketches of the way words and pictures could be arranged. With a yardstick, lightly draw on guidelines with a pencil, or use a chart liner, figure 18-8; page 256. Next, lightly make words in printscript. Go over the printscript later with a felt pen or a dark crayon. Magazines, old elementary school workbooks, old children's books, and photographs are good sources for pictures. Brads or paper fasteners can be used for movable parts. Book pockets or heavy envelopes provide a storage place for items to be added later to the chart.

Experience Charts
Purpose:
    Recognize that spoken words can be put in written form.

Materials:
    Large paper sheets (newsprint), felt pen or black crayon.

Activity:
    After an interesting activity such as a field trip, special speaker, party, celebration, or cooking experience, the teacher can suggest that a story be written about the experience. A large sheet of paper or chart sheet is hung within the children's view, and the children dictate what happened. The teacher prints on the sheet, helping children sort out what happened first, next, and last, figure 19-9.

    Figures 19-10, 19-11, and 19-12, show examples of other word and picture charts that the teacher can use.
    Homemade chart stands, figure 19-13, can be made by teachers. Commercial chart holders, chart stands, and wing clamps are sold at school supply stores. The alphabet patterns in figure 19-14 are useful for teacher-made games, wall displays, and bulletin boards.

The Picnic

We had lunch
in the park
We sat
on the grass

FIGURE 19-9 An example of an experience chart

PARENT COMMUNICATION

A conversation with or note to the parents of a child who has asked about or started printing might include the following comments:

- Teacher has noticed the child's interest in printing alphabet letters, numerals, and/or words.
- Teacher is including a printscript and numeral guide for parents who wish to show their child the letter forms that he will be using in kindergarten.
- The early childhood center encourages printing attempts but does not try to teach printscript to every child. Many children are not interested and others would find it too difficult at their present level.
- A parent can help by having paper and writing tools for the child at home, and by noticing and praising the child when he comes to the parent with written letters.
- Children who start printing early often write letters and numerals in their paintings. The printing may be backwards or sideways; this is to be expected.

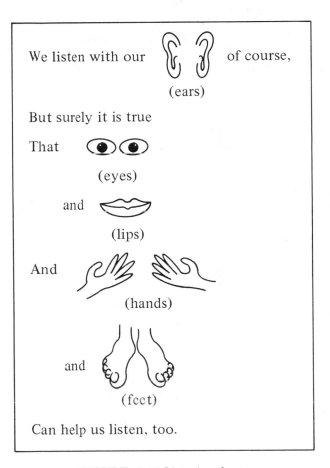

We listen with our ⟨ears⟩ of course,

But surely it is true

That ⟨eyes⟩

and ⟨lips⟩

And ⟨hands⟩

and ⟨feet⟩

Can help us listen, too.

FIGURE 19-10 Listening chart

SUMMARY

Equipment and settings for giving each child an opportunity to explore printing are available in a childhood center. Materials are arranged within reach. Printing seen on wall displays and charts helps motivate interest.

Printscript is used in a variety of ways. The most common is in planned activities and labeling artwork. A name or sentence should start in the upper left-hand corner and move toward the right.

Teachers need to examine printscript closely and practice so that good models can be sup-

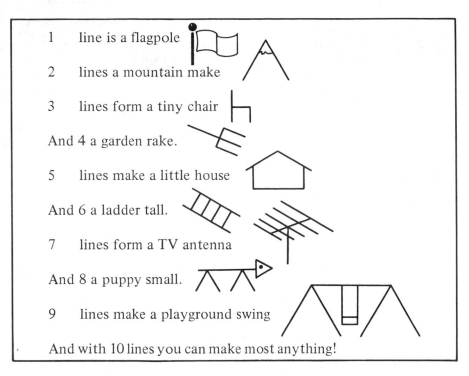

1   line is a flagpole

2   lines a mountain make

3   lines form a tiny chair

And 4 a garden rake.

5   lines make a little house

And 6 a ladder tall.

7   lines form a TV antenna

And 8 a puppy small.

9   lines make a playground swing

And with 10 lines you can make most anything!

FIGURE 19-11 Lines chart

plied. It is also important to encourage children and to recognize their effort, even if they cannot make correct forms yet.

Parents should be alerted to children's printing attempts and to the center's feelings concerning this language arts skill.

Learning Activities

- Obtain an order catalog from a preschool supply store or company. Most companies will send the catalogs free of charge. Professional magazines such as *Instructor, Early Years,* and *Scholastic Teacher* are good sources for addresses. Make a list of any pieces of equipment or supply items that could be used to promote printing.

- Watch the children's use of crayons or other writing tools. Take notes. Make observations about the following:
  a. Time spent with marking tools.
  b. Manner used — How do they hold the crayons?
  c. Do they have good control of both paper and tool?

- Place a pile of paper and two or three soft drawing pencils on a table. (Pencils are not used often because they need sharpening and are not always safe.) *Supervise the activity closely* — let only two or three children

FIGURE 19-12 "I like" chart

work at a time. How many of the children tried to make letters? How many said "yes" when you asked them if they wanted you to add their names to their papers?

- Make three sketches of an early childhood chart that uses printscript words. Design one which will involve child interaction rather than just looking.

- Design and make one preschool chart.

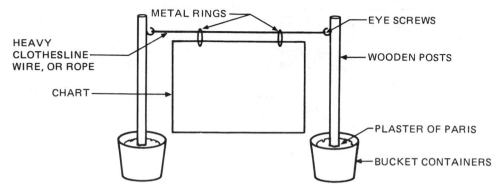

FIGURE 19-13 Homemade chart stand

- Take a blackboard test. Print the uppercase and lowercase alphabet in printscript. Ask your instructor to circle forms that are not exactly right.

Unit Review

A. Answer the following questions.
1. If a child comes to a teacher to show letters he has drawn, how should the teacher react?
2. If two children are arguing over the name of a letter, how should the teacher handle the situation?
3. List three ways a teacher can use printscript during the school day.

B. Print the printscript alphabet in both uppercase and lowercase. Also print the numerals 1 through 10.

C. Referring to figure 19-15, list all of the things the teacher might have done to encourage the children's attempts.

D. Select the correct answer. All have more than one.
1. When a child's name is to be printed on his work, it should be
   a. in the center on top.
   b. in the upper right-hand corner.
   c. in the upper left-hand corner.
   d. done with an uppercase first letter and then lowercase letters.
2. The size of the printscript used with young children
   a. doesn't really matter.
   b. should be large enough to see.
   c. can be of any size.
   d. should be at least an inch high.

FIGURE 19-14 These letters are about 2″ high. They are useful patterns for games, wall displays, and bulletin boards.

FIGURE 19-14 Cont.

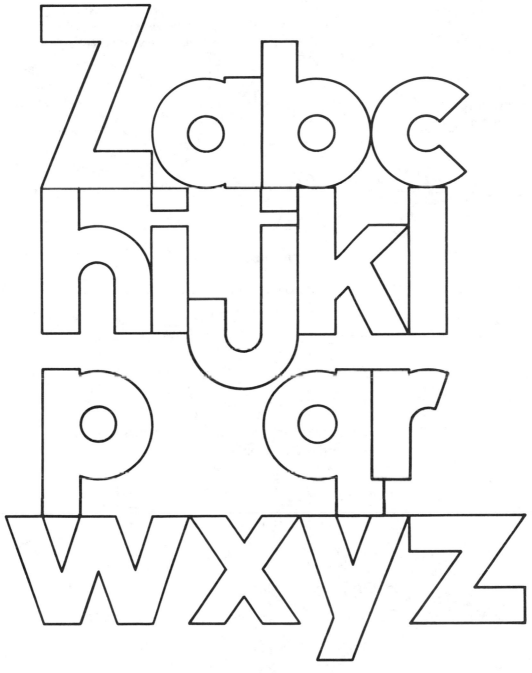

FIGURE 19-14 Cont.

FIGURE 19-15

1. Lines should be straight — perpendicular to the edge of the paper.

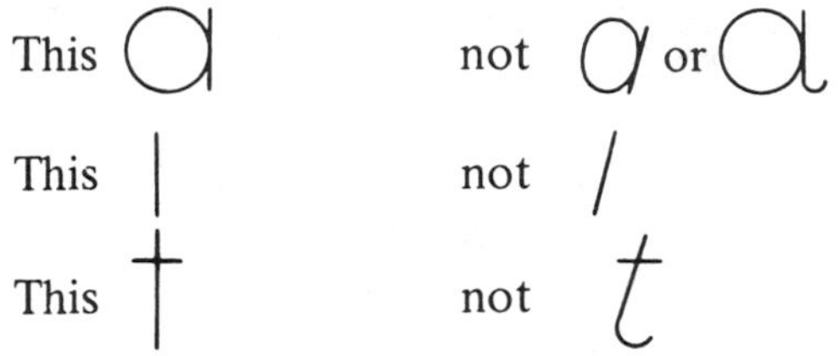

    This ⊂⟩   not ⊂⟩ or ⊂⟩

    This | not /

    This †   not *t*

2. The circular parts of small letters are half the length of large ones.

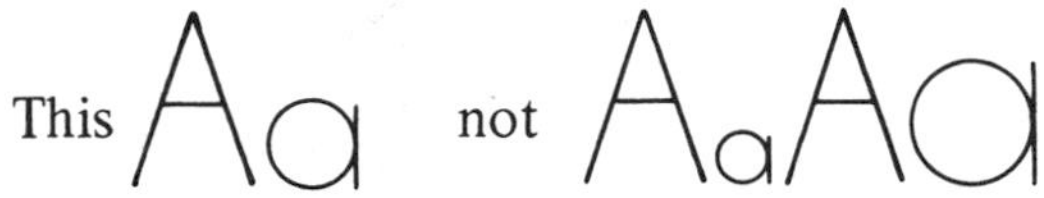

    This A⊂⟩   not A⊂⟩A⊂⟩

3. Circles on letters are full ones.

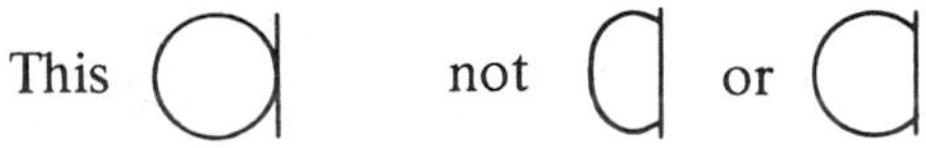

    This ⊂⟩   not ⊂⟩ or ⊂⟩

4. Circles and lines bisect each other.

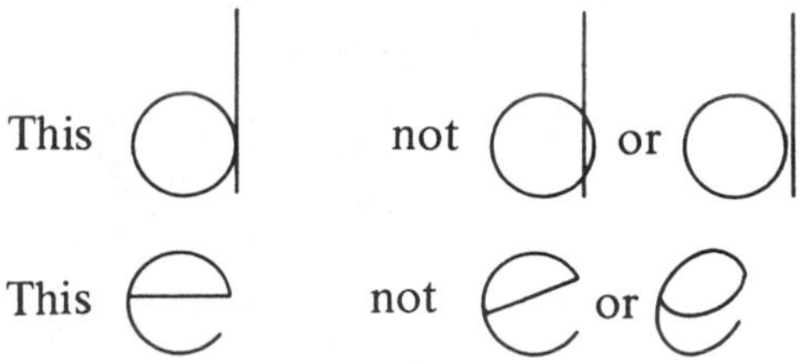

    This ⊂⟩| not ⊂⟩| or ⊂⟩|

    This e   not *e* or *e*

FIGURE 19-16 Common errors in printscript form

3. The teacher who does not know how to form printscript letters can
   a. practice.
   b. use an individual style.
   c. get a copy from an elementary school.
   d. write instead.

E. Print your full name and address in printscript.

F. A note to the parents of a child who is interested in learning to print should include what kind of information? Give four points to bring out.

G. Describe your handling of the following situations:
   1. Mrs. Mason (parent) insists her child must learn to print because her child's friend has learned.
   2. Betsy never wants her name written on her artwork.
   3. Chris says, "My *a* is better than Sam's, huh, teacher?"

H. Study figure 19-16, then look back at your own printing in Review Question E. How many and which letter forms need improvement?

Unit 20
Activities With Printscript

OBJECTIVES

After studying this unit you should be able to

- describe a variety of printscript and symbol activities.
- plan and present a printscript activity.

Activities in this unit deal with symbols, letters, and words. The objectives range from printscript readiness activities with symbols such as circles, squares, triangles, and other geometric and common shapes, to those in which the child comes in contact with printscript letters and words.

Clay-on Patterns
Purpose:
Small manipulative muscle use, tracing symbols.

Materials:
Clay and contact-covered cardboard sheets with patterns, figure 20-1.

Activity:
Child rolls and forms clay over the cardboard patterns, figure 20-2.

Dot-to-dot
These can be made quickly by the teacher and used as a free-play choice, figure 20-3.

Purpose:
Small muscle use, forming and recognizing symbols.

Materials:
Paper, writing tool (dittos can be used).

Variation:
Chalk and chalkboard dot patterns.

Activity:
Dots are connected to form symbols, figure 20-4.

Sorting Symbols
Purpose:
Small muscle use, discriminating symbol differences.

Materials:
Paper, writing tool, scissors, paste.

Activity:
After cutting symbols in squares from sheets, child is asked to mix them all together and then find the ones that are the same to paste on another sheet of paper.

FIGURE 20-1 Patterns

FIGURE 20-2 Clay-on patterns activity

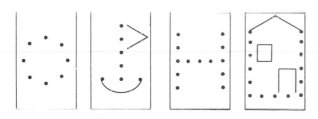

FIGURE 20-3 Dot-to-dot activity

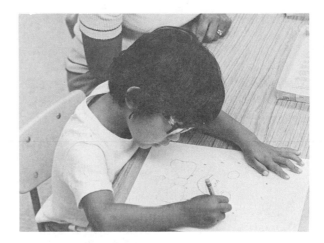

FIGURE 20-4 When dots are connected, they will form symbols.

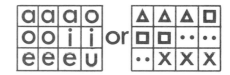

FIGURE 20-5 Symbol cards for sorting game

| Aa | Bb | Cc | Dd | Ee | Ff | Gg | Hh | Ii | Jj |

FIGURE 20-6 Printscript alphabet line

Variation:
Teacher can make a cardboard set as a table game, figure 20-5.

Alphabet Song Game
Purpose:
Recognizing letter names.

Materials:
A long, printscript alphabet line, figure 20-6.

Song:
"ABCDEFG
HIJKLMNOP
QRSTU and V
WX and Y and Z.
Now I've said my ABCs,
Tell me what you think of me."

Activity:
Children sing the song while one child or the teacher touches the corresponding letter on the alphabet line. Teacher can ask the group to sing slowly, quickly, in a little and a big voice, in a high and then low voice.

Alphabet Potato Prints

Purpose:

Recognizing letter names.

Materials:

Potatoes, sharp knife (for teacher's use), thick paint, paper, flat containers. Teacher cuts potato halves into letters or symbols. Some letters need to be reversed for printing.

Activity:

Prints are made by children.

Alphabet Macaroni Prints

Purpose:

Discriminating shapes; small muscle activity.

Materials:

Alphabet soup macaroni (sand, rice, or salt can also be used), glue and brushes, paper, felt pen.

Activity:

Child traces by name by painting over lines with thinned white glue. Macaroni is then spooned over. When dry, shake those macaroni that did not stick into a container. The end result will be raised textured letters, figure 20-7. The teacher should demonstrate this process.

ABC "Paste-on" Group Wall Poster

Purpose:

Small muscle use, recognizing symbols.

FIGURE 20-7 Alphabet macaroni pictures

Materials:

Alphabet letters or words cut or torn from magazines or newspapers.

Activity:

A montage effect is created by having children paste letters where they choose on a piece of paper. During a period of one week, the children can return to the work and paste on more letters.

Alphabet Eaters

Purpose:

Large muscle use, visual discrimination.

Materials:

Cards with printscript alphabet letters small enough to be slipped in animal's mouth. Sturdy boxes on which animal heads and alphabet strips are glued. (Cut a hole in the opposite side so child can reach in for cards.)

Activity:

Child selects a card and "feeds" it to the animal which has a similar alphabet letter on the strip under its mouth, figure 20-8.

Footprint Alphabet Walk

Purpose:

Large muscle use, recognizing symbols.

Materials:

Large cardboard (or cloth) on which 26 footprints have been traced. Cardboard footprint cutouts each with a printscript alphabet letter (3 sets can be made — lowercase, uppercase, and numerals, if desired), covered with clear contact paper or made from plastic-like material.

Activity:

Children place cutout footprints over footprint of the correct letter, figure 20-9.

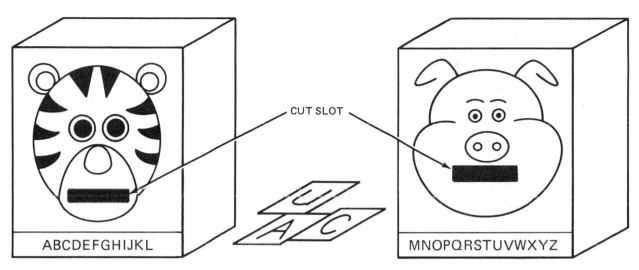

FIGURE 20-8 Alphabet "eaters" and cards

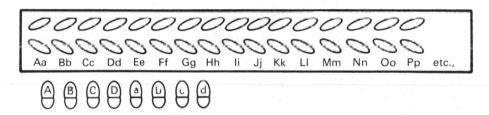

FIGURE 20-9 Footprint alphabet walk

Tracers

Tracers can be used over and over again. Waxy crayons wipe off with a soft cloth, figure 20-10.

Purpose:

Recognizing and discriminating symbols; coordinating small muscles.

Materials:

Acetate or clear vinyl sheets, cardboard, scissors, strapping or masking tape, paper, felt pen.

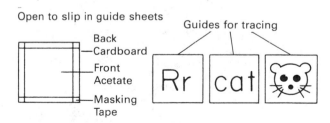

FIGURE 20-10 Tracers

Construction:

Attach acetate to cardboard leaving one side open to form a pocket. Make letter or word guide sheets. Simple pictures can also be used.

Activity:

Child or teacher selects sheet and slips it into tracer pocket. A wax crayon is used by the child to trace the guide sheet. A soft cloth erases the crayon, figure 20-11.

Alphabet Bingo

Purpose:

Recognition and discrimination of letters.

Materials:

Cardboard, felt pen, scissors, pencil, ruler, paper, old pack of playing cards, glue, clear contact paper.

FIGURE 20-11 The child uses a tracer and wax crayon to make a picture.

Construction:

Cardboard is cut to make four or more 8½ x 11 sheets (any similar size is also suitable). Each sheet is divided into nine or twelve sections. An alphabet letter is added to each section. Make sure each sheet has a different combination of letters. Cover sheet with clear contact paper. Turning to the pack of old playing cards, glue paper to the front side of each playing card. Add letters of the alphabet. Covering with clear contact paper will make these cards more durable. For markers, cut paper into small pieces; bottle caps or poker chips may also be used.

Activity:

Teacher passes out the sheets to the children. Holding up a playing card (with a letter on it), the teacher asks if any child has that letter on his sheet. If so, the child should cover it with a marker. The game ends when a child covers all the letters his sheet. At that time, all markers are removed and a new game begins. The child who wins the game by being the first to cover all his letters takes the place of the teacher and holds up the playing cards for the next game.

His and Hers

Purpose:

To help children learn to form letters and write legibly, figure 20-12 (EARLY YEARS Magazine, 1973).

FIGURE 20-12 "His and Hers" activity

Materials:

Cardboard, paper clips, writing paper, scissors, clear contact paper.

Construction:

Cut a 13 x 15 piece of cardboard. Place a 9 x 12 sheet of writing paper on the cardboard close to the bottom. Just above the top of the paper in the center of the board, cut out a rectangular shape. Put a paper clip through this opening and slip the writing paper under the clip. Print the child's name on a strip of the writing paper, place it above the opening in the cardboard, and cover it with clear contact paper.

Activity:

The child may now use this pad to practice writing his name. Make similar practice pads for words, sentences, or paragraphs. (Note: using clear contact paper on handmade learning devices will make them last longer. It is great for preserving magazine pictures, too.)

Popcorn Names

Purpose:

Small muscle use, recognizing symbols.

Materials:

Alphabet letters drawn by teacher on 8½ x 11 sheets. Liquid white glue with brush or stick applicator. Popcorn can be colored by shaking in a bag with dry tempera paint.

Activity:

Children paste popcorn on lines forming letters, figure 20-13.

Variation:

Colored fish tank rocks, fresh peas, pebbles, seeds, small marshmallows, rice, or salt can also be used.

DISPLAYS AND BULLETIN BOARDS

Interesting eye-level wall and bulletin board displays capture the children's attention and promote discussion. Children's work, names, and themes based on their interests increase their feelings of "my room," as well as pride in accomplishment.

Displays that involve active child participation are suggested. Many can be designed to change on a daily or weekly basis.

Printscript is used on bulletin boards with objects, pictures, or patterns. Book pockets, picture hooks, ¼-inch elastic attached to clothespins, and sticky bulletin board strips allow pieces to be added and removed. A helpful teacher resource for bulletin board ideas is *Nursery School Bulletin Boards,* Fearon-Pitman, 6 Davis Drive, Belmont, CA 94002.

One bulletin board idea is shown in figure 20-14. The child selects a spot to paste his picture (photo) and name. A colored line is drawn between photo and name. Later, colored lines can be drawn connecting friends' pictures.

BLACKBOARD ACTIVITIES

One of the most under-utilized instructional items in early childhood centers can be the

FIGURE 20-13 Popcorn names

blackboards. The following blackboard activities are suggested to help children's language development.

- Tracing templates and colored chalk

    Cut plastic coffee can lids with a sharp tool into a variety of patterns, figure 20-15. Suspend the patterns on cord (or elastic with clothespins) over the blackboard.
- Pattern games with tracing template

    Draw figure 20-16 on the blackboard. Ask the children what shape comes next in the pattern. Then draw figure 20-17, and see if they can make a line path from the dog to

the doghouse. These activities are very good for developing left-to-right skills needed for reading.

- Guessing rebus messages (for older preschoolers)

    The sets of pictures in figure 20-18 are put up on the blackboard. The teacher asks the children to find the message by guessing the word for each picture. The teacher writes the correct words underneath the pictures.
- Labeling pictures

    Tape pictures like the ones in figure 20-19 on the board with masking tape. Write identifying names dictated by children underneath each picture,
- Daily helper identification

    Make up a chart with the children's names printed next to a picture of their job for the day. See figure 20-20.

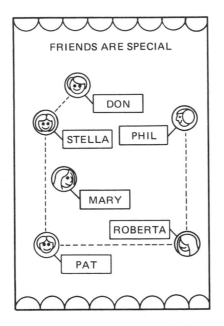

FIGURE 20-14 Bulletin board idea

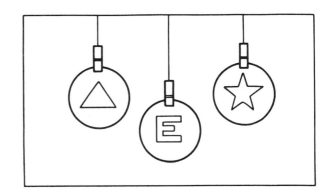

FIGURE 20-15 Coffee lid blackboard activity

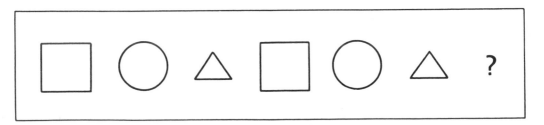

FIGURE 20-16 What comes next in the pattern?

FIGURE 20-17 A left-to-right skill builder

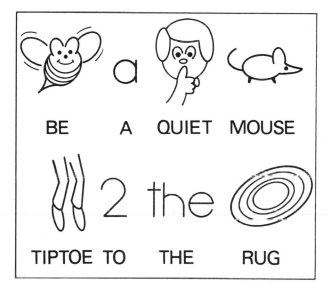

FIGURE 20-18 Rebus messages

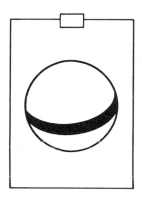

FIGURE 20-19 Children help identify the pictures.

Drawing on the Blackboard

A "line fence" on the blackboard between children helps each to know his drawing area.

OTHER DRAWING ACTIVITIES

Words on Drawings

Purpose:

Attaching word labels to pictures.

Materials:

Felt pen or crayons.

Activity:

Teacher asks each child individually if words can be added to his painting, drawing, or illustration. Make sure the child realizes the teacher is going to write on his work. It is a good idea to show the child what has been

Chalk Talk

Purpose:

Motivating interest in letter forms.

Materials:

Chalk, chalkboard, chalkboard eraser.

Activities:

Teacher presents the rhyme and drawings on the chalkboard, figure 20-21. When the activity ends, ask if anyone would like a turn at the blackboard.

Peggy (Fish Feeder)

John (Waste Basket Passer)

FIGURE 20-20 Daily helper chart

done to another child's picture beforehand. Most children will want words added, but some will not. It is best to limit this activity to the children who are making symbols of faces, figures, houses, etc. in their work. Younger children might not be able to decide if asked, "Would you like me to put a word name on something you've drawn in your picture?"

COMMERCIAL MATERIALS

A number of school supply manufacturers provide items which encourage or sustain an interest in alphabet letters. A partial list follows:

- Desk Tape Manuscript Letter Line by **Instructo**
- Magnetic Alphabet Picture Board by **Child Guidance**

DRAW A FISH

1. *I'll draw an oval*
Like an egg in the sky.
What comes next
2. *Why it's a little eye.*
3. *Next comes a mouth*
4. *And a tail to swish*
Look at that
I've made a fish!

FIGURE 20-21

- Alphabet Practice Cards by **Ideal Toy Co.**
- Beaded Tactile-kinesthetic Manuscript Cards by **Ideal Toy Co.**
- Wooden Alphabet Letters by **Instructo**

Teachers can sometimes gain ideas and "homemade" game-making ideas from commercial suppliers' catalogs.

Learning Activities

- Collect five printscript activity ideas from other resource books or create them yourself. Use the following format:

Title	Activity
Purpose	Construction (if any)
Materials	Variations (if any)

- Create a blackboard activity.

- Use one of the activities from this unit with a group of children, or with one child, and answer the following questions.
  1. Was it of interest to the child or children?
  2. What was the purpose of the activity?
  3. How were printscript letters or symbols used?

4. Were the children successful in the activity?

• Make up your own "chalk talk." A rhyme or simple story works well. Try out your creation on young children, and write a description of their reactions.

• Design an early childhood bulletin board. Specify how children will be involved.

Unit Review

A. Name common symbols that might be used in designing activities with symbols.

B. What is the purpose of a line fence between children during blackboard activities?

C. Why involve children in bulletin board displays?

D. List 5 ideas using printscript and child involvement in a wall display or bulletin board.

E. Describe ways bulletin boards and wall displays could be used to increase children's language arts skills.

Reference

EARLY YEARS MAGAZINE, Reprinted with permission of the publishers, Allen Raymond, Inc., Darien, CT, January, 1973.

Section 5
Reading —
A Language Art

Unit 21
Readiness for Reading

OBJECTIVES

After studying this unit you should be able to

- describe reading readiness.
- list three methods used to teach reading.
- discuss the teacher's role in reading.

At one time, it was thought that there was an age when all children became *ready* for reading instruction. That idea has changed to realize that no two children learn exactly the same way or at the same age. That is probably why it is possible to find children who read in early childhood centers and kindergartens. Some have picked up the skill on their own; others have spent time with an older brother or sister, parents, or other family members.

Although reading is considered the fourth language art, this unit does not intend to suggest, or even induce, reading instruction for groups of young children, or even encourage "sitdown" instruction to those 1–5% who can read words during preschool years.

READING

A language arts approach to reading views reading as one part of the communication process. The language arts are interrelated — not separate, isolated skills. The teacher is responsible for showing the child the relationship between the various areas of language arts. In other words, the goal is to help the child to understand that communication is a total picture in which speaking, listening, written symbols,

and the reading of those symbols are closely connected, figure 21-1.

In past years, the logical connection between listening, speaking, written words, and reading was overlooked. The subjects were often taught as separate skills, and the natural con-

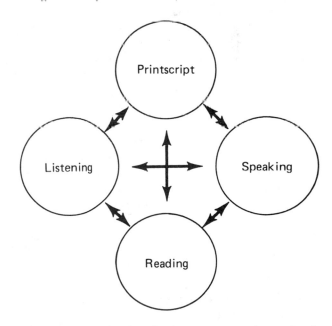

FIGURE 21-1 The four language arts are interrelated and interdependent.

nection between each area was not clear to children. In a language arts approach, the *connection* (the way these areas fit together) is emphasized.

The Task Force Report on Early Childhood Education by the State of California (1971) states:

> Concern should be given to the nature of the written language material used in early reading instruction and the degree of fit between this material and the child's oral language style. Attention should also be devoted to representing the child's oral language in written form with very little teacher editing. In this way the child comes to understand the relationship between speech and writing as a basis for reading instruction.

The teacher realizes that certain skills and abilities appear in children before others appear. Early learning in listening and speaking serve as beginnings for further language and communication.

Activities with young children can move easily from listening, speaking, seeing, or using printscript to beginning reading attempts: from passive to active participation. It is not uncommon for preschool youngsters to be able to read most of the names of the children in their group, after being exposed to an activity in which the children's names are used.

The ability to read is present if the child understands and acts appropriately when he sees a printed word. In other words, the child must be able to understand the *concept* that (1) all "things" have a name, (2) the name of the thing can be a written word, (3) the two are interchangeable, and (4) that the "word symbols" can be read.

Beginning to Read

Most teachers have had children "read" to them from a favorite, memorized storybook. Generally, a word from the book will not be rec-

ognized out of context and read by the child when seen elsewhere, however.

A child may develop the ability to recognize words because of an interest in printing letters. Another child may pick up the sounds of alphabet letters by listening and finding words that start with the same letter. Books and stories can also lead children into early interest and recognition of words, figure 21-2. Some children have the ability to distinguish one word from another word by sight and can easily remember words.

Early readers are children who have a desire to read. They also have had the opportunities and interactions with others who have answered their questions and stimulated their interest. A few children will read between the ages of four and five, but many will not have the capability or interest to read until a later age. Learning to read involves a variety of skills which are interwoven in the other three areas of language arts. The child who has "reading readiness" is one who has displayed some success in reading a few words.

FIGURE 21-2 An interest in books can lead to an interest in printed words.

READINESS SKILLS

A teacher should be aware of a child's capabilities. In daily observations and verbal conversations, a child's responses give valuable clues. The wrong answers are as important as the right ones.

Some language activities include the introduction and practice of skills that will be used when the child learns to read. These are often called *reading readiness activities*.

Readiness allows one to proceed without hesitation, delay, or difficulty. It includes skills, motivation, desire, attitudes concerning the task, and how the child feels about himself. Reading is a complex task which involves eye and hand muscles. It requires a degree of reasoning ability (mental maturity) and a degree of motor (physical) development. Figure 21-3 is a checklist of attitudes toward reading.

The ideal situation for a child learning to read is a one-to-one child/teacher ratio, with the reading task suited to the child's individual capacity, learning style, and individual interests. This is difficult to fulfill in an early childhood learning center due to not only the number of children per teacher but the many other duties required of a teacher. Other difficulties can include: the teacher's amount of training, knowledge of a variety of methods to teach reading, and the teacher's ability to suit the book to the child.

PART I: FOR CHILDREN WHO DO NOT YET READ

YES   NO   1. Asks to be read to, or asks for story time.
YES   NO   2. Hurries to be near the reader when story time is announced.
YES   NO   3. Comes willingly when story time is announced.
YES   NO   4. Likes to leaf through picture books.
YES   NO   5. Talks aloud (pretends to read or reads) as books are examined.
YES   NO   6. Looks over shoulder at what another child is "reading."
YES   NO   7. Picks books to "read" with some care (after examining more than one).
YES   NO   8. Has memorized some of the words from some books.
YES   NO   9. Has memorized most the words in some books.
YES   NO   10. "Reads aloud" to others.
YES   NO   11. Usually enjoys hearing stories read aloud.

PART II: FOR CHILDREN WHO CAN READ

YES   NO   12. Borrows books from library.
YES   NO   13. Takes books home to read with no urging by teacher or parents.
YES   NO   14. Laughs aloud or smiles when reading funny material.
YES   NO   15. Asks others to listen as he reads something (of interest to him) aloud.
YES   NO   16. Treats books with care.
YES   NO   17. Volunteers to read aloud.
YES   NO   18. Tries to write books, poems, or plays without teacher prompting.
YES   NO   19. Asks for help locating book on specific topics.
YES   NO   20. Asks for help locating book about particular characters.
YES   NO   21. Collects books (starts own library).
YES   NO   22. Gets "lost" in books and ignores activities in the room.

FIGURE 21-3 Checklist for reading attitudes of young children *(Adapted from George Mason,* A Primer on Teaching Reading, *F. E. Peacock Publishers, Inc., 1981)*

As Goetz (1979) states:

Unfortunately, few early childhood specialists have been trained to assess reading readiness or teach beginning reading in a manner suited to the developmental level of very young children.

Early childhood teachers looking for indicators to identify children who possess readiness need to realize that simple recognition of a few sight words is but one area of skill. A more complete listing is outlined by Emery (1975). They are considered "primary indicators":

- Oral vocabulary
- Reading curiosity
- Auditory discrimination as it relates to clear speech and learning letter sounds
- Visual discrimination of letters

His "secondary indicators" include:

- Attention
- Compliance
- Memory as it relates to the general idea of a story
- Concepts such as, top/bottom, up/down, open/closed, etc.
- Writing in terms of copying straight lines, circles, etc.
- Page turning

OBJECTIVES

Programs which choose to include reading readiness among their instructional goals (objectives) plan activities which promote the following skills and attitudes.

- Recognizing incongruities — the ability to see the lack of fitness in a situation or statement, such as "The mouse swallowed the elephant."
- Recognizing context clues — realizing that pictures on the same page give visual clues to the words.
- Acquiring the ability to listen.

- Building vocabulary through first-hand experiences
  a. recognizing likenesses and differences
  b. identifying through sight and sound
  c. rhyming
  d. increasing memory span
  e. recalling sequence and content
  f. following directions.
- Increasing speech output
  a. developing attitudes of each child's ability and worth
  b. increasing imaginative and creative speech.
- Building critical thinking and problem solving with language
  a. identifying through clues
  b. classifying, sorting and organizing
  c. concept and relationship development
  d. anticipating outcomes
  e. seeing cause and effect relations.
- Developing self-confidence — attitudes of self-competence.
- Increasing interest and motivation through enjoyment and success in language activities.
- Developing left and right awareness.
- Developing positive attitudes toward books and skills in book use
  a. turning pages
  b. storage and care

DEVELOPMENT OF READING READINESS

The following has been identified as a sequence in the development of reading and writing abilities.

In the absence of adult intervention that emphasizes another sequence, children generally seem to develop reading and writing abilities as follows:

1. The child develops an awareness of the functions and value of the reading and

writing processes prior to becoming interested in acquiring specific knowledge and skills.

2. The child is likely to give greater attention to words and letters that have some personal significance, such as his or her own name or the names of family, pets, etc.

3. The child develops both reading and writing skills simultaneously as complementary aspects of the same communication processes, rather than as separate sets of learning.

4. The child develops an awareness of words as separate entities (as evidenced when he or she dictates words slowly so that the teacher can keep pace in writing them down) before showing awareness or interest in how specific letters represent sounds.

5. The child becomes familiar with the appearance of many of the letters through visually examining them, playing games with them, etc., before trying to master their names, the sounds they represent, or their formation.

6. The child becomes aware of the sound similarities between high-interest words (such as significant names) and makes many comparisons between their component parts before showing any persistence in deciphering unfamiliar words by blending together the sounds of individual letters (Lay, Dopyera, 1977).

As stated earlier in this unit, the teacher will probably encounter a few preschool children who have already learned how to read simple words and simple books. Another group of children, usually older four-year-olds, seem quite interested in alphabet letters, words, and writing. Teachers should ask questions about the center's goals for each child.

It is important for teachers to be able to help the child's existing reading abilities, and actively plan for future reading skill.

Any teacher of young children over the age of three can anticipate working with some children who already have interest in and abilities for reading and writing. As a teacher you should be aware of the various processes involved in learning to read and be able to assess and assist in their development. This is no less true for the teachers of three-, four-, and five-year-olds than for teachers of six- and seven-year-olds (Lay and Dopyera, 1977).

Parents often know that reading skill is important to school success. Many want their children to have early opportunities to gain skills which will make the complicated learning process as easy as possible, figure 21-4. Studies have been made to try to pinpoint the *best* method

FIGURE 21-4 A library can become a familiar place to visit.

for teaching children to read. Most of these studies have concluded there is no proven best method. The important factors seem to be (1) the teacher's enthusiasm for the method or technique used, and (2) the teacher's understanding of the method used.

METHODS

There are many methods of teaching reading skills to young children. Since educators do not agree that there is a best way for every child, each school decides which method or methods will be used in that particular school.

Three popular reading instruction approaches will be discussed in this text:

1. Whole word recognition — sight vocabulary (Look-Say)
2. Language experience
3. Phonetic decoding, figure 21-5

Many more approaches to reading instruction exist, and combinations of methods are commonplace.

Look-say Method

Most of the children who do read during preschool years have learned words through a "look and say" method. That is, when they see the written letters of their name or a certain word, they can identify the name or word. They have recognized and memorized that group of symbols. It is felt that children who learn words in this fashion have memorized the shape or configuration of the word (see earlier in unit). They often confuse words that have similar outlines such as *Jane* for *June*. They may not know the alphabet names of the letters or the sounds of each letter (phonics). In a phonetic approach to reading, the child breaks the word into sounds and decodes it.

Approach	Strategy
Whole Word-sight Vocabulary	• Teaches reading by using visual memory skills; child recognizes total words.
	• Develops abilities to recognize a large number of basic word list words, then saturates primers with memorized words repeated often. (Referred to as Look and Say reading.)
Language Experience	• Uses meaningful activities in all language arts areas: speaking, listening, prewriting, and reading readiness are interrelated.
	• Makes use of the child's own language, interests, and experiences.
Phonetic Alphabet (See appendix for alphabet letter pronunciation guide.)	• Begins reading instruction by associating individual letters of the alphabet with the sound (or sounds) of the letter.
	• Then teaches combined sounds.
	• Commonly called "The ABC Method"

FIGURE 21-5

Language Experience Approach

A language arts approach to reading introduces children to written words through their own interests in play; their enjoyment of speaking; and by listening to language. Often children's first experience with written words comes from their own speech and actions. A sign that says, "John's Block Tower" or "Free Kittens" may be a child's first exposure to reading. The emphasis is on the fact that words are part of daily living; words are not only important during planned reading instruction in school.

The language experience approach is often associated with the work of Van Allen (1967). Stauffer (1970) points out specific features of the language experience approach which he feels make it especially appropriate for young children:

1. Its base in children's language development and first-hand experiencing.
2. Its stress on children's interests, experiences, and cognitive and social development.
3. Its respect for children's need for activity and involvement.
4. Its requirement for meaningful learning experiences.
5. Its integration of school and public library resources with classroom reading materials.
6. Its encouragement of children's creative writing as a meaningful approach to using and practicing reading-writing skills.
7. Its requirement for self-regulated but teacher-directed learning activities.

Robinson (1983) also recommends the language experience approach to young children's teachers when she remarks ". . . a very natural way to build on children's expressive and cognitive activities . . ." and ". . . because of its flexibility and adaptability. . . ."

She suggests new teachers collect a large repertoire of activities from the many writers who have contributed to the development of this method. (Van Allen and Allen's *Language Experience Activities* is a valuable resource.) Since no one reading method is superior, Robinson continues: "teachers should be able to use features of phonic, linguistic, or sight-word recognition that seem useful at any given time." In other words, combine methods.

Decoding-phonetics Approach

Decoding using a phonetic approach to reading instruction is based on teaching children (or letting them self discover) the 44 language sounds (phonemes) which represent 26 alphabet letters and combinations (graphemes). Though phonetic approaches differ widely, most users believe that when children know which sounds are represented by which letters or letter combinations, they can "attack" an unknown word and "decode" it. Some approaches begin decoding sessions when all sounds have been learned, others expose children to select sounds and offer easily decoded words early. A few phonetic approach systems require teachers to use letter sounds exclusively, and later introduce the individual letter names, such as a, b, c, . . . etc.

Five "word attack" (or decoding) skills are helpful in the complicated process of learning to read.

Picture clues. Using an adjacent picture (visual) to guess at a word near it (usually on the same page).

Configuration clues. Knowing a word because you remember its outline.

Context clue. Guessing an unknown word by known words that surround it.

Phonetic clue. Knowing the sound a symbol represents (see the Appendix for English alphabet letter pronunciation guide).

Structural clue. Seeing similar parts of words and knowing what these symbols mean.

Attitudes of the Teacher and Parent

Whichever prereading or reading method is used, it is important for the child to recognize that "talk" can be written, and that "written talk" can be read.

The staff in early childhood centers closely examines the advantages and disadvantages of various methods. Individual plans for individual children are formed and activities increase the child's interest while developing his skill.

Staff members facing "the back-to-academics" push need to be both prepared and articulate. If they can discuss the real basics necessary in beginning reading and the benefits of a well rounded developmental curriculum which includes physical, social, intellectual, and creative opportunities and plenty of play, they may be able to curb pressure for more limited "academic" program types.

Most parents can relate to and understand the importance of their child's perceptions of their abilities as learners; they want teachers to encourage natural curiosity, to promote searching, questioning minds, and prompt a joy in discovery and problem solving. Parents realize the skill of reading can be *taught* and that the process can breed a thorough dislike for the activity. Many also can relate to the "commercial sell," and the trend to hurry children in our increasingly technological society. Thinkers, movers and shakers, and socially integrated and creative people will always be our most precious national resource. Educational research simply does not support the "earlier the better" position in the teaching of reading.

RECOGNIZING THE EARLY READER

Teacher observation is perhaps the best way to assess a child's skill development and interest in reading. Assessment tests and checklists offer teachers a systematic approach, and are useful in identifying children's skill. A checklist of readiness skills is included in the Appendix.

Hillerich (1977) has pinpointed nine skills and abilities which serve as a foundation for reading.

1. Development of an adequate oral language, including both sentence patterns and vocabulary;
2. Awareness of their ability to use oral context to anticipate a word;
3. Ability to discriminate minor differences between letter forms;
4. Understanding of what is meant by "the beginning" of a spoken word;
5. Experience in classifying spoken words according to beginning sounds;
6. Association of consonant letters with the sounds those letters represent at the beginning of a word;
7. Ability to apply the skill of using oral context along with the consonant sound association for the first letter of a printed word in order to read that word;
8. Familiarity with the patterns of the literary language from having been read to;
9. Experience with certain high-frequency words, enabling instant recognition of these printed words.

Speaking about a readiness program and individual differences, Hillerich states:

The typical child who has experienced the prereading skills program in or before kindergarten will be ready about the end of kindergarten or beginning of first grade to make use of these skills in actual reading. Of course, there will be some children entering first grade who are well beyond this level and others who have not yet mastered the necessary prereading skills, even though they may have been exposed to them.

READING READINESS ACTIVITIES

All activities found in this text can be considered readiness skill activities because each involves an area of language arts. The following activities deal with the development of the ability to use picture clues and configuration clues, both useful to the beginning reader.

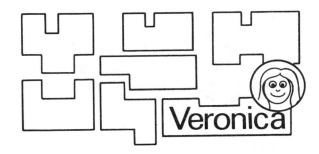

FIGURE 21-6 Name puzzle

Picture Clue Activities

1. Draw several shapes on a piece of paper. Ask the child for a word label for each. Print the word beneath the picture. Ask the child what he wants to do with the paper. (Some will want to cut it, color it, or take it home.)
2. Using coloring book pages, encourage the child to name all parts of each picture. After recording the child's words, show him the results.
3. Tell the child you are going to draw objects on the blackboard, and he can guess their names. Record the child's guesses next to each object.

Configuration Clue Activities

1. Use chartboard or newsprint to make a large wall chart called a Name Puzzle. Post it so the children can see it. Make the configuration outline of each child's and teacher's name.
2. Introduce the activity to interested children by printing your name on a strip of colored construction paper. Outline the name as shown in figure 21-6, and then cut it out. Move to the chart, finding the matching shape. If photos are available, paste these above the shape after pasting the configuration name shape over the matching chart shape.
3. Draw a picture of some simple objects (jar, eraser, scissors, classroom toy, etc.). Have

the child match each drawing with the real object.

4. Trace around objects on the blackboard. Have the child reach into a bag and feel the object, then guess its name. Write the guess under the blackboard outline.
5. Outline a place mat. Have the child place the matching object over the drawn outline. Include an outline of the child's name on the place mat. Three configuration outlined names are placed with the objects. The child is usually able to choose the name that fits. The teacher can assist, either by saying, "The name you've placed here is Brett," or by placing the name over the outline saying "This is a spot for Brett's name."

THE ROLE OF STORYTIMES AND BOOK-READING EXPERIENCES

Most elementary school teachers who are faced with the responsibility of teaching reading feel that ease in learning to read is directly related to the amount of time a child has been read to by parents, teachers, and others. Think of the difference in *exposure hours* between a child who's had a nightly bedtime storybook and one who has not.

Books have a language of their own; conversation is quite different. Books aren't just written oral conversation but include descriptions, primarily full sentences, a rhythm of their own, dialog, and much more. Listen to adults as they read books to young children — they adopt special voices and mannerisms and communicate much differently than in everyday speech. Through repeated experience children learn that illustrations usually reflect what a book is saying; this knowledge helps them make educated guesses of both meanings and printed words adjacent to pictures, figure 21-7.

Storybook sessions are reading readiness sessions and greatly affect the child's future with books. If teachers wish to evaluate how well they are doing in making books important to children in their programs, the following set of questions (Cazden, 1981) will help.

- During free-choice periods, how many children go to the library corner and look at books by themselves?

- How many requests do adults get to "read to me" during a day?
- How many children listen attentively during story time?
- How many books have been borrowed by parents during the week?
- Which books have become special favorites, as shown by signs of extra wear?

BASAL READERS IN ELEMENTARY CLASSROOMS

About 90% of elementary schools use basal readers to teach reading. Basal readers are packaged in sets or series which are used through as many as seven or eight grade levels. Readers (books) are collections of stories, facts, activities, poems, assignments, and other things of increasing difficulty. As age increases (1) print

FIGURE 21-7 Look at the deep concentration and focus.

becomes smaller, (2) illustration less frequent, and (3) book length is greater. Teachers' manuals accompanying a series need considerable study on the part of teachers if goals are to be realized. Lesson plans recommend specific activities and procedures and workbooks are provided to follow-up and elaborate readings. Many basal series packages use a combination of reading method approaches, including sight recognition and phonetic decoding.

PARENTS AND READING READINESS

Parents often want to find ways to help their children succeed in school. Since the ability to read is an important factor in early schooling, parents may seek the advice of the teacher.

Many programs keep parents informed of the school's program and goals, and of their child's progress. An early childhood center's staff realizes that parents and teachers working together can produce a carryover between things learned at home and at school.

The following are suggestions for parents who want to help their children's language skill development. Many are similar to suggestions for teachers in early childhood centers.

- Show an interest in what your child has to say. Answer, giving clear, descriptive, full statements in response.
- Arrange for your child to have playmates and to meet and talk to people of all ages.
- Make your child feel secure. Encourage and accept his opinions and feelings.
- Develop a pleasant voice and offer the best model of speech you can. Shouting and loud voices can create tension.
- Encourage your child to listen and to explore by feeling, smelling, seeing, and tasting when possible.
- Enjoy new experiences. Talk about them as they happen. Each community has interesting places to visit with the young child

— parks, stores, museums, zoos, buses, and trains are only a few suggestions.
- Read to your child and tell him stories; stop when he loses interest. Try to develop the child's enjoyment of books and knowledge of how to care for them. Provide a quiet place for your child to enjoy books on his own.
- Listen to *what* your child is trying to say rather than *how* it is said.
- Have confidence in your child's abilities. Patience and encouragement help language skills grow.
- Consult your child's teacher if you have questions about the child's language skill.
- Consult a speech-language specialist or your child's teacher if you feel your child is more than six months behind in his language development.

SUMMARY

The fourth area of the language arts is reading. Although many early childhood centers do not offer formal reading instruction as such, some preschoolers can read.

The goal of the teacher is to blend the language arts skills: listening, speaking, reading, and printscript; into successful experiences. Because the skills are so closely connected, one activity can flow into another activity in a natural way. This gives young children a clearer picture of communication.

Experiences in language provide a background for reading readiness. Abilities, skills, and understandings grow at an individual rate. There are many methods of teaching reading; each center decides which course of action or activities are best suited for attending children.

A teacher's knowledge of reading skills aids in the identification of beginning readers, and helps developmental activity planning. Parents and teachers work together to give children the opportunity to gain prereading skill and to keep children's interest alive and personally rewarding.

Learning Activities

- Invite a kindergarten teacher and a first-grade teacher to discuss their experiences and knowledge about young children and reading.

- Observe a kindergarten class. List and describe any activities which increase a child's reading readiness.

- Make a chart of printscript words (common ones such as dog, cat, and highly-advertised words such as commercial beverages or cereals; include children's names found at a local preschool). Test these words with a group of four-year-olds in a "gamelike" way. Describe the children's response to your game.

- Borrow the Edward Dolch Basic Reading word list from a library. Share it with the group. Note the date it was developed. (Dolch, Edward W., *A Manual for Remedial Reading,* Champaign, IL: Garrard Publishing Co., 1939).

- Create an activity that has:
  a. speaking and printscript.
  b. listening and printscript.
  c. printscript and reading.

- In a small group, discuss what you would do and what your limitations would be if you were working with a group of young children and found that two of them were reading a few words.

- Stage a debate. Divide the class into two groups: one representing the disadvantages in teaching young children to read before first grade and the other representing the advantages. Do some research at the library. Have each group discuss its position separately, before the debate begins. Substantiate your arguments by citing experts' opinions.

Unit Review

A. Discuss the following situations briefly.
1. A child asks you to listen to him read his favorite book.
2. You have noticed a young child who is able to read all of the printscript in the playroom.
3. A parent notices her child is reading a few words and asks advice as to what to do.

B. How can a teacher include the four language arts in activities?

C. Explain what is meant by:

reading	phonics
readiness	configuration
method	incongruities

D. Select the phrase which best completes each of the following sentences.
  1. Between the ages of 4 and 5 years old,
      a. many children learn to read.
      b. a few children learn to read.
      c. children should be given reading instruction.
      d. most children will be ready to read.
  2. The language arts are
      a. reading, printscript, and listening.
      b. speaking, reading, and listening.
      c. listening, speaking, printscript, and reading.
      d. reading readiness, listening, speaking, and alphabet knowledge.
  3. Children may begin reading because they
      a. have an interest in alphabet letters.
      b. have an interest in books.
      c. want to see what they say written down.
      d. have an interest in speaking, listening, or writing (printscript).
  4. Reading readiness
      a. includes a variety of skills, motives, and attitudes.
      b. can be defined as showing an interest in reading.
      c. means at a certain age a child will perfect all the skills he needs to read.
      d. means that reading should be taught to most preschoolers.
  5. Parents and early childhood teachers work together so that
      a. parents will teach their children to read at home.
      b. teachers can teach reading during preschool years.
      c. at home learnings and at school learnings are understood by both parents and teachers.
      d. children will have the same experiences at home that take place at school.

E. List five skills which are basic to learning to read.

References

Ashton-Warner, S., *Teacher,* New York: Bantam, 1961. (An unforgettable account of a creative teacher who uses children's own dictated words as the basis for reading instruction.)

Cazden, Courtney, *Language in Early Childhood Education,* N.A.E.Y.C., 1981.

Goetz, Elizabeth M., *Early Reading,* Young Children, July 1979.

Emery, Robert, *Early Readers,* Holt, Rinehart, and Winston, 1975.

Hillerich, Robert L., *Reading Fundamentals for Preschool and Primary Children,* Columbus, OH, Charles E. Merrill Publishing Co., 1977.

Lay, Margaret Z. and John E. Dopyera, *Becoming a Teacher of Young Children,* Lexington, MD, D. C. Heath & Co., 1977.

Mason, George E., *A Primer on Teaching Reading,* F. E. Peacock Publ., Inc., 1981.

Montessori, Maria, *The Discovery of the Child,* Ballantine Books, 1965.

Robinson, Helen F., *Exploring Teaching in Early Childhood Education,* Allyn and Bacon, Inc., Boston, 1983.

Stewig, John Warren, *Teaching Language Arts in Early Childhood,* Holt, Rinehart and Winston, 1982.

Task Force Report on Early Education, Dept. of Education, State of California, Sacramento, 1971.

Van Allen, Roach, *Language Experiences in Early Childhood,* Encyclopedia Britannica, Chicago, 1969.

Van Allen, Roach and Claryce Allen, *Language Experience Activities,* Houghton Mifflin Co., 1982.

Suggested Readings

Goetz, Elizabeth M., *Early Reading,* Young Children, July, 1979.

Mason, George, E., *A Primer on Teaching Reading,* F. E. Peacock Publ., Inc., 1981.

Unit 22
Language Development Materials

OBJECTIVES

After studying this unit you should be able to

- explain the need for materials in language development activities.
- assist teachers in the care, storage, and replacement of materials.
- describe early childhood language games.

This text has emphasized the need to provide children with a wide variety of interesting classroom materials, objects, and furnishings. The importance of materials, particularly in keeping programs alive, fascinating, and challenging needs to be recognized.

Classroom materials and objects promote language skills in many ways.

- They provide the reality behind words and ideas.
- Exploration using the sense organs increases children's knowledge of relationships and identifying properties.
- Materials capture attention, motivate play, and build communication skill.
- Familiar and favorite materials can be enjoyed over and over, with the child deciding how much time to devote to self-chosen tasks.
- Many materials isolate one language and perceptual skill so it can be practiced and accomplished.
- Materials can help motivate creative expression.

TYPES OF MATERIALS

Materials are described here as objects or items used by either teachers or children. Materials may be staff-made or commercially made. A partial listing of the many commercial early childhood materials suppliers is found in the Appendix. Additional addresses are available in early childhood professional magazines.

Some materials are made for teachers' use only. Other materials are used by both teachers and children. Still others are made solely for the child's use, figure 22-1.

STAFF-MADE MATERIALS

Every center has budget limitations. Staff-made items can increase the variety of materials available for language development activities, figure 22-2.

Many materials are creatively designed for special language teaching purposes. Some have been made from ideas obtained from other centers, other teachers, commercially manufactured items, resource magazines, or teacher workshops.

FIGURE 22-1 Children playing with a teacher-made card game

FIGURE 22-2 Some materials are designed for children to use without teacher's help.

Staff-made materials are based on the interests and developmental levels of each particular group of children. They can be devised and designed to motivate and stimulate. This is part of the challenge of teaching — to keep a program continually inviting, expanding, and interesting to a unique group of individual children.

The Teacher's Role

As a member of the staff, the teacher's role in providing staff-made materials includes:

- designing and creating appropriate materials which minimize competition and emphasize task completion.
- constructing and preparing materials.
- use of materials with children.
- care, storage, and replacement of existing materials.

Appropriateness, cost, and sturdiness must be considered in the design and construction of materials. Most teacher-made materials are appreciated and welcomed by the entire staff, and enjoyed by the children, figure 22-3.

FIGURE 22-3 Teacher-made materials are welcomed by teachers and children.

COMMERCIALLY-DEVELOPED MATERIALS

There is a wide variety of commercially-manufactured materials for early childhood language development. They are available from teachers' supply stores and from educational media and equipment companies. Pictures, books, puppets, games, toys, audiovisual items, and idea resource books for early childhood teachers are just a few of the many items manufactured.

Magazines for teachers are a good source for addresses of companies who will send free catalogs to interested people upon request.

In addition to single items, special kits and sets are made to promote language development. These kits and sets may include various combinations of pictures, objects, games, charts, puppets, and audio-visual aids, such as records and filmstrips.

Most large kits include a teacher's manual with daily, planned suggestions and directions for a language development program. The goals of each activity are explained in detail along with suggestions for teachers and specific directions instructing what the teacher is to say during the activity. Most of the kits are based on sound educational principles and have been designed by early childhood educators. Many of the kits are developmental — starting with basic language arts skills and progressing to more mature levels. Often the set has been developed for use with language-disadvantaged children. Goals cited in kits and sets include the following items.

- Vocabulary development
- Development of thought processes and problem-solving techniques
- Practice with basic sentence patterns of standard English
- Use of existing syntax and new syntax patterns
- Interpretation of feelings and points of view
- Use of creative language
- Providing enjoyment and development of positive attitudes
- Development of a self-concept
- Teaching standard English as a second language

The Teacher's Role

Teachers have different opinions on the use of language development kits. Some prefer one kit over another; others prefer to plan their own program; still others combine kit activities with self-planned ideas.

Teachers have expressed concern that a language kit might become the total program. They maintain that if this should happen, language arts might be offered only one way and at only one time of the day. They also point out that activities should be planned with regard for a particular group's current interests and past experiences. Kits that are based only on the life experiences of children who live in large cities may lack reality for rural children; kits based on the familiar experiences of the middle-class child may not be appropriate for children in disadvantaged areas.

Care, proper storage, repair, and replacement of commercial language development materials is part of the teacher's duties. Some kits are rather expensive, making teacher use, storage, and care even more important.

Figure 22-4 provides a listing of commercial kits and programs.

RESOURCES FOR TEACHER-MADE MATERIALS

Materials used in the construction of teaching materials can be obtained from a variety of community resources. Some are free or inexpensive; others are higher in cost. Local resources include these.

Businesses/Often displays and advertising material can be adapted. Boxes, containers, and

ALG. Young. *Amazing Life Games,* Boston: Houghton Mifflin.

BECP. Nedler. *Bilingual Early Childhood Program,* TX: Southwest Educational Development.

Blank. Blank. *Teaching Learning in the Preschool: A Dialogue Approach,* Columbus, OH: Merrill.

Bowmar. Jaynes; Woodbridge; Curry; and Crume. *Bowmar Early Childhood Series,* Los Angeles: Bowmar.

DISTAR. Engelmann and Osborn. *DISTAR, Language 1,* Chicago: Science Research.

Focus. Tough. *Focus on Meaning,* London: George, Allen and Unwin, 1973. (Published in the United States as *Talking, Thinking, Growing,* New York: Schocken Books.)

Goal. Karnes. *Goal Program: Language Development,* East Long Meadow, MA: Milton Bradley.

Intellectual Skills. Hobson and McCauley. *Intellectual Skills and Language,* Tucson, AZ: Arizona Center for Educational Research and Development.

Minicourse. Ward and Kelley. *Developing Children's Oral Language, Minicourse 2,* Beverley Hills, CA: Macmillan Educational Services.

Murphy and O'Donnell. Murphy and O'Donnell. *Developing Oral Language with Young Children,* Cambridge, MA: Educator's Publishing Service.

Oral English. Thomas and Allen. *Oral English,* Oklahoma City, OK: Economy.

Peabody. Dunn; Horton; and Smith. *Peabody Language Development Kit, Level P,* Circle Pines, MN: American Guidance Service.

SELF. Monolakes and Scian. *Self,* Morristown, NJ: Silver Burdett.

Simonds. Simonds. *Language Skills for the Young Child,* San Francisco: R & E Research Associates.

SWRL. Southwest Regional Laboratories. *Communication Skills Program: Expressive Language, Blocks 1 and 2,* Lexington, MA: Ginn.

FIGURE 22-4 Commercial language development program and kits

packaging material are also available for the asking.

Outgrown, Recycled, Second-hand Shops/Besides flea markets, garage sales, and so forth, these shops offer various kinds of resources.

Home Discards/Food packaging and mail advertising materials are plentiful. Items that are no longer useful, such as children's games with missing parts, can be restored and adapted to preschool playroom use.

Elementary School Discards/Old workbooks can be a good source for patterns and pictures.

School Supply Stores, Stationery Stores, Variety Stores, Five and Dime Stores/Dice, small plastic items, game spinners, colorful decals, decorative stamp packs, plastic and clear contact paper, construction paper and chartboard, binding tape, and so forth, are available.

Out-of-town Companies and Public Agencies/ Many national companies send teachers educational and promotional materials involving their products.

Printed Resource Guides to Free and Inexpensive Materials/Some examples include:

Garlitz, Edward, *Resource Guide to Free and Inexpensive Materials,* American Association of Elementary Kindergarten-Nursery Education, NEA Center, Washington, D.C. (Public Resources)

Free and Inexpensive Learning Materials, Div. of Surveys and Field Services, George Peabody College for Teachers, Nashville, TN 37203 (about $3.50.) (Product Company resources)

Construction Tips

The extra time devoted to protective coverings and sturdy storage containers on teacher-made items adds extra life, figure 22-5. Clear contact paper, strapping tape, and plastic book-binding tape are often used to seal edges and

FIGURE 22-5 These sturdy, teacher-made puzzles are covered with clear plastic adhesive and made from coloring book pages mounted on cardboard. *(Colored by elementary school children.)*

protect surfaces. A lamination process is available to some centers. Material which is compact and can be folded is a must when storage space is limited.

Volunteer help and parents' talents and efforts are often used to construct classroom materials. Simple directions for construction prepared in advance minimizes the need for teacher's directions. One or more parent meetings a year is often devoted to construction of useful child language materials.

Teacher-made Language Development Materials

Pictures and Picture File Collections/ Magazine ads, calendar art, photographs, coloring book pages, or drawings mounted on same-size construction paper, filed in catego-ries, can be used in a variety of child activities and displays. Butterfly wall clips at the children's eye level add to display ideas.

Suggestions:
a. Use pictures in a conversational way. The child selects a picture of his choice to talk about.
b. Children can make their own picture books or picture dictionaries.
c. A series of pictures can motivate a child to tell a story.
d. Pictures, drawings, or photos can be pasted to heavy paper or cardboard and easily cut into puzzles. Store puzzles in flat boxes or flapped envelopes.

Patterns and Silhouettes/Seasonal shapes, animal and object shapes, and so forth, can be used in many interesting ways.

Suggestions:
a. Games with matching or classifying.
b. Tracing activities.
c. Chart, mural, and display visuals.
d. Shadow stories and overhead projector stories.
e. Blank book cover shapes.
f. Flannel board activity shapes.

Storage: Categorized patterns stored in see-through envelopes help teachers find shapes quickly. Small patterns can be enlarged using projectors.

Resources for patterns:
a. Senini, Megan L., *Contemporary Shapes for Books,* Prentice-Hall Learning Systems Inc., P.O. Box 47X, Englewood Cliffs, NJ 07632
b. *Animals to Color,* A Whitman Book, Western Publishing Co., Inc., Racine, WI 53401

Activity Books/Commercial materials for children's activities and play books offer teachers a variety of ideas. Activities can be packaged separately for stories, games, patterns, and language activities.

Resources:

a. *Ladybird Books Ltd.,* Loughborough, Leicester, England. Play Book 1 and 2, available in local children's toy stores. (Nice large print.)

b. *Sticker Fun and Stamp Books,* Western Publishing Co., Inc. Education Div. 150 Parish Drive, Wayne, NJ 07470

Dittos/Dittos, although rarely used, interest some children. Dittos may be helpful for children with advanced skills, who like using pencil and paper, or cutting activities. Blank ditto masters can be used by children and duplicated for another child or the total group. Teachers occasionally design activities themselves using dittoed forms. (A spirit duplicating machine is necessary.)

Resources:

a. *Unit 1 Paths A,* or *Alphabet Skills,* The Continental Press, P.O. Box 554, Elgin, IL 60120

b. *Directional Concepts,* F.A. Owens Publishing Co., Dansville, NY 14437

Tracing Tablets/Materials needed include acetate (or X-ray film or heavy plastic see-through paper), cardboard, masking or cloth mending tape.

Construction:

Tape acetate and cardboard together, leaving three sides open (can be constructed for younger children leaving only one side open).

LANGUAGE GAMES

Language games are defined as games in which children use communication skills. Played inside or outside, there are many game possibilities. The following concentrates on language arts games involving indoor teacher-made materials which emphasize skills in prereading, speaking, and prewriting areas. They are noncompetitive. Each child finishes the task at his own rate of speed.

Children often make up their own games with their own rules. The games that follow usually need some direction and demonstration by the teacher before children proceed on their own.

Teachers' supervision of games includes:

- eliminating undue competition.
- monitoring, maintenance, and repair.
- assisting children to help them succeed, when necessary.
- positive comments noting children's completion of tasks and proper handling of materials.

Hints and tips in constructing games include the following.

- Be sure the games are sturdy. Flimsy parts or frustrating tasks should be avoided. Reinforce edges and folds.
- Package each game as a complete unit in an attractive container.
- Make games that are colorful and attractive.
- Experiment with clear contact covering, with the aid of a helpful friend.
- Base games on observed child interests. If Yogi is an often-talked-about character, perhaps a game with a bears theme would immediately motivate the children.
- Include children's names, teachers' names, familiar school and community names and settings.
- Monitor children's game playing. Be watchful for instances when a child needs helpful teacher company.
- Be open to children's ideas, for example; find new ways to play a game or devise new rules. If games are changed, be sure the revised game makes good use of materials, so materials are not destroyed.
- Discover book binding, plastic and strapping tape, book pockets, tongue depressors, and brads.
- Obtain inexpensive plastic and metal spinners from school suppliers.
- Design games using materials such as seeds, leaves, or wood.
- Design flat and standing type games.
- Common preschool games often use the following materials:

  tongs and tweezers

  dice and spinners

marbles, small balls, bean bags
interesting textures and coverings
small toys — metal cars, airplanes, small dolls, animal figures, etc.
rubber bands, nails, pegs
shoe strings and colored pipe cleaners
commercial stamp sets
hooks, clothespins, snaps
small, colored blocks and rods
magnets, paper clips
discarded playing cards, figure 22-6
dowcling or wood scraps

Resources

Game Component Collection
Creative Publications, Inc.
Box 10328
Palo Alto, CA 94303

Components include blank game boards, blank playing cards, wooden pawns, dice, spinners, shape and number pressure-sensitive stickers, felt game mats, and brightly colored storage boxes for the games created.

Reading Readiness
Early Childhood Education Gameboards #2032

FIGURE 22-6 A teacher supervises while children enjoy a table top activity with cards.

Communications Skill Building, Inc.
817 E. Broadway
P.O. Box 6081-E
Tucson, AZ 85733

GAMES

Matching Clothesline Game

Materials:

Two lengths of clothesline rope, colorful clothespins, storage box, and a collection of paired, matching items, (such as cards, alphabet letters, felt shapes, pictures).

Procedure:

One child (or teacher) pins one of the pair of picture cards on the first line. Another child matches the cards in sequence on a second line.

Lotto

Sets can be made to be difficult or easy, depending on the matches and the complexity of card figures.

Materials:

Cardboard or tagboard sheets, ruler, pictures, pen, clear contact paper, scissors, small box for storing set, colorful contact paper for storage box (paper cutter optional).

Construction:

Make enough small cards to cover each square on each large Lotto card.

Procedure:

The game is played until all cards are drawn. The first child who finishes covering all the squares on his large card draws cards in the next game.

Word and Picture Dominoes

Materials:

Oblong divided cards, small stamps or pictures, felt pen, ruler, scissors, paste, clear contact paper, tape (optional), playing board (optional), storage box.

Procedure:

Cards are dealt face down. The second child to play matches one side of the first-played card, or passes.

Classification Game

Materials:

Three boxes, cards with dog, fruit and bird pictures (many other categories are possible — fish, people, cars, farm, jungle, food), knife, paint (or scenes can be made from construction paper), glue, and felt pen.

Construction:

Remember to cut a door in the back of the box so cards can be retrieved.

Procedure:

The child slips a card into the correct box, figure 22-7.

Dice Games

Board and matching games which use dice are popular for language activities. Figure 22-8 shows a pattern for a large die. Games using one, two, or more dice are possible.

Matching Wheel Games

Pictures, spots, alphabet letters, etc. are matched, figure 22-9.

Large-Snake Floor Alphabet Puzzle

Draw a large snake on newsprint to be used as a pattern. Make segments large enough to printscript the alphabet in lowercase and uppercase. Cut segments; trace on cardboard pieces. Print the alphabet. Cover with clear contact paper. Store in a large box.

Matching Tongue Depressors

A design is made in pairs on the tongue depressor. Bright paint is preferred. Children match the designs.

Spinner and Board Games

There are many possible game ideas. Old gameboards or new gameboards are easily designed, figure 22-10.

Card Games

Simple games made with commercial card sets save construction time. Pictures are colorful and card sets are available on many themes — cars, flowers, fish, animals, and so forth.

Resource:

EDU-CARDS
Binney and Smith, Easton, PA 18042

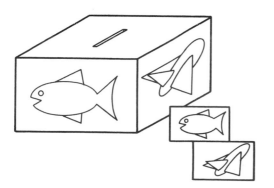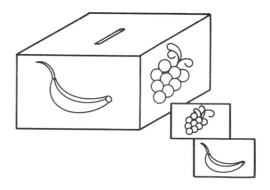

FIGURE 22-7 Classifying cards in correct box

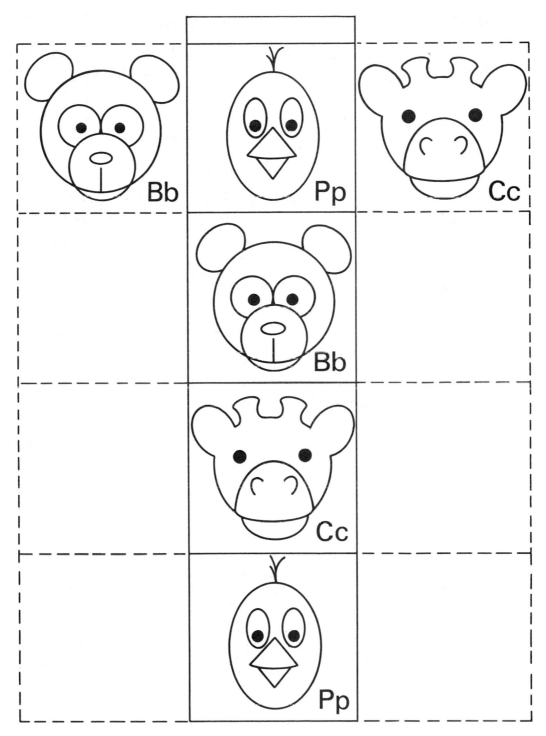

FIGURE 22-8 Dice patterns

Puzzle with Words

Teachers can add word labels to large cardboard puzzle pieces. This helps increase children's awareness of written words.

Example:

Magic Cottage Popout Puzzle
Bank St. College of Education
Published by Intelicor Products and Services, Inc.
New York, NY 10018
(available at toy stores and school supply stores)

Body Part Matching Game

Materials:

Cardboard (or tagboard), scissors, felt pens, pencil, clear contact paper.

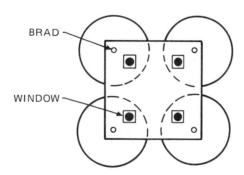

FIGURE 22-9 Wheel games

Construction:

Trace a child's foot and hand. Draw a large ear and eye pattern. Cut out the patterns. Trace the patterns on tagboard and cut matching pairs. Each set of two is different (change color or details).

Procedure:

The child picks out matching pairs from the collection.

SKILLS INCORPORATED IN GAMES

Table games often are designed to develop the following skills and abilities:

- Small muscle manipulation
- Sorting ability — color, size, weight, shape, symbols
- Visual matching of objects, symbols, patterns, colors, classification categories
- Sequence and ordering skills
- Following game patterns and directions
- Noticing likenesses and differences
- Verbal and vocabulary development and labeling skill
- Noting relationships
- Visual memory
- Tactile discrimination
- Predicting outcomes

A game can be played until everyone finishes, and two or more turns can be given to

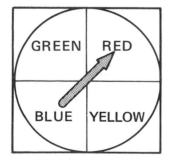
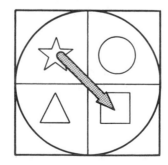
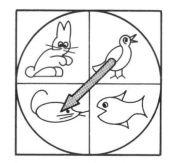

FIGURE 22-10 Spinners for game boards

speed this process and to avoid waiting time for early completors in group games. Many games are solitary pursuits or joint efforts with a friend or two.

When a new game is introduced, make statements like: "We play until everyone gets his marker on the 'pot of honey'," or "If you've finished your friends may need an extra turn to catch up," or "Everyone finishes in the game. You keep spinning until you reach the end." Help reinforce this concept of noncompetitive play, figure 22-11.

RESOURCES FOR GAME IDEAS

The following references contain additional ideas for early childhood language games.

FIGURE 22-11 Playing, rather than winning, is emphasized.

1. Barrata-Lorton, Mary, *Workjobs*, Addison-Wesley Publishing Co., 1972.
2. McCord, Andy and Ross, Shirley, *Animal Rhythms*, 1973, Personal Learning Association, P.O. Box 886, San Jose, CA 95106
3. Day, Barbara, *Open Learning in Early Childhood*, New York: Macmillan Publishing Co., Inc., 1975.
4. Belton, Sandra and Terborgh, Christine, *Sparks*, Human Service Press, 4301 Connecticut Ave., N.W., Washington, DC, 1972.
5. *Sesame Street Magazine*, 1 Lincoln Plaza, New York, NY, 10023.
6. *Playbooks*, 1970, Ladybird Books Ltd., Loughborough, Leicester, England (available in many local toy stores).
7. Kaplan, Sandra; Kaplan, JoAnn; Madsen, Sheila; and Taylor, Bette K., *Change for Children*, Goodyear Publishing Company, Inc., Pacific Palisades, CA, 1973.

COMPUTERS — THE NEW AUDIOVISUAL

Preschool educators taking a serious look at microcomputer use by preschool children are hard put to find features which don't mesh well with their professional educational philosophy and practice. Many are as downright enthusiastic as the children who are lucky enough to experience them. It's now felt that computers will neither replace or dispace either the teacher or any presently-planned activities. Instead they will add immeasurably to children's first-hand learning opportunities.

Software programs developed for 3- and 4-years-olds which run on a wide variety of microcomputers are quickly being designed and manufactured. Prices vary, but are no more expensive than other preschool play equipment in many cases (after the microcomputer investment). Programs designed by knowledgeable developers are highly participatory, sensitive to child self-esteem, and aesthetically pleasing —

besides being novel and fun. The child may listen to, talk to, create, express, make decisions, talk to others about, learn by making choices, actively explore, build and destroy, repeat over and over, or solve problems, all while feeling a sense of power.

Research studies, while few in number, have begun to make the following generalities concerning young children (in group programs) and microcomputers.

- Most four- and five-year-olds are interested.
- Waiting lists are necessary, and time-allowed periods can be set.
- A knowledgeable, clear demonstration on operation and care is necessary.
- Children tend to work and discuss in small groups.
- After becoming proficient, some prefer working alone.
- They average about 20 minutes a seating.
- They adopt computer descriptor terms quickly: disk, boot, save, etc.
- Graphic programs which allow them to "draw" capture their fancy.
- They learn to use joysticks, paddles, and hand controls after brief introduction.
- A standard keyboard doesn't intimidate them.
- The girls are as interested as boys. They are not viewed as a "boy" toy.
- Children seem rewarded and don't seek or need outside teacher reinforcement.
- Both color and sound add to experiences.

From the evidence, it seems that microcomputers will take their place in children's minds and hearts and become as beloved as blocks, puzzles, books and the sandbox. A computer can do what educators planning other experiences for children hope for — capture interest and make children feel competent. They are here to stay. How fast or slowly they become standard preschool equipment really depends on staff and school budget. Early childhood teachers are increasingly facing parents' questions, and will be opening more and more computing centers in their classrooms.

The Teacher's Task

Where should a preschool teacher start? You'll need "hands on" experiences; many county and city offices of education already have computer education centers for teachers which are equipped with personnel and software programs. Local computer stores gladly provide demonstrations. Local computer clubs abound with experts, or perhaps a parent can serve as a school resource.

Many language arts, prereading, and prewriting skills are already part of existing preschool level software programs. *Software Magazine* listed about sixty in its November, 1983 issue ranging in price from about $5 to $50. Software programs need serious previewing by preschool teachers before they enter the program into the curriculum. The software curriculum should advance a school's goals rather than serve as a gimmick to increase enrollment. Teachers — as mentioned before — will have to have mastered a software program themselves to be effective co-explorers and resourceful guides. Fortunately this will not be difficult, but time consuming instead.

A listing of software programs recommended by other early childhood educators is found in figure 22-12.

SUMMARY

A variety of materials and media is used to promote language development in early childhood centers. Materials can:

- motivate and stimulate.
- promote play and interaction.
- introduce new learnings.
- keep children interested.
- provide variety.

Above/Below, Right/Left (The Learning Company)
Teaches spatial concepts by dividing the keyboard into quadrants. Any key in a particular area will activate the desired response.

A Clock Game (Edutek Corp.)
Makes a game of telling time.

Alphabet (Steketee Educational Co.)
Press the keys and the letters of the alphabet appear in color while the Apple sings the alphabet song.

Bumble Plots (The Learning Co.)
Six games feature Bumble, a fantasy creature. Guessing secret numbers and logical thinking skills taught.

Children's Carrousel (Dynacomp, Inc.)

Color Guess (Ideatech Company)
Teaches reading and spelling of color words by associating the color with the current color word as displayed on the screen.

The "E" Game (Eric Software Publ.) Ages 4 and up.
Matching alphabet letters and learning their names.

Electronic Playground (Software Entertainment Co.) Age 3–6.
Counting, number recognition, and matching.

Gertrude's Secrets (The Learning Co.) Ages 4–9.
Identify and classify objects by color and shape plus "logic" puzzles.

Juggle's Rainbow (The Learning Co.) Ages 3–6.
Above, below, right, left, symmetry includes prereading and classfication skill development.

Magic Spells (The Learning Co.)
A word and spelling game.

Proto the Robot (Educational Software)
Coloring pictures, composing songs, and a storybook with game pages.

Reader Rabbit and the Fabulous Word Factory (The Learning Co.)
Visual memory and matching skills.

Teacher's Pet (Dynacomp, Inc.)
Introduction to computers and a learning tool for letter/word recognition.

Teddy's Magic Balloon (Program Design Inc.)
An interactive story with voice narration. Child guides balloon through the sky.

The Toddler's Turtle (Logo Association)
Turtle moves in all directions and makes large and small circles.

Working With the Alphabet (Random House)
Alphabetical order and letter recognition.

FIGURE 22-12 Software programs have been designed for use with young children.

- offer opportunities to manipulate and explore.

Materials can be made by staff members or purchased. Staff-made items help provide a variety of activities. The needs, motivations, and interests of each particular group of children serve as the basis for the design of sturdy and inexpensive materials.

Commercial language-development kits and sets are also available. They differ in goals, activity plans, and types of items included. Most of the kits are sequential, starting with the simple and moving toward higher and broader levels of development. Teacher manuals should be studied closely before using the kits with children.

There are many teacher-made language game ideas where skills are learned through game participation. Inexpensive materials for staff-made games come from a variety of sources.

Microcomputers may take their place alongside traditional preschool materials as software programs for young children are developed at a fast pace. Selecting programs in tune with a school's goals could become an early childhood teacher's task, as well as serving as a resource person for both children and parents. Use of well-designed computer programs may contribute to young children's educational opportunity.

Learning Activities

- Visit an early childhood center; list and describe staff-made materials for language development.

- In small groups, compare language-development materials found in catalogs. Make comparisons between companies. Find 5 to 10 items your group feels would be valuable for a center's language development program.

- Visit a local stationery and supply store. Describe five items or materials to use in developing staff-made materials, or describe five commercially manufactured language development materials or media.

- Develop a list and description of language development kits used in local programs.

- Obtain a language kit. Read the teacher's manual and outline the goals of the program. Present an activity in class, with other students playing the role of the children.

- Design a dice game which uses a language arts skill. Draw a sketch if necessary. List materials needed.

- Design a language developing spinner and board game. Draw a sketch and list materials needed.

- Invite an early childhood teacher to speak with the class, to describe use of teacher-made and commercially-made materials.

- Invite a manufacturer's representative of an early childhood language kit to describe the company's products to the class.

- Visit a computer center and preview a preschooler's software program.

• Discuss your feelings about microcomputers and young children with a group of fellow students. Record your ideas and share with the group.

Unit Review

A. Briefly discuss the following statements.
1. Many different types of media and materials are used to promote language arts in young children.
2. A teacher can add to a center's program by being aware of commercial materials for use in the language arts.
3. In designing and constructing materials for young children, there are several important considerations.
4. One of the duties of the teacher is the care of materials.

B. Match each item in Column I with the statement that best suits it from Column II.

Column I	Column II
1. games	a. free upon request
2. local business	b. categorized collection
3. picture file	c. usually less expensive
4. staff-made items	d. a construction concern
5. sturdiness	e. storage, proper use, and replacement
6. care	f. resource for materials
7. catalogs	g. a collection of teaching materials
8. kit or set	h. every child wins
9. goals	i. from simple to complex
10. a sequence	j. objectives

C. Discuss the positive and negative features in the use of commercial language development kits or sets.

D. Select the best answer.
1. A large quantity of language materials
   a. makes a center interesting to young children.
   b. may not make a center interesting unless materials are also appropriate.
   c. assures language arts will be enjoyed.
   d. assures appropriateness of materials.
2. Teachers can obtain valuable materials ideas from
   a. catalogs
   b. school supply stores.
   c. resource books.
   d. visiting preschools.
   e. All of the above.

3. Materials can be purchased
   a. as single items or in groups.
   b. directly from manufacturers.
   c. at teachers' supply stores.
   d. All of the above.
4. A teacher who notices a child becoming frustrated with a language game should
   a. distract the child and suggest another activity.
   b. tell the child he's chosen a game which is too difficult.
   c. subtly help the child by asking problem-solving questions or completing parts for the child.
   d. make sure the game is withheld from the classroom for a few months until the child is ready for it.
5. Language-development kits should be used
   a. without question because they are usually designed by expert educators.
   b. as the total language program.
   c. when the staff wants a sequential program.
   d. when staff members clearly understand goals and methods.
6. The main goal of teacher-made language games is
   a. enjoyable child skill development for all players.
   b. to help winners gain self-esteem.
   c. reducing budget expenditures.
   d. teacher-child interaction.

E. Discuss "A preschool teacher's role in offering microcomputer programs is _____."

References

Bartlett, Elsa Jaffe, "Selecting an Early Childhood Language Curriculum," in *Language in Early Childhood,* Revised ed., Courtney B. Cazden, ed., N.A.E.Y.C., 1981.

Personal Software Magazine, Nov. 1983, Hayden Publishing Co.

Piestrup, Ann M., "Young Children Use Computer Graphics," *Harvard Computer Graphics Week,* Harvard Univ. Graduate School of Design, copyright Ann M. Piestrup, 1982.

Swigger, Kathleen M., "Is One Better?", *Educational Computer,* Nov./Dec., 1983.

Watt, Molly, "Electronic Thinker Toys," *Popular Computing,* June 1983.

Suggested Readings

Bits and Pieces — Imaginative Uses for Children's Learning, A.C.E.I., 11141 Georgia Avenue, Suite 200, Wheaton, MD 20902, 1982.

"Children in the Age of Microcomputers," Steven Silvem, Guest Editor, *Childhood Education,* March/April, 1983.

Language in Early Childhood, Courtney B. Cazden, ed., N.A.E.Y.C., 1981.

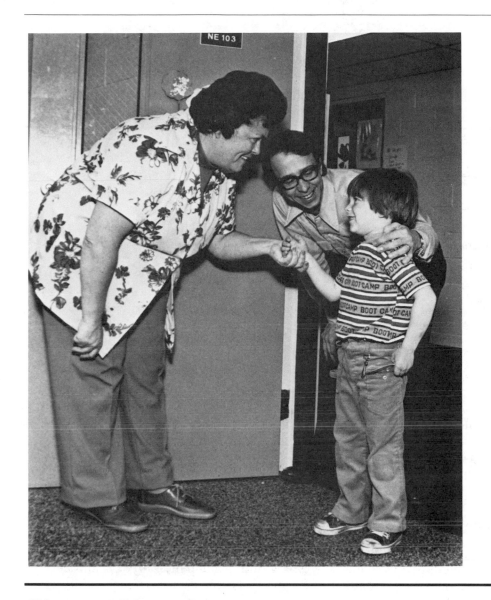

Section 6
Language Arts — in Class and at Home

Unit 23
Classroom Language Arts Area

OBJECTIVES

After studying this unit you should be able to

- describe the advantages of a classroom's early childhood language arts center.

- list ten items of equipment or furnishings suggested for a language arts center.

- make a sketch of a classroom language arts center labeling furnishings and equipment.

An inviting, comfortable language arts center can become a child's favorite place in the school. Language materials within easy reach, and soft textures to lean on or lie upon in a quiet screened area, offer a different type of setting than do active and vigorous play areas.

ADVANTAGES

Language activities are always available for children to choose when a language arts center is part of an early childhood classroom. Materials placed at children's eye level motivate the children to explore, and offer the opportunity for them to follow individual interests.

Well-stocked, well-supervised language centers full of "things to do" encourage the development of language art skills. Listening, speaking, prereading, and prewriting activities are all available. Individual and group work areas plus quiet play spots are provided.

In language arts centers, related instructional materials are located in one convenient area. Stocking, supervision, and maintenance of materials, furnishings, and equipment is easily accomplished.

LANGUAGE CENTER AREA

Full of communication-motivating activities, every inch of floor and wall space of a language arts center is used. Small room areas enlarged by building upward with lofts or bunks solve floor-space problems in crowded centers, figure 23-1. Adding "climb into" areas is another useful space-opening device.

Language center areas have three main functions: they provide looking-listening activities for children, they give children an area for working with material activities, and they provide for storage of materials. The ideal area has comfortable, soft furnishings together with ample work space, proper lighting, and screening to block the sights and sounds of active classrooms. Language arts centers are quiet places separated from the more vigorous activities of the average playroom. Suggested furnishings are listed by category.

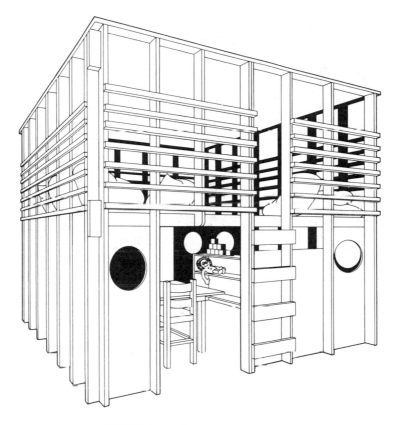

FIGURE 23-1 Language center area

General Use Materials
- One or more child-size tables and a few chairs
- Shelving
- Dividers (screens)
- Soft cushioned rocker, easy chair, or couch
- Soft pillows
- "Crawl into" hideaways, lined with carpet or fabric, figure 23-2
- Book rack which displays book covers, figure 23-3
- Individual work space or study spots
- Audiovisuals and electrical outlets
- Chalkboard
- Flannel board
- Pocket chart
- Children's file box, figure 23-4

- Bulletin board
- Carpet, rug, or soft floor covering
- Chart stand or wall-mounted wing clamps
- Storage cabinets
- Wastebasket

Writing and Prewriting Materials
- Paper — scratch, lined, typing
- Table
- File or index cards
- Storage shelf, figure 23-5
- Writing tools — crayons, felt markers, soft pencils in handy contact-covered containers
- Primary typewriter
- Small typewriter table

FIGURE 23-2 A crawl-into area for quiet language activities

- Word boxes
- Picture dictionary
- Wall-displayed alphabet guides
- Cutout, colorful alphabet letters
- Tabletop blackboards with chalk
- Blank book skeletons
- Scissors
- Tape
- Erasers
- Tracing envelopes, patterns, wipe-off cloth
- Large, lined chart paper (or newsprint)
- Magnet board with alphabet letters

Reading and Prereading Materials

- Books (including child-made examples)
- Book and audiovisual combinations

- Favorite story character cutouts
- Rebus story charts

Speech Materials

- Puppets and puppet theaters
- Flannel board sets
- Language games

Audiovisual Equipment

- Record player, headsets, jacks, figure 23-6
- Story records
- Tape recorder (cassette)
- Language master, recording cards, figure 23-7
- Picture files

Adults usually supervise use of audiovisual equipment in a language center, although a

FIGURE 23-3 Book covers can be easily seen when displayed on a child-level book rack.

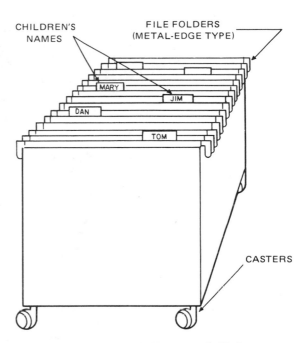

FIGURE 23-4 Children's work file box

number of the simpler audiovisuals can be operated by children after a brief training period. Tape recorders and headsets require careful introduction by the teacher.

TEACHER'S ROLE

Teachers are congenial, interested companions for the children: sharing books; helping them with projects; recording their dictation; playing and demonstrating language games; making words, word lists, signs or charts, (figure 23-8); and helping children use the center's equipment.

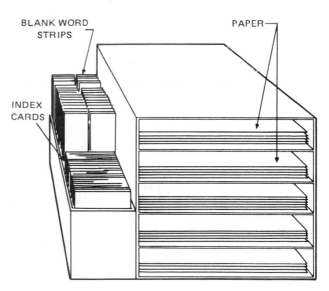

FIGURE 23-5 Tabletop paper holder

FIGURE 23-6 Individual listening places have record players and headsets for private listening.

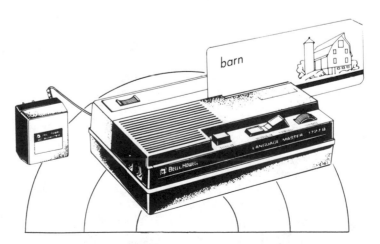

FIGURE 23-7 Language master instructional device

Hurt no living thing:
Ladybug nor butterfly,
Nor moth with dusty wing,
Nor cricket chirping cheerily
Nor grasshopper
    so light of leap,
Nor dancing gnat,
Nor beetle fat,
Nor harmless worms
    that creep.

FIGURE 23-8 Language center chart

Children who have been given clear introductions to a language center's materials, and clear statements concerning expectations in use of the center's furnishings, may need little help. It may be necessary, however, to set rules for the number of children who can use a language center at a given time.

The teacher explains new materials which are to become part of the center's collection. The materials are demonstrated before they are made available to the children.

Pasting children's work on the center bulletin board, and planning blackboard activities and messages catch the children's attention. Plants and occasional fresh flowers in vases add a pleasant touch.

AUDIOVISUAL EQUIPMENT

Budgets often determine the availability of audiovisual materials in a center. Care of equipment and awareness of operating procedures are important. Special fund-raising projects, rental agreements, borrowing arrangements, or seeking donations can secure audiovisuals for some programs. The machine's instruction manual should be studied for the proper care and operational maintenance necessary for efficient use.

The following audiovisuals enrich a center's language arts equipment.

Camera/Polaroid or standard-type cameras provide photos that are useful in speaking activities, displays, games.

Slide Projector and Slides/Common house, school, field trip, and community scenes can be discussed, written about (experience stories), or used for storytelling.

Super 8 Projector and Film Loops/Group and private showings are enjoyed. Tape accompanying children's or teacher's stories can be created.

Dukane Projector/Used with or without headsets, this projector provides filmstrip and sound presentations of language arts materials available from commercial suppliers.

Overhead Projectors and Transparencies/Stories with silhouettes or numerous transparency activities can be designed. Small patterns and alphabet letters are enlarged and copied by teachers or children for a variety of uses, figure 23-9.

Opaque Projector/Pages of picture books are projected on wall areas, offering a new way to read books. Guessing games are also possible.

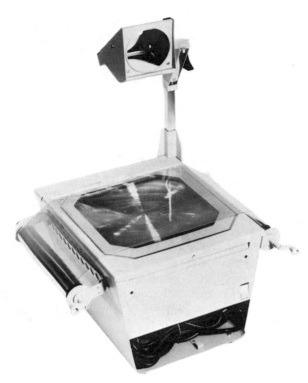

FIGURE 23-9 Audiovisual equipment (overhead projector)
(Photo courtesy of Buhl, Inc.)

Picture book characters become companions.

Filmstrip Projector and Filmstrips/Easy operation and low cost make this equipment popular. Teacher-made filmstrips can be created.

16 mm Film Projectors, Films, and Screens/Many films are made for use with preschool children. Often libraries stock films. Programs attached to public school systems have film catalogs listing available titles. Screens are optional. (Blank walls can also be used.)

Language Master/This machine instantly records and plays back. Children can easily operate this equipment. Words and sounds are paired. Prepackaged language development programs can be purchased. For additional information contact: Bell and Howell, Audio-

visual Products Division, 2100 McCormick Road, Chicago, IL 60645.

Record Player/Most centers have this piece of equipment.

Tape Recorders/A popular audiovisual aid, and in frequent use in early childhood centers, the tape recorder opens up many activity ideas. Suggestions for language development activities follow:

a. Record children's comments about their artwork or projects. "Tell me about _____" is a good starter. Put tape and work together in the language center, available for the children's use.

b. Let the children record their comments about a group of plastic cars, people, animals, and so on, after they arrange them as they wish.

c. Have children discuss photographs or magazine pictures.

d. Record a child's comments about a piece of fruit he has selected from a basket of mixed fruit.

e. Record a "reporter's" account of a recent field trip.

f. Gather a group of common items, such as a mirror, comb, brush, toothbrush. Let the child describe how these items are used.

g. Record a child's description of peeling an orange or making a sandwich with common spreads and fillings.

h. Record a child's comments about his block structures.

(NOTE: If the teacher takes the child's dictation instead of using the tape recorder, words should be recorded in a word-for-word fashion, without teacher editing.)

COMMERCIAL SOURCES FOR AUDIOVISUALS

AA Records, 250 W. 57th Street, New York, NY 10019

ABC School Supply, 437 Armour Circle N.E., Box 13084, Atlanta, GA 30324

A. B. LeCrone Company, 819 N.W. 92nd Street, Oklahoma City, OK 73114

Argosy Music Corporation, Motivation Records, 101 Harbor Road, Westport, CT 06880

Bilingual Educational Services, 816 So. Fair Oaks, South Pasadena, CA 91030

Bowmar, P.O. Box 3623, Glendale, CA 91201

Capital Records, Inc., 1750 N. Vine St., Hollywood, CA 90028

Childcraft Education Corp., 20 Kilmer Road, Edison, NJ 08817

Children's Record Guild (CRG), 225 Park Avenue South, New York, NY 10003

David C. Cook Publishing Co., 850 N. Grove Avenue, Elgin, IL 60120

Decca Records, 445 Park Avenue, New York, NY 10022

Disneyland Records, 800 Sonora Avenue, Glendale, CA 91201

Droll Yankees, Providence, RI 02906

Encyclopedia Britannica Ed. Corp., 425 N. Michigan Avenue, Chicago, IL 60611

Educational Activities, Inc., P.O. Box 392, Freeport, NY 11520

Folkways Records, 43 W. 61st Street, New York, NY 10023

Golden Records, 250 W. 57th Street, New York, NY 10019

Happy Time Records, 8016 43rd Avenue, Long Island City, NY 10001

Kimbo Educational, P.O. Box 246, Deal, NJ 07723

KTAV Publishing House, Inc., 120 E. Broadway, New York, NY 10022

Learning Arts, P.O. Box 179, Wichita, KS 67201

Mercury Record Productions, Phonogram, Inc., One IBM Plaza, Chicago, IL 60611

MGM Record Corporation, 7165 W. Sunset Blvd., Los Angeles, CA 90046

Miller-Brody Productions, Inc., 342 Madison Avenue, New York, NY 10017

Peter Pan Industries, 88 St. Francis St., Newark, NJ 07105

Pickwick Records, 135 Crossways Park Drive, Woodbury, NY 11797

RCA Records, 1133 Avenue of the Americas, New York, NY 10036

Rhythms Productions, P.O. Box 34485, Los Angeles, CA 90034

Scholastic Book Services, Audiovisual Dept., 904 Sylvan Ave., Englewood Cliffs, NJ 07632

W. Schwann, Inc., 137 Newbury Street, Boston, MA 02116

Scott, Foresman and Company, 1900 E. Lake Avenue, Glenview, IL 60025

Singer Society for Visual Education, Inc., 1345 Diversey Parkway, Chicago, IL 60614

Tikva Records, 22 E. 17th Street, New York, NY 10003

UNICEF, U. S. Committee for UNICEF, 331 E. 38th St., New York, NY 10016

United Synagogue Book Service, 155 Fifth Avenue, New York, NY 10010

Westminster Press, Witherspoon Bldg., Rm. 905, Philadelphia, PA 19107

Young People's Records (YPR), 225 Park Avenue South, New York, NY 10003

RECORD AND PICTURE BOOK COMBINATIONS

Children's Press, 1224 W. Van Buren St., Chicago, IL 60607

Scholastic Book Services, Audiovisual Dept., 904 Sylvan Ave., Englewood Cliffs, NJ 07632

Viking Penguin Audiovisual Catalog, Charles Wieser Assoc., P.O. Box 538, El Toro, CA 92630

CHILDREN'S BOOK PUBLISHERS

(Many publishers also supply audiovisual materials.)

Abelard-Schuman Limited, 6 W. 57 Street, New York, NY 10019

Allyn & Bacon, Inc., 470 Atlantic Ave., Boston, MA 02110

American Book Company, 55 Fifth Avenue, New York, NY 10003

Atheneum Publishers, 122 E. 42 Street, New York, NY 10017

Beacon Press, 25 Beacon Street, Boston, MA 02108

The Bobbs-Merrill Co., Inc., 4300 W. 62 Street, Indianapolis, IN 46206

Children's Press, Inc., 1224 W. Van Buren St., Chicago, IL 60607

Chilton Book Company, 401 Walnut St., Philadelphia, PA 19106

Coward-McCann, Inc., 200 Madison Ave., New York, NY 10016

Thomas Y. Crowell Company, 201 Park Ave. S., New York, NY 10003

The John Day Company, Inc., 62 W. 45 St., New York, NY 10036

The Dial Press, Inc., 750 Third Ave., New York, NY 10017

Doubleday & Company, Inc., 277 Park Ave., New York, NY 10017

E. P. Dutton & Co., Inc., 201 Park Avenue South, New York, NY 10003

Farrar, Straus & Giroux, Inc., 19 Union Square West, New York, NY 10003

Follett Publishing Company, 1010 W. Washington Blvd., Chicago, IL 61820

Funk & Wagnalls, 380 Madison Ave., New York, NY 10016

Ginn and Company, Statler Building, Back Bay, P. O. 191, Boston, MA 02117

Golden Press, Inc., 850 Third Avenue, New York, NY 10022

Grossett & Dunlap, Inc., 51 Madison Avenue, New York, NY 10010

Harcourt, Brace and World, Inc., 757 Third Ave., New York, NY 10017

Harper & Row Publishers, 49 E. 33 St., New York, NY 10016

Harvey House, Inc., Publishers, 5 S. Buckhout St., Irvington-on-Hudson, NY 10533

Hastings House, Publishers, Inc., 151 E. 50 Street, New York, NY 10022

Hawthorn Books, Inc., 70 Fifth Avenue, New York, NY 10011

Holiday House, Inc., 18 E. 56 Street, New York, NY 10022

Holt, Rinehart & Winston, Inc., 383 Madison Ave., New York, NY 10017

Houghton Mifflin Company, 2 Park Street, Boston, MA 02107

Alfred A. Knopf, Inc., 501 Madison Ave., New York, NY 10022

Lantern Press, Inc., 257 Park Avenue South, New York, NY 10010

Lerner Publications Company, 241 First Avenue, N., Minneapolis, MN 54401

J. B. Lippincott Company, East Washington Square, Philadelphia, PA 19105

Little, Brown and Company, 34 Beacon Street, Boston, MA 02106

Lothrop, Lee and Shepard Company, Inc., 419 Park Ave. South, New York, NY 10016

Robert B. Luce, Inc., 1244 19 Street, N.W., Washington, DC 20036

McGraw-Hill Book Company, 330 W. 42 Street, New York, NY 10036

David McKay Co., Inc., 750 Third Avenue, New York, NY 10017

The Macmillan Company, 866 Third Avenue, New York, NY 10022

Melmont Publishers, Inc., 1224 W. Van Buren Street, Chicago, IL 60607

William Morrow & Co., Inc., 425 Park Ave. South, New York, NY 10016

Thomas Nelson and Sons, Copewood & Davis Streets, Camden, NJ 08103

W. W. Norton and Company, Inc., 55 Fifth Avenue, New York, NY 10003

Parents' Magazine Press, 52 Vanderbilt Avenue, New York, NY 10017

Platt & Munk Company, Inc., 200 Fifth Avenue, New York, NY 10010

Prentice-Hall, Inc., Route 9 W, Englewood Cliffs, NJ 07632

G. P. Putnam's Sons, 200 Madison Avenue, New York, NY 10022

William R. Scott, Inc., 333 Avenue of the Americas, New York, NY 10014

Scott, Foresman and Company, 1900 East Lake Avenue, Glenview, IL 60025

Charles Scribner's Sons, 597 Fifth Avenue, New York, NY 10001

Silver Burdett Company, Park Avenue and Columbia Rd., Morristown, NJ 07960

Summy-Birchard Company, 1834 Ridge Avenue, Evanston, IL 60204

Vanguard Press, Inc., 424 Madison Ave., New York, NY 10017

The Viking Press, Inc., 625 Madison Avenue, New York, NY 10022

Henry Z. Walck, Inc., 19 Union Square West, New York, NY 10003

Frederick Warne & Co., Inc., 101 Fifth Avenue, New York, NY 10003

Albert Whitman & Co., 560 W. Lake St., Chicago, IL 60606

The World Publishing Company, 2231 W. 110 Street, Cleveland, OH 44102

FILM DISTRIBUTORS

Association Films, 600 Grand Avenue, Ridgefield, NJ 07657

Avis Films, P.O. Box 643, Burbank, CA 91503

Bailey Films, Inc., 6509 DeLongpre Avenue, Los Angeles, CA 90028

Charles Cahill and Associates, Inc., 5746 Sunset Blvd., Los Angeles, CA 90028

Churchill Films, 662 N. Robertson Blvd., Los Angeles, CA 90069

Coronet Films, 65 E. South Water Street, Chicago, IL 60601

Walt Disney Productions, 350 S. Buena Vista Ave., Burbank, CA 91503

Encyclopedia Britannica Educational Corporation, 425 N. Michigan Avenue, Chicago, IL 60611

Film Associates of California, 11559 Santa Monica Blvd., Los Angeles, CA 90025

Indiana University Audiovisual Center, Indiana University, Bloomington, IN 47405

Sterling Films, 241 E. 34 Street, New York, NY 10016

CHILDREN'S FILMS

Chick Chick Chick. Robert and Michael Brown. Churchill Films, New York, NF 1977 (ages 4–10). A hatching egg, chicks, and barnyard life are accompanied by bluegrass music.

Kuumba: Simon's New Sound. Carol Munday Lawrence, Beacon Films, Norwood, Mass., NF 1980 (ages 4–10). A boy invents a steel drum during a carnival in Trinidad.

Little Tim and the Brave Sea Captain. Weston Woods Studios, Weston, Conn., NF 1978 (ages 4–8). A boy and a sea captain experience a storm in Edward Ardizzone's story.

Lullaby. Cyörgy Csonka. International Film Bureau, Chicago, NF 1979 (ages 3–8). A lullaby sung in Hungarian provides a musical background for a dreamlike setting.

A Frog Went A-Courting. Evelyn Lambart. National Film Board of Canada, Films Incorporated, Wilmette, Ill., NF 1977 (ages 3–6). The folk song is illustrated with animated cutouts.

Local libraries may have children's films which can be borrowed.

FILMSTRIP SUPPLIERS

McGraw-Hill Early Learning Materials, Paoli, PA 19301

Stanley Bowmar Co., Inc., 12 Cleveland St., Valhalla, NY 10595

Eye Gate House, Inc., 146-01 Archer Ave., Jamaica, NY 11435

The Jam Handy Organization, 2821 East Grand Blvd., Detroit, MI 48211

Society for Visual Ed., Inc., 1345 Diversey Parkway, Chicago, IL 60614

PLANNING LANGUAGE CENTERS

Centers begin when staff members designate room locations. Materials are then classified into "looking and listening" or "working with" categories. Display, storage, working space, and looking and listening areas are determined. Activities which require concentration are screened off when possible. Many different arrangements of materials and equipment within a language arts center are possible. Most centers rearrange furnishings until the most functional arrangement is found. For sample arrangements with different functions, refer to figure 23-10.

SUMMARY

When there is a language arts center within an early childhood playroom, language development materials are arranged in one central room location. Children follow their own interests, according to their preferences. This increases the children's interaction with materials, which in turn expands their language skills.

A language center's material can include a wide range of teacher-made and commercially-purchased items. Activities in listening, speaking, prewriting, and prereading (or combinations of these) are side by side, promoting the child's ability to see relationships among them.

Audiovisual materials and equipment are useful language center devices. Costs sometimes limit their availability. Training in the use and care of audiovisual machines is necessary for efficient operation.

Learning Activities

- Observe an early childhood program. Describe the use and storage of language development materials.

- Listen to three story records. Judge and compare the quality of the recordings.

- Invite an audiovisual company's sales representative to the class to demonstrate the company's product.

- Develop a price list for five pieces of audiovisual equipment found in this unit.

- Interview two early childhood teachers on their use of audiovisuals in their language arts curriculum. Report the findings to the group.

- Sketch a language arts center to promote dramatizing favorite stories. Label each item and furnishing.

- Plan and conduct an activity for a group of preschoolers using a tape recorder.

Unit Review

A. List the advantages of an early childhood language arts area. What are the disadvantages?

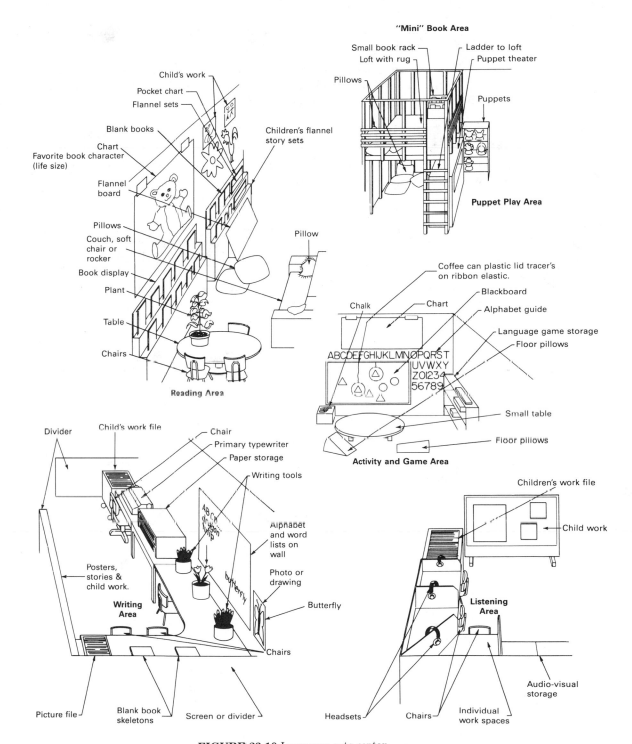

"Mini" Book Area

Small book rack
Loft with rug
Pillows
Ladder to loft
Puppet theater
Puppets

Puppet Play Area

Child's work
Pocket chart
Flannel sets
Blank books
Children's flannel story sets
Chart
Favorite book character (life size)
Flannel board
Pillows
Couch, soft chair or rocker
Book display
Plant
Table
Chairs
Pillow

Reading Area

Coffee can plastic lid tracer's on ribbon elastic.
Blackboard
Alphabet guide
Chalk
Chart
Language game storage
Floor pillows
ABCDEFGHIJKLMNØPQRST
UVWXY
ZO1234
56789
Small table
Floor pillows

Activity and Game Area

Divider
Child's work file
Chair
Primary typewriter
Paper storage
Writing tools
Alphabet and word lists on wall
Photo or drawing
Posters, stories & child work.
Butterfly
butterfly

Writing Area

Picture file
Blank book skeletons
Screen or divider
Chairs

Children's work file
Child work

Listening Area

Headsets
Chairs
Individual work spaces
Audio-visual storage

FIGURE 23-10 Language arts center

B. List the teacher's duties in a well-functioning classroom language arts center. (Example: supervision)

C. Describe or draw a picture of an imaginary language arts center "crawl into," bunk, or loft. It should be a place where a child could be alone, to enjoy a book.

Suggested Reading

Children are Centers for Understanding Media, A.C.E.I., 11141 Georgia Avenue, Suite 200, Wheaton, MD 20902, 1978.

Unit 24
The Parent-center Partnership

OBJECTIVES

After studying this unit you should be able to

- describe the parent-teacher partnership which affects language arts programs.
- list types of parent-school communications.
- identify ways parents can help in a center.

Although parents and teachers are partners in children's education, parents are always the child's foremost teacher and model, figure 24-1.

Schools differ widely in both the amount of written home-school communication and actual time spent just talking or meeting. Considering what's ideal and best for young children, most preschool teachers desire more time, more conversations, and additional written communication. This suits many young parents very well since they seem to be seeking supportive assistance in child rearing.

Each parent group and center is unique, consequently a tremendous difference exists in the degree preschools and parents are able to work together. Considering the many factors that work against the desire to work jointly, most centers try to have some type of parenting assistance.

Parent-school contacts usually take place in at least four ways:

1. Daily conversations
2. Written communications
3. Planned parent meetings, workshops, social events
4. Individual conferences

ON THE FLY

Teachers have a good chance to share a child's interests and favorite school activities with the parent in the brief moments at pick-up time: books, play objects, and child-created or constructed work can be mentioned. Children spend time with and talk about what excites them; the observant teacher keeps aware of the attending children's "at school" play and work. Parents are usually interested in hearing what their child has shared about his home and "out-of-school" activities.

Bulletin Boards

Many schools use "parent" bulletin boards as a communicative device. Language-developing local happenings and activities can be advertised to parents. Short magazine and newspaper articles of interest get posted at eye-catching levels.

FIGURE 24-1 Parent and child in intimate, warm conversation

PLANNED MEETINGS

Conferencing

Parents need to know how the school plans for their child's individual interests and growth. When a child has an interest in alphabet letters, dramatizing, or special-topic books, joint thinking on planned at-school and possible at-home activities can be discussed.

Goal Identification Meetings

Discussion meetings with parents and staff identify language arts areas and parents' wishes and concerns. A center's language arts goals reflect the ideas of parents and staff. Parents, as well as teachers, value the development of a young child's listening, speaking, prewriting, and prereading skills. Teachers contribute ideas and play integral roles in the home-school partnership.

Methods and Materials
Review Meetings

A meeting can be planned to take a closer look at the center's planned language program, materials, and language art classroom center. Parents get a first-hand look and an opportunity to explore. Teachers conduct sample activities and demonstrate material and equipment use. Parents may ask questions about their child's use of or interest in a center's planned opportunities.

Parent-teacher Study Meetings

Some possible themes of study meetings include (1) the effects of television viewing on a child's language (2) bilingualism or (3) free and inexpensive home toys which promote language. The center's staff, parents, outside experts, or films can present ideas to be studied and discussed. This type of meeting helps inform all who are present. Differing views may be stated and are respected.

It's a good idea to analyze what's really important to translate to parents concerning children's language arts development. The following items are the author's high priority topics:

1. So many parents show concern over their children's articulation and vocabulary. Assuring parents the school's staff monitors fluency, while sharing typical child speech characteristics, is helpful. Such discussions often relax parents and dispel their fears. Hints concerning simple modeling of correct forms is well received by most parents.
2. Sharing information on school interaction techniques which the staff uses to increase children's speech by listening, following children's leads, and expanding interest in daily conversation is very important. Mention rewarding children's speech attempts.
3. Parents need to know how important they are in modeling an interest and attitude toward reading, writing, and speaking. Their ability to listen closely to ideas rather than judging correctness of grammar or ideas should be discussed.
4. Talking to parents about the warm, "unpressured" social environments which promote conversations about pleasurable happenings is another topic.
5. Reading picture books and sharing stories with the family at home "whets the appetite" for more. Discussion of quality books and *advertising books* to children can perhaps combat a television dominance in the home, figure 24-2.
6. The child's access to creative materials, drawing and marking tools in his at-home "work station" is important.
7. Last but not least, parents have many questions about early reading and writing of alphabet letters. Both reading and

FIGURE 24-2 Parents need information concerning quality books.

writing acquisition is aided by a widely enriching home and preschool curriculum which preserves children's feelings of competence by offering that which is slightly above each child's level and related closely to that child's present interests.

DAILY CONTACTS

Greeting both parents and children as they arrive starts a warm, comfortable atmosphere, encourages talking, and sets the tone for conversation. Short, personal comments build parent-school partnership feelings, and help children enter the school discussing the morning's happenings, figure 24-3. The child is offered choices of possible activities through certain statements such as "We've put red play dough on the table by the door for you," or "The matching game you told me you liked yesterday is waiting for you on the shelf near the birdcage."

Parent mailboxes can hold daily teacher messages. Important milestones, such as the child's first interest or attempt at printing alphabet letters or his name, or first created stories, should be shared. A short note from the teacher about a child's special events is appreciated by most parents. Special daily happenings such as "I think Toni would like to tell you about the worm she found in the garden," or "Saul has been asking many questions about airplanes," keep parents aware of their child's expanding interests.

One center sends home (about once a week) an index card with a colorful sticker and a positive comment, such as pictured in figure 24-4.

Written Communication

Often centers prepare informal letters or newsletters which describe school happenings or daily themes. Figures 24-5 and 24-6 are two examples of this type of teacher-parent communication.

FIGURE 24-3 Teacher and parent can work together to help reinforce the child's language skills.

I like the way _____ listened at story time. Ask her about Babar's problem.

FIGURE 24-4 Positive comments may be written informally and sent home to the child's parents. *(Courtesy of Janet Johnston.)*

BIG, BIGGER, BIGGEST

Dear Parents,

At school we are learning to talk about the size of things. Sometimes we compare the size of two things. Sometimes we compare more than two.

We listen for the sounds at the end of the size words, especially for *-er* and *-est*. When we compare two objects or people, we hear and say the *-er* form. (Example: Alonzo is *bigger* than Antonio.) When we compare more than two, we hear and say the *-est* form. (Example: Alonzo is the *biggest* boy in the class.)

Here are some suggestions you can use at home to help your child learn to talk about the size of things:

1. Place some objects such as boxes, small containers, buttons, or cards, in a box or on the floor. Let your child arrange them according to size:

   smallest to largest
   largest to smallest
   same sizes together.

   During the arranging, talk about which are bigger, which are smaller, and which is biggest or smallest of all.

2. Play games of "smaller but larger."
   - Find something smaller than your hand, but larger than your finger.
   - Find something smaller than the clock but bigger than a penny.
   - Find something smaller than an orange but larger than a pea.

3. Play size games while walking around. Say, "I see something tall. It is a telephone pole. Can you find something taller? Or shorter?" Keep playing until no one can find anything taller or shorter, wider or narrower, etc.

   Use many words that tell the size of things.

   Sincerely,

FIGURE 24-5 Informal teacher letter describing a concept the child is learning in school *(From Roach Van Allen and Claryce Allen,* Language Experiences in Early Childhood, *Chicago: Encyclopaedia Britannica Ed. Corp., 1969.)*

A written communication may concern the following:

- Local library addresses or a description of services or programs such as story hours or puppet shows.
- Local children's theater or drama productions.
- Children's book stores.
- Film presentations of interest to the young child.
- Special community events.
- Adult programs, workshops, meetings, and so forth, which include topics concerned with the development of children's language arts.
- Requests for "junk" materials useful in language arts games or activities.

PARENT RESOURCES

Centers sometimes provide informational articles, magazines, and books which may be borrowed for short periods, or available at the

Dear Parents:

This week we've talked about many means of transportation — of how we use animals and machines to take us from one place to another.

We built things, painted things and learned songs and heard stories about different vehicles such as bikes, cars, trucks, buses, boats, trains, airplanes, horses and wagons, etc., and even took a bus ride.

Here are some suggested home activities to reinforce school learnings:

- Talk about places you go together in your car.
- Save large cardboard boxes — line them up, and pretend they're railroad cars.
- Save old magazines. Let your child find "Vehicles that move things from place to place." They may want to find, cut and paste pictures.
- Take a walk, and find all the moving vehicles you can.
- Sing a train song, "I've been Working on the Railroad," or any other.
- Plan a ride on or in a vehicle that's new to the child.

As you enjoy life together you may want to point out and talk about transportation.

Sincerely,

P.S. Here's a rebus poem to share.

Sam wanted to go to the zoo.

The family wanted to go there too.

The was out of gas.

And the didn't go past

their , so what could they do?

How could they get to the zoo?

FIGURE 24-6 A partnership letter

school's office. Xeroxed magazine articles in manila folders which have been advertised on the school's parent bulletin board are a good resource for busy parents.

Descriptions of home activities aiding children's language development can be either created by the teacher, or commercially prepared. One such commercial kit is:

Author	Title	Publisher	Date
Arno, Ed	The Gingerbread Man	Crowell	1962
Baum, Arline and Joseph	One Bright Monday Morning	Random House	1962
Bonne, Rose and Mills, Alan	I Know an Old Lady	Rand McNally	1961
Brandenberg, Franz	I Once Knew a Man	Macmillan	1970
Brown, Marcia	The Three Billy Goats Gruff	Harcourt	1957
Burmingham, John	Mr. Grumpy's Outing	Holt	1970
Charlip, Remy	What Good Luck! What Bad Luck!	Scholastic	1969
Charlip, Remy and Supree, Burton	Mother Mother I feel Sick Send for the Doctor Quick Quick Quick	Scholastic	1966
Chwast, Seymour	The House That Jack Built	Random House	1973
Emberly, Barbara and Ed	One Wide River to Cross	Prentice-Hall	1966
Flack, Marjorie	Ask Mr. Bear	Macmillan	1932
Galdone, Paul	The Three Billy Goats Gruff	Seabury	1973
Graham, John	I Love You, Mouse	Harcourt	1976
Hogrogian, Nonny	One Fine Day	Macmillan	1971
Hutchins, Pat	The Surprise Party	Collier	1969
	Rosie's Walk	Macmillan	1968
Kraus, Ruth	Bears	Scholastic	1948
Langstaff, John	Oh, A-Hunting We Will Go	Atheneum	1974
	Soldier, Soldier, Won't You Marry Me?	Doubleday	1972
Leodhas, Sorche Nic	All in the Morning Early	Holt	1963
Martin, Bill, Jr.	Brown Bear, Brown Bear, What Do You See?	Holt	1970
	A Ghost Story	Holt	1970
	The Haunted House	Holt	1970
	Tatty Mae and Catty Mae	Holt	1970
	Ten Little Squirrels	Holt	1970
	Welcome Home, Henry	Holt	1970
	When It Rains . . . It Rains	Holt	1970
Merriam, Eve	Do You Want To See Something?	Scholastic	1965
Sendak, Maurice	Chicken Soup with Rice	Scholastic	1962
Shaw, Charles B.	It Looked Like Spilt Milk	Harper	1947
Shulevitz, Uri	One Monday Morning	Scribner's	1967
Slobodkina, Esphyr	Caps for Sale	Scholastic	1947
Spier, Peter	The Fox Went Out on a Chilly Night	Doubleday	1961
Stover, JoAnn	If Everybody Did	McKay	1960
Viorst, Judith	Alexander and the Terrible, Horrible, No Good, Very Bad Day	Atheneum	1972
Zolotow, Charlotte	If It Weren't for You	Harper	1966

FIGURE 24-7 From George Mason, A PRIMER ON TEACHING READING, 1981. Permission to reprint from F. E. Peacock Publishers, Inc., © copyright 1981.

Learning Language at Home by Merle B. Karnes, published by the Council for Exceptional Children, 1920 Association Dr., Reston, VA 22091 (about $35). It offers parents 1,000 ideas for home activities.

For information on children's books, consult:

Larrick, Nancy, *A Parent's Guide to Children's Reading,* Bantam Books.

Kimmel, Mary Margaret and Elizabeth Segal, *For Reading Out Loud!: A Guide to Sharing Books With Children,* Delacorte Press.

Trelease, Jim, *The Read-Aloud Handbook,* Penquin Books, 1982.

Carr, J., *Beyond Fact: Nonfiction for Children and Young People,* American Library Association.

Figure 24-7 contains a list of "predictable books" for young children. Parents can enjoy the shared experience in which the child becomes an active participant — guessing and telling what comes next.

PARENTS AS PROGRAM VOLUNTEERS

Most parent groups include willing volunteers who donate their time, talents, skills, and abilities, or share hobby collections with the children. Some of the ways parents can contribute are listed:

Celebrating "Book Week"/

Explaining Occupations/Police officer, baker, typist, bricklayer, waiter, telephone installer, and so forth. Encourage these speakers to bring in items used in their occupations and to wear the clothing associated with their job.

Special Skills and Hobbies/From yoga to weaving, simple demonstrations interest children.

Collections/Butterfly, coin, shells, whatever. Many children sit for brief presentations.

Cooking Demonstrations/Tortillas, Chinese noodles, or simple apple pie demonstrations can add to children's language knowledge.

Field Trips/Parents may volunteer their time or suggest places to go.

Organizing Fund Raisers/

In addition to volunteering their time, parents can be good resources of materials. Many

FIGURE 24-8 Parent volunteers are a welcomed resource.

parents often work in businesses where useful language arts materials are discarded such as scrap paper, cardboard, and so forth. The parent is usually more than willing to obtain these previously discarded materials, especially if they are unable to volunteer their time to the center.

Through the joint efforts of home and school, centers are able to provide a wider range of language-developing experiences for attending children as they acquire skills in the language arts.

SUMMARY

Schools differ in both the amount and type of interactions between families and the center. School personnel need to clarify priorities which they wish to communicate to parents concerning child language and its development. Working together, school learnings can be reinforced and expanded by parents who are children's most important language models and educators.

Contact with parents takes place in a variety of ways both planned and unplanned, including daily conversations, written notes and letters, and various types of conferencing. Centers are interested in promoting the reading of quality books in the home and alerting parents to community opportunities. Parent volunteers can aid goal realization in the language arts by sharing their talents, hobbies, labor, time, and energy. Together, home and school can work toward children's language growth and competence.

Learning Activities

- Xerox the following. Cut into cards. Rate each card before joining a group of classmates to discuss ratings.

Rating Scale

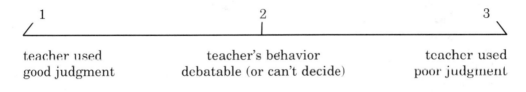

1	2	3
teacher used good judgment	teacher's behavior debatable (or can't decide)	teacher used poor judgment

A field trip is in progress. Mrs. Winkler, a parent, is acting as a volunteer supervisor. A teacher overhears Mrs. Winkler tell her group to be quiet and listen to her explanation of what is happening at the shoe factory. The teacher tactfully suggests to Mrs. Winkler that the children may wish to ask questions.	During a study meeting, two parents are having a heated discussion concerning television's value. A teacher offers her views. Her views happen to support one side of the argument.
Mr. Sousa is a violinist. He is also Tami's father. Tami's teacher sends a special note to Mr. Sousa, inviting him to share his talents with the class. The note mentions he will be allowed to play the violin for a 5-minute period.	Mr. Thomas, a teacher, knows about a book sale at a local children's book store. He includes the item in the school's newsletter to parents.

Sending written messages to parents is not personal, Ms. Garcia (a teacher) feels. She telephones parents in the evenings with news of milestones their children have accomplished in the school's language arts program.	Parent bulletin board posting is part of Miss Alexian's duties. She feels parents rarely read posted materials. At a staff meeting, she asks others for helpful ideas for displays that would grab parents' attention.
Mr. Washington, a teacher, greets the children by waving from across the room or saying, "Hi, Mark, I'm glad you're here."	"Oh, that's not the right way to ask a child about his artwork," Mrs. Yesmin, a teacher, says to Patsy's father.
"You're her teacher. Why ask me what she does at home? It's what goes on at school I'm interested in!" says Mrs. McVey, Pam's mother. "Knowing how Pam spends her time at home helps me plan school activities," explains Mrs. Lerner, Pam's teacher.	"Do you read to your child?" Miss Hernandez asks Mike's mother. "Of course, didn't you think I did?" the child's mother answers.
"There's an article on the parent bulletin board about children's use of slang words that you might want to look over, Mrs. Roades," says Mr. Benjamin (a teacher) to one of the parents.	During a parent-teacher meeting, Mrs. Texciera says, "Jill's work is always so messy." Miss Flint, the teacher, answers, "With time, it will improve. She's working with small puzzles and painting. This will give her more practice and control."

- Plan a parent newsletter for a local preschool center with helpful information concerning children's language development.
- Invite a school's director to discuss parent involvement in a school's language arts goals.

- Identify three books which might help parents understand children's language development, or might provide at-home activity ideas. Cite title, author, and copyright date.

- Find three magazine articles which might be useful in a discussion concerning home television use.

- Interview a few parents of preschoolers. Ask, "What three communication skills do you feel are important for your child's success in public elementary school (which he will attend after preschool)?"

- Discuss the following statement with a classmate. "Many parents are so busy and tired after work that parent meetings are just an added burden."

Unit Review

A. In a short paragraph, describe parent involvement in an early childhood center's language arts program.

B. List the teacher's duties and responsibilities in school-home communications.

C. What is the meaning of the following statement? "Early childhood centers reinforce home learnings just as homes can reinforce centers' learnings."

References

Kimmel, Mary Margaret and Elizabeth Segal, *For Reading Out Loud!: A Guide to Sharing Books With Children*, Delacorte Press.

Larrick, Nancy, *A Parent's Guide to Children's Reading*, Bantam Books.

Trelease, Jimm, *The Read-Aloud Handbook*, Penquin Books, 1982.

Suggested Readings

Bibliography of Books for Children, Association for Childhood Education International, 11141 Georgia Avenue, Suite 200, Wheaton, MD, 1983.

Excellent Paperbacks for Young Children, American Library Association and A.C.E.I., 1979.

Appendix

EARLY CHILDHOOD COMMERCIAL ASSESSMENT INSTRUMENTS

Bellugi-Kiima, Ursula, *Evaluating the Child's Language Competence: Grammatical Comprehension Test,* National Laboratory on Early Childhood Education, Illinois University National Coordination Center, Urbana, IL 61801

Dunn, L. L. Peabody, *Picture Vocabulary Test,* American Guidance Service, Inc., Circle Pines, MN 55014

Foster, C. R., et al., ACLC: *Assessment of Language Comprehension* (Research Edition) Consulting Psychologists Press, Inc., 577 College Ave., Palo Alto, CA 94306

Frankenberg, W. K., *The Denver Developmental Screening Test,* University of Colorado School of Medicine, 4200 E. 9th Ave., Denver, CO 80220

Goldman, Ronald, et al., *Test of Auditory Discrimination,* American Guidance Service, Inc., Circle Pines, MN 55014

Mecham, Merlin, *Verbal Language Developmental Scale,* American Guidance Service, Inc., 720 Washington Ave. SE, Minneapolis, MN 55414

Scholastic, *Comprehensive Language Program,* C.L.P., Scholastic Testing Service, 480 Meyer Road, Bensenville, IL 60106

Resource for additional information:

Educational Testing Service, *An Annotated Bibliography of References to Tests and Assessment Devices,* Princeton, NJ 08540

NONFICTION BOOK LIST

Basic Science Education Series, New York: Harper and Row, Primary Level.
Encyclopaedia Britannica True-to-Life Books, Chicago: Encyclopaedia Britannica, Inc.
Golden Library of Knowledge Series, New York: Golden Press.
Golden Nature Guide Series, New York: Simon and Schuster.
How and Why Wonder Books, New York: Grosset & Dunlap.
"Learn About" Series, Racine, WI: Whitman Publishing Company.
Let's-Read-and-Find-Out Science Books, New York: Thomas Y. Crowell Co.
Question and Answer Series, New York: Golden Press.
Webster Beginner Science Series, New York: McGraw-Hill Book Company.

ADDITIONAL STORIES (UNIT 10)

THE LITTLE ELF WHO LISTENS
— Author Unknown

Do you know what an elf is? No one ever saw an elf, but we can pretend it is a little boy about the size of a squirrel. This elf I'm going to tell you about lived at the edge of a big woods.

He played with chattering chipmunks, with bushy-tailed squirrels, and with hopping rabbits. They were his best friends.

Now, this little elf had something very special. His fairy godmother had given him *three pairs* of listening ears! That would be *six* ears, wouldn't it?

There was a *big* pair of ears, a *middle-sized* pair of ears, and a *tiny* pair of ears.

When the little elf wore his *big* ears, he could hear the faintest (smallest) sounds in the woods — leaves falling from the trees, the wind whispering to the flowers, the water rippling over stones in the little stream. He could hear the dogs barking far, far away. The little elf always told his friends, the squirrels, the chipmunks, and the rabbits, about the dogs, so they could run and hide. They were very thankful.

The little elf wore his *tiny* ears when the storms came and the wind blew loud and fierce, and when the thunder roared and crashed. The little animals, who had only one pair of ears apiece, were frightened by the loud noises, but their friend, the elf, told them that the wind and the thunder were important. After them would come the rain, and the rain was needed to help the food to grow.

Most of the time the little elf wore his *middle-sized* ears. He liked them best of all. He listened to all the middle-sized sounds with them, not the very loud and not the very soft sounds.

One morning some children came to the woods to pick flowers. "What shall we do with our pretty flowers?" a little girl asked.

A boy called Billy said, "Let's take them to school." "Let's!" the little girl agreed. "We can show them to the other children."

The little elf listened, and he wished that he could go to school. He wanted to see and hear what the children did at school.

He told his friends, the squirrels, the chipmunks and the rabbits, about it, but they said, "No, an elf can't go to school. School is just for children."

The little elf decided he would go to school anyway. So the next morning he crept out of his warm bed of leaves under the toadstool and skippety-skipped down the road toward the school.

Soon he came to a big building. Girls and boys were playing out on the playground. There was a red, white and blue flag flying high on a pole, so the little elf knew this was really the school.

Just then a bell rang, and the children all went inside. The little elf quietly slipped inside too.

You were the girls and boys playing outside. You are the children that the little elf followed.

Which pair of ears do you think he will have to use?

— His *big* ears because you talk too low, as if you were afraid of your own voice?

— His *tiny* ears because you talk so loud that you sound like a thunderstorm?

— Or his *middle-sized* ears because you are talking just right — loud enough so everyone in the room can hear, but not so loud that you seem to be shouting? Remember, the little elf likes his *middle-sized* ears best!

Suggestion: It's a good idea to show tiny, middle-sized and big ears drawn on the chalkboard or on paper, or on the flannelboard.

(A followup to this story could be sorting objects into three groups by size.)

LITTLE DUCK

A good group participation story. Children imitate the actions with teacher (Scott, 1968).

Run	= Slap thighs quickly.
Walk	= Slap thighs slowly.
Big Steps	= Thump fists on chest.
Swim	= Rub palms of hands together rapidly.
Bang	= Clap hands once.

Little Duck was scolded for eating too many bugs, so he said to his mother, "I am going to run away. Then I can eat anything I like."

So Little Duck left the barnyard and his own dear mother who loved him. He walked down the road on his little flat feet. (Action)

Little Duck met a cow who was munching hay.

"Have some," offered the cow.

Hay was much too rough for Little Duck to eat because he had no teeth to chew it. He thanked the cow for her thoughtfulness and walked on. (Action) Suddenly, he heard a big BANG. (Clap) Little Duck trembled with fright.

"Oh, oh, that must be a hunter with a gun," he cried.

Little Duck ran away from there fast. (Action) Then Little Duck heard some BIG LOUD steps coming toward him. (Action) He hid in some bushes until the big steps went by.

"Why, that was only a HORSE," said Little Duck happily.

Little Duck met a dog with a bone.

"Have some," said the dog.

"No, thank you," said Little Duck as he walked on. (Action)

Little Duck came to a pond. He jumped into the water and swam across the pond. (Action) He climbed out of the water and walked on. (Action)

Suddenly Little Duck heard a fierce sound, "Grrrrrrowl, Rrrrrrruff."

Right in front of Little Duck sat a fox!

"Yum, yum," said the fox, smacking his lips. "Duck for dinner!"

"Oh, oh!" cried Little Duck as he began to run. (Action)

He ran and ran faster and faster. (Action) He came to the pond and swam across. (Action) The fox was right behind him.

Suddenly there was a loud BANG. (Action) When the fox heard the big noise, he turned and ran away. (Action)

Little Duck felt safer now, but he kept right on running. (Action)

He passed the horse — and the cow — and the dog with a bone. Soon he was back in the barnyard with his own dear mother who loved him.

He said:

"I'm a little duck as you can see,
And this barnyard is the best place for me."

Little Duck knew that being scolded was for his own good, and he never ate too many bugs again. He never ran away again, either.

Ask: "What made the big bang?"

I'M GOING TO CATCH A LION FOR THE ZOO

I'll get up in the morning (yawn and stretch)
I'll put on my clothes (go through motions)
I'll take a long piece of rope down from the wall (reach up)
I'll carry it over my shoulder (push up arm to shoulder)
Open the door (pretend to turn door handle)
And close the door (clasp hands)
I'm going on a lion hunt, and I'm not afraid (slap hands on knees)
Whoops — comin' to a hill (climbing with hands)
Now I'm crossing a bridge (pound closed fists on chest)
And I'm crossing a river (motion as though swimming)
Now I'm going through tall grass (rub hands together)
Whoops — I'm walking in mud (poke air-filled cheeks)
I'm going on a lion hunt, and I'm not afraid (slap hands on knees)
Comin' to a lion territory — want to catch a lion
With green stripes and pink polka dots
Have to go tippy-toe (finger tips on knees)
I'm climbing up a tree (climb up and look all around)
No lion!

Going in a dark cave (cup hands around eyes and look around)

Oh, a lion!

(The trip back home is exactly the same, only in reverse and faster. *The cave* is first and *slam the door* is last)

Home at last. I'm not going on any more lion hunts. I've found a lion, and I'm afraid.

(This story is full of child participation and action. It takes teacher practice, but is well worth the effort.)

HOW SAMMY SNAKE GETS A NEW SKIN
by Pauline C. Peck (1968)

"My skin is too small,"
said Sammy Snake.
"I need a new skin."
Sammy met Toby Turtle.
"I need a new skin,"
said Sammy.
"Where can I get one?"
"I don't know," said Toby,
"I never need a new skin."
Sammy met Katy Caterpillar.
"I need a new skin,"
said Sammy.
"Where can I get one?"
"I know," said Katy.
"Spin a cocoon, the way I do."
"I can't do that," said Sammy.
And he slid away.
Sammy met Grampa Snake.
"I need a new skin,"
said Sammy.
"Where can I get one?"
"I know," said Grampa.
"You just wiggle and wiggle."
Sammy wiggled and wiggled.
He wiggled his old skin right off!
And do you know what?
Underneath his old skin
there was a shiny new skin
that was JUST RIGHT!

HALLOWEEN HOUSE

(For this story, a large sheet of orange construction paper and a pair of scissors are needed.)

Hugo, the bear, and his friend, Bitsy, the mouse, wanted to give a Halloween party for all of the forest animals, but they didn't have a house, just a small den and a hole.

They thought about the fun they'd all have wearing scary costumes and telling ghost stories. Hugo wanted to make honey cookies, and Bitsy knew how to make a delicious mouse candy from maple sugar and pine nuts.

But, alas, they had no house.

One day while walking through the forest together, Hugo found a large piece of orange paper. Running as fast as he could, carrying the paper in one hand and Bitsy in the other, Hugo went straight to his den.

"Watch this," he said, putting Bitsy down. Hugo folded the paper and cut a round house shape with a big door.

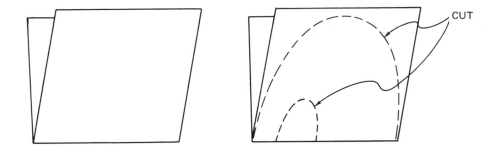

"You need a window," said Bitsy. So, Hugo cut a window.

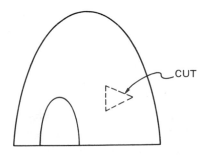

"But, I need a small door, too," Bitsy said. Hugo cut a small door.

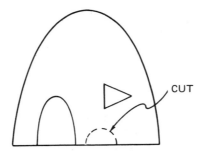

"Now we can invite all our friends to a Halloween party, whoopee!" said Hugo.
"Wait a minute. Just wait a minute," said Bitsy. "We need a jack-o-lantern!"
"We already have one!" Hugo said.
(Unfold the house.)

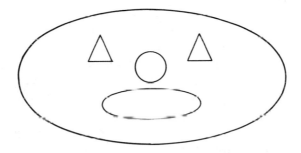

THE CROOKED MOUTH FAMILY

There are many versions of this action story. This one, however, appeals to young children and never fails to bring laughter and requests to have it repeated. Before beginning the story, quietly light a candle — preferably a dripless one.

Once there was a family called The Crooked Mouth Family.
The father had a mouth like this.
   (Twist mouth to the right.)
The mother had a mouth like this.
   (Twist mouth to the left.)
The Big Brother had a mouth like this.
   (Bring lower lip over upper lip.)
The Big Sister had a mouth like this
   (Bring upper lip over lower lip.)
But the Baby Sister had a pretty mouth just like yours.
   (Smile naturally.)

(Repeat mouth positions as each character speaks.)

One night they forgot to blow the candle out when they went upstairs to bed.

The father said, "I'd better go downstairs and blow that candle out."

(With mouth still twisted to the right, blow at the flame being careful not to blow it out.)

"What's the matter with this candle? It won't go out."

(Repeat blowing several times.)

"I guess I'd better call Mother. Mother! Please come down and blow the candle out."

Mother said, "Why can't you blow the candle out? Anybody can blow a candle out. You just go like this."

(She blows at the flame, mouth still twisted to the left.)

"I can't blow it out either. We'd better call Big Brother."

(Change to father's mouth.)

"Brother! Please come down and blow the candle out."

Big Brother said, "That's easy. All you have to do is blow hard."

(With lower lip over upper, hold the candle low and blow.)

Father said, "See. You can't blow it out either. We'll have to call Big Sister. Sister! Please come down and blow the candle out!

Big Sister said, "I can blow it out. Watch me."

(With upper lip over lower, candle held high, blow several times.)

Father said, "That's a funny candle. I told you I couldn't blow it out."

Mother said, "I couldn't blow it out, either."

Big Brother said, "Neither could I."

Big Sister said, "I tried and tried, and I couldn't blow it out."

Father said, "I guess we'll have to call Baby Sister. Baby! Please come down and blow the candle out."

Baby Sister came downstairs, rubbing her eyes because she had been asleep. She asked, "What's the matter?"

Father said, "I can't blow the candle out."

Mother said, "I can't blow it out either."

Big Brother said, "Neither can I."

Big Sister said, "I can't either."

Baby Sister said, "Anybody can blow a candle out. That's easy." And she did.

Author Unknown

THE BIG MOUTHED FROG

A small big mouthed frog decided to leave home and see the world. The first creature the frog met went "Quack, quack." "Hi, I'm a big mouthed frog and I eat bugs. Who are you and what do you eat?" "I'm a duck and I eat seeds and grain," said the the duck.

"So long Mr. Duck, I'm off to discover the world!" "Meow, meow." "Hi, I'm a big mouthed frog! I eat bugs. Who are you and what do you eat?" "Silly child, I'm a cat and cream is what I prefer — purr purr," said Ms. Cat. "Goodbye Ms. Cat. I'm off to discover the world and all that's in it!" "Bow wow. Bow wow." "Hi there, I'm a big mouthed frog, and I eat bugs. Who are you, and what do you eat?" "I'm Bowser the Beagle and I chew on bones." "You're a bowser?" "Nope, I'm a dog!" "See you later, I'm off to discover the world and all that's in it." "Moo, moo." "Hi up there," yelled the big mouthed frog, "I'm a big mouthed frog, I eat bugs. Who are you, and what do you eat?" "I'm a cow and I eat grass — watch out, move aside, I might step on you." "Goodbye cow I'm off to see the world." "Hiss Hiss." "Hi there I'm a big mouthed frog and I eat bugs. Who are you, and what do you eat? "I'm a SNAKE AND I EAT BIG MOUTHED FROGS!!!!" "Ooooo oooo you don't say," said the frog. (This last line is said with the mouth compressed in a small circle!)

Courtesy of Katherine Blanton

References

Peck, Pauline C., Special permission granted by *My Weekly Reader I,* published by Xerox Education Publications, Xerox Corporation, 1968.

Scott, Louise Binder, *Learning Time with Language Experiences for Young Children,* New York: McGraw-Hill, 1968.

ADDITIONAL FLANNEL BOARD STORIES AND PATTERNS (UNIT 12)

Note: Patterns in this section have been reduced to fit the page size. It is suggested that students enlarge these patterns for child activities on the flannel board. This can be done by using an overhead opaque projector, and then cutting pieces with enlarged patterns. Consult your instructor.

THE PUMPKIN THAT GREW

Pieces: Green Leaves for Vine (5 or 6)
Large Vine
Finished Pumpkin
(green stem, orange face)

Pumpkins in Three Different Sizes
small (dark green)
medium (light green)
big (yellow)

Action: See story in Unit 12.

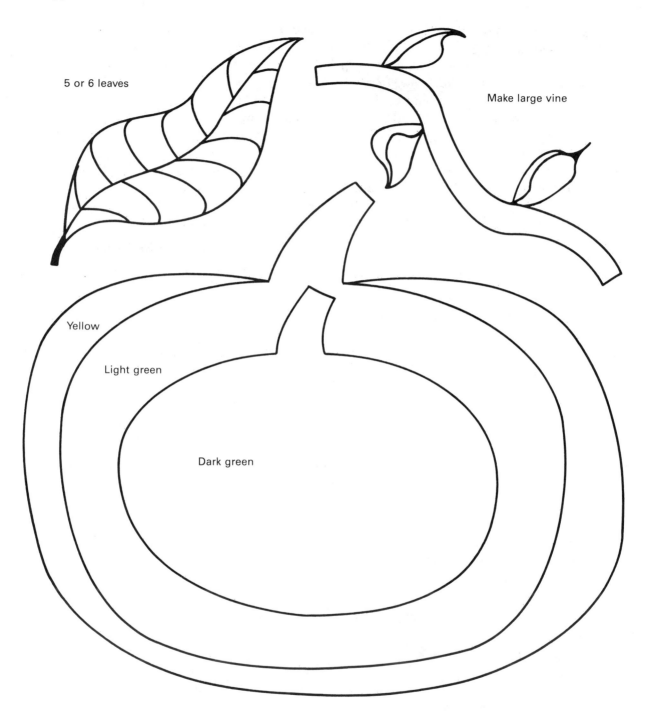

5 or 6 leaves

Make large vine

Yellow

Light green

Dark green

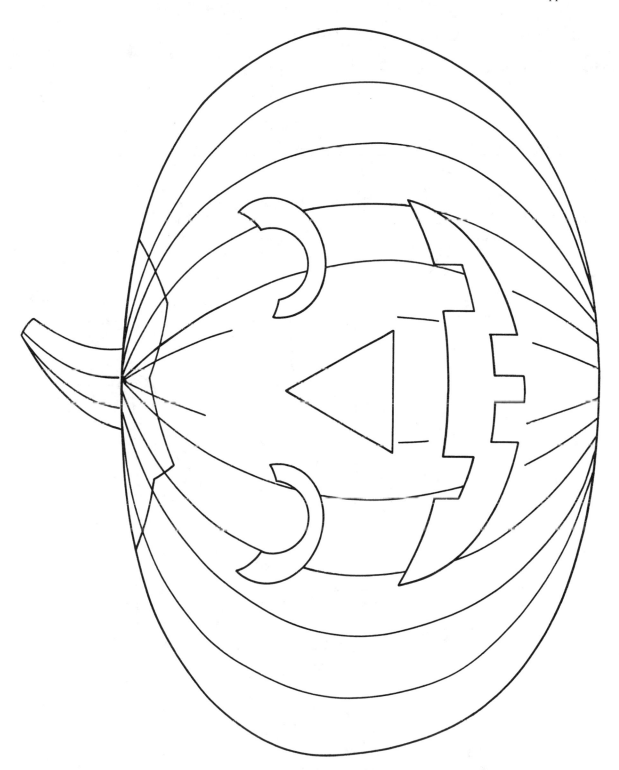

THE SEED

Pieces: Small Roots   Seed   Beaver
         Green Shoot   Bird   Large Tree
         Deer   Small Trunk   Apples (5 or 6)
         Mr. Man   Leaves

Action: See story in Unit 12.

JUST LIKE DADDY

Pieces: Little Brown Bear   Green Fish (large)

Little Bear's Blue Vest   Green Fish (small)

Flower   Brown Mother Bear

Brown Father Bear   Red Boots for Little Bear

Red Boots for Father Bear   Blue Vest for Father Bear

Yellow Coat for Father Bear   Yellow Coat for Little Bear

Purple Vest for Mother Bear

Action: See story in Unit 12.

Little bear's
Blue vest (cut 1)

Little brown bear (cut 1)

Flower (cut 1)

Brown father bear (cut 1)

Green fish (cut 2)

Small green fish (cut 1)

Brown mother bear (cut 1)

Red boots
for father bear
(cut 2)

Red boots
for little bear
(cut 2)

Yellow coat
for father bear
(cut 1)

Blue vest
for father bear
(cut 1)

Yellow coat
for little bear
(cut 1)

Purple vest
for mother bear
(cut 1)

THE TREE IN THE WOODS

Pieces: Grass   Bird's Nest
               Tree   Bird's Egg
               Tree Trunk   Bird
               Tree Limb   Wing
               Tree Branch   Feather

Action: See story in Unit 12.

Tree top

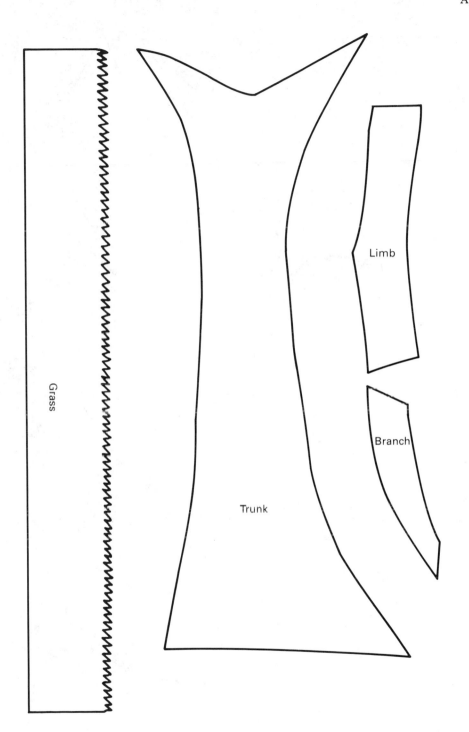

Board assemblage — for tree in the woods

Tree top

Grass

THE LION AND THE MOUSE

Pieces: Lion Awake   Tree   Mouse
               Lion Sleeping   Rope   Two Hunters

Action: See story in Unit 12.

Patterns from *Adventures in Felt* by Jeanne M. Machado, © 1972.

FORTUNATELY/UNFORTUNATELY

Pieces: Boy   Haystack   Shark
                  Plane   Pitchfork   Tiger
                  Parachute   Water   Cave
                  Snake   Birthday cake

Action: See story in Unit 12.

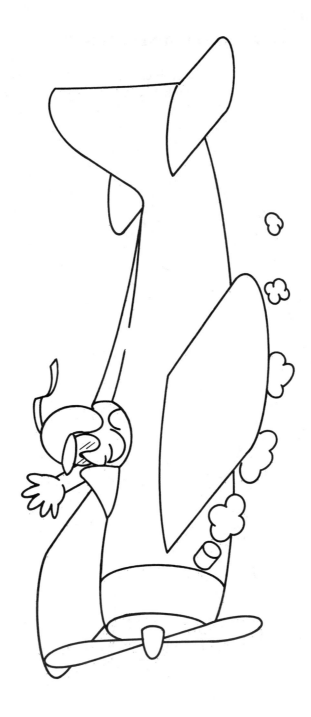

APPLE AND WORM

Pieces: Apple, Worm

Action: Move the worm to fit the following positional words:

in	on	front	side	bottom	behind
out	off	back	top	under	

THE HARE AND THE TORTOISE
Adapted from Aesop

Pieces: Rabbit   Dog   Rabbit running   Finish Line   Tree
          Turtle   Hen   Rabbit sleeping   Flag

One day the rabbit was talking to some of the other animals; "I am the fastest runner in the forest," he said. "I can beat anyone! Do you want to race?"

"Not I," said the dog.

"Not I," said the hen.

"I will race with you," said the turtle.

"That's a good joke," said the rabbit. "I could dance around you all the way and still win."

"Still bragging about how fast you are," answered the turtle. "Come on, let's race. Do you see that flag over there? That will be the finish line. Hen, would you stand by the flag so that you can tell who wins the race?"

"Dog, will you say the starting words — get on your mark, get ready, get set, go!"

"Stand there," said the dog. "Get on your mark, get ready, get set, go!"

The rabbit ran very fast. He looked over his shoulder and saw how slowly the turtle was running on his short little legs. Just then he saw a shady spot under a tree. He thought to himself — that turtle is so slow I have time to rest here under this tree. So he sat down on the cool grass, and before he knew it, he was fast asleep.

While he slept, the turtle was running. (Clump, Clump — Clump, Clump) He was not running very fast, but he kept on running. (Clump, Clump — Clump, Clump) Pretty soon the turtle came to the tree where the rabbit was sleeping. He went past and kept on running. (Clump, Clump — Clump, Clump)

The turtle was almost to the finish line. The hen saw the turtle coming and said, "Turtle, keep on running. You've almost won the race."

When the hen spoke, the rabbit awoke. He looked down by the finish line and saw the turtle was almost there. As fast as he could, rabbit started running again. Just then he heard the hen say, "The turtle is the winner!"

"But I'm the fastest," said the rabbit.

"Not this time," said the hen. "Sometimes slow and steady wins the race."

Put on turtle, dog, hen, rabbit at left edge of board.

Add finishing line flag on right edge of board. Move hen by flag.

Put on running rabbit. Remove standing rabbit.

Add sleeping rabbit while removing running rabbit.

Change sleeping rabbit to running rabbit.

FIVE YELLOW DUCKLINGS
(A Flannel Board Poem)

Pieces: 5 yellow Ducklings   1 Mother Duck   1 Pond (large enough for 5 ducklings)

Special permission granted by *Adventures in Felt* © 1972 by Jeanne M. Machado.

Cut pond
as separate
piece.

Cut as
separate
piece.

Special permission granted by *Adventures in Felt* ©1972 by Jeanne M. Machado.

Five yellow ducklings went swimming one day,
Across the pond and far away.
Old mother duck said, "Quack, Quack, Quack,"
Four yellow ducklings came swimming back.

Four yellow ducklings went swimming one day,
Across the pond and far away.
Old mother duck said, "Quack, Quack, Quack,"
Three yellow ducklings came swimming back.

Three yellow ducklings went swimming one day,
Across the pond and far away.
Old mother duck said, "Quack, Quack, Quack,"
Two yellow ducklings came swimming back.

Two yellow ducklings went swimming one day,
Across the pond and far away.
Old mother duck said, "Quack, Quack, Quack,"
One little duckling came swimming back.

One yellow duckling went swimming one day,
Across the pond and far away.
Old mother duck said, "Quack, Quack, Quack,"
No little ducklings came swimming back.
Old mother duck said, "Quack, Quack, Quack," (very
   loudly)
Five yellow ducklings came swimming back.

Place pond, mother duck and 5 ducklings on flannelboard.
Remove 1 duckling.

Remove 1 duckling.

Remove 1 duckling.

Remove 1 duckling.

Remove last duckling.

Add 5 ducklings.

Suggestions:

Have children listen and participate when mother duck says "Quack, Quack, Quack." The last "Quack, Quack, Quack" should be louder than the first five. This is a good poem for children to dramatize. Outline a pond area with chalk, tape, or use an old blue blanket. Decide which child (duckling) will not return in the order of the poem. Teacher reads poem as five ducklings swim across pond. Teacher can demonstrate how ducklings waddle, and how hands can be used for ducks' beak. This poem leads well into discussions about loud and soft, or "inside and outside" voices.

THE BIG, BIG TURNIP
(Traditional)

Pieces:	Farmer	Turnip	Daughter	Cat
	Farmer's Wife	Large Piece of Ground	Dog	Mouse

A farmer once planted a turnip seed. And it grew, and it grew and it grew. The farmer saw it was time to pull the turnip out of the ground. So he took hold of it and began to pull.

He pulled and he pulled and he pulled and he pulled. But the turnip wouldn't come up.

So the farmer called to his wife who was getting dinner.

Fe, fi, fo, fum
I pulled the turnip
But it wouldn't come up.

And the wife came running, and she took hold of the farmer, and they pulled and they pulled and they pulled and they pulled. But the turnip wouldn't come up.

So the wife called to the daughter who was feeding the chickens nearby.

Fe, fi, fo, fum
We pulled the turnip
But it wouldn't come up.

And the daughter came running. The daughter took hold of the wife. The wife took hold of the farmer. The farmer took hold of the turnip. And they pulled and they pulled and they pulled and they pulled. But the turnip wouldn't come up.

So the daughter called to the dog who was chewing a bone.

Fe, fi, fo, fum.
We pulled the turnip
But it wouldn't come up.

And the dog came running. The dog took hold of the daughter. The daughter took hold of the wife. The wife took hold of the farmer. And the farmer took hold of the turnip. And they pulled and they pulled and they pulled. But the turnip wouldn't come up.

The dog called to the cat who was chasing her tail.
Fe, fi, fo, fum
We pulled the turnip
But it wouldn't come up.

And the cat came running. The cat took hold of the dog. The dog took hold of the daughter. The daughter took hold of the wife. The wife took hold of the farmer. The

Place farmer on board. Cover turnip so that only top is showing with ground piece, and place on board.

Move farmer next to turnip with hands on turnip top. Place wife behind farmer.

Place daughter behind farmer's wife.

Place dog behind daughter.

Place cat behind dog.

farmer took hold of the turnip. And they pulled and they pulled and they pulled. But the turnip wouldn't come up.

So the cat called the mouse who was nibbling spinach nearby.

Fe, fi, fo, fum
We pulled the turnip.
But it wouldn't come up.
And the mouse came running.

"That little mouse can't help," said the dog. "He's too little." "Phooey," squeaked the mouse. "I could pull that turnip up myself, but since you have all been pulling I'll let you help too."

So the mouse took hold of the cat. The cat took hold of the dog. The dog took hold of the daughter. The daughter took hold of the wife. The wife took hold of the farmer. The farmer took hold of the turnip. And they pulled and they pulled and they pulled. And up came the turnip.

Place mouse behind cat.

And the mouse squeaked, "I told you so!"

Remove ground.

THE LITTLE RED HEN

Pieces: Cottage   Sticks   Fox
         Little Red Hen   Fire   Sack
         Mouse   Pot   2 Large Rocks
         Rooster   Table

It was morning. In the cottage where the little red hen, and the rooster, and the mouse lived, little red hen was happily setting the table for breakfast.

Place cottage, table and hen on board.
Add rooster.
Add mouse.

"Who will get some sticks for the fire?" said little red hen.

"I won't," grumbled the rooster.

"I won't," squeaked the mouse.

"Then I'll do it myself," said the little red hen, and off she went to gather them.

Remove hen.

When she returned with the sticks, and had started the fire she asked, "Who will get water from the spring to fill the pot?"

Replace with hen and sticks. Place fire over sticks.

"I won't," grumbled the rooster.

"I won't," squeaked the mouse.

"Then I'll do it myself," she said and ran off to fill the pot.

"Who will cook the breakfast?" said the hen.

"I won't," grumbled the rooster.

"I won't," squeaked the mouse.

"Then I'll do it myself," said the hen and she did.

When breakfast was ready, the hen, the mouse and the rooster ate together but the rooster spilled the milk and the mouse scattered crumbs on the floor.

"Who will clear the table?" said the hen.

"I won't," grumbled the rooster.

"I won't," squeaked the mouse.

"Then I'll do it myself," said the hen. So she cleared everything and swept the floor.

The lazy rooster and mouse by this time has moved close to the fire, and had fallen fast asleep.

"Knock, knock, knock," the noise at the door awakened them. "Who's that?" said the rooster. "Oh it might be the mail carrier with a letter for me," so the mouse went to the door and opened it without looking out the window first to see who was there.

It was a fox. "Help," said the mouse, but the fast old fox, quick as a wink, caught not only the mouse, but also the rooster and the little red hen. Quickly he popped them all into his sack, and headed off toward home thinking about the fine dinner he was bringing to his family.

The bag was heavy, and home was a long way so the fox decided to put it down and rest.

"Snore, Snore, Snore," went the fox.

Little red hen said to the rooster and mouse, "Now we have a chance to escape. I have a pair of scissors and a needle and thread in my apron pocket. I've cut a hole in the bag, hurry and jump out, find a rock, the biggest one you can carry and bring it back quickly. "Snore, Snore, Snore," went the fox. Soon the mouse and the rooster returned with large rocks, they pushed them into the sack and the hen sewed the hole up. Off they ran to their home, they closed the door and locked it, they bolted the windows. They were safe now.

Place pot over fire.

Move hen, mouse and rooster near table.

Move rooster and mouse near the fire.

Place fox and sack on board. Hide fox, mouse and hen behind sack. Remove cottage.

Put fox in horizontal position.

Add rocks.
Move rocks behind sack.

The fox didn't know he'd been fooled until he got home and opened his sack.

The mouse and the rooster were so happy to be home that they didn't grumble and fight anymore, they even helped to cook the dinner with smiles on their faces.

Remove fox and sack.

Place cottage, hen, rooster and mouse beside it on board.

HUSH, LITTLE BABY
Flannel Board Song

Pieces: Mother   Looking Glass
         Sleeping Baby   Billy Goat
         Crying Baby   Cart and Bull
         Mocking Bird   Dog
         Ring   Horse

Courtesy of *Adventures in Felt* © Copyright 1972

Hush, little baby, don't say a word, Mama's going to buy you a mocking-bird.

Place mother and crying baby on her lap.

If that mocking-bird won't sing, Mama's going to buy you a diamond ring.

Add ring.

If that diamond ring turns to brass, Mama's going to buy you a looking glass.

Add looking glass.

If that looking glass gets broke, Mama's going to buy you a billy-goat.

Add billy-goat.

If that billy-goat won't pull, Mama's going to buy you a cart and bull.

Add cart and bull.

If that cart and bull turn over, Mama's going to buy you a dog named Rover.

Add dog.

If that dog named Rover won't bark, Mama's going to buy you a horse and cart.

Add horse and move cart from bull.

If that horse and cart break down, YOU'LL be the sweet-est little baby in town.

Lullaby, baby sweet of mine, you'll be asleep by half-past nine.

Replace crying baby with sleeping baby.

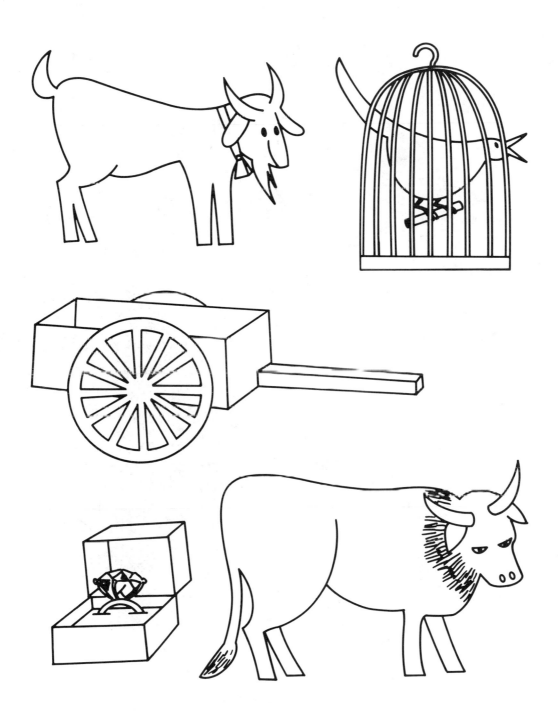

ADDITIONAL PUPPETRY IDEAS AND PATTERNS (UNIT 16)

Paper Bag Puppets

Construction: Draw a face on the upper part of bag; color. Stuff with cotton or newspaper. Put neck cylinder into head and tie string around neck. (Neck cylinder is made by rolling a piece of tag board and taping together. The roll should fit around the first finger.)

If the puppet needs hair, paste on. Add other distinguishing characteristics. Cut hole in paper or cloth and stick neck cylinder through the hole. Paste, sew, or otherwise fasten. Add hands or paws cut from tag board.

Materials: 5″ x 8″ paper bag   Paste
String   Crepe paper or cloth for dress
Crayons or paint   Scissors
Newspapers or cotton

Movement: Holding   forefinger   in neck tube.

Potato or Tennis Ball Puppets

Construction: Cut a hole the size of your forefinger in the bottom of a fairly smooth evenly shaped potato. Insert neck tube. Paint face. Add hair. It may be fastened with pins stuck into the potato. Sew dress to neck tube. Add tag board hands and feet.

Same procedure for the tennis ball.

Materials: Potato or tennis ball   Cloth for dress
Scissors or paring knife to cut hole   Material for hair
Tag board

Stuffed Cloth Puppet

Construction: Draw head pattern and cut around it on a fold of cloth (white, tan, or pink). Sew around front and back, turn inside out, and stuff with cotton or rags. Insert neck tube and tie. Paint on face. Cut dress and sew to neck tube. Add hands and feet.

Materials: Cloth (for head and dress)   Tag board for hands and feet
Scissors   Material for hair (cotton, yarn, etc.)
Needle and thread

Stuffed Paper Puppet

Construction: Have the child draw himself or any character he chooses on a piece of butcher paper. Then trace and cut second figure for the back.

Paper Bag Puppet Face — Lamb

Basic Puppet Body

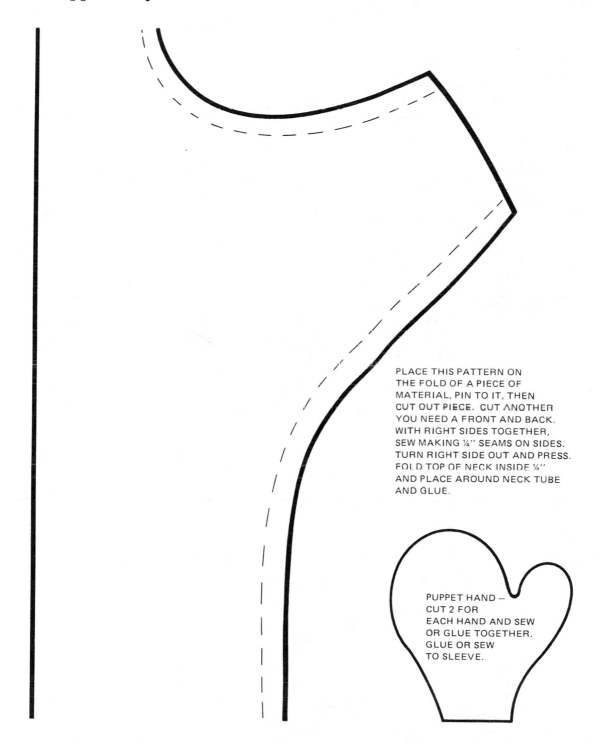

PLACE THIS PATTERN ON
THE FOLD OF A PIECE OF
MATERIAL, PIN TO IT, THEN
CUT OUT PIECE. CUT ANOTHER
YOU NEED A FRONT AND BACK.
WITH RIGHT SIDES TOGETHER,
SEW MAKING ¼″ SEAMS ON SIDES.
TURN RIGHT SIDE OUT AND PRESS.
FOLD TOP OF NECK INSIDE ¼″
AND PLACE AROUND NECK TUBE
AND GLUE.

PUPPET HAND —
CUT 2 FOR
EACH HAND AND SEW
OR GLUE TOGETHER.
GLUE OR SEW
TO SLEEVE.

Frog and Bird Puppet Patterns

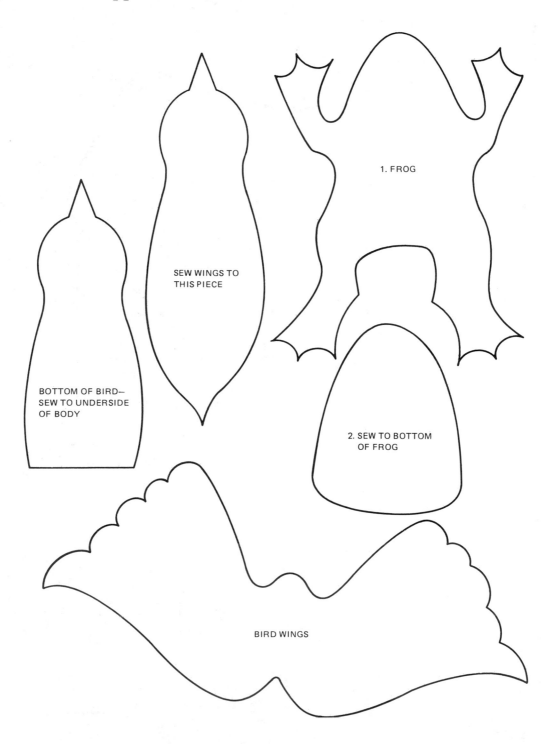

BOTTOM OF BIRD—
SEW TO UNDERSIDE
OF BODY

SEW WINGS TO
THIS PIECE

1. FROG

2. SEW TO BOTTOM
OF FROG

BIRD WINGS

Large Cloth Hand Puppet Pattern

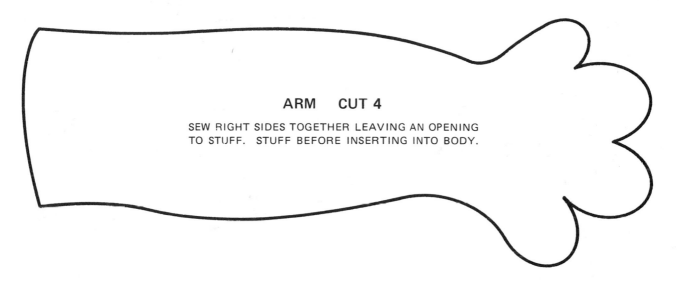

ARM   CUT 4

SEW RIGHT SIDES TOGETHER LEAVING AN OPENING
TO STUFF.   STUFF BEFORE INSERTING INTO BODY.

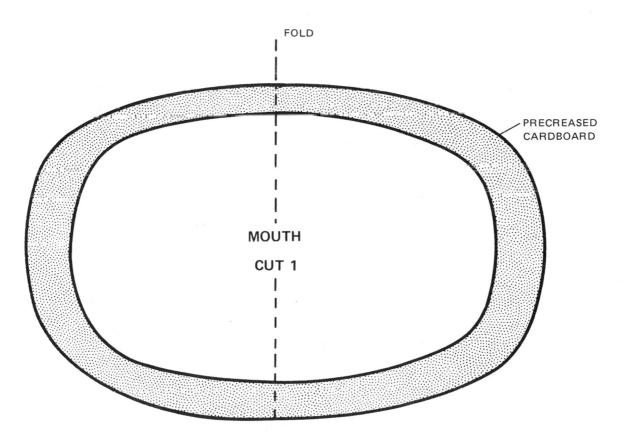

FOLD

PRECREASED
CARDBOARD

MOUTH

CUT 1

Large Cloth Puppet Pattern

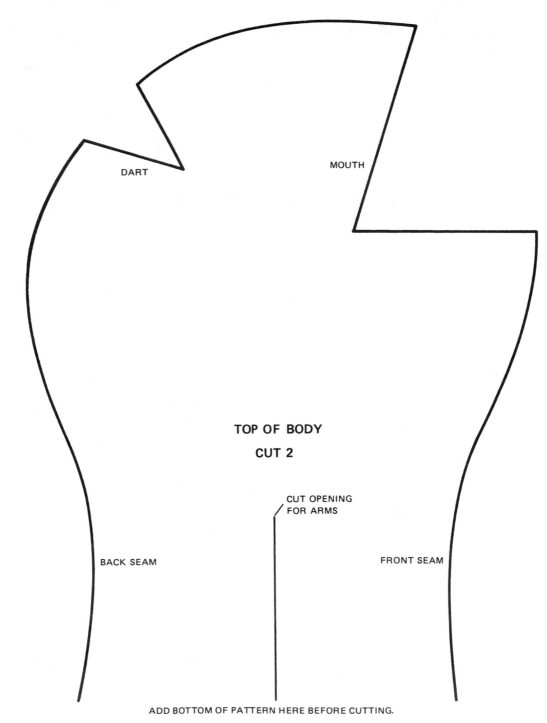

DART

MOUTH

TOP OF BODY

CUT 2

CUT OPENING
FOR ARMS

BACK SEAM

FRONT SEAM

ADD BOTTOM OF PATTERN HERE BEFORE CUTTING.

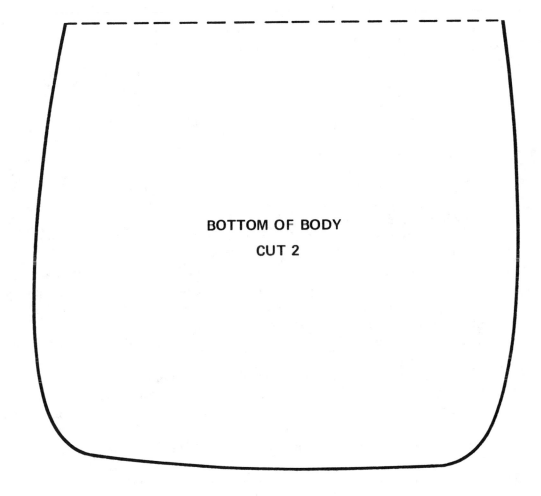

BOTTOM OF BODY

CUT 2

There was an Old Woman Who Swallowed a Fly

Materials Needed: 2 large pieces of white posterboard
18″ x 36″ piece of plywood
1 skein black rug yarn
1 clear plastic drop cloth or ½ yd clear plastic
½ yd material (any color or pattern)
marking pens
fishing line (about 18 inches)
2 black pipe cleaners
2 wiggly eyes
colored feathers
craft glue
woodworking glue
clothespins
thumbtacks and a hammer OR a staplegun

Instructions:

Old Woman

Step 1:   Trace the pattern of the old woman onto the posterboard and onto the plywood.

Step 2:   Transfer all of the details onto the posterboard old woman. Cut out, including the inner square for the stomach.

Step 3:   Use an electric jigsaw and cut out the plywood old woman — including the inner square for the stomach.

Step 4:   Using the woodworking glue, spread a thin layer over the entire plywood old woman. Lay the posterboard old woman on top and clip with clothespins around the outer and inner edges. Let dry thoroughly before removing the clothespins. If necessary, sand the outer and inner edges to make them smooth.

Step 5:   Spread a thin layer of the craft glue on the bottom half of the posterboard, up to the neckline.

Step 6:   Lay the piece of material wrong side down on top of the glue. Let dry thoroughly.

Step 7:   Cut off the excess material from the outer edges and inner stomach.

Step 8:   Starting at the outer edges of the hairline, use craft glue to glue the rug yarn onto the posterboard. Glue the yarn around and around, filling in the whole area. Glue small pieces of yarn on for the eyes and eyebrows. Let the hair dry thoroughly.

Step 9:   Turn the old woman over to the backside.

Step 10: Cut a piece of 18″ x 72″ clear plastic. Fold the plastic in half widthwise to form two 18″ x 36″ pieces with a fold at the bottom.

Step 11:   Place the plastic on the back of the old woman, with the fold down at the bottom of the stomach hole.

Step 12:   Open the plastic, leaving the bottom layer in place on the old woman.

Step 13:   Using tacks or a staplegun, attach the bottom layer of plastic around the outer edge of the old woman's body, mouth, and head, making sure the plastic is smooth and tight.

Step 14:   Bring the second layer of plastic back up and tack or staple it at the very bottom of the stomach hole. Push the top layer of plastic in from the edge of the bottom piece, forming a loose bag or pocket. Tack the second layer in place up to the neckline in the side with the mouth. NOTE: do not tack the mouth shut!! Leave that portion of the plastic open for putting in the animals. Continue tacking at the top of the head and tack the rest of the plastic, continuing to push the plastic in to form a pocket. Trim the excess plastic from around the edges.

Animals

Step 1:   Trace each animal onto the posterboard. Color each one appropriately and cut out.

Step 2:   Glue two wiggly eyes onto the spider.

Step 3:   Cut each pipe cleaner into fourths and glue four on each side of the spider for legs.

Step 4:   Tie one end of the fishing line to the top of the spider's head. Attach the other end to one of the tacks at the top of the old woman's head (wind the line around the tack or tie a loop).

Step 5:   Place the spider inside the bag so that it extends down into the old woman's stomach. The spider is a permanent part of the old woman and should be left as it is.

Step 6:   Another addition you can make is to add colored feathers to the bird's tail.

Use: Place the Old Woman against a wall or in front of you. Remove the spider and hold onto it until time to place it back inside the plastic stomach. As you sing, place the appropriate animal in the mouth, letting it drop down into the stomach. The spider can be wiggled and jiggled on each verse by holding the fishing line and bouncing it up and down.

from Magic Moments
P.O. Box 53635
San Jose, CA. 95135

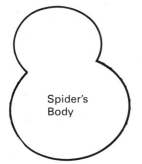

Spider's
Body

Little Miss Muffet

Materials Needed: 1 large piece white posterboard
4 black pipe cleaners
12″ x 12″ piece black velour
2 large wiggly eyes
craft glue
felt pens
black rug yarn
black marker
clothes pins
1 tongue depressor

Instructions:

Miss Muffet

Step 1:   Trace the Miss Muffet pattern onto the posterboard. Add the details with the black marker. Use the felt markers to color in the hair and face. Cut out.

Step 2:   Glue the tongue depressor onto the back of Miss Muffet. Let dry.

Spider

Step 1:   Trace the spider pattern onto the posterboard twice. Cut out.

Step 2:   Glue one of the spiders onto the wrong side of the black velour. Let dry. Cut off the excess material from around the posterboard.

Step 3:   Cut each pipe cleaner in half for the legs. On the wrong side of the posterboard, position 4 legs on each side of the body so that two-thirds of each pipe cleaner is extending out. Glue down and let dry.

Step 4:   Put a generous amount of glue all over the wrong side of the spider, being sure to put glue over the legs. Place the second spider on top of the glue and secure all the way around with clothespins. Let dry.

Step 5:   Glue the 2 wiggly eyes onto the black velour side of the spider.

Step 6:   Punch a hole into the top of the spider's head. Cut a piece of black rug yarn about 24 inches long. Tie the yarn securely through the hole and tie a loop at the top end of the yarn for a handle.

Use: You will need two children to participate in this dramatic play activity. Have Little Miss Muffet sit on a small stool or on the floor. As you and the other students recite the poem, the child holding the spider will walk over to Miss Muffet and Miss Muffet will run away.

from Magic Moments
P.O. Box 53635
San Jose, CA. 95135

Miss Muffet

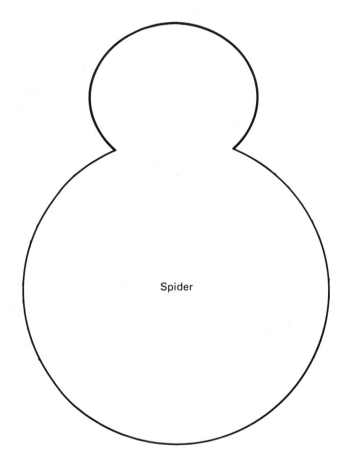

Spider

CHECKLIST FOR THE DEVELOPMENT OF READING BEHAVIORS

1 YEAR

_____ Handles books without necessarily verbalizing.

_____ Crumples, tears, and chews books.

_____ Ignores print.

15 MONTHS

_____ Turns book pages in random order.

_____ Verbalizes while pointing to pictures in books.

_____ Points to pictures of known objects when objects are named.

_____ Pats pictures of things liked.

_____ Points to round things (circles, balls, the letter O).

18 MONTHS

_____ Orients pictures to line of vision.

_____ Asks for pictured objects and animals to be named.

_____ Demonstrates pictured action.

_____ Tells a "story" related to pictures on pages.

_____ Answers questions about story which has been read aloud several times.

_____ Shows concern for book's condition.

_____ Guesses outcomes when hearing new story.

2 YEARS

_____ Has a favorite book.

_____ Pretends to read (holds book and talks).

_____ Turns pages right-to-left.

_____ Asks for stories to be read aloud.

_____ Remains attentive as story is read.

_____ Remembers names of pictured book characters.

_____ Recalls plots of stories read aloud.

_____ Asks what the printed words say.

30 MONTHS

_____ Can turn to the front of a book when asked.

_____ Can turn to the back of a book when asked.

_____ Can point to the top of a page when asked.

_____ Can point to the bottom of a page when asked.

_____ Pretends to pick up objects pictured on pages.

_____ Enjoys looking through picture books.

_____ Likes hearing and repeating nursery rhymes.

_____ Completes oral sentence by saying the last word omitted by an adult.

_____ Talks to book characters (slaps, kisses, etc.).

_____ Reacts emotionally to story content.

_____ Repeats sentence verbatim.

_____ Asks for a book about a particular topic to be read aloud.

_____ Rejects changed oral version of a familiar story.

_____ Tells purpose of coloring book.

_____ Can tell what common adjectives are not (wet is not dry).

_____ Notices capital letters in color.

3 YEARS

_____ Remains attentive as story is read aloud, even when pictures are not visible.

_____ Can choose two pictures as being the same when given three to choose from.

_____ Can draw a cross (+ or ×) after being shown one.

_____ Can relate activities in the order in which they occurred.

_____ Can name some of the capital letters in own name.

_____ Asks to see pictures when listening to someone read aloud.

4 YEARS

_____ Can rearrange a set of pictures in an order appropriate for a story.

_____ Can name six or more capital letters.

_____ Points to printed area of page as the place to look when you read.

_____ Chooses a set of letters when given letters and numbers and asked to point to a word.

_____ Copies letters, reversing only a few.

_____ Can retell the plot of a short story after hearing it only once.

5 YEARS

_____ Can spell three or more words orally.

_____ Asks what letter sequences spell.

_____ Recognizes letters comprising own name.

_____ Recognizes words from signs, food containers, and television commercials.

_____ Can select and order letters to form own name.

_____ Can point to capital (or "big") letters on a page of print.

_____ Copies letters from books on separate paper.

_____ Tells story appropriate to newspaper comic strip.

ALPHABET PRONUNCIATION GUIDE (UNIT 21)

Symbols	Sounds as in the Words	Symbols	Sounds as in the Words
a	fat, apple, ask	m	him, me, custom
ā	ate, name	n	sun, not, even
b	rib, big	o	ox, on, not
c	traffic, cat	ō	go, open, home
d	lid, end, feed	p	sip, pat
e	end, wet, pen	r	ran, rip, very
ē	me, Elaine, eat	s	kiss, so, last
f	if, leaf, full	t	hit, top
g	rag, go	u	up, rug, custom
h	hat, how, high	ū	useful, unite
i	it, individual, pin	v	give, have, very
i̯	piece, niece	w	we, win, watch
ī	ice, while	x	box
j	jump, jeep	y	yea, you
k	lick, kiss, milk	ȳ	my, cry
l	will, late, little	z	zoo, fuzz

COMMERCIAL SOURCES FOR LEARNING MATERIALS (UNIT 22)

ABC School Supply Inc., 437 Armour Circle N.E., Box 13084, Atlanta, Georgia 30324

Afro Am Publishing Co., Inc., 1727 S. Indiana Avenue, Chicago, Illinois 60616

Angeles Nursery Toys, 4105 N. Fairfax Drive, Arlington, Virginia 22203

Ashland Co., 22221 Drury Lane, Shawnee Mission, Kansas 66208

Bailey Films, Inc., 6509 DeLongpre Avenue, Hollywood, California 90028

Beckley-Cardy, 1900 N. Narragansett Ave., Chicago, Illinois 60639

Binney and Smith, Inc., 380 Madison Avenue, New York, New York 10017

Bowmar, P.O. Box 3623, Glendale, California 91201

Childcraft Education Corporation, 20 Kilmer Road, Edison, New Jersey 08817

Child Guidance, Questor Education Products Co., 200 Fifth Avenue, New York, New York 10010

Childhood Resources, 5307 Lee Highway, Arlington, Virginia 22207

Community Playthings, Rifton, New York 12471

Constructive Playthings, 1040 E. 85th Street, Kansas City, Missouri 64131

Creative Playthings, A Division of CBS Inc., Princeton, New Jersey 08540

Creative Publications, P.O. Box 10328, Palo Alto, California 94303

David C. Cook Publishing Co., 850 No. Grove Avenue, Elgin, Illinois 60120

Dennison Manufacturing Co., 67 Ford Avenue, Framingham, Massachusetts 01701

Developmental Learning Materials (DLM), 7440 Natchez Avenue, Niles, Illinois 60648

Ed-U-Card/Ed-U-Card Corporations, Subsidiaries of Binney & Smith, 60 Austin Boulevard, Commack, New York 11725

Educational Performance Associates, 563 Westview Avenue, Ridgefield, New Jersey 07657

Educational Teaching Aids Division (ETA), A. Daigger & Co., Inc., 159 W. Kinzie Street, Chicago, Illinois 60610

Eureka Resale Products, Dunmore, Pennsylvania 18512

Fisher Price Toys, A Division of Quaker Oats Co., East Aurora, New York 14052

GAF Corporation, Consumer Photo Products/ViewMaster, 140 West 51st Street, New York, New York 10020

Growing Child Playthings, 22 North Second St., P.O. Box 101, Lafayette, Indiana 47902

Gryphon House, 1333 Connecticut Ave., N.W., Washington, D.C. 20036

Hayes School Publishing Co., Inc., 321 Pennwood Avenue, Wilkinsburg, Pennsylvania 15221

Holcomb's, 3000 Quigley Road, Cleveland, Ohio 44113

Ideal School Supply, 11000 S. Lavergne Avenue, Oak Lawn, Illinois 60453

Information Center on Children's Cultures, Administrative Offices, 331 East 38th Street, New York, New York 10016

Instructo Corporation, Subsidiary of McGraw-Hill Inc., Cedar Hollow and Mathews Roads, Paoli, Pennsylvania 19301

Judy Instructional Aids, The Judy Company, Sales Office, 250 James Street, Morristown, New Jersey 07960

Lakeshore Equipment Company, P.O. Box 2116, 1144 Montague Avenue, San Leandro, California 94577

Lauri Enterprises, Phillips-Avon, Maine 04966

Learning Products, Inc., 11632 Fairgrove Industrial Blvd., St. Louis, Missouri 63043

Lego Systems, Inc., P.O. Box 2273, Enfield, Connecticut 06082

Mab-Graphic Products Inc., 310 Marconi Boulevard, Copiague, New York 11726

Mead Educational Services, B & T Learning, 5315-A Tulane Drive, Atlanta, Georgia 30336

Milton Bradley Company, Springfield, Massachusetts 01100

National Dairy Council, 111 N. Canal Street, Chicago, Illinois 60606

National Geographic Society, 17th and M Streets N.W., Washington, D.C. 20036

National Wildlife Federation, 1412 16th St., N.W., Washington, D.C. 20036

Parker Brothers Inc., Division of General Mills, Fun Group Inc., Salem, Massachusetts 01970

Playskool Incorporated, Milton Bradley Company, Springfield, Massachusetts 01100

Practical Drawing Company, P.O. Box 5388, Dallas, Texas 75222

Romper Room Toys, Hasbro Industries, Inc., Pawtucket, Rhode Island 02861

Scholastic Early Childhood Center, 904 Sylvan Avenue, Englewood Cliffs, New Jersey 07632

Scott Foresman and Co., 1900 E. Lake Avenue, Glenview, Illinois 60025

Scripture Press, Victor Books, 1825 College Avenue, Wheaton, Illinois 60187

Shindana Toys, Division of Operation Bootstrap, Inc., 6107 S. Central Avenue, Los Angeles, California 90001

Standard Publishing Co., 8121 Hamilton Avenue, Cincinnati, Ohio 45231

Trend Enterprises, P.O. Box 3073, St. Paul, Minnesota 55165

Uniworld Toys, P.O. Box 61, West Hempstead, New York 11552

Glossary

Acquisition — to gain possession by one's own endeavor (such as acquiring a skill), or by purchasing something (such as acquiring a piece of equipment).

Acuity — how well or clearly one uses senses — the degree of sharpness.

Articulation — the adjustments and movements of the muscles of the mouth and jaw involved in producing clear oral communication.

Assimilation — the process which allows new experiences to merge with previously stored mental structures.

Auditory discrimination — the act of perceiving different sounds, such as the differences of sounds within words.

Categorize — to place items, events, ideas (etc.) in the correct class, group, division (etc.).

Classify — the act of systematically grouping things according to identifiable common characteristics; for example, size.

Cognitive behavior — thinking process behavior. Also, the act or process of knowing, including both awareness and judgement.

Cognitive structure — a system of organized and integrated perceptions.

Communication — the giving (sending) and receiving of information, signals, or messages.

Concept — a commonly recognized element (or elements) which identifies groups or classes, usually a given name which is a symbol of the concept.

Conceptual tempo — a term associated with Jerome Kagan's theory of different individual pacing in perceptual exploring of objects.

Configuration — the figure, shape contour, or pattern produced by the relative arrangement of parts.

Cooing — an early stage during the prelinguistic period in which vowel sounds are repeated, particularly the u-u-u sound.

Curriculum — an overall plan for the content of instruction to be offered in a program.

Decoding — the process by which the individual is able to translate written language forms into their oral counterparts. Strategies used in this process range from grapheme/phoneme relationships and letter-pattern/sound-pattern generalizations to structural analysis.

Deprivation — being kept from acquiring, using, or enjoying.

Dialect — a variety of spoken language unique to a geographical area or social group. Variations in dialect may include phonological or sound variations, syntactical variations, and lexical or vocabulary variations.

Directionality — the ability to understand right, left, up, down, north, south; directional orientation.

Discrimination; auditory — ability to detect differences in sounds.

Discrimination; visual — ability to detect differences in objects seen.

Dramatic play — acting out experiences.

Echolalia — a characteristic of the babbling period. The child repeats (echoes) the same sounds over and over.

Equilibrium — a balance attained with consistent care and need satisfaction which leads to security feelings and lessens anxiety.

Fluency — a ready flow of ideas, possibilities, consequences, and objects.

Grammar — the word order and knowledge of "marker" word meanings necessary to send communications to (and receive them from) another in the same language.

Holophrases — the expression of a whole idea in a single word. They are characteristic of the child's language from about 12–18 months.

Infer — draw a conclusion.

Inflections — the grammatical "markers" such as plurals. Also, a change in pitch or loudness of the voice.

Impulsivity — a quick answer or reaction to either a simple or complex situation or problem.

Intonation — varying the tone, pitch, or inflection of the voice in speaking.

Intonational patterns — variations in voicing, such as loudness and pitch variations, that help convey meaning.

Language — the means by which a person communicates ideas or feelings to another in such a way that the meaning is mutually understood.

Large motor skill — ability to make one's large muscles perform in a coordinated way.

Linguistics — the study of human speech in its various aspects.

Markers (language markers) — the two types in the English language are function words (such as a, an, the, with) and suffixes (such as -s, -ing). Markers often identify classes (such as nouns), specify relations, or signal meanings (such as -ing, an ongoing activity, or -s indicating plurality).

Modifier — giving special characteristic to a noun (for example, a *large* ball).

Morpheme — the smallest unit in a language that by itself has a recognizable meaning.

Morphology — the study of the units of meaning in a language.

Neonate — newborn baby.

Nonstandard English — a dialect that deviates from standard English in pronunciation, vocabulary, or grammar.

Objectives — purposes to be realized through activities, sometimes stated in behaviors.

Overregularization — the tendency on the part of children to make the language regular, such as using past tenses like -ed on verb endings.

Perception — mental awareness of objects and other data gathered through the five senses.

Phonation — exhaled air passes the larnynx's vibrating folds and produces "voice."

Phonology — the sound system of a language and how it is represented with an alphabetic code.

Rate — speed with which sounds, syllables, or words are spoken.

Reflection — taking time to weigh aspects or alternatives in a given situation.

Resonation — amplification of laryngeal sounds using cavities of the mouth, nose, sinuses, and pharynx.

Rhythm — uniform or patterned recurrence of a beat, accent, or melody in speech.

Semantics — the study of meanings, of how the sounds of language are related to the real world and our own experiences.

Sensory motor development — the control and use of sense organs and the body's muscle structure.

Small motor skill — ability to make one's small muscles perform in a coordinated way (such as holding a pencil and writing, or playing the piano.)

Stress — emphasis in the form of prominent loudness of a syllable, word, or between compound words and noncompound words and phrases.

Syllable — a part word (or whole word) pronounced with a single uninterrupted sounding of the voice, usually blending vowel and consonant sounds.

Symbol — something standing for or suggesting (such as pictures, models, word symbols, etc.)

Symbolization — using symbols to convey a message or meaning.

Syntax — the arrangement of words as elements in a sentence to show their relationship.

Telegraphic speech — a characteristic of early child sentences in which everything but the crucial word is omitted, as if for a telegram.

Bibliography

BOOKS

Alda, Alan, *A Guide to Nonsexist Children's Books,* Chicago: Academy Press Ltd., 1976.

Almy, Millie, *The Early Childhood Educator at Work,* New York: McGraw-Hill Book Co., 1975.

Anderson, Paul, *Storytelling with the Flannel Board,* Book One and Book Two, T. S. Denison and Co., 9601 Newton Ave. S., Minneapolis, MN.

Anglin, J. M., *Work, Object, and Conceptual Development,* New York: Norton Publishers, 1977.

Arbuthnot, May H. and Shelton L. Root Jr., *Time for Poetry,* Scott, Foresman and Co., 1968.

Aston-Warner, Sylvia, *Teacher,* New York: Bantam Books, Inc., 1965.

Bailey, Carolyn, and Clara Lewis, *For the Children's Hour,* New York: Platt and Munk, 1943.

Barker, Larry L., *Listening Behavior,* New Jersey: Prentice-Hall Inc., 1971.

Beaty, Janice J., *Skills for Preschool Teachers,* 2nd. ed., Charles E. Merrill Publishing Co., 1984.

Beckman, Carol, et al., *Channels to Children,* P.O. Box 25834, Colorado Springs, CO 80936.

Belton, Sandra and Christine Terbough, *Sparks: Activities to Help Children Learn at Home,* Human Services Press, 4301 Connecticut Ave. NW, Washington, DC 20008.

Bentley, William G., *Learning to Move and Moving to Learn,* New York: Citation Press, 1970.

Berg, Leila, *Reading and Loving,* Henley and Boston: Routledge and Kegan Publ., 1977.

Bettelheim, Bruno, *The Uses of Enchantment,* New York: Alfred A. Knopf, 1976.

Biber, Barbara, Edna Shapiro, and David Wickens, *Promoting Cognitive Growth: A Developmental Interaction Point of View,* Washington, DC: National Association for the Education of Young Children, 1971.

Bloodstein, O., *A Handbook on Stuttering,* National Easter Seal Society of Crippled Children and Adults, Chicago, 1975.

Brake, Rachel G., *Developing Prereading Skills,* New York: Holt, Rinehart, and Winston, Inc., 1972.

Brashears, D. and Sharron Werlin, *Circle Time Activities for Young Children,* 1 Corte Del Rey, Orinda, CA 94563.

Broman, Betty, *The Early Years,* Chicago: Rand McNally College Publishing Co., 1978.

Brophy, Jere E., *Child Development and Socialization,* Chicago: Science Research Associates, Inc., 1977.

Brown, Margaret W., *Nibble, Nibble,* Addison-Wesley, 1959.

Bruner, Jerome, et al., *Studies in Cognitive Growth,* New York: John Wiley and Sons, 1966.

Bulletin of the Center for Children's Books, The University of Chicago Press, 580 Ellis Ave., Chicago, 1973.

Cazden, Courtney B., *Child Language and Education,* New York: Holt, Rinehart, and Winston, Inc., 1972.

_____. *Language in Early Childhood Education,* N.A.E.Y.C., 1981.

Chambers, Dewey W., *Storytelling and Creative Drama,* Dubuque, IA: William C. Brown Co., 1970.

Chandler, Bessie E., *Early Learning Experiences,* The Instructor Publications, Inc., Dansville, NY 14437.

Children's Books of the Year, Child Study Children's Book Committee, Bank Street College, 610 West 112th St., New York, 1983.

Chomsky, Noam, *Language and Mind,* New York: Harcourt, Brace, and World, 1968.

Chukovsky, Kornei Ivanovich, *From Two to Five,* Berkeley, CA: University of California, 1963.

Clarke-Stewart, R. and Joanne Barbara Koch, *Children,* John Wiley and Sons, Inc., 1983.

Clark, Leonard, *Poetry for the Youngest,* The Horn Book, 1969.

Clement, John, "Promoting Preschool Bilingualism," *KEYS to Early Childhood Education,* Vol. 2, No. 3, March 1981.

Cochran, K. V., *Teach and Reach That Child,* Mountain View, CA: Peek Publishers, Inc., 1971.

Coglin, Mary Lou, *Chants for Children,* Coglin Publ., Box 301, Manilius, NY, 13104.

Coody, Betty, *Using Literature With Young Children* 3rd ed., Wm. C. Brown Company Publishers, 1983.

Corcoran, Gertrude B., *Language Experience for Nursery and Kindergarten Years,* Itasca, IL: F. E. Peacock Publishers, Inc., 1976.

Croft, Doreen J. and Robert Hess, *An Activities Handbook for Teachers of Young Children,* Houghton Mifflin Co., 1983.

Danoff, Judith, Vicki Breitbart, and Elinor Barr, *Open for Children,* New York: McGraw-Hill Book Co., 1977.

Day, Barbara, *Open Learning in Early Childhood,* New York: Macmillan Publishing Co., Inc., 1975.

Dee, Rita, *Planning for Ethnic Education: A Handbook for Planned Change,* Revised ed., Illinois State Board of Education, Jan. 1980, ERIC ED191 976.

de Villiers, Peter A., and Jill G. de Villiers, *Early Language,* 3rd ed., Harvard University Press, 1982.

Dillard, J. L., *Black English,* Random House, 1972.

Donoghue, Mildred, *The Child and the English Language Arts,* Dubuque, IA: William C. Brown, 1975.

Durkin, Dolores, *Children Who Read Early,* Teachers College Press, NY, 1969.

_____. *Teaching Young Children to Read,* Boston, MA: Allyn and Bacon, Inc., 1972.

Eisenson, Jon, *Is Your Child's Speech Normal?,* Reading, MA: Addison-Wesley Publishing Co., 1976.

Ellis, Mary Jackson, *Finger Play Approach to Dramatization,* T. S. Denison and Co., Inc., Minneapolis, MN.

Engel, Rose C., *Language Motivating Experiences for Young Children,* Educative Toys and Supplies, 6416 van Nuys Blvd., Van Nuys, CA 91401.

Erikson, Erik, *Childhood and Society,* New York: W. W. Norton, 1950.

EPIE Report - Educational Product Report, No. 68, EPIE Exchange Institute, 1975, p. 77.

Finger Frolics, Gryphon House, 1976.

Fleming, Bonnie Mack and Darlene Softley Hamilton, *Resources for Creative Teaching in Early Childhood Education,* New York: Harcourt, Brace, Jovanovich, Inc., 1972.

Flores, Manna I., "Helping Children Learn a Second Language," *KEYS to Early Childhood Education,* Vol. 1, No. 6, July, 1980.

Fostering Growth in Language Skills and Social Concepts, Macmillan Co., Threshold Division, 866 Third Ave., New York, NY 10022.

Frank, Josette (ed.), *Poems to Read to the Very Young,* New York: Random House, 1961.

Freeman, Ruth S., *Children's Picture Books,* New York: Century House, 1967.

Frost, Joel, *Early Childhood Education Rediscovered,* (Readings) New York: Holt, Rinehart, and Winston, Inc., 1968.

Frost, Joel and Joan Kissenger, *The Young Child and the Education Process,* New York: Holt, Rinehart, and Winston, Inc., 1976.

Garvey, Catherine, *Play,* Cambridge, MA: Harvard University Press, 1977.

Georgio, C., *Children and Their Literature,* Prentice-Hall, 1969.

Glazer, Tom, *Eye Winker Tom Tinker Chin Chopper: Fifty Musical Fingerplays,* Doubleday and Co., Inc., 1973.

Goetz, Elizabeth M., "Early Reading," *Young Children,* July 1979.

Grayson, M., *Let's Do Fingerplays,* Robert B. Luce, Inc., 1962.

Green, Margaret, *Learning to Talk,* New York: Harper and Brothers, 1960.

Greenberg, Dr. Herbert M., *Teaching with Feeling,* Indianapolis, IN: The Pegasus Press, 1969.

Greene, Allen and Madalynne Schoenfeld, *A Multimedia Approach to Children's Literature,* American Library Association, 1972.

Hartwell, P., "Dialect Interference in Writing: A Critical View," *Research in the Teaching of English,* 14 (May 1980).

Heathers, Anne and Frances Esteban, *A Handful of Surprises,* New York: Harcourt, Brace, and World, 1961.

Hendrick, Joanne, *The Whole Child,* St. Louis: The C. V. Mosby Company, 1975.

_____. *The Whole Child,* Times Mirror/Mosby, 1984.

Hennings, Dorothy Grant, *Communication in Action,* Rand McNally, 1978.

Herr, Selma, *Learning Activities for Reading,* Dubuque, IA: William C. Brown Co., 1970.

Hillerich, Robert L., *Reading Fundamentals for Preschool and Primary Children,* Columbus, OH: Charles E. Merrill Publishing Co., 1977.

Hoban, Russell, *Egg Thoughts and Other Frances Songs,* Harper and Row, 1972.

Hoggart, Richard, *Speaking to Each Other,* Volume II. About Literature, Chatto and Windus, London, 1970.

Holmes, Deborah L. and Frederick J. Morrison, *The Child,* Monterey, CA: Brooks-Cole Publishing Co., 1979.

Huck, Charlotte, *Children's Literature in the Elementary School,* 3rd ed., New York: Holt, Rinehart and Winston, 1976.

Hunt, J. McVicker, "How Children Develop Intellectually" in Guy R. LeFrancois (ed.) *Little George,* Belmont, CA: Wadsworth Publishing Co., Inc., 1974.

_____. *Intelligence and Experience,* New York: The Ronald Press, 1961.

Jackson, Marilyn, *Finger Play and Flannelboard Fun,* Box 124, Basking Ridge, NJ, 1978, (More activity ideas.)

Kable, Gratia, *Favorite Finger Plays,* T. S. Denison and Co., Inc., Minneapolis, MN.

Kaplan, Sondra Nina, Jo Ann Kaplan, Shuta Madsen, and Bette Gould, *A Young Child Experiences,* Monica, CA: Goodyear Publishing Co., Inc., 1975.

Karnes, Merle B., *GOAL Language Development Program,* Springfield, MA: Milton Bradley Co., 1972.

_____. *Helping Young Children Develop Language Skills: A Book of Activities,* The Council for Exceptional Children, 1411 S. Jefferson Davis Highway, Suite 900, Arlington, VA 22202.

Katz, Bobbi, *Bedtime Bear's Book of Bedtime Poems,* Random House, 1983.

Kimmel, Mary Margaret and Elizabeth Segal, *For Reading Out Loud!: A Guide to Sharing Books With Children,* Delacorte Press.

Kirk, S., J. McCarthy, and W. Kirk, *Illinois Test of Psycholinguistic Abilities,* Urbana, IL: University of Illinois Press, 1968.

Knight, Lester N., *Language Arts for the Exceptional,* Itasca, IL: F. E. Peacock Publishers, 1974.

Landreth, Catherine, *Preschool Learning and Teaching,* New York: Harper and Row, 1972.

Larrick, Nancy, *A Parent's Guide to Children's Reading,* 4th ed., Bantam Books, 1975.

Lay, Margaret Z. and John E. Dopyera, *Becoming A Teacher of Young Children,* Lexington, MA: D. C. Heath and Co., 1977.

Lee, Laura L., "The Relevance of General Semantics to Development of Sentence Structure in Children's Language" in Lee Thayer (ed.) *Communication: General Semantics Perspectives,* New York: Spartan Books, 1970.

Lenneberg, Eric H., *Biological Foundations of Language,* New York: John Wiley and Sons, Inc., 1967.

Lewis, Claudia, *Writing for Children,* Bank St. College, 610 West 112th St., New York, 1982.

Lewis, M. M., *Language, Thought, and Personality,* New York: Basic Books, Inc., 1963.

Lorton, Mary, *Workjobs: Activity-Centered Learning for Early Childhood Education,* Addison-Wesley, 1972.

Lundsteen, Sara W., *Children Learn to Communicate,* Prentice-Hall, Inc., 1976, Chap. 4.

Machado, Jeanne and Helen C. Meyer, *Early Childhood Practicum Guide,* Delmar Publishers Inc., 1984.

Magic Moments, P.O. Box 53635, San Jose, CA 95153–0635.

Manson, Beverlie, *Fairy Poems for the Very Young,* Doubleday, 1983.

Margolin, Edythe, *Teaching Young Children at School and Home,* New York: Macmillan Publ. Co., 1982.

Mason, George, E., *A Primer on Teaching Reading,* F. E. Peacock Publ., Inc., 1981.

Mayesky, M., Neuman, D., and Wlodkowski, R., *Creative Activities for Young Children,* Albany: Delmar Publishers, 1985.

McCandless, Boyd R., *Child Behavior and Development,* New York: Holt, Rinehart, and Winston, Inc., 1967.

McCandless, Boyd R. and Ellis Evans, *Children and Youth: Psychosocial Development,* Hinsdale, IL: The Dryden Press, 1973.

Meers, Hilda J., *Helping Our Children Talk,* New York: Longman Group Limited, 1976.

Montessori, Maria, *The Absorbent Mind,* New York: Holt, Rinehart, and Winston, 1967.

_____. *The Discovery of the Child,* (translated by M. Joseph Costelloe), New York: Ballantine Books, 1967.

Moore, Vadine, *Preschool Story Hour,* New Jersey: Scarecrow Press, 1972.

Nedler, Shari, "A Bilingual Early Childhood Program" in *The Preschool in Action,* Mary Carol Day and Ronald K. Parker (eds.) Boston, MA: Allyn and Bacon, Inc., 1977.

Norton, Donna E., *Through the Eyes of a Child,* Chas. E. Merrill Publ. Co., 1983.

Osborn, Janie Dyson and D. Keith Osborn, *Cognition in Early Childhood,* Athens, GA: Education Associates, 1983.

Peck, Johanne, Richard Goldman, and Stephen Lelane, *Looking at Children,* Atlanta, GA: Humanics Limited, 1976.

Peralta, Chris, *Flannel Board Activities for the Bilingual Classroom,* La Arana Publ., 11209 Malat Way, Culver City, CA 90232. (A collection of Latin-American traditional stories for the flannel board, patterns included.)

Personal Software Magazine, Nov. 1983, Hayden Publishing Co.

Pflaum, Susanna Whitney, *The Development of Language and Reading in the Young Child,* Columbus, OH: Charles E. Merrill Publishers, 1974.

Piaget, Jean, *The Language and Thought of the Child,* London: Rutledge and Kegan Paul, 1952.

_____. *The Origins of Intelligence in Children,* New York: International Universities Press, 1952.

Poltarnees, Welleran, *All Mirrors are Magic Mirrors,* The Green Tiger Press, 1972.

Pushaw, David R., *Teach Your Child to Talk,* Dantree Press Inc., 1976.

Rainey, Ernestine W., *Language Development for the Young Young Child,* Atlanta, GA: Humanics Press, 1978.

Rapsberry, W., "Reading, Writing and Dialect," *Young Children,* Nov. 1979.

Robinson, Helen F., *Exploring Teaching in Early Childhood Education,* 2nd ed., Boston, MA: Allyn and Bacon, Inc., 1983.

Ryle, Gilbert, *The Concept of Mind,* London: Hutchinson House, 1949.

Sawyer, Dorothy, *The Way of the Storyteller,* New York: Viking, 1969.

Schimmel, Nancy, *Just Enough to Make a Story,* Berkeley, CA: Sister's Choice Press, 1978.

Scott, Louise B., *Developing Communication Skills,* New York: McGraw-Hill Book Co., 1971.

_____. *Learning Time with Language Experiences for Young Children,* New York: McGraw-Hill Book Co., Webster Division, 1968.

Sebesta, Sam Leaton, and William J. Iverson, *Literature for Thursday's Child,* Science Research Assoc., Inc., 1975.

Simonds, Lynn, *Language Skills for the Young Child,* R. and E. Research Associates, 4843 Mission St., San Francisco, CA 94112.

Skinner, B.F., *Verbal Behavior,* New York: Appleton-Century Crofts, 1957.

Slobin, Dan, *Psycholinguistics,* Glenview, IL: Scott, Foresman, and Co., 1971.

Smith, Charles and Carolyn Foat, *Once Upon a Mind,* North Central Regional Extension Publication, Kansas State University, 1982.

Smith, James A. and Dorothy M. Park, *Word Music and Word Magic: Children's Literature Methods,* Boston, MA: Allyn and Bacon, Inc., 1977.

Spitzer, Dean R., *Concept Formation and Learning in Early Childhood,* Columbus, OH: Charles E. Merrill Publishing Co., 1977.

Spodek, Bernard, *Teaching in the Early Years,* Englewood Cliffs, NJ: Prentice-Hall, 1972.

Stevens, Joseph H. and Edith King, *Administering Early Childhood Education Programs,* Boston, MA: Little, Brown, and Co., 1976.

Stewig, John Warren, *Teaching Language Arts in Early Childhood,* Holt, Rinehart and Winston, 1982.

Stone, L. Joseph and Joseph Church, *Childhood and Adolescence,* New York: Random House, 1973.

Sutton-Smith, Brian, *Child Psychology,* New York: Appleton-Century-Croft, 1973.

Sweeney, Mary and Jeff Fegan, *Flanneltales,* 310 Sequoia Ave, San Jose, CA 95126.

Tarrow, Norma B. and S. W. Lundsteen, *Activities and Resources for Guiding Young Children's Learning,* McGraw-Hill Book Co., 1981.

Thompson, Richard A., *Energizers for Reading Instruction,* West Nyack, NY: Parker Publishing Co., 1973.

Threshold Program for Early Learning, Vol. III, Language Skills and Social Concepts, New York: Macmillan, 1970.

Tiedt, Sidney and Iris Tiedt, *Language Arts Activities for the Classroom,* Penguin, 1971.

Todd, V. E. and H. Heffernan, *The Years Before School: Guiding Preschool Children,* New York: Macmillan, 1970.

Tooze, Ruth, *Storytelling,* New Jersey: Prentice-Hall, 1959.

Tough, J., *Focus on Meaning: Talking to Some Purpose With Young Children,* George, Allen and Unwin, Ltd., 1973.

Townsend, John Rowe, *Written for Children,* The Horn Book, Inc., 1965, 1974.

Trelease, Jimm, *The Read-Aloud Handbook,* Penguin Books, 1982.

Van Allen, Roach, *Language Experiences in Early Childhood,* Encyclopedia Britannica, Chicago, 1969.

Van Allen, Roach and Clarye Allen, *Language Experience Activities,* Houghton Mifflin Co., 1982.

Van Riper, C., *Teaching Your Child to Talk,* New York: Harper and Row, 1950.

Vonk, Idelee, *Storytelling with the Flannel Board,* Book Three, T. S. Denison and Co., 9601 Newton Ave S , Minneapolis, MN.

Watson, Clyde, *Catch Me and Kiss Me and Say It Again,* Collins, 1983.

Weiss, Curtis E., and Herold S. Lillywhite, *Communicative Disorders,* 2nd Ed., The C. V. Mosby Co., 1981.

Wilmes, Liz and Dick, *Everyday Circle Times,* Gryphon House Inc., P.O. Box 275, Mt. Rainier, MD 20712.

Winn, Marie, *The Plug-In Drug,* New York: Viking Press, 1977.

Yamamoto, K., *The Child and His Image,* Boston, MA: Houghton Mifflin Co., 1972.

Yawkey, Thomas et al, *Language Arts and the Young Child,* F. E. Peacock Publishers, Inc., 1981.

ARTICLES

Balaban, Nancy, "What Do Young Children Teach Themselves?", *A.C.E.I. International,* 1980.

Bartlett, Elsa Jaffe, "Selecting an Early Childhood Language Curriculum" in *Language in Early Childhood,* revised ed., Courtney B. Cazden, ed., N.A.E.Y.C., 1981.

Bellugi, Ursula, "Learning the Language" in Robert Schell (ed.) *Reading in Psychology Today,* New York: Random House, 1977.

Braine, M. D. S., "The Ontogeny of English Phrase Structure: The First Phase" in C. A. Ferguson and D. I. Sloben (eds.) *Studies of Child Language Development,* New York: Holt, Rinehart, and Winston, Inc., 1973.

Brenner, Nancy Dreifus, "Helping Children Consolidate Their Thinking," *Young Children,* July 1977.

Brittain, W. Lambert, "Analysis of Artistic Behavior in Young Children" Final Report, Cornell Univ., 1973.

Carew, J. V. "Experience and the Development of Intelligence in Young Children at Home and in Day Care," *Monographs of the Society for Research in Child Development* 45 (1980). Serial No.187.

Carini, Patricia, "Building a Curriculum for Young Children from an Experiential Base," *Young Children,* March 1977, p. 14.

Children in the Age of Microcomputers, *Childhood Education,* March/April 1983, Steven Silvern, Guest Editor.

Chomsky, Carol, "Write Now, Read Later," *Childhood Education,* 47, 1971.

Douglass, Robert, "Basic Feelings and Speech Defects," *Exceptional Children,* March 1959.

Elkind, David, "Cognition in Infancy and Early Childhood" in John Eliot (ed.) *Human Development and Cognitive Processes,* New York: Holt, Rinehart, and Winston, Inc., 1971.

Eveloff, Herbert H., "Some Cognitive and Affective Aspects of Early Language Development" in S. Cohen and T. Comiskey (eds.) *Child Development Contemporary Perspectives,* Itasca, IL: F. E. Peacock Publishers, Inc., 1977, p. 149.

Honig, Alice Sterling, "What Are the Needs of Infants?", *Young Children,* Vol. 37, no. 1, Nov, 1981.

Huey, J. Francis, "Learning Potential of the Young Child," *Educational Leadership,* November 1965, v. 23.

Irwin, D. Michelle, "Making Your Own Games," *Day Care and Early Education,* May/June 1977, pp. 32–33.

Johnson, Kenneth, "Pedagogical Problems of Using Second Language Techniques for Teaching Standard English to Speakers of Nonstandard Negro Dialect," *Linguistic Cultural Differences and American Education,* ed. by Aarons, Gordon and Stewart, Florida FL. Reporter, 1969.

Kane, Frances, "Thinking, Drawing — Writing, Reading," *Childhood Education,* May/June 1982.

Katz, Susan, "Is Your Toddler's Language Delayed?" *American Baby,* August 1977, p. 16.

Kitano, Margie, "Young Gifted Children: Strategies for Preschool Teachers," *Young Children,* Vol. 37, No. 4, May 1982.

Klopf, Donald W., "Educating Children for Communication in a Multicultural Society," *Paper presented at the Conference on Developing Oral Communication Competence in Children,* Australia, July, 1979, ERIC ED180 026.

Lake, Alice, "New Babies are Smarter Than You Think," *Readings in Early Childhood Education 77/78,* Guilford, CT: Duskin Publishing Group, Inc., 1977.

Lamberts, Frances, et al., "Listening and Language Activities for Preschool Children," *Language, Speech and Hearing Services in Schools,* April 1980.

Lenneberg, Eric H., "The Natural History of Language," in John Eliot (ed.) *Human Development and Cognitive Processes,* New York: Holt, Rinehart, and Winston, Inc., 1971.

List, Hindy, "Kids Can Write The Day They Start School," *Early Years,* Jan. 1984.

Markham, Lynda R., "De Dog and De Cat" Assisting Speakers of Black English as They Begin to Write, *Young Children,* May 1984.

Marten, Milton, "Listening Review," *Classroom-Relevant Research in the Language Arts,* Assoc. for Supv. and Curriculum Development, Washington, DC, 1978.

Paul, R., "Invented Spelling in the Kindergarten," *Young Children,* 31, Mar. 1976.

Pellegrini, Anthony and Lee Galda, "Effects of Thematic-Fantasy Play Training on the Development of Children's Story Comprehension," *American Educational Research Journal,* vol. 19, no. 3, 1982.

Piestrup, Ann M., "Young Children Use Computer Graphics," *Harvard Domputer Graphics Week,* Harvard Univ. Graduate School of Design, copyright Ann M. Piestrup, 1982.

Swan, Raymond, "Memo to Caretakers: On Children's Learning Styles," *Child Welfare,* Vol. LV #5, May 1976, p. 335.

Swigger, Kathleen M., "Is One Better?", *Educational Computer,* Nov./Dec., 1983.

Van Allen, Roach "The Write Way to Read," *Elementary English,* XVIV, May 1967.

Vukelich, C. and J. Golden, "Early Writing: Development and Teaching Strategies," *Young Children,* 39, Jan. 1984.

Watt, Molly, "Electronic Thinker Toys," *Popular Computing,* June 1983.

Weir, Mary E., and Pat Eggleston, "Teachers First Words," *Day Care and Early Education,* Nov./Dec., 1975.

Answers to Review Questions

Unit 1 Beginnings of Communication

A. Answers will differ.

B. Be responsive and attentive to each infant.
   Be sensitive, alert and loving.
   Read infant's nonverbal and vocalized cues.
   Be physically warm; touching and holding often.
   Note individualness.
   Hold firmly yet gently.
   Interact playfully.
   Imitate child sound.
   Talk to infants about what's happening to them.
   Speak clearly.
   Engage in word play.
   Plan "first-hand" experiences.

C. Phonation = Exhaled air which passes the larynx and produces voice.
   Echolalia = A characteristic of the babbling period when the child repeats or echoes.
   Resonation = The amplification of sounds by the mouth area.

D. Understand the reciprocal nature of adult-infant conversations, and are responsive, attentive, and at times playful.

E. 1. Heredity and environment.
   2. By satisfying infant needs consistently, responding to infant's nonverbal and verbal messages, providing learning opportunities, respecting infant individuality, providing pleasurable social interaction, showing love and attention, and providing speech for the child to hear.
   3. Possible speech mechanism exercise or self entertainment, although the purpose of babbling is not clearly understood.
   4. Language requires mutual understanding, and infers a reciprocal circumstance for at least two individuals.
   5. Ears, eyes, skin surfaces, mouth, and throat area.
   6. Perceptions.

F. 1. b　　　　　　2. c　　　　　　3. b　　　　　　4. a　　　　　　5. c

G. Communication is defined as sending and receiving information, signals, or messages. Language is defined as communicating ideas, feelings, etc., in such a way that the meaning is mutually understood.

H. 1. k　　　4. c　　　6. e　　　8. j　　　10. l　　　12. d
   2. a　　　5. h　　　7. i　　　9. b　　　11. m　　　13. f
   3. g

Unit 2 The Tasks of the Toddler

A. 1. f   2. e   3. c   4. b   5. a   6. d   7. g

B. Answers will differ.

C. Needle — thin, sharp, used with thread, used in sewing, pointed
   Giraffe — four legs, spots, long neck, eats leaves, found in zoos

D. Answers will differ.

E. Period of fastest language growth; child starts using sentences he creates; vocabulary increases dramatically; time of active language-sending; child has tremendous learning capacity

F. See Glossary in text, or refer to a dictionary.

G. 1. a   2. c   3. c   4. c   5. d

H. Supplying words; tying words to sensory experiences; being active listeners; answering child speech in a positive way; being accepting of child's ability; being warm, responsive companions

Unit 3 Characteristics of Preschool Language

A. *Younger Preschoolers (age 2–3)*
   telegram sentences
   repetitions
   substitutions
   omissions of letter sounds
   nonverbal communication
   talking about what one is doing
   stuttering
   talking through an adult

   Older Preschoolers (age 4–5)
   75% perfect articulation
   "Look, I'm jumping."
   name-calling
   adultlike speech
   2,000–2,500 word vocabulary
   role playing
   planning play with others
   rhyming and nonsense words
   bathroom words

B. 1. a, c   3. b, c, d   5. a, b, c   7. a, b, c   9. b
   2. a, b, d   4. a, b, c   6. a, b, d   8. a, b, c, d   10. a, b, c, d

Unit 4 Growth Systems Affecting Early Language Ability

A. See unit material for definition.

B. See unit material.

C. 1. b   4. b   7. c   10. a or b   13. a
   2. c   5. b   8. b   11. b   14. b
   3. a   6. c   9. a   12. c   15. c

D. 1, 3, 4, 5, 6, 7, 9

E. Vision is in the 20/45–20/30 range, and hearing is essentially mature at ages 4 and 5.

F. It's important for a teacher to respect and understand individual differences.

G. 1. a   2. c   3. d   4. a   5. d

Unit 5 Identifying Goals and Planning the Language Arts Curriculum

A. Listening, speaking, prewriting, and prereading

B. Answers will differ.

C. Answers will differ.

D. 1. a, b, d   3. a, b, d   5. b, c, d   7. c
   2. b, c, d   4. a, b, c, d   6. b, d   8. a, b

Unit 6 Teaching Language

A. Modeling speech behavior and attitudes; providing opportunities for language growth; interacting with the children

B. *Models*
   speech
   intonation
   pitch
   articulation
   attitudes
   actions
   grammar
   sentence patterns
   standard English
   courtesy words
   listening
   pronunciation
   enthusiasm
   care and concern
   problem solving
   curiosity

   Provides
   opportunities
   activities
   equipment
   materials
   words
   information
   the necessity to speak
   group situations
   listening
   an accepting classroom atmosphere
   physical contact
   variety

   Interacts
   focusing attention
   asking questions
   motivating
   planning repetitions
   giving feedback
   reinforcing
   taking advantage of unplanned events
   listening
   wonders out loud
   notices children's interest
   affirms children's statements
   links new learnings to old
   daily personal conversation

C. *Appropriate*
   attempts to focus attention on the activity
   use of "please"
   full sentences
   clear, concise speech
   use of standard English

   Inappropriate
   negative reinforcement of child's desire to speak
   denies child's perceptions
   not answering
   not listening
   fails to ask clarifying questions
   fails to supply words
   doesn't pursue conversation about child's interest
   makes speaking a task instead of a pleasure
   omits any positive reinforcement of child's speaking

D. The child's developmental level and individual needs

E. 1. a, b   2. a, b   3. a, b, c, d   4. a, b, d   5. a, c   6. a, b, c

F. Answers will differ.

G. *First Mother:*   Explains in specific terms; encourages child in task.
   Second Mother: Tells child in general terms in commanding way; criteria for classifying by color is not verbalized.

H. Adult adds words but does not increase the child's interest or discovery.

Unit 7 *Developing Listening Skills*

A. 1. creative listening   3. appreciative listening   5. purposeful listening
   2. critical listening   4. discriminative listening

B. Sustain attention span
   Follow directions or commands
   Listening to details
   Identify and associate sounds
   Discriminate by tempo, pitch, or intensity between sounds
   Use auditory memory

C. 1. b, d   2. b, c   3. a, b, c, d   4. a, b   5. a, b, c

D. Intensity = an extreme degree of strength, force, or energy
   Pitch = the highness or lowness of sound
   Tempo = the rate of speed

E. Answers will differ.

Unit 8 *Listening Activities*

A. Answers will differ.

B. Finger plays, body-action plays

Unit 9 *Reading to Children*

A. 2, 3, 12, 15, 16

B. 1. It may be inappropriate for young children. A teacher should be familiar with the content so the book
      can be presented enthusiastically. The teacher is better prepared for discussions which promote goals.
   2. Model this behavior with statements and actions.
   3. The teacher can make the experience successful in relation to reading goals and assessing children's
      interest.

C. 1. e   3. a   5. c   7. f   9. j   11. l
   2. g   4. b   6. d   8. h   10. i   12. k

Unit 10 *Storytelling*

A. 1. f   2. c   3. a   4. b   5. e   6. d

B. 1. It involves close personal contact between teachers and children while using language.
      It promotes children's storytelling.
      Teachers model speech usage and gestures.
      It is one way teachers can share their own experiences and attitudes with children.
      Children can create their own mental pictures as stories are told.
      School or life problems can be dealt with in storytelling experiences.
      New vocabulary can be introduced.
      Listening is promoted.
   2. Sharing problems
      Physical aggression problems
      Adjusting to a new baby at home

Fears of animals, bodily harm, the dark, etc.

Almost every type of social or emotional problem in the lives of young children

3. Include brief, simple definitions during the storytelling.

Repeat the new words and facts, and provide first-hand experiences when possible.

Purposefully include them, and stress them in the context of the story.

4. Books, children's magazines, movies, other teachers, stories created by the teachers

5. They present one generalized type when many varieties exist. Example: People with glasses are studious and shy.

6. Women shown only as housewives (and other stereotyped roles)

Dated word usage

C. 1. a, b, c, d   2. a, d   3. b, c   4. b, d   5. a, b, c, d

Unit 11 Poetry

A. 1. It promotes language development.
2. Children enjoy poetry's rhythm, fast action, and imaginative aspects.
3. Children can learn new words and concepts.
4. It is easy to learn and remember for many children, therefore, it builds children's self-confidence.
5. It is a language arts form that promotes children's speaking.
6. Many poems add humor to the language arts program.

B.
1. j	4. f	7. g	10. k	13. o
2. e	5. d	8. i	11. m	14. a
3. c	6. b	9. h	12. n	15. 1

C. 5, 6, 7, 8, 10

Unit 12 Flannel Boards and Activity Sets

A. Wood, heavy cardboard, composition board, foam

B. Pellon, felt, flannel, paper with any backing that sticks (such as sandpaper or fuzzy velour paper)

C. Answers will differ.

D. Focuses attention; adds a visual representation for words used during activities

E. 3, 4, 2, 5, 7, 6, 10, 1, 8, 9

F. Answers will differ.

G. 1. Pieces stick better on board
2. It is good for storage, carrying, changing locations
3. "These pieces are to look at; other ones that you can play with are in the language center."
4. They stick better when flat
5. Weight, low cost, can be used with pins
6. It is breakable

Unit 13 Realizing Speaking Goods

A. 1. Activities which teachers have planned and prepared during which they actively lead and direct the participation
2. Words that show ownership
3. Words implying a denial or refusal; saying "no"

    4. A relational word that connects a noun, pronoun, or noun phrase to another part of a sentence (such as: in, by, for, with, to)

    5. A word that compares one thing with something else, or examines in order to observe or discover similarities or differences (examples: more, less, equal, big, bigger, biggest)

B. 1. Planned activities, daily staff-child interaction, use of equipment and materials
    2. Be interested and focus attention on details.
    3. Lighting, heating, adequate movement, space, soft textures, seating arrangements
    4. Children's eye level

C. 1. c   2. a, b, d   3. a, c   4. a, d   5. c

D. 1. Plan many activities where children have speaking successes.
    2. Listen and respond to their speaking.
    3. Appreciate their communication efforts
    4. Reward their speaking with smiles and answers.
    5. Do not make verbal comparisons of children's speaking abilities.

E. 1. e   2. d   3. a   4. b   5. c   6. f

    1. divergent   3. recall   5. recall   7. divergent or convergent
    2. convergent   4. evaluative   6. divergent or convergent   8. convergent

Unit 14 Speech in Play and Routines

A. Child's play in which children act out past experiences and creatively improvise new ones

B. 1, 2, 3, 5, 6, 8, 9, 11, 12, 13, 14

C. 1. A collection of items, clothing, or other props that would stimulate children's activity and play; centered around one theme such as fire fighter, nurse, and so forth
    2. Children feel pressured to speak; children become restless and bored

D. 2, 3, 4, 5, 9

E. Answers will differ.

F. Bonnie, you didn't say it. You were playing with your hair ribbon.
Say it now, Bonnie.
Speak louder, Susie, we can't hear you.
Not "I'm present," Brett. Say "I'm here, Mrs. Brown."
David, you must answer when I call your name!
No, Andy, say "I'm here Mrs. Brown" not "I'm here" and that's all.
I don't know what's the matter with all of you; you did it right yesterday.
We're going to stay here until we all do it right.
I can't understand what you said, Dana; say it again.
No, it's not time to talk to Ronnie now; it's time to speak up.
I give up, you'll never learn.

Unit 15 Circle and Group Activities

A. 1. It allows for a smooth dispersal
    2. Building group spirit and identity; teaching customs and values
    3. Active, enthusiastic, prepared, accepting, appropriate, clearly stated concepts, familiar, novel, relaxed, sharing

B. Children learn finger plays easily, and the plays involve body motion. The children experience "groupness" and a sense of belonging. They can exhibit a learned skill to others. Once learned, they produce a feeling of security and competency. Children enjoy rhyming and word play.

C. 3, 2, 6, 5, 8, 4, 1, 7

D. Bell, flicking light switch, finger play, short song, teacher statement

E. Actively participate, encourage, and monitor child attention; move closer to a child when the child is distracted

F. 1. G 3. G 5. P 7. P 9. P
   2. P 4. G 6. P 8. P 10. G

Unit 16 Puppetry and Simple Drama

A. Puppets increase speech usage, help children coordinate speech and actions, build vocabulary, and build audience skill. A puppet is a useful teacher technique for holding and focusing attention, helping children develop auditory memory skills, promoting creative imagination.

B. 1. − 2. + 3. + 4. + 5. −

C. 1. a 2. c 3. b 4. e 5. c 6. a

Unit 17 Understanding Differences

A. 1. A teacher can learn about the cultural background of the child by visiting the home and observing the neighborhoods and communities in which the particular children reside. Parents are valuable resources in giving teachers more insights into understanding the lives and customs of the home.
   2. The teacher accepts and values them as individuals just as they are, not "as they could be."

B. 1. The teacher did not continue the conversation with a comment that would motivate or stimulate the child's speaking further in greater detail.
   2. The teacher was admonishing and making a moral evaluation of the child's behavior. A better answer could have been "It hurts when someone hits us. Ask Johnny for a turn with the truck when you want to play with it."
   3. The teacher has already received three verbal responses from the child without rewarding his request. The child simply gives up, and does not want to play a verbal game where he must ask for things in exactly the right way.
   4. The teacher could have shown interest, and discussed with the child where the bug was found, how it was caught, the bug's color or other distinguishing characteristics, with questions which would have promoted the child's putting his ideas into words.
   5. In this case, the child is speaking words, not sentences. To define "fellow" is probably offering too much. A better response would have been "Here's the yellow one, Lindy," for the child's words were spoken as a question.
   6. The child probably does not understand the question. The teacher could have tried rewording the question: "What kind of ice cream do you like?"

C. Refer to text glossary or dictionary.

D. 1. "You are playing with the ball. Throw the ball up like this." (Demonstrate)
   2. "Oh, you went to get the crayon. What are you going to do with it?"
   3. "Does it have a name?"
   4. "I like chicken soup, too. Do you like the chicken pieces or the noodles best?"

5. "That's right, we don't run into the street. We walk after looking both ways for cars."
6. "If you don't want to play with them, what are you going to choose to play with?"

E. 1. a, b, c   2. b, c, d   3. a, b, c, d   4. b, c, d   5. b, c, d   6. a, b, c, d

Unit 18 Printscript

A. 1. b, d   2. a, b, c   3. b   4. a, b, c, d

B. 1. b, a, c   2. b, c, a   3. b, c, a   4. b, a, c   5. a, b, c

C. 1. They have had access to writing tools. They have seen others writing. Parents have shown interest in alphabet letters or numbers.
2. Crayons; small manipulative toys; chalk; puzzles; string beads; any toy that involves small finger, hand, or arm muscle use
3. It is correct for their geographical area, large enough for young children to see, written in a left-to-right fashion, a good model for children.
4. Children do not come to school with the same home experiences or with the same maturity or interests as other children.
5. Other factors include a child's interest, motivation, mental readiness, and past experiences with symbols.
6. Say, "Yes, that is the alphabet letter named *m*."
7. Wait for the child's lead and plan a stimulating environment with lots of interesting things to do.
8. Say, "It's an alphabet letter just like *f* but it's called a *b*." Plan interesting activities which name *b* and involve tracing the outline of the letter.

Unit 19 Practicing Printscript

A. 1. Recognize the child's effort with positive comments.
2. Use the situation to direct them to a printed alphabet in the room where, with the teacher's help, the argument could be settled and become a learning situation for both.
3. During roll taking; labeling possessions or objects; making signs which fit into children's play situations; writing children's names on artwork; preparing bulletin boards or charts

B. In accordance with local printscript of elementary schools

C. 1. Printed Bob's name in correct form
2. Printed Chris' name over his shoulder
3. Asked Chris' permission to write his name on his paper
4. Answered Bob with more interest, positive reinforcement, and enthusiasm
5. Answered Sue; printed her name and encouraged her to trace and then write it for herself

D. 1. c, d   2. b, d   3. a, c

E. Student prints name and address in printscript

F. 1. The teacher has noticed the child's interest in printing and alphabet letters.
2. The teacher would like the parent to have a copy of the forms the child should learn. (The printscript alphabet obtained from a local elementary school.)

3. Children's early attempts are often upside down or backward, but this is nothing to worry about.
4. Whether the child writes or not at this age is not very important; a child's interests change.
5. The preschool will supply activities and materials in the area of printing as long as the child has continued interest in these activities.

G. Answers will differ.

H. Answers will differ.

Unit 20 Activities with Printscript

A. Circles, squares, triangles, rectangles, stars, dots, moon shapes, or any other commonly recognized shapes, geometric or other

B. It helps each child know the limits of his drawing area.

C. Answers will differ.

D. Answers will differ.

E. Answers will differ.

Unit 21 Readiness for Reading

A. 1. The teacher should listen approvingly whether the child is really reading or has just memorized the story, or is retelling the story in his own words. A positive comment by the teacher is helpful, such as "Thank you for sharing your favorite book with me."
2. Since the child has demonstrated both his ability and interest, the teacher should plan activities to expand his beginning skill.
3. Teachers suggest that the family provide for the child's interest by borrowing library books, and spending time with the child in reading activities. It is helpful for parents to know that supplying words when the child asks and offering to read words found naturally in home environments will increase the child's beginning attempts.

B. Make every effort to interrelate or combine activities, stressing how they fit together in the communication process.

C. Reading = to understand the meaning of a symbol or group of symbols by interpreting its characters or signs; to utter or repeat aloud words of written or printed material
Readiness = a state that allows one to proceed without hesitation, delay or difficulty
Method = a regular, orderly, definite procedure or way of teaching
Phonics = the use of elementary speech sounds in teaching beginners to read
Configuration = outline or shape of a word
Incongruities = lack of fitness or appropriateness; not corresponding to what is right, proper, or reasonable

D. 1. b   2. c   3. d   4. a   5. c

E. 1. Recognizing incongruities
2. Recognizing context clues
3. Ability to listen
4. Building vocabulary
5. Increased speech

Unit 22 Language Development Materials

A. 1. Almost all real objects (with the exception of those which are dangerous or too large to explore) can be used to promote firsthand exploration and language development. Pictures and drawings are also useful.
2. Most programs use visuals and materials which are both commercially manufactured and teacher-made. By continually reviewing new materials, programs improve and remain interesting to the children.
3. Sturdiness, teaching goals, children's individual or group interests, the maturity level of the group or child using them
4. Periodic checking of materials, repairing worn parts or replacing them is part of the teacher's responsibility. Creating and constructing materials for individual and group interests is another.

B. 1. h   3. b   5. d   7. a   9. j
   2. f   4. c   6. e   8. g   10. i

C. There are many possible answers. These are a few.

Positive	Negative
Most have sequentially planned experiences.	A set or kit could become the total language arts program.
Activities are included with teacher instructions.	Set or kit goals could differ from a particular program's goals.
Most have been designed by experts in language development.	The set or kit may not take into consideration the needs of individual children.
Kits and sets include commercially made visuals and teaching materials	Some commercial materials may not hold up under heavy use.

D. 1. b   2. e   3. d   4. c   5. d   6. a

E. Answers will differ.

Unit 23 Classroom Language Arts Area

A. Advantages
   1. Supplies and equipment are centrally located.
   2. Inviting language arts activities promote the interrelated language arts areas.
   3. There are spaces for individual exploration.
   4. There is comfortable seating.
   Disadvantages
   1. The space used may not serve other play and learning activities.
   2. Supervision of audiovisuals may require additional staff.

B. 1. supervising children's activity
   2. maintaining supplies and equipment
   3. periodic changing of display areas
   4. providing new activities and materials
   5. taking child dictation
   6. listening to child conversation
   7. serving as a resource in finding or securing materials

C. Students draw their own ideas of a language arts "crawl into" area

Unit 24 The Parent-Center Partnership

A. Answers will differ.

B. Answers will differ.

C. Answers will differ.

Acknowledgments

The author wishes to express her appreciation to the following individuals and agencies.

Nancy Martin, David Palmer, Ann Lane, and Joseph Tardi Associates for the photographs

Theresa and Caryn Macri for appearing in photos for Unit 1

The students at San Jose City College, AA Degree Program in Early Childhood Education

Arbor Hill Day Care Center, Albany, NY

San Jose City College Child Development Center Staff

Marcy Pederson of Magic Moments

Evergreen Valley College Child Development Center personnel, San Jose, CA

James Lick Children's Center, Eastside High School District, San Jose, CA

Lowell Children's Center, San Jose Unified School District, San Jose, CA

Piedmont Hills Preschool, San Jose, CA

Pineview Preschool, Albany, NY

St. Elizabeth's Day Home, San Jose, CA

Sunnymont Nursery School, Cupertino, CA

John Wiley and Sons, Inc. for permission to use figures 3–5 and 13–1 from *Psychology of the Child* by R. I. Watson and H. C. Lindgren, 1973.

Katrina Elena Machado and Coleen Colbert for proofreading, research, and technical assistance.

The staff at Delmar Publishers, Inc.

My fellow colleagues, Cia McClung and Roberta Immordino, whose supportive assistance and understanding have been of immeasurable help

In addition, special appreciation is due the reviewers involved in the development of the Third Edition:

Margaret Budz, Triton College, River Grove, Illinois

Paul Chesler, DeAnza College, Cupertino, California

Mary Anne Curtin, Anoka Technical Education Center, Anoka, Minnesota

Lillian Escobar, Cerritos College, Norwalk, California

Janet Johnston, Gaston College, Dallas, North Carolina

Lydia Harris, West Valley Community College, Saratoga, California

Sue Stuska, Front Range Community College, Westminster, Colorado

Paula Zajan and Minerva Rosario, Hostos Community College, Bronx, New York

The author is also grateful for the opportunity to have this text classroom-tested at the San Jose City College, San Jose, California.

Index